934

British Flight Testing

The Supermarine Spitfire was one of the very many
types tested at Martlesham Heath. (Flight)

British Flight Testing: Martlesham Heath 1920–1939

by

T MASON

in collaboration with
T HEFFERNAN

PUTNAM

To my wife, Penny

© Tim Mason 1993

First published in Great Britain in 1993 by
Putnam Aeronautical Books, an imprint of
Conway Maritime Press Ltd,
101 Fleet Street
London EC4Y 1DE

British Library Cataloguing in Publication Data
Mason, Timothy
British Flight Testing: Martlesham Heath, 1920-39
I. Title
623.7

ISBN 0 85177 857 7

Typeset and designed by Swanston Graphics Ltd, Derby
Printed and bound in Great Britain by
Butler & Tanner Ltd, Frome and London

Contents

Foreword

by
J M Bruce, ISO, MA, FRAeS, FRHistS

As long as aeroplanes exist they will have to be tested. In the last decade of the twentieth century, inexorably increasing complexity and vertiginously spiralling costs of research, design, development, operation and maintenance, demand that testing at all stages be rigorous and comprehensive. Yet, no matter how many applications of high technology are employed in the creation of a new aircraft design, the end product still has to undergo exhaustive flight testing in the hands of human pilots and other test personnel.

Viewed in long retrospect, the kind of flight testing that was practised in the earliest years of aviation might seem to have been barely better than perfunctory. Assessments were quickly made; satisfaction or condemnation was unhesitatingly expressed. Thus it was at the outbreak of war in 1914, when sudden urgency demanded the hasty requisition of many aircraft of dubious value. Soon, however, procedures of testing began to evolve. In Britain, an Experimental Flight was formed at the Central Flying School, Upavon, tasked with evaluating new types for the Royal Flying Corps. As the volume and variety of the work increased, armament testing was transferred to a new and separate establishment at Orfordness; and late in 1916 all flight testing of experimental aeroplanes was also removed from CFS.

The testing staff, organisation and equipmentwerethen moved to Martlesham Heath.

By that time, trial reports had become increasingly more informative, reflecting improved techniques and practices in test flying. The whole business of this highly specialised aspect of flying had developed greatly since the rudimentary exercises and sketchy reports of 1914. A foundation had been laid.

The post-Armistice period brought many problems to the Royal Air Force, foremost among them the matter of its survival, which was soon threatened. The implementation of unrelenting demands for economy gravely reduced the effectiveness of those RAF units that did survive.

Financial constraints tended to vitiate official specifications for new types of aircraft, many of which perpetuated functions and weaponry rooted in the First World War; some, indeed, compelled compromises that impaired effectiveness. Yet aircraft manufacturers, their future dependent on orders that were few and often small, submitted many prototypes for consideration. With few exceptions, these were tested at Martlesham Heath.

Those widely varying aircraft of the two decades that separated the two World Wars are the fascinating subjects of this book. Their appraisements by Martlesham's pilots – succinct, mordant, witty as they often were – provide, in their gritty factuality, vivid impressions that quite often differ from other accounts that are unduly flattering of their subjects.

These surviving assessments have now been brought together, authoritatively and concisely, in this volume by Tim Mason, himself a pilot of great and widely varied experience in experimental flying, and therefore admirably well qualified to interpret and correlate their contents. His book is a unique and invaluable record that gives an instructive insight into a period of British aviation history that was part of the brief interlude between the two World Wars.

In the first of these appalling conflicts, military aviation developed at an astonishing pace; in the second, it played a dominant and determining role. Had that role been foreseen in 1919, our inter-war aviation might have been less parsimoniously and more energetically developed, our aircraft specifications more realistically drawn up, and – perhaps most significant of all – greater importance attached to aero-engine design and to weaponry. Many lessons are implicit in the history related in this book; but above all it bears witness to the skill, courage and dedication of a distinguished body of test pilots who plied their profession at Martlesham Heath.

Preface

Martlesham is known today as the home of BT's telecommunications laboratories but until the second decade of this century Martlesham was just another small Suffolk village. In between, the village gave its name to an active military airfield, which from 1917 to 1939 was the site for testing all aeroplanes intended for the Royal Air Force and its Fleet Air Arm. Testing of air armament was added in 1924, and later, civil aeroplanes for their Certificates of Airworthiness.

This book is a history of the Establishment charged with the responsibility for making the tests between 1920 and 1939, Part I describes in general terms what was done, where, how and who did it. Particular emphasis has been given to those who were responsible for setting the standards that became so universally accepted and respected, together with an assessment of the Establishment's influence. Sources used for this Part are the limited number of official records, published papers of learned bodies, some of the Establishment's own reports and, above all, the personal reminiscences collected

by my collaborator Terry Heffernan who has so generously given me access to his extensive archives.

Part II is based almost exclusively on such of the Establishment's own reports that survive – fortunately some 75 percent. Where reports have not been found, largely for the period 1924 to 1929, pilot's comments in their log-books, where available, have been quoted. Photographs are predominantly from the collection at Boscombe Down, and most in Part II are Crown Copyright, and reproduced with the permission of the Controller of Her Britannic Majesty's Stationery Office. No apology is made for using the standardised views of aeroplanes on the ground – the aim has been to include a picture of the aeroplanes as tested – the very purpose for which official photographs were taken. To keep this volume to manageable proportions, it has been necessary to reduce descriptions of tests to the essential minimum; every aeroplane known to have been used at Martlesham Heath in the period 1920 to 1939 has been included.

Opinions expressed are the

author's own except where quoted from the Establishment's reports.

The author gratefully acknowledges the help given by the Aircraft and Armament Evaluation Establishment (late Aeroplane and Armament Experimental Establishment), and in particular to staff of the Science Library and Photographic Group over many years, and to recent Commandants and Superintendents of Flying. Research has been made possible by the Defence Research Agency (late Royal Aerospace Establishment), Farnborough; the Public Record Office, Kew; the Royal Air Force Museum and the Ministry of Defence Library, Whitehall.

People who have helped me include Keith Bolton, Jack Bruce, Sherri Carnson, Kenneth Chesterson, Robert Forrester-Addie, Brian Foskett, Keith Ingle, Jyz and Daz James, Philip Jarrett, Brian Kervell, Gordon Kinsey, Richard Lovekin, Geoffery Quick, George Randall, Richard Searle, Ray Sturtivant, and last but by no means least, Jayne Fox with Mandy Freer who have processed my every word. My thanks to them all.

Part I

The First Years of Peace 1920–1924

The need for aeroplanes and their equipment to be assessed before Service use evolved during the Great War, starting in 1914 with the earliest bombsights. The unit chosen for this testing was the Central Flying School at Upavon in Wiltshire. It was the only military flying unit with experienced pilots remaining in the country after the departure to France of all four fully-formed squadrons. Soon, Upavon was sent other equipment and then aeroplanes with a view to accepting or rejecting them for the Royal Flying Corps. By the end of 1914 a separate Experimental Flight was in existence and as the demands for this work increased so did the Flight until it outgrew the capacity of Upavon, already struggling to maintain its output of trained pilots. Armament testing moved to Orfordness in Suffolk in October 1916, followed by aeroplane testing to nearby Martlesham Heath in January 1917. The latter was by then known as the Aeroplane Testing Squadron, a title changed in the following October to the Aeroplane Experimental Station.

In the course of these changes in location and nomenclature, the terms of reference for the unit remained the same – seeking the answer to the question, will the aeroplane do the job for which it was designed when it is flown by the young pilots in squadrons in the field?

A form of questionnaire evolved in which the aeroplane was itemised to include constructional details, dimensions, weights, engine and propeller types, performance in the climb, level speed and handling; later details of armament and its accessibility were added. Actual air firing and bomb dropping trials remained the responsibility of Orfordness. By the end of the war extensive measurements of the airframe were made before flying began together with ground firing of guns, and then weighing and Centre of Gravity (CG) calculation. Handling remained throughout the war a largely subjective exercise, but with the benefit of wide yet untutored experience of the test pilots. It is in the measurement of performance that the greatest progress was made. Among the handful of academically qualified officers at Martlesham was Captain Henry T Tizard. In 1917 he read a paper to the Aeronautical Society in which he explained how the speed, rate of climb and ceiling of aeroplanes were calculated, and, in particular, how the data recorded by the pilots were used to produce accurate performance figures independent of weather conditions at the time of the flights. Using observations by the Meteorological Office, Tizard obtained data on the average pressure, temperature and density of the air up to about 20,000ft above sea level, and thereby deduced a standard atmosphere for East Suffolk.

His was remarkably close to the standard internationally adopted shortly after the First World War. He had stated that the whole performance of an aeroplane depended on the density of the air in which it was flying, and that to obtain accuracy, pressure and temperature had to be obtained to calculate the divergence of the density from the standard. Having determined the divergence, the standard (or true) height could be determined by applying the relevant factor. A complication (at least until 1925/6) was the altimeter itself, adapted from an aneroid, and graduated to show altitude assuming a constant +10 deg C. This temperature was far too high for the conditions encountered, and the resultant error could be as much as 2,000ft at 16,000ft (minus 25 deg C in winter) when the altimeter would show 18,000ft. Tizard devised a table for correcting the error. Speeds, heights, temperatures and other data were recorded many times per flight and the reduction process was laborious.

By the time of the Armistice in 1918, standard methods were being applied to every new aeroplane and its derivatives. The almost universal configuration was a tractor biplane, constructed with a wooden frame and fabric covering, and powered most commonly by a single engine.

Aeroplane types proliferated but differences were small – handling being more affected by choice of rotary or static engine than by stability and control characteristics.

Cancellation of production orders for over 10,000 aeroplanes was not extended to any large degree to new designs already on order at the end of 1918. Thus in the months following the war Martlesham received several new types – many powered with the ill-fated ABC Dragonfly radial engine – at a time of general demobilisation of Service personnel.

Towards the end of 1919, the final wartime civilian employees left, including two women computers, one of whom was Dr Alice Lee, an expert at the tedious calculations involved in performance reduction. Among those remaining under the Chief Technical

Officer, Sqn Ldr T M Barlow, were Flt Lt C E Nightingale, four airmen draughtsmen and one civilian clerk E W Robinson (still with AAEE in 1966).

Setting the Standards

Anyone connected with British aviation between the two World Wars would have recognised the name Martlesham Heath and associated it with aeroplane testing. To those who served there between 1920 and 1939 life was full of interest, was challenging and shared with fellow enthusiasts. Writing in 1962 Grp Capt W F Dry sets the scene as follows:

'I arrived at the Aeroplane Experimental Station (soon changed to the Aeroplane Experimental Establishment) in December 1919, and so began six of the happiest years of my Service life. The station, on flat, heather-covered heathland between Woodbridge and Ipswich, with a few semi-permanent hangars with tarmac surrounds, workshops and offices and a couple of well built large permanent hangars which seemed rather grand affairs, had an atmosphere which was quite unique. Within days of arrival there, the newcomer sensed this was no ordinary station – it was not only that the flying personnel of the place were experts in their own right but, additionally, some friendly bond

seemed to be established at once between all ranks of the place. In 1920 the Establishment was organised on a three flight basis.

'A' Flight (single-seat fighters) and 'C' Flight (two- and three-seat aircraft) in the semi-permanent hangars right on the main Woodbridge–Felixstowe road which ran through the camp, while 'B' Flight (big multi-engined aircraft) was housed in the two permanent hangars on a short stretch of road near the aerodrome boundary.'

This account summarises the organisation during the first period under review (1920-1924); more significantly Dry's memoirs reflect the less tangible but equally real spirit of the Establishment experienced throughout the inter-war period. Without exception, all who have contributed to this history remember their days at Martlesham with great affection, and usually as the highlight of their working lives. In the peacetime routine from 1920, initiative was encouraged and officers, NCOs and airmen had ample opportunity to develop their individual talents. Command passed rapidly from Sqn Ldr A Sheckleton to Sqn Ldr A C Maund, both having distinguished wartime careers, and then early in 1922 to the first Wing Commander – Napier John Gill who did as much as anybody to establish the character and reputation of his station. He had an austere presence and an acid tongue combined with a

The members of 'B' Flight early in 1920. Left to right: Flt Sgt in charge of Flight groundcrew, Flg Off B McEntegart, Flg Off Jephson, Flg Off Fraser, Flg Off W F Dry, Flt Lt G Barrett, commanding B Flight, Flt Lt E M Pizey, Sgt (pilot) and groundcrew. The aeroplane is the Bristol Braemar Mk II.

wealth of humanity, a sense of humour and clarity of vision. When the hangar burnt down in October 1922, one of the first on the scene in the small hours of the morning was Gill, immaculately turned out, including cane. On another occasion, an officer came to the CO's office to ask for 24 hours leave as his wife had just given birth to twins; 'Poor man', said Gill, 'You'd better have a fortnight'.

Above all, the respect commanded by Gill stemmed from his principle of making the good name of Martlesham the highest priority, by his support of subordinates, and from his insistence on the highest standards at work. By 1924, the 'Trade' (the aircraft industry whose products were under test) had come to accept without demur the opinions and objective results of Establishment testing; yet all business was conducted in the friendliest atmosphere.

Among the lasting innovations originating in Gill's time was the annual Contractors' Dinner, the first of which was held in 1922 in the Officers' Mess. The idea was to return the hospitality extended by designers and test pilots of companies whose aircraft were undergoing test, and who, when staying in the vicinity, invited Martlesham officers to dine, play tennis and golf. From the first, the Dinners attracted managing directors as well as designers and pilots of the twenty or so independent companies that made up the 'Trade'. The reverse of the menu card for 1923 is reproduced (*see* Appendix H), and is representative of the following years. Several of the guests were invited to sing for their supper, and most notable of the speakers was Frederick Handley

The signatures of those attending the Contractors' Dinner in December 1923. The names are in Appendix H, and are typical of other years.

Page, who attended for most years. Activities continued after the formalities, including four-a-side squash played in dinner jackets and mess kit. On another occasion, a perilous ascent, well after midnight, of the mast of the anemometer was made to rotate the head at a fiendish speed to indicate a freak wind on the recorder below; the perpetrators were disappointed when this jape went unnoticed.

Gill had under him many whose abundant inventiveness and initiative he encouraged, with, no doubt occasional misgivings. From July 1923 'A' Flight (single-seat fighters) was commanded by Flt Lt A H Orlebar who had a striking yellow Citröen in which he visited his girlfriend. Every spare

minute was spent on preparing the car – known as the 'split lemon' – for the following weekend; such was the rush that the wiring was cross connected and the horn sounded every time he touched the brake pedal. Orlebar went on to command the High Speed Flight in 1931 after setting a World Speed Record of 357mph in 1929. Another pilot, Flg Off Oliver Stewart, became well known as the Editor of the magazine *Aeronautics*, and later as commentator at the SBAC's Farnborough Air Displays in the 1950s.

Flt Lt R Ivelaw-Chapman was adjutant for a time and later on 'B' Flight (twin-engines); in 1929 he flew many of the relief flights from India to Kabul, and retired with the rank of Air Chief Marshal and contributed several of the anecdotes related here. Other early pilots who reached Air rank were Flg Offs A Gray and H V Battle, the latter recording his Service career in book form – one of the few Martlesham people to do so (*see* Bibliography).

Organisation and Building

Until well into the Second World War the work at Martlesham was directed by the Air Ministry (after 1924, the Director of Technical Development), while administration and discipline remained with the Royal Air Force. The latter exercised its authority through a succession of Group, Area and Command Headquarters*, the changes being brought about initially by the rapidly evolving command structure of the infant air service following the First World War, and latterly by the expansion before the Second. In practice the very distinct division of responsibility between the two masters caused few, if any, difficulties.

In April 1920 the title of the unit was changed to the Aeroplane Experimental Establishment (Home);

---

* 1921 No.1 Group
  1922 Coastal Area
  1923 No.3 Group
  1926 No.21 Group
  1934 Inland Area
  1936 Training Command
  1937 No.24 Group

the suffix appears rather quaint as no overseas establishment was formed, nor seriously planned. Also at home were aeronautical establishments at the Isle of Grain (Marine Aircraft Experimental Establishment), South Farnborough (Royal Aircraft Establishment), Biggin Hill (Instrument Design Establishment), Pulham (Airship Experimental Establishment) and South Kensington (laboratory).

In the search for economy in 1920, the Air Ministry formed an internal committee, under Air Commodore H R M Brooke Popham, to investigate what savings might be achieved by amalgamating some of the establishments. Among matters of concern to the committee was the end of the lease in November 1923 of the 800 acres of Martlesham Heath. The committee, strengthened after its second meeting by a Treasury representative and Professor H Tizard by then with the Department of Scientific and Industrial Research, soon concentrated on two possibilities including the move of AEE from Martlesham to Grain. The annual saving identified was £8,000, while capital costs were broadly similar whether or not Martlesham was retained. Tizard, who had practical experience of the Martlesham area, advised the committee that Grain was not a suitable airfield for large aircraft, that Martlesham was among the finest aerodromes and in good country for forced landings (to which experimental aircraft could be expected to be prone) and, furthermore, near the bombing and gunnery range at Orfordness and near the major town of Ipswich.

Tizard's quiet advocacy carried the day, and in its final report of 31 May, 1921, the committee recommended that the AEE should remain in situ, and that steps should be taken to purchase the site. The committee's other recommendation resulted in the move of the Instrument Design Establishment from Biggin Hill to Farnborough. An earlier and apparently independent decision to move the armament work to Grain was implemented when Orfordness closed in June 1921.

As a result of the committee's decision, the Lands Directorate of the Air Ministry reviewed the existing rental agreement of the land at Martlesham Heath. The original owner, the Rt

The Aeroplane Repair Section on fire in October 1922. (G Kinsey)

Hon E G Pretyman MP, had received a peppercorn rent for the duration of the war. Following the Armistice a temporary agreement to run from 11 November, 1918, was subsequently agreed at an annual rent of £200 for five years with the Air Ministry being obliged to remove all buildings by 11 November, 1923. The only objection by the owner to the Service use of the land arose over the closure of the public road during flights along the one-mile speed course, but the owner retained shooting, hunting and other rights and did not press his objection. During the negotiations in 1922-3 for the long term lease of the land, minor boundary changes were agreed, but the main objection was lodged by the local vicar, Rev F E Doughty, who pointed out first that existing hangars obstructed Rights of Way and second that parishoners' Rights of Common (on the northern part of the airfield) would be lost. The Air Ministry proposed a £5 per annum compensation for the former, and £125 lump sum for extinguishing the latter, although no statutory documentation could be found to substantiate the parishioners' claims. The matter was, however, finally resolved and a 999 year lease agreement was signed on 1 May, 1925, between the President of the Air Council and Mr G M T Pretyman (the MP's son) at an annual rent of £350 for 730 acres; this arrangement overcame the possible difficulty of a Member of Parliament receiving profit from the Crown.

By 1929 the increase in aircraft speed had led to the need for a further 65 acres on the extreme west side of the aerodrome for manoeuvring on to the line of the one-mile speed course; negotiations were protracted, but another agreement was reached in June 1931 and an additional annual rent of £75 fixed. Thus the heathland south of the village of Martlesham, and divided by the main Woodbridge to Felixstowe road, remained from 1920 until 1939 the country's only venue for testing landplanes intended for military use.

The main and public road also divided the buildings of the Establishment with five aircraft hangars on the west side and ancillary buildings such as administration and power house on the east side. To the south were the domestic quarters, also split by the road so that officers living on one side had to cross over for meals and the public rooms of the Officers' Mess. The main road at least gave easy access from the living quarters to the technical areas and every working day airmen marched northwards early in the morning and after lunch and southwards at midday and in the evenings. On Sundays, church parades marched to service in Martlesham village for Church of England adherents while those of other religions made their own way to Woodbridge churches. The former arrangements were changed in 1922 when Wg Cdr Gill altered the wartime Womens' Quarters into a church and an education centre.

Service life was very much centered on the station for officers, NCOs

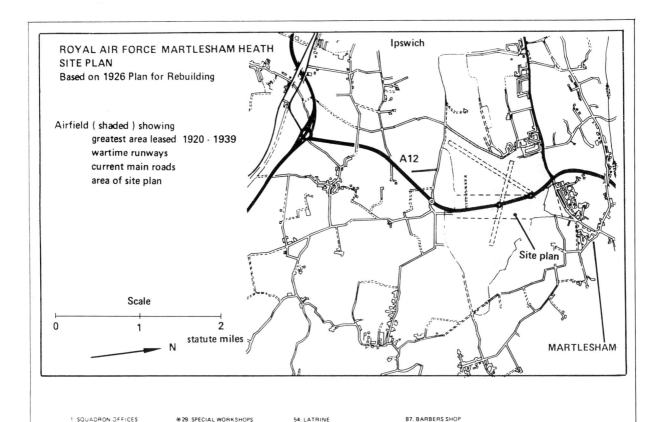

ROYAL AIR FORCE MARTLESHAM HEATH
SITE PLAN
Based on 1926 Plan for Rebuilding

Airfield (shaded) showing
greatest area leased 1920 - 1939
wartime runways
current main roads
area of site plan

Ipswich

A12

Site plan

MARTLESHAM

Scale

0   1   2
                                    statute miles
N

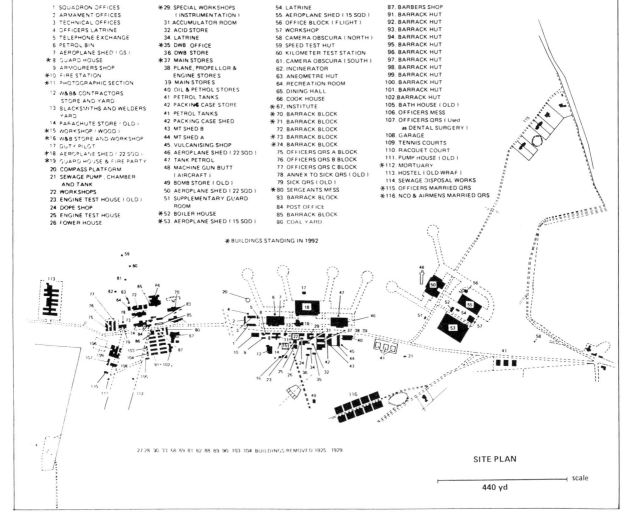

1 SQUADRON OFFICES	*29. SPECIAL WORKSHOPS	54. LATRINE	87. BARBERS SHOP
2 ARMAMENT OFFICES	(INSTRUMENTATION)	55. AEROPLANE SHED (15 SQD)	91. BARRACK HUT
3 TECHNICAL OFFICES	31. ACCUMULATOR ROOM	56. OFFICE BLOCK (FLIGHT)	92. BARRACK HUT
4 OFFICERS LATRINE	32. ACID STORE	57. WORKSHOP	93. BARRACK HUT
5 TELEPHONE EXCHANGE	34. LATRINE	58. CAMERA OBSCURA (NORTH)	94. BARRACK HUT
6 PETROL BIN	*35. DWB OFFICE	59. SPEED TEST HUT	95. BARRACK HUT
7 AEROPLANE SHED (GS)	36. DWB STORE	60. KILOMETER TEST STATION	96. BARRACK HUT
*8 GUARD HOUSE	*37. MAIN STORES	61. CAMERA OBSCURA (SOUTH)	97. BARRACK HUT
9 ARMOURERS SHOP	38. PLANE, PROPELLOR &	62. INCINERATOR	98. BARRACK HUT
*10 FIRE STATION	ENGINE STORES	63. ANEOMETRE HUT	99. BARRACK HUT
*11 PHOTOGRAPHIC SECTION	39. MAIN STORES	64. RECREATION ROOM	100. BARRACK HUT
12 W&B& CONTRACTORS	40. OIL & PETROL STORES	65. DINING HALL	101. BARRACK HUT
STORE AND YARD	41. PETROL TANKS	66. COOK HOUSE	102. BARRACK HUT
13 BLACKSMITHS AND WELDERS	42. PACKING CASE STORE	*67. INSTITUTE	105. BATH HOUSE (OLD)
YARD	41. PETROL TANKS	*70. BARRACK BLOCK	106. OFFICERS MESS
14 PARACHUTE STORE (OLD)	42. PACKING CASE SHED	*71. BARRACK BLOCK	107. OFFICERS QRS (Used
*15 WORKSHOP (WOOD)	43. MT SHED B	72. BARRACK BLOCK	as DENTAL SURGERY)
*16 W&B STORE AND WORKSHOP	44. MT SHED A	*73. BARRACK BLOCK	108. GARAGE
17 DUTY PILOT	45. VULCANISING SHOP	*74. BARRACK BLOCK	109. TENNIS COURTS
*18 AEROPLANE SHED (22 SQD)	46. AEROPLANE SHED (22 SQD)	75. OFFICERS QRS A BLOCK	110. RACQUET COURT
*19 GUARD HOUSE & FIRE PARTY	47. TANK PETROL	76. OFFICERS QRS B BLOCK	111. PUMP HOUSE (OLD)
20 COMPASS PLATFORM	48. MACHINE GUN BUTT	77. OFFICERS QRS C BLOCK	*112. MORTUARY
21 SEWAGE PUMP , CHAMBER	(AIRCRAFT)	78. ANNEX TO SICK QRS (OLD)	113. HOSTEL (OLD WRAF)
AND TANK	49. BOMB STORE (OLD)	79. SICK QRS (OLD)	114. SEWAGE DISPOSAL WORKS
22 WORKSHOPS	50. AEROPLANE SHED (22 SQD)	*80. SERGEANTS MESS	*115. OFFICERS MARRIED QRS
23 ENGINE TEST HOUSE (OLD)	51. SUPPLEMENTARY GUARD	83. BARRACK BLOCK	*116. NCO & AIRMENS MARRIED QRS
24 DOPE SHOP	ROOM	84. POST OFFICE	
25 ENGINE TEST HOUSE	*52. BOILER HOUSE	85. BARRACK BLOCK	
26 POWER HOUSE	*53. AEROPLANE SHED (15 SQD)	86. COAL YARD	

✱ BUILDINGS STANDING IN 1992

27 28 30 33 68 69 81 82 88 89 90 103 104 BUILDINGS REMOVED 1925 1929

SITE PLAN

440 yd   scale

and airmen, but recreation facilities in the early 1920s were restricted to outdoor sports, a canteen (in addition to the three messes) and an education centre. Competition was fostered in sport and in domestic arrangements – each Flight having its own, separate, accommodation. Early in the 1920s Martlesham soon gained and held many of the Royal Air Force's Station, Command and Service sporting trophies. The rugby team captained by Sgt McGlasson was particularly successful. Among all ranks there soon developed a strong esprit-de-corps from their sporting, social and above all their working activities.

Once the Air Ministry committee had reached its decision and the long-term tenure of the land been secured, rebuilding was planned. One event, on the night of 6 October, 1922, had added urgency to this reconstruction as the Aeroplane Repair Section (the centre of the three semi-permanent hangars) had burnt down, destroying the aeroplanes inside including an Avro Bison and some German machines; the belief was that the fire had been started by an airman in the course of stealing petrol. By the time the local fire brigade arrived with horse drawn appliance, the station fire fighting team had the blaze contained and damage was restricted to the single hangar.

Testing – Methods and Development

Throughout this first period following the First World War, the scope of aeroplane testing remained as laid down by Tizard in 1917 with the performance results reduced to the standard conditions he had derived. On the ground, increasing attention was given until 1927 to measuring the physical dimensions and weights of new types, including their propellers and such minutiae as carburetter jet size. Calibrated airspeed indicators, altimeters and thermometers aided accuracy, but fuel consumption was measured only on an experimental, and highly capricious basis. Armament was tested at Orfordness and from 1921 to 1924, on the Isle of Grain. By the standards of even a few years later, 'full' tests in the early 1920s produced a voluminous report, with only a small proportion relating

to speed, climb, ceiling and stability. Take-off and landing distances measurements were tedious, and only considered necessary for the larger machines. The opinions of pilots found little place in the official reports, and the more colourful descriptions were saved for informal contact with Establishment technical staff, and with the makers, designers and pilots. Once the physical characteristics were noted and the usually limited performance measurements made, the new aeroplanes were available, sometimes for considerable periods, for general flying by Establishment pilots.

This arrangement was known as having aircraft 'on hire', and greatly broadened the basis of informed opinion on the merits of individual machines, opinions eagerly sought by the designers. The content of full test reports relied on the most accurate measurement possible of performance. Airspeed indicators (ASI), required correction not only for density error, but also for errors induced by the position and angle of the pitot head. To measure the latter, two methods were employed. First was the speed course which required the pilot to fly at about 50ft at various speeds while his time between two points a known distance apart on the ground was noted. The wind, which needed to be less than 5mph, was also measured. The second method used two camera obscura lenses suitably arranged so that the passage of the aeroplane could be manually plotted every second using the image cast on the table. The wind was measured by plotting a smoke puff, fired by the pilot at the required height, usually between 4,000ft and 6,000ft. A number of speeds were flown, each being flown twice in each direction but the difficulty of maintaining height accurately led to the abandonment of this method. In both methods the calculated ground speed was compared with the pilot's airspeed, and after allowing for the wind and height (ie density), the airspeed indicator error was derived.

Three items of equipment were evolved at Martlesham to assist in performance testing: a thermometer with expanded scale, usually taped to a strut (this can be seen in many of the photographs), and two instruments

modified from thermos flasks (so described by Tizard). The 'flasks' were both connected via a transparent tube with a restricted orifice to atmosphere. One type was arranged to show maximum differential pressure and thus maximum rate of climb; this type appears to have been used only briefly after 1920. The other type, known as a statoscope, was arranged so that a bubble of liquid was central in the transparent tube when the aircraft was maintaining height precisely; this type remained in general Service use until at least 1939.

Thus in the early postwar period, performance testing at Martlesham was in accordance with the method laid down by Tizard. Aeroplanes for test were fitted with thermometers and at least a statoscope; airspeed indicators and altimeters were calibrated on the ground, refitted and the pilot armed with pencil, writing pad, a stopwatch and lots of warm clothing. At least two and usually three climbs to ceiling were made, the pilot noting the temperature and time every 1,000ft, and the airspeed and engine revolutions periodically. Airspeed calibration was usually but not invariably completed before the climbs. On landing, the data recorded was analysed using prepared graphs, slide rules, logarithms and a great deal of laborious arithmetic; the task fell to male scientific assistants.

It is difficult to overstate the importance of Tizard's scientific basis of determining the performance of aeroplanes; in the period 1920-39 and later the principles remained unchanged. Later more accurate instruments and increased aeroplane performance led to a change in the basis of reduction. In February 1922 Sqn Ldr T M Barlow, who was the Chief Technical Officer from the end of the war until 1923, gave a lecture at Cambridge University; it was very similar to Tizard's 1917 lecture. Barlow noted the work at Farnborough which indicated that engine torque varied with pressure rather than density. However, since the latter produced small and acceptable errors and was, in any case, more convenient, density remained the basis of performance reduction for several years after 1920 until more accurate instruments and increased aeroplane performance led to a change.

To complement the accuracy of the performance work, aeroplanes were very accurately weighed – first without fuel, oil and military load, then with known fuel and oil quantities and finally with the load required by the Air Ministry Specification. Each weighing provided a check of the others. Finally, at least one loading was used as the basis of calculation of the Centre of Gravity and was measured in the flying attitude and with tail down; this procedure gave both horizontal and vertical position of the CG. Aerodynamic features of every aeroplane fully tested were measured, and details of petrol and other systems noted, and drawn to scale for inclusion in the subsequent reports which in many cases were to become voluminous tomes.

Armed with accurate weight and CG the pilots made initial handling tests to determine the best climbing speed at various heights, and then made the speed course measurements. Following the climbing and speed tests at various heights, on larger machines, the standard routine ended with take off and landing measurements, any special tests and consumption calculations. The last were stopped after a few years for reasons which are not entirely clear – due largely no doubt to the inaccuracy of early flowmeters, the amount of test flying necessary and due also to the requirement of the Air Staff for aeroplanes in Service to be operated at maximum engine revolutions at the maximum altitude irrespective of any range benefit accruing from a small reduction in engine speed.

In July 1920 the first annual Royal Air Force Pageant (later Display) was held at Hendon. By 1922 an item on every programme was 'New Types', featuring aircraft at, or soon to be tested at, Martlesham, and flown at Hendon by Establishment pilots to preserve the Service nature of the occasion. In most years, some new types appeared in the hands of Martlesham test pilots after the briefest of tests by the manufacturer following maiden flights.

Military Aeroplanes

During the 1920s there was a large number of different military prototypes, of which the majority did not proceed beyond Martlesham trials. A feature was the damning of several designs for apparently trivial shortcomings in, say, cockpit layout or draught, and the abandonment of the type without a serious attempt to improve matters. New propellers were frequently tried to improve revolutions and thus climb and speed, but only occasionally were aerodynamic fixes tried. A notable exception was the Blackburn Swift, which quickly gained a larger rudder following complaints at Martlesham of inadequate control. This situation arose partially from the system whereby a proliferation of military Specifications appeared every year, and, if a designer's offering did not please, the solution was to produce another type the following year, and thus avoid wasting time on a remedy for the shortcomings of the current model. Later, as the system evolved for testing several contenders against a single Specification, one or more of the prototypes was chosen for further development before the final selection was made.

At the beginning of 1920 well over half the new types at AEE were powered by the recalcitrant ABC Dragonfly engine; the group included fighters, army reconnaissance machines and twin-engined bombers. When the engine could be persuaded to run for more than a few minutes at a time, some impressive performance figures were produced (see Part II). However, in spite of a Mk II version in which exhaust heated inlet muffs cured cutting out on take off, the fundamental design fault remained, and many engines vibrated themselves and the aircraft they powered to smithereens. Some later engines achieved 50hr flying on endurance tests, usually involving a change of airframe because the vibration broke rigging wires, among other components.

On the large aircraft Flight in 1920-21, the large Bristol, Vickers and Handley Page types rarely flew – indeed the conservative pilots so disliked the enclosed cockpit of the Bristol Pullman that the arrangement was rejected and the type abandoned. The Establishment was able to confirm the opinion of pilots of No.7 Squadron that even the best of their Vickers Vimys had an appalling performance in 1923, well below that of the prototypes in 1917. The replacement, the Virginia, was scarcely better, and became worse as the type was developed over the years.

The first of what later became recognized as competitions occurred in 1922, between the Blackburn Dart and the Handley Page Hanley torpedo droppers. The former was well liked but rejection of the latter followed a damning handling report by Martlesham. Another comparison, in 1922-3 and also of deck landing aeroplanes, was made between the Avro Bison and Blackburn Blackburn Fleet Spotters. Martlesham found both acceptable, the Bison marginally so; both types entered service.

In 1923, the large Armstrong Whitworth Awana was rejected following the Establishment's adverse comments on its size and lack of rigidity. Fortunately, the Vickers Victoria to the same Air Ministry Specification had already been found acceptable by Martlesham and during Service trials in Iraq. In these three early instances, as later, Martlesham's opinion was supported either by trials elsewhere or by Service use, and was upheld when decisions were made by the Air Ministry between competing types.

Civil Aeroplanes

The testing of civil aeroplanes at Martlesham between the wars was in three distinct periods. The first phase began in January 1920. While routine testing continued on a few military types ordered during the war, preparations were put in hand for the forthcoming Civil Aeroplane Competition sponsored by the recently created Director General of Civil Aviation at the Air Ministry. Initially, a new speed measuring course was established by Flt Lt Nightingale and Flt Sgt B H Rolles after surveying an east–west course exactly one statute mile in length and marked at each end by a timing hut interconnected by landline. The speed course with a minor realignment remained in use until 1939, but was by then being superceded by the five-mile course.

While accurate low-level speed measurement was made possible by the mile course, similar success did not attend the measurement of take-off and landing distances; the problem was never entirely successfully solved up to 1939. For the 1920 Civil

Competition three concentric circles were marked on the aerodrome for landings – the touchdown point being marked by two brave and active airmen and the distance to rest measured; take offs were recorded by camera set at right angles to the run of the aircraft.

Among recurring difficulties were fickle winds and human pilots – both liable to render measurement more an art than a science. However, work on the facilities at Martlesham for the 1920 Competition resulted in definite progress to accuracy in gathering quantitative data.

Unlike normal Establishment procedure where every machine was flown by several pilots, each Competition aircraft was flown by a single civilian pilot employed by the makers; every pilot therefore had a vested interest in his mount, and any shortcomings in handling were not identified in the trial. The judges, under Sqn Ldr T O'B Hubbard of the Air Ministry (and lately Commanding Officer at Martlesham), awarded prizes, announced on 2 October, 1920, to the Vickers Vimy Commercial (2nd prize – the 1st was not awarded) in the large class, the Westland Limousine in the small class and the Vickers Viking III in the amphibian class. None of the competitors was tested by the Establishment (with the exception of the Vickers Vimy Commercial), and in Part II of ths work they are excluded from the description of aircraft tested. On 12 December, 1921, the speed course was used by Gloster to establish a British speed record of 196.4mph in their diminutive Bamel. In modified form the aeroplane was tested by the Establishment the following year. The Civil Competition occupied the facilities of the entire Establishment which was officially closed for three months until September, 1920.

In the second phase, which lasted until 1928, the Establishment played only a small part in tests for the Certificate of Airworthiness (C of A). The 1920 scheme for awarding a C of A to new civil types and their development involved first strength scrutiny, based on plans, by the Air Ministry, then certification of materials by the Aeronautical Inspection Department during construction, and third the witnessing of the constructor's flight trials by a representative of the Air Ministry. Finally, the official check consisted of a single flight by a Service pilot, usually from Farnborough and usually undertaken at the constructor's aerodrome. Accurate weighing, when necessary, was done at Martlesham.

In 1919, the Director of Research, Air Commodore H R M Brooke Popham, initiated a parallel scheme to enable the country's aeroplane makers to send their products intended for civil use for normal performance tests and comment by AEE. The scheme was formalised by the issue of a Notice to Airmen (No.5) in January 1920, under which, for a nominal fee of £20, a company would have responsibility only for delivery and removal; the company still bore the risk of damage to its machine and during testing was required to effect repairs. This scheme appears to have been used even when civil aeroplanes were constructed to Air Ministry Specifications and with official financial assistance.

It is hardly surprising that the very limited test flying for a C of A failed, in many instances, to reveal poor features which were abundantly clear to Martlesham from the latter's more searching assessment of the same machines. Yet the official requirements for granting a C of A remained largely unchanged before 1939.

The third phase of involvement for the Establishment began in 1928.

Safety and Parachutes

It is now difficult to assess whether Martlesham suffered more or fewer accidents during the inter-war period when compared with the Service as a whole. Surviving statistics on accidents and engine failures exclude experimental flying, and records of individual accidents up to about 1935 are sketchy. From an analysis of known crashes and total hours flown, a comparison with RAF accident rates indicates that Martlesham's record was probably no worse and arguably better than other units. This conclusion is surprising in view of the large number of untried and diverse types flown and the nature of the flying involved. The reasons why the demanding test flying did not result in more accidents in a period when a normal squadron could expect a 'smash' on average at least once a month in the early 1920s, and less frequently by 1939, are several. First and foremost was the greater experience of the pilots at Martlesham, who were almost invariably posted to test flying only after an assessment of above average ability from previous Service flying. Next was the control exercised on all test flights which were, throughout the period, increasingly carefully briefed to achieve specific results. All flying took place near the airfield, over flat, generally open land suitable for forced landings, free from inconvenient hills, and over an area which became well known to pilots. Although of usually new design, aeroplanes, engines and equipment were subject to greater scrutiny and servicing on the ground, not only by the Establishments's own excellent NCOs

The remains of Bristol Braemar C4297 in August 1921, after the crash in which Flt Lt O M Sutton and AC Sheriden were killed: the remains of D.H.9A H3629 are also visible. (G Kinsey)

and airmen but often with the benefit of assistance from representatives of the designing firm. Finally, test flights were usually required to be flown in weather conditions better than those tolerable to Service units.

In the early postwar period (1920-24), the first fatal accident occurred on 16 August, 1921, when Flt Lt O M Sutton (inventor of the Sutton seat harness universally used in British military aircraft until after the Second World War) swung left on take off in the second Bristol Braemar and hit a hangar. The front of the aircraft was demolished; Sutton and Aircraftman Sheridan were killed. The cause was not determined, but it was Sutton's first flight in the Braemar, and his first in a four-engined aeroplane. The tandem undercarriage was suspected for an unspecified reason by the Accident Committee, who commented on the aeroplane's total airborne time of only 11 hr 50 min in its two and half year life.

More fortunate in July 1922 was the pilot, Flt Lt A H Orlebar, of the third Westland Weasel after a malfunction to its very early Bristol Jupiter engine caused a fire which was still burning following a hurried landing on the airfield. Orlebar scrambled clear only slightly singed.

The second Short Springbok, which had metal covered wings, was subjected to spinning tests shortly after arrival. On 30 November, 1923, it failed to recover, and the pilot, Flg Off E Bird, and Corporal Ball, on his first flight and his last day in the RAF, were killed. The cause was traced to lack of tail effectiveness, and possibly blanking of the rudder, but not, as was first thought from eye witness reports, separation of the wing covering.

Of these accidents perhaps the second fatality could have been avoided by the pilot wearing a parachute. Work at Martlesham had been underway since 1920 in the Parachute Section, testing various designs, but by mid-1922 results had been so disappointing that only one officer remained. The Section had had the task of developing techniques for aeroplane use of the wartime balloon type of parachute – the Guardian Angel, made by Calthrop; 500 had been ordered in 1919. It was operated by a static line attached to the aeroplane, often with ingenious routeing of the line around the fuselage. Only dummies were used, and problems with both types included difficulty of escape if the aircraft was in an unusual attitude, unreliable opening and inconsistent rates of descent. Two makes were soon discarded after determining that much of the trouble stemmed from fouling of the hemp ropes used for rigging. Some success was achieved with a third make, Salvus, when the rigging lines were meticulously folded; also an acceptable quick release fastening was developed for all types of harness.

Notwithstanding the results of Martlesham trials, the Air Ministry decided, in 1923, to fit parachutes in bombers, and on 1 April, 1924, the Parachute Section was reopened, with Flt Lt J Potter as Commanding Officer, Sgt Hawkings and ten airmen together with two aeroplanes – a Bristol Fighter and a Fairey Fawn. Potter had already had some success with parachutes of his own design for dropping containers. He had persisted, in spite of many early disasters with smashed containers, with the

One of the makes of parachute, The Guardian Angel, extensively tested by the Parachute Section in 1920-21. The lower photograph shows the tightly packed rigging lines which were prone to tangling.

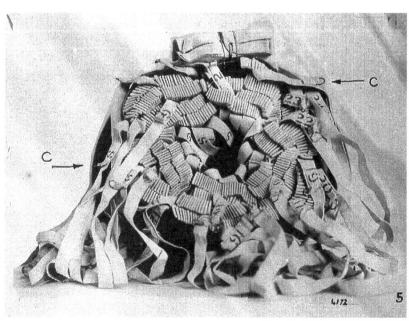

5

help of Flg Off, later Flt Lt, McKenna the Establishment engineering officer, to achieve a reliable system which later saw widespread Service use overseas.

Potter was less fortunate when testing one of many locally designed harnesses by first jumping from the top of a cupboard. The ceiling attachment broke, and he went about for some time afterwards with his face covered in plaster. Potter also became involved in discussion at a guest-night in the Officers' Mess about the terminal velocity of a man. The specific gravity was obviously required, and Potter, who was well built, grabbed a nearby officer and plunged him into a full bath, mess kit and all. Results from this trial were hotly disputed – largely because it could not be agreed how much water had been absorbed by the clothing.

Testing in the new section was soon under way not only with dummies but soon live drops using the recently purchased trial batch of Irvin

parachutes from the United States. In December 1924 the Air Ministry decided to adopt the Irvin type, which was self contained, had silk cords and was deployed by manually pulling a rip cord. Many of the early live jumps were made by two airmen, Corporal East and Aircraftman 'Brainy' Dobbs; the latter established a reputation for delayed opening of his parachute. By early 1925, the Fawn, modified with a ladder on the port side, was used for giving all who would 'volunteer' a chance for a jump. Safety decreed that a second, chest mounted, parachute should be worn which always seemed to get caught in the rungs of the ladder.

Inevitably, some drops did not go according to plan. The procedure was for the pilot to instruct the victim to descend the ladder when approaching the airfield and to give the thumbs up signal to drop for a landing in the middle of the airfield. On one occasion, Flt Lt C McKenzie-Richards decided to

The Establishment Officers – late in 1923.

Standing left to right: Flg Off T G Bird, Flg Off W F Dry, Flg Off J A Gray, Flg Off J D Breakey, Flg Off J H B Carson, Flg Off R Ivelaw-Chapman, Flg Off A C Clinton, Flg Off F C Griffin, and Flg Off M C Head

Seated left to right: Flt Lt T J West, Flt Lt H B Greene, Flt Lt R A de H Haig, Sqn Ldr C H Nicholas, Wg Cdr N J Gill, Mr T M Barlow, Flt Lt A H Orlebar, Flt Lt R C Savery, and Flt Lt J Potter

delay pulling the rip cord, but omitted to tell the pilot with the result that he landed on the apex of the steep sided roof of a hangar. It took half an hour of careful work by 'Works and Bricks' (the Air Ministry Works Dept) with ladders to get him down. After introducing the joys of free-fall parachuting to the Establishment, Potter and his section moved to Henlow in mid-1925.

The Years of the Squadrons 1924-1934

Organisation

In 1922, when the Royal Air Force in the United Kingdom could boast only a handful of front-line land-based aeroplanes, it was decided to create two Home Defence bomber squadrons (No.15 and No.22) near the East Coast. Both were intended to fly D.H.9As and as a first step the existing three Flights at Martlesham were given the title of No.22 Squadron; the change passed almost unnoticed. Work continued exactly as normal, without the new aeroplanes, and members of the squadron learnt of their new status on 24 July, 1923 (formation was officially ante-dated to 1 May, 1923). Arrangements for the second squadron were less straightforward, although throughout 1923 various branches of the Air Ministry, including the Works Department, each played their part, apparently unco-ordinated, to create the new formation. To accommodate the new squadron two temporary Bessonneau hangars were to be supplied, the technical stores enlarged and various improvements made to the existing officers', NCOs' and airmens' accommodation, and the armoury was to be reconditioned. It was October 1923 before details were agreed and May 1924 before all the work was completed, including an additional four steel-framed Baghdad hangars. The period between decision in 1923 and completion the following year gave Wg Cdr Gill, the Commanding Officer, many somewhat bizarre if frustrating experiences. As early as May 1923, the Equipment Branch sent five D.H.9As (Lion Engines); their imminent arrival gave the station commander his first intimation of the formation of the new squadron. He quickly cancelled their arrival; only the first was accepted, unpacked and used later for trials. In October 1923 the Stores Depot, which had already supplied the Bessonneau tents, asked for their return even before they had been erected. In December, Gill wrote testily to the Record Office, which was anxious to post in a squadron's worth of airmen, as follows, 'Your letter bears little relation to fact, and it is no use continuing correspondence re-15 Squadron'.

Meanwhile, the decision of the Air Ministry committee to close Grain resulted in the need for a new home for armament testing. It appears that this requirement and the intention of forming a new squadron were fortuitous and coincidental. By early 1924 sufficient accommodation was ready at Martlesham, and a small group of personnel, stores and aeroplanes moved from Grain to form the first flight of No.15 Squadron for armament testing. Of more significance was the effect of their arrival on the role of the station, and, to reflect the broadened responsibilities, on 20 March, 1924, the title was changed to The Aeroplane and Armament Experimental Establishment. To regularise the new organisation, an Air Ministry Weekly Order (No.395 of 1924) was issued, stating that the station had a Headquarters, Workshops, No.15 (Bombing) Squadron and No.22 (Bombing) Squadron; the second and third Flights of 15 Squadron were formed on 5 May, 1924. The order gave the composition of each squadron as three Flights of four D.H.9As for home defence duties, but that 'for the present' No 22 Squadron would not receive the standard aircraft, but use 'any experimental aircraft'. No.15 Squadron had two further functions – that of armament

The large new hangar under construction in April 1929.

experiments for which an additional two Vickers Vimys and two Bristol Fighters were received, and of training in accordance with the normal annual routine, using the third Flight. The control of the Establishment remained divided between the Director of Technical Development at the Air Ministry (all testing matters) and the Air Officer Commanding Inland Area (Service administrative matters).

Many noted the political sleight of hand involved in the creation of two new squadrons, but even cynics kept their observations private. The Chief of the Air Staff, Air Marshal Trenchard was no doubt content to see the observance of his dictum:

'The expansion of the power of materiel and personnel without increasing either'.

Armament Testing

Demands on No.15 Squadron for armament testing soon expanded beyond the capacity of the Vimys and Bristol Fighters. In addition to increasing use being made of the D.H.9As for bomb and gun tests and other non-routine tasks, the squadron was called upon to assess the armament features of new types. In 1926 another order (AMWO 33 of 1926) was issued, reflecting the changing emphasis of the work of the squadron, by removing from two Flights their eight standard aeroplanes; the training duties of the third remained – bolstered by a further two reserve aircraft. The Air Ministry's desire for pilots to complete at least some training continued to be frustrated, and the

Training Flight effectively ceased to operate at the end of 1927. The demise of the Training Flight may have been influenced by an incident in 1926; of five aircraft of the Flight landing at Larkhill for an annual bombing exercise, four crashed and No.15 Squadron was unable as a result to take part. An order (AMWO 686 of 1928) regularized the cessation of training, but it was 1932 before a final order (AMO A 84 of 1932) formally recorded abolition of all flying training; at the latter date the duties of No.15 Squadron were given as two Flights on experimental armament work and the third on W/T test work. No.22 Squadron continued as before, with 'A', 'B' and 'C' Flights. During the ten years 1924-34, neither squadron took part in a major Air Exercise.

Squadron Leader P C (Pat) Sherren led No.15 Squadron for over three years after its formation, and the first Flight Commander was Flt Lt A M Wray; they were joined later by Flt Lts J W Jones and W N Plenderleith for the other flights. The full complement of D.H.9As was received, but most were infrequently flown. The two Vimys seem to have quickly disappeared, and the routine armament trials (*eg* proof testing of batches of bombs, assessment of gun mountings) were increasingly flown on the D.H.9A and the experimental aircraft after tests of the latter's own armament. The training flight received Hawker Horsleys in 1927 and that year flew 282 hours of the total of 763 hours by the squadron. Flying hours steadily increased throughout the period (*see* Appendix G), but remained well below the totals achieved by regular squadrons.

The closure of Grain necessitated another site for dropping and firing weapons; Orfordness, 13 miles east of Martlesham was reopened in May 1924. Facilities were run down, and unsuitable at first for much of the firing and bomb dropping; as a result the smaller bombs and explosive devices for testing continued to be dropped onto the aerodrome at Martlesham. RAE Farnborough had responsibility for maintenance of Orfordness, and soon had the facilities in working order for use by the three Establishments – RAE, AAEE and MAEE Felixstowe. The Officer commanding No.15 Squadron was responsible for

The Officers' Mess in 1928, looking north. The silver birch at centre left is visible in the two early group photographs.

running the range, and daily sent out parties of airman for plotting and other recording duties; road transport was soon supplemented by air travel when the old but very small and uneven aerodrome on the Ness was reopened. This arrangement lasted until personnel were permanently stationed on site in 1931.

A major improvement in the scope of testing was achieved with the opening of the new ballistic hut at Orfordness on 1 January, 1934. Among benefits was the ability, using recently developed equipment, to determine accurately the ballistics of the bombs, flares and markers with the consequent improvement in calculation of release point.

Each Establishment sent a technical or service officer to the range to supervise its own trials; Martlesham, the major user, usually sent N E Rowe until replaced in 1929 by S Scott-Hall, Flt Lt T LeG 'Nippers' Pynches or Flg Off M H Garnons-Williams; 'Garney-Bill', was a character held in high esteem by his contemporaries, not least for his unique living accommodation in an old red bus parked near the Officers' Mess. Pynches was replaced in 1928 by Flt Lt A E Groom who served for eleven years as the Gunnery expert; Groom had been a wartime gunner in the Royal Navy, and in the ten years since the war had also become an expert in bombing installations.

In fine weather, days spent at Orfordness were usually enjoyable as the salt marshes provided ample opportunity for wild fowling, and oysters were readily, if not completely honestly, available. Midday breaks involved being rowed to the mainland where a plate of oysters and a pint of beer for lunch at a local hostelry cost one shilling and sixpence (7$\frac{1}{2}$p). Not surprisingly such rural delights attracted numbers of visitors from the Air Ministry, RAE and the Royal Arsenal at Woolwich to witness the end results of their work. In summer, for sports afternoons and at weekends, air or surface transport could be found to take those who had not been volunteered for sports to the Ness to enjoy the benefits of the sea and sand.

Records exist for much of the work of No.15 Squadron, and are contained in the armament sections of the M, or type, reports and in the M/Arm series; the latter started in 1924 and are summarised later. The wide range of warlike equipment described gives a comprehensive picture of the Squadron's duties which were nevertheless of a more routine and less hazardous nature than those of the Performance Squadron.

Even routine flights could, however, pose risks – especially for the occupant of the tail position in the later Vickers Virginias who not only had an unpleasant ride if the weather was at all bumpy, but who also was well advised to keep his head down on long flights since the pilots were obliged to react to calls of nature by standing and facing rearwards.

In 1930, a Virginia flown by Flt Lt

Seton Broughall crashed on the aerodrome. An onlooker rushed to the wreckage and forced his way inside to look for survivors; shortly afterwards the doctor arrived and seeing a large bottom sticking out of the fuselage, and thinking the owner was trapped and in agony, thrust his hypodermic needle well into the backside and gave the would-be rescuer a large squirt of morphia. All occupants, in fact, survived even without the benefit of the drug.

Among other incidents recalled by members of No.15 Squadron are the first occasion, in 1926, on which Italian magnesium flares for photography were dropped at night off Orfordness. The illumination was spectacular and lit up the coast for miles around – with the result that not only were the photographs remarkable but the local and not-so-local populace rushed to the village of Orfordness in the middle of the night in various stages of undress demanding to know if a new war had started.

Among the series of long running trials was the search for an acceptable fuse for anti-submarine bombs which had to function underwater after hitting the surface at high speed. Preliminary tests consisted of dropping the fuse onto a concrete floor from a height of six feet; very many were damaged and rejected but eventually a successful model was devised. However, so beautifully constructed were these mechanisms by the Royal Arsenal at Woolwich, that in the opinion of the armament experts at Martlesham, the fuses were impractical for mass production. A further series of trials was mounted against HMS *Marlborough*, decommissioned before being broken up, and acting as a target to assess the effectiveness of armour piercing bombs; several relatively small areas of the ship had had the armour removed and to the frustration of all concerned, some bombs usually found an unarmoured area, and fell straight through the ship without exploding. The *Marlborough* trials coincided with the first tests of the electro-magnetic cartridge fired release unit and the widespread use of high frequency wireless telegraphy (HF W/T) for communications and navigation. On at least one occasion a 500lb bomb (which was not required for the trial) was missing on landing;

The Beardmore Inflexible being refuelled in 1930.

after much head scratching it was established that use of the radio could induce a current into the firing system and operate the cartridge. This phenomenon in 1931 was the first recorded incidence of what later became known as Electro Magnetic Interference, and was initially cured by increasing the current needed to fire the release cartridge. Later aircraft were designed to minimise the interference, and by 1935 AAEE tests routinely included investigation into Electro Magnetic effects.

Wireless (W/T) was gradually introduced into the RAF in the 1920s, and from 1928 the equipment on new aeroplanes was tested by No.15 Squadron. From March 1931 the newly installed mobile W/T trailer was used, manned by A O Roberts (a Junior Technical Officer) with S A Dean as assistant. 'Sid' Dean was still with AAEE in 1970. Pairs of frequencies within the HF band were used for both voice and Morse communication; quality and range of the former was invariably poor until at least 1936. Testing electrical systems and their windmill driven generators was the responsibility of Roberts's section. Electrical intercommunication on multi-seat types was also gradually introduced, and led to at least one attempt at recording pilots' commentary being tried. In 1932 the Blattnerphone wire recorder was tested on the Vickers Vellore and Fairey Fox; results were indifferent due to lack of recording time and the freezing of the microphone at altitude. The Blattnerphone engineer, a German named von Heising insisted on being

present during trials, and made a nuisance of himself by riding around the station on his bicycle and showing unwanted interest in activities completely unconnected with his work.

The Station

With No.15 Squadron ensconced in its new, if temporary accommodation and the future of the station settled, thoughts turned to the provision of more permanent buildings with suitable workshops, fuel storage and other accommodation. Plans were agreed by Wg Cdr Gill, but it fell to his successor to implement them. Wg Cdr Harold Blackburn was a bluff North-countryman whose conversation started 'Eee, chaps ......', and whose dislike of ceremonial soon became well known. The annual inspection by the Air Officer Commanding in September, 1925 found both drill and turn out lamentable; officers in particular had old fashioned and stained uniforms. The following year things had improved somewhat; in 1927 arms and equipment were exceptionally clean, and in 1928 the CO was complemented on the high quality of the voluntary band, some 38 strong. During Blackburn's four years in post the major rebuilding programme was largely completed, having started in 1925. The dominant new structure was the hangar on the North side of the 'B' Flight road, so called because the original 'B' Flight hangar of 1918 was located there. The plan (on page 14) gives details of the 1920s rebuilding work which included new barrack blocks, sports grounds and extra fuel storage capacity. The aerodrome itself received little attention, and continued to be a source of trouble to undercarriages, particularly tail-skids. The heather was cut periodically following a major effort starting in January 1927 and lasting six months. Fire in the surrounding scrubland remained a constant hazard, and an outbreak in August 1930 smouldered for over three weeks but did not damage the aerodrome. Improvements on the airfield were limited to the laying out in 1921 in large chalk letters the name MARTLESHAM HEATH and in late 1927, the permanent landing circle, 450ft in diameter and 4 in wide. The following year, a strip to the north of 'B' Flight road was prepared for the first take off of the Beardmore Inflexible – a very large machine with three 650hp Rolls-Royce Condor engines and a span of 140ft – which had been brought with great difficulty by road to the Establishment and erected on site. With the wind finally in the right direction, Sqn Ldr Noakes, commanding No.22 Squadron, took off having taken only a fraction of the run prepared. The machine completed its trials over the following three years, during which it also flew as a novelty item at air shows, including the RAF Display. Its pilot eventually left the Service with the rank of Air Commodore. The previous year, in June 1927, the aerodrome had been the venue for the successful forced landing of the severely overladen Hawker Horsley, flown by Flt Lt C R Carr, when an attempt at the world's long distance record had to be abandoned shortly after take off from Cranwell.

While the Inflexible and Horsley incidents reflect favourably on the 'Heath', the destructive effect of the rough surface was more usually manifest. Many undercarriages broke, but, in 1929 the CAC Monoplane suffered not only the indignity of a collapse of the main wheels, but also of the engine breaking loose when five engine bearers gave way. Three years later the de Havilland Fox Moth needed a new undercarriage leg after landing. Both types had previously been approved for strength by the structural experts of the Airworthiness Department at RAE. In a way, the nature of the aerodrome surface provided an additional, if unintended, hurdle for both military and civil types to pass before achieving the Establishment's blessing.

The domestic building programme included a handful of substantial houses for use as Officers' married quarters at the far end of 'B' Flight road, and twenty of a smaller type for airmen in the northeast corner of the aerodrome. The latter were very convenient for those NCOs on the Married Establishment of the RAF who qualified for occupancy under the time-honoured points system; the houses were initially little more than basic dwellings. Among those who sought to improve the amenities, both for families and for those living in single accommodation on the station, were the doctor, Sqn Ldr B F 'Fritz' Haythornthwaite and his wife Mary. They provided musical entertainment, arranged for children's swings and slides to be built, and were for ever active in the general well being of all ranks. They were also generous in lending their German sailing canoe, moored on the River Deben nearby. The commanding officer for three years from November 1928 was Victor O Rees, initially as a Wg Cdr, but from January 1930 as a Group Captain – a promotion reflecting the increased responsibilities of his growing station. Rees was friendly with a local landowner, with the result that lorry loads of trees were imported from the latter's estate and transplanted around the station. He also instituted a prize for the best kept garden among the airmen's quarters. Rees, who had a reputation as a disciplinarian, undoubtedly lost a little of his *amour propre* one day while 'tearing a strip' off a defaulter. Rees fell from his swivelling chair in mid-tirade, but, nothing daunted and without batting an eyelid, continued from the prone position to exhort the defaulter to behave himself in future.

The building programme and what would now be called landscaping were significant alterations, but, even in 1939, the station still possessed rural charm and unsophistication. Many an officer from the Air Ministry and the other Establishments found compelling reasons for visiting Martlesham Heath, but the price of the large number of visitors, most of whom had to be entertained in the Officers' Mess, lay in the very high messing charges levied on resident officers – charges reputed to be the highest in the Service at four shillings (20p) a day in 1932 for a Flying Officer, when one shilling (5p) was more normal.

The Role of Martlesham Heath

In 1924-5 a table was circulated within the Air Ministry illustrating how it took over five years from the time that even a small new aeroplane requirement was conceived until the first series production aircraft was delivered. The table is reproduced here as it shows Martlesham's place in the scheme of normal military development – a scheme that was followed until shortly before the Second World War.

As an example of the gestation period for a large aeroplane, a replacement for the Vickers Virginia was first considered in April 1926, and the first full production aircraft was delivered to the Service in August 1934, as the Handley Page Heyford Mk II; the

Aeroplane Size	Small	Medium	Large
		(months)	
Preparation of Specification, tendering and selection of two or three types of prototypes.	13	15	19
Construction of prototypes	12	16	24
Martlesham trials	6	10	10
Service trials and reporting	4	4	4
Specification amendment, order for one squadron to delivery of 1st* aircraft.	13	13	17
Development, order of full production to delivery of 1st* aircraft.	18	20	22
Total Months	66	78	96

*First aircraft for short trials at Martlesham.

total period was thus 100 months. The prototype had arrived at AAEE late in 1931, and the first development production aircraft late in 1933.

The table shows typical development timescales of the successful designs; most of the remainder failed to proceed beyond the first Martlesham visit or, for a few, Service trials. The Establishment's power in the matter of selection was considerable, and great pains were taken for objective assessment and reporting. Impartiality was the watchword at all levels, but the presence of representatives of firms whose designs were under test added to the difficulty of making fair assessments. One doctor slyly remarked in later years that so keen were the competing firms for the success of their own aeroplanes that, Kings Regulations notwithstanding, pilots were tempted with weekends on private yachts, hospitable entertainment and even the odd gold cigarette case.

The ten years 1924-1934 saw the bulk of the aircraft Competitions, so much a feature of Martlesham's work (*see* Appendix D). The twenty recognizable competitions are described later; a further seven took place in 1935-8. All save two were mounted to find the best design to meet a particular Air Ministry Specification. Usually, two or three manufacturers were chosen for offical sponsorship of single prototypes, and other firms encouraged to submit Private Venture types. Dates were fixed for delivery of the rival designs to Martlesham, with the aim of assembling all types together for comparison. This aim was rarely

An ever present hazard in the summer - a heath fire; this one was in August 1930. (G Kinsey)

achieved in toto as inevitably there would be late-comers, often causing delay in the deadline. Once the first aeroplane (of up to eleven types in the case of smaller machines) arrived the Establishment started work – stripping, reassembling, measuring, speed course, climb speeds, climbs to ceiling, diving, stability tests, perhaps measuring take off and landing, completing gunnery and bombing trials, timing maintenance and finally writing the report – all this for every type in every competition. In 1928 alone there were four competitions. Before final selection, about three of the most promising contenders completed Service trials with an operational squadron. Once selection was made on the basis of the performance (a generic term including handling, stability, view and accessibility as well as speed and climb) of the prototype, occasionally without military equipment fitted, further testing followed with any modifications necessary plus incorporation of Service equipment. The inevitable increases in weight and drag frequently caused a significant decrease in performance – a matter of great disappointment to the Air Staff. The Armstrong Whitworth Atlas and Bristol Bulldog are but two examples; the latter suffered further in Service, the actual deterioration being measured at Martlesham.

The unique position in British aviation held by AAEE gave it a very comprehensive view of aeronautical

developments and the Establishment played its part in the progress made; parachutes in the early 1920s provide an example. In general, however, Martlesham's role was to assess novel features as they appeared, usually on several different types at around the same time. The following list is a selection of the more widely used developments: Metal airframes gradually replaced wood in the period 1924-1930 for front-line types. Handley Page slots (more properly slats which formed a slot when open), first tested in 1927 on the Avro Buffalo, were assessed on a further eleven types[*] in the following twelve months. Antifreezing lubricating oil for controls was first successful in the Bristol Bulldog in 1929 flying at 27,000ft where the temperature was minus 33 deg C. Wheelbrakes, first intended to assist deck manoeuvring on aircraft carriers, became common in the 1930s, although early methods of actuation left much to be desired. Townend rings, usually for fighters, were briefly in vogue for radial engines to increase cooling and reduce aerodynamic drag. Retractable undercarriages were not widely used by 1934 – the first to be tested was on a civil machine, the Airspeed Courier, in 1933. Several types of fighters and their trainer derivatives were re-tested with varying sizes of mass balances on the control surfaces. Later developments, after 1934, included flaps, variable-pitch propellers, enclosed cockpits, and monoplane wings.

As advances in aeronautical techniques were made, so the Establishment became the repository of knowledge, gleaned from a broad spectrum of types of aeroplanes incorporating the new features. The wealth and breadth of experience on phenomena such as spinning and stalling, and engine characteristics was unique. The benefit of this experience for future developments was passed on in a number of ways. First was the infor-

---

[*] Handley Page Harrow, Blackburn Ripon, Westland Wapiti (two versions) Hawker Woodcock, de Havilland D.H.9A (for Wapiti), Armstrong Whitworth Atlas (five versions), Handley Page Hyderabad, Fairey IIIF, Blackburn Dart, Vickers Virginia, and Hawker Horsley.

mal contact of Martlesham pilots and technical people with industry; then there was the passing of reports on aeroplanes to their designers, who were able to remedy shortcomings by modification or in new designs. Next, the Air Ministry was aided in determining new requirements, both civil and military, by the constant flow of reports on existing designs. Finally, and of great importance in the more fundamental and general areas, was the formal relationship with the Aeronautical Research Council (ARC) the country's premier forum for collation, consideration and dissemination of aeronautical matters of moment. The ARC was sent such reports as it required, and, on occasion, also sponsored trials. Thus, while Martlesham developed techniques and methods for its own use, it also indirectly but significantly contributed to the general advance of aviation knowledge.

Civil Aircraft

Notwithstanding the shortcomings apparent in 1924, of the procedures for granting a C of A, using arrangements apparently designed for the convenience of the manufacturer as far as the flying tests were concerned, the procedure was, in fact, changed on financial rather than technical grounds.

In the twelve months to the end of January 1927 the Airworthiness Department of the RAE calculated that C of A work cost £3,250.9s.4d, against a total income from applicants of £936.6s.0d. The resulting changes included creation of the Approved Firms Scheme (officially introduced by an Air Navigation Directive in November 1929 which included sixteen firms*) to reduce official oversight at factories, and the designation of Martlesham as a site for technical appraisal and flying tests. The first C of A test at Martlesham was on the Simmonds Spartan in December 1928, some five months after the type had flown privately in the King's Cup Race in the hands of Flt Lt S N

---

* Armstrong Whitworth, Avro, Blackburn, Boulton and Paul, Bristol, de Havilland, Fairey, Gloster, Handley Page, Hawker, Parnall, Saunders-Roe, Short Brothers, Supermarine, Vickers and Westland.

Webster of No.22 Squadron. Thereafter, C of A tests were regularly completed at AAEE which gradually took over the official testing from RAE. To modern eyes the tests were superficial, frequently being completed in under two days. The technical appraisal was an examination under the supervision of the Senior Technical Officer, a post held by Flt Lt (retaining the rank of Squadron Leader on retirement in 1928) H W McKenna throughout this middle inter-wars period. His great experience and critical eye missed little, and on his brief but intensive probing depended the success or otherwise of the application. Such was McKenna's influence that designers were known to include old tried and trusted features which would please him, rather than risk an improvement which he might find a trifle novel and unacceptable.

In fact reports usually recommended issue of a Certificate, but often with caveats regarding the necessity of incorporating improvements before issue. Flying involved a measured take off, landing and climb, determination of maximum level speed and a dive to 150 per cent of the level speed. In 1929, the requirement to remain under control at a speed less than 55mph (measured by the static head) was stated. For the take off, public transport aeroplanes were required to achieve a height of 66ft within 546yd of starting take off (into a 5mph wind) and of climbing to 1,378ft within 3 min. Private category machines had less demanding requirements, and those in the aerobatic category required satisfactory completion of standard aerobatic manoeuvres.

It is an interesting fact that, in 1929-31 at a time of national economic depression, Martlesham (only one of three sites for official trials for C of A) alone flew fourteen new types in 1929, ten in 1930 and nine in 1931. More remarkable is the enthusiasm of the constructors who produced the aeroplanes, and who, with one or two exceptions, could expect only a handful of orders. The exception was de Havilland, who made the Moth series; Martlesham's comments on the Puss Moth in 1930 were soon reflected in sales. Indeed, such was his reputation at the Establishment that in 1934 it was sufficient (if ill advised) to say of the D.H.86 that it was 'as good as the

usual de Havilland'. Later in service the early D.H.86 suffered unexplained crashes.

The design and manufacture of civil aeroplanes, particularly for the private owner, attracted many people new to the business. Martlesham was often the first place where any fundamental shortcomings became apparent. It is not surprising that most comments were critical; many examples are given later. What is surprising is that so many of the serious handling deficiencies reported were allowed by the Airworthiness authorities to pass unrectified on granting a C of A. Perhaps the most notable example was the four-seat Seagrave Meteor in 1930, for which a C of A was recommended in spite of doubts about passenger safety, the inability to fly on one engine due to excessive rudder force and a propensity to enter an immediate spin at the stall. Larger aeroplanes were expected to have better handling, but even so some of them were granted a C of A with the need for trimming to achieve round-out on landing. The system was, indeed, far from perfect in the 1920s and 1930s.

Some innovations on civil machines, such as the first retractable undercarriage on a British production aeroplane on the Airspeed Courier in 1933, posed few problems for testing. Others, particularly the Cierva Autogiro in 1932, were so novel that existing tests were felt to be inappropriate and the Establishment's comments somewhat tenuous as a result, and the report lacked performance data. Handling qualities in general improved as designer's knowledge of such features as control hinge moments increased; the improvements were progressive, and possibly largely unnoticed. When the Handley Page Hamilton G-EBIX returned for further testing in 1930 after a gap of six years, the elevators and ailerons were found to be excessively heavy, and the machine to be very unstable laterally. These features had apparently been considered unworthy of comment on the earlier occasion.

Civil machines in general were less advanced than their military counterparts and produced fewer interesting handling charactertistics. Nevertheless a tragic accident to a civil aircraft in this period occurred on 21 October, 1933. Trials earlier in 1933 of the

Boulton Paul P.64 Mailcarrier had revealed alarming directional characteristics, in which yaw could be contained only by prompt use of asymmetric power; the rudder lacked sufficient control. Auxiliary fins were fitted, and Flt Lt G L G Richmond took off to confirm another pilot's opinion of the modification. At 1,200ft the aircraft suddenly dived into the ground and Richmond was killed. Excessive fuselage side-area ahead of the CG was held to blame.

Among the less serious incidents was one caused by Martlesham's notorious surface which caused the pin holding the left port oleo strut to shear and the wheel to swing free on the Westland Wessex. Alerted by ground staff holding up a wheel, the pilot, Flt Lt S N Webster had the craft lightened by jettisoning ballast while he flew around using up fuel. On landing the port wingtip struck the ground and the machine keeled over while coming to rest. The most alarming moment for one passenger (Victor Gaunt of Westland) was after landing when he was startled by the ripping noise of the escape panel as it was opened by the other passenger (Stuart Scott-Hall).

On another occasion, the Vickers Viastra was prepared for the Hendon Display in 1931. It had only flown twice after reconversion to three engines (from two) before being taken over by Flt Lt Langford-Sainsbury under the normal arrangements whereby AAEE Service pilots flew the New Types at this RAF event. On both flights during rehearsals the centre engine cut out on take off and the pilot declined to fly it again. The Viastra did not fly in the Display, and Vickers' people were dismayed; the fault was traced to a miscalculation of the fuel feed rates during acceleration.

Performance Measurement

In April 1923 the post of Chief Technical Officer was filled by R S Capon on the departure of T M Barlow to Fairey Aviation. Capon joined from the Air Ministry having been a Martlesham pilot briefly in 1919; he was an Australian astronomer and took the post as CTO as short term employment pending the completion of an observatory in Canberra;

in fact he completed an eventful four years at AAEE, until becoming Superintendent of Scientific Research at RAE. In 1923, the scope of Martlesham reports was expanded from an average of four pages to a total approaching forty (*see* Appendix F) for a complicated large aeroplane. Capon's first task was to expand the technical staff to meet the demands of the reports; that he was successful (assistants increased from one to seven) at a time of unprecedented financial stringency is a tribute to his power of persuasion. However, of even more importance to the work and status of the Establishment was Capon's work on the development of testing methods to produce the most accurate and comprehensive performance data. His aims were first to improve existing methods and second to devise ways of reducing flying time while increasing the usefulness of results.

Standard tests of maximum speeds were refined by the use of airspeed indicators calibrated for temperature, the introduction of Farnborough's 'suspended static head' for position error determination, and the use of cameras on the speed course; the second of these greatly reduced the need for the third. Climb to ceiling trials were preceded by partial climbs through 1,000ft at various speeds to determine the best. The single needle altimeters in use throughout the interwars period could give unacceptable errors over small changes in height and Capon introduced the Askania statoscope (a considerable refinement of Tizard's thermos flask) which was ideal for measuring accurately changes of pressure over 1,000ft. Finally, the altimeters themselves were accurately calibrated in a low-temperature and low-pressure chamber supplied by Farnborough. Having improved the accuracy of the raw performance data, Capon set about quantifying the errors possible from the use of the two methods of reducing the data to standard atmospheric conditions. The pressure basis proved to be considerably more accurate than the density basis – the discrepancy increasing as temperature variation from standard increased. The pressure basis was adopted at Martlesham, at least temporarily, from about 1926. The final area to be investigated in the attempt

to improve the quality of standard performance was the error in recording (*ie* the pilots' observations) and in analysis; perhaps surprisingly, Capon concluded that recording errors were negligible.

The improvements in standard test techniques, worthwhile though they were, still included approximations for some variables, *eg* the cosine of the angle of climb being replaced by unity and the slipstream effect on lift being neglected. Capon set about determining the effect of the variables which could account for the final two or three percent of accuracy in performance. Building on earlier research work, Capon developed a system of non-dimensional quantities from which families of curves could be produced once the basic performance had been established for a particular type. By a further limited number of flight tests with, say, increased weight or a new propeller, it was possible to calculate the whole performance at the new condition. Further, it was possible to determine whether the penalty on performance of, for example, carrying bombs under the wings, was due to increased weight or extra drag, and the relative contribution of each. The effect of the changes on test flights was to make the briefing to pilots very specific as to engine revolutions, height, speed and meteorological conditions.

From early 1925 a special Research Flight was formed to develop and refine the new methods; Flt Lt Arthur Scroggs was succeeded by Flt Lt Atholl Paish in command of the Flight. The Flight was used initially to validate theoretical work and later to apply the results to specific types when they could be spared for the extra flying after initial trials. Examples in 1930-31 are the Westland Wizard, Handley Page Hare and prototype Westland Wapiti. Most of the improvements at Martlesham in test techniques and accuracy of measurement, together with increased understanding of performance and control characteristics came from the work of the Flight. After nine years it was disbanded, probably because its work was increasingly of a nature more properly conducted at Farnborough.

The Scientific method of testing, as Capon's work became known, continued in use until the war. The first major development after Capon's

2 N. 525. P.
MARTLESHAM. HE
4·9·29.
F/10"   500'

To Woodbri

The northern end of Royal Air Force Martlesham Heath in September 1929. The large hangar (38) is numbered 53 on the site plan.

departure resulted from further work on the performance of aeroplanes with supercharged engines. In 1928, N E Rowe (earlier one of Capon's assistants) reported a series of tests which indicated that the power of supercharged engines varied as a function of density. Further work in 1929 confirmed this result, and, in 1930 when the terms moderate supercharging (full power to 4,000ft) and full supercharging (full power to 10,000ft) were introduced, trials refined but did not alter the earlier conclusion. The continuous search for the most accurate measurement of performance led to a series of reports in 1932 by J L Hutchinson, E Finn and R W Blundell which concluded that the performance of aeroplanes with all types of engine could be determined accurately and simply by reducing the data by the 'half and half' method *ie* apply half the correction from the density method and add half from the pressure method. It is of interest that this series of reports with the prefix M/Res included the authors' names;

all other reports were issued in the name of the Establishment.

Handling Assessment

Throughout the 1920s and early 1930s there were few changes in the handling tests which formed part of the standard assessment routine. Stability investigations were straightforward; in each axis in turn the aeroplane was settled into the required configuration of speed and engine revolutions, then the appropriate control was used to induce a disturbance and then released. Longitudinal behaviour was assessed by a recording airspeed indicator; having held the trimmed condition for 20 seconds, the elevator was used to increase or decrease speed by 10mph. Stability was indicated by the speed tending to return to the trimmed figure, instability by the tendency to increase or decrease after the controls were released. A high, medium and a low trim speed were usually investigated. Laterally and directionally, the technique was less simple

since there were usually no trimmers to prevent the minor roll or yaw tendencies of the aircraft. Included in standard performance tests of all but large twin-engined machines were spins.

In the early years aeroplanes were spun at standard loading (but without free guns or bombs) for four, later eight, turns using the accepted, *ie* control reversal recovery technique; reports were limited to stating the pilots' opinion on recovery behaviour – usually 'normal'. The position of the tail incidence was of great importance, and the first series of spins was made with the gear set to the mid position; a comment was usually included in the report of the best setting, and any difficulty with recovery from even a prolonged spin with other settings. A recalcitrant aircraft in a spin was the prototype Bristol Bulldog; the difficulty in recovery was resolved by progressively increasing the fin area, and then lengthening the fuselage so that a satisfactory and repeatable spin was achieved before Service use in 1929. The reverse situation was the case in the Hawker Hart and its developments; the original Hart was straightforward, but changes in wing design and increasing the amount of equipment and its distribution led to unsatisfactory characteristics, particularly in the Osprey Fleet Air Arm version. The solution was partially similar to the Bulldog in that the fin area was increased. In later years weight and CG were varied if considered necessary, and comments on differences in behaviour between left and right spins, and a note on whether the engine (which was invariably at idling) stopped; there never seems to have been difficulty in restarting. By 1934 when eight turn spins were the norm, a more scientific technique was in use involving timing of turns (using two thigh-mounted stop watches) and noting the number of turns and height needed to effect recovery. Some research was also completed on the normal accelerations in spins and in recovery using a maximum recording accelerometer. In 1930, it was concluded that all manoeuvres correctly performed by skilled pilots rarely exceeded 3G; presumably these included looping manoeuvres.

Spinning caused several accidents and near-accidents; among the latter was the first two-seat Gloster Grebe, flown by Flt Lt H V Rowley in 1927. Entry was at 15,000ft and recovery attempted above 10,000ft but without response. Several turns later full power was applied as a desperate measure at the same time as full forward stick; recovery followed and level flight regained at 4,000ft. It was later concluded that the head and shoulders of the tall pilot in the rear seat had blanked the rudder. Less fortunate was Flt Lt H S Broughall in October 1931 in the Amstrong Siddeley Panther-engined Hawker Hart; he had to bale out when the aircraft failed to recover from a righthand spin with a forward CG. The wreckage indicated that the aircraft had recovered; it was concluded that the experimental radial engine and its cowling had upset the airflow over the tail. The following year the Vickers Jockey monoplane

failed to recover from a righthand spin and Flt Lt V S 'Lovely' Parker baled out; wheel spats added just before the spin were thought to have upset recovery. Sometime before this accident, Parker, who was a strikingly handsome man, had rolled his Austin Seven car and had to have a plaster of paris collar to immobilise his neck; he was sent on leave not at all happy with his appearance. When higher authority learnt of his case, he was ordered to hospital at RAF Halton where he was immobilised with sandbags on a bed and watched over by adamantine Sisters.

Stalling was a vexed subject for many years between the wars and received much thought and ingenuity; the primary objective was docile behaviour at the lowest possible speed. It seems that, at least in the 1920s, it was taken as axiomatic that pilots would stall their aeroplanes inadvertently on occasions – even experienced pilots of transport types; there was no emphasis on identifying aerodynamic or other phenomena which would warn the pilot of the approaching stall – other than his low airspeed. At Martlesham, the standard test, for civil and military machines, was to fly the aircraft at the slowest possible speed for one minute; the highest speed noted on a recording airspeed indicator during that time was taken as the stalling speed. Usually a trailing static head was used to overcome pressure errors; presumably the appropriate correction was applied to the figure found so that pilots in service without the benefit of a trailing static head would be aware of the indicated stalling speed. In 1927 the only requirement under the head of 'controllability' for a civil C of A was the one sentence, 'Must glide under control at less than 55mph (as shown by suspended static head)'.

Just as the accuracy of climb and speed performance methods was improved, so was the precision of recording take-off and landing distances improved. To modern eyes, there is a surprising number of variables which were either not considered, or ignored. 'Stick and unstick' as the tests were colloquially known were made into wind. The surface of the aerodrome was covered with short heather and other growth, and was notoriously uneven although essen-

tially level. However, the effect of surface and its variable retarding effect appears not to have been taken into account.

In 1928 an investigation by the Research Flight was reported on the effects of altitude, temperature, wind and weight on take-off and landing performance; the results were inconclusive, probably because of the limited range of temperatures and the location of the trials near sea level. The report appears to have had no effect on the conduct of routine tests since temperature was not noted and the effect of reducing weight during a series of tests was ignored. Both would have been minor factors. The wind was always recorded (10mph maximum but ideally only 5mph for civil types), but at least until the mid-1930s no attempt was made to correct take-off (the more critical manoeuvre) and landing distances to a standard wind speed. The figures quoted in the performance tables in Part II, therefore, are not strictly comparable. Perhaps the Establishment's view of these tests can be gauged by the fact that take-off and landing distances were not measured as a routine on fighters and similar high performance aeroplanes, at least until after 1930. However, where measurements were made definite improvements in accuracy and convenience were achieved from the earliest method which employed airmen with flags to mark the start of the take-off run and the point of unstick (which involved much running and guesswork) and a similar procedure to note touchdown and the point of coming to rest; measurement soon relied upon the use of cameras. By 1926, a system of two plate cameras, one aimed along the line of take-off and the other at right angles was used; as the subject aeroplane passed the second camera (aligned with a pair of measured posts), both cameras were operated. The image from the second camera, corrected for tracking error from the first, gave an accurate height at the so called screen. Accuracy was enhanced, but convenience cannot have been improved because any change in wind direction involved moving the whole set up. In 1931, a multi-exposure camera developed by the RAE greatly simplified the measurement process and did away with the need for the tracking camera but increased the work of

analysis. The new camera also revealed that take offs and landings were made at speeds much below stalling speeds, particularly on monoplanes (the Vickers Vireo was the first case in point). Further research in 1931 established that piloting technique had a large effect on distances to the screen, and that within half a span of the ground, the wing produced usable lift at a speed lower than the lowest achievable in free air. In 1932, a trial using two types of Armstrong Whitworth Atlas and several pilots concluded that landing distance achieved was dependent much more on the pilot than on the difference between the aircraft. There is no record of any action to standardise piloting techniques for landing.

Air Ministry Instructions

In April 1924, while No.15 Squadron was being assembled, the Establishment's 'boss' at the Air Ministry changed from the Director of Research to the Director of Technical Development (DTD); the latter was one of two new Directorates created by dividing the responsibilities of the former. One effect of the change at the Air Ministry was a steady flow of formal instructions to Establishments, the first to affect AAEE being issued in October 1924. This instruction concerned the loading of aeroplanes for Squadron trials on completion of Martlesham's work. Other instructions issued between 1924 and 1934 included the requirement for armament test results in reports (March 1925), the need to preserve aircraft parts which had failed on test (February 1926), the importance of tests of the oiling system (January 1928) and the need for all test aircraft to be fitted with an oil thermometer

(February 1928), the effect on performance of rear guns in different positions, (July 1930), the need for armament trials to be combined with performance tests (September 1932), and the need to consider the advisability of flying trials above continuous cloud cover (October 1933).

The DTD instructions had varied impact, although most tended to increase the amount of flying and thus the bulk of the report on each type; a few, such as the instruction to limit the details of construction (December 1925), reduced the work of reporting. Other subjects were of more importance, and often give an insight into the scope and conduct of tests.

In 1928 a Bulldog was making a climb to ceiling. The limited, free flowing, oxygen supply was usually switched on above 15,000ft; on this occasion the switch was not properly put on and the pilot became unconscious. He recovered as the aircraft descended out of control. In May 1929, DTD decreed that the maximum altitude for AAEE tests was to be 25,000ft due to the shortcomings of existing oxygen systems. Pilots no doubt greeted the limitation with amusement since 20,000ft was regularly achieved without any oxygen equipment and, as early as mid-1925, supercharged Siskins had climbed (with the benefit of the unreliable liquid oxygen system) to 29,000ft.

Strenuous efforts were made to improve oxygen systems, and leading Martlesham's contribution was Flg Off J R Addams who made many high-level flights with experimental liquid and gaseous systems between 1928 and 1931. He frequently suffered when the systems failed to work properly, but always recovered sufficiently to make a safe landing; he was awarded the Air Force Cross for his work. Addams had a second spell at AAEE

in 1936-7 and later retired as a Group Captain; his daughter Dawn became a film star.

Pilots may have noted that no direction was issued by DTD to limit flying at altitude without serviceable heated clothing. Until enclosed cockpits were the norm, cold was the worst enemy, a discomfort experienced many times a month in winter by test pilots, unlike pilots in operational squadrons who rarely had to fly above 5,000ft. At Martlesham, 'A' Flight (Fighter) in particular, wore huge Sidcot flying overalls, several pairs of gloves and socks, and thick fur lined boots together with a couple of extravagant scarves and a fur-lined helmet and goggles. Electrically heated clothing routinely either failed to work at all, or overheated causing alarming smouldering until the wires could be disconnected. A common cause of many failures was the unreliable electrical supply from the generator driven by a windmill in the propeller slipstream; some tests were made to improve matters but appear to have met with little success. There were many instances of frostbite of the face and hands; the latter was caused by the need to remove at least the more cumbersome gloves to write data on the inevitable kneepad. Frequently, a pilot had to be helped out of the open cockpit after landing from a high-altitude flight where temperatures could be as low as minus 60 deg C as recorded on the strut mounted thermometer. There are several instances of pilots being reduced to tears in the hour or so after landing as they thawed out. Another phenomenon of high-altitude flying, the vapour trail, was first noted at Martlesham in 1926 when Flt Lt A O (Robbo) Lewis-Roberts was doing runs at about 20,000ft in the Vickers Vixen. Observers on the ground thought that the aircraft was on fire, and were surprised when the Vixen landed to find the frozen pilot oblivious of the fire – he is reported as saying that the heat would almost have been welcome.

Fuel Consumption

As noted, fuel comsumption trials at AAEE were not routinely completed on types under test in the inter-wars period. The reasons were manifold. Most important was the RAF's attitude to range and endurance calculations. In 1924 the Air Staff calculated the radius of action by taking the maximum level speed at a specified height (8,000ft for bombers, 10,000ft for fighters) as reported by AAEE, and multiplying this figure by the endurance found by applying the consumption of the engine (as given by ground tests of the engine type) to the capacity of the fuel tank; an allowance of 30 min for take off, climb and emergencies was made. Thus the radius of the Avro Aldershot was established at 248 miles, based on the test speed of 90mph at 8,000ft. The shortcomings of this method were recognized, and DTD issued an instruction in April 1926 for Martlesham (and Felixstowe) to include consumption data in reports. After briefly attempting to comply, AAEE abandoned routine consumption trials for several years due to the practical difficulties. There was no reliable flowmeter; an RAE type tested in 1928 had technical shortcomings. Also measurement of fuel useage by tank selection in the cruise was impractical in most types.

Nevertheless between 1926 and 1932 several trials were made to discover the conditions for maximum range. In 1926, using an extra fuel tank with suitable calibrations, a useful increase in range was achieved by increasing height from 5,600ft to 18,000ft. In 1931, a further increase in range resulted from use of the mixture control to reduce engine RPM; a 3

percent reduction was the optimum. When a variable timing engine was available (a Bristol Jupiter VIIIF in a Wapiti), even greater economy was achieved by advancing the ignition; this trial confounded earlier forecasts which had indicated that a weak mixture combined with the greatest retardation of the ignition would give maximum range at any height. It is of interest that in 1931-3 versions of the Fairey IIIF and Fairey Gordon were tested with external long range tanks. Of primary concern to the Air Ministry, who called for the trials, was the adequacy of the oil supply; no requirement for range measurement was specified.

Meanwhile, the Air Staff in 1932 were obliged to use the 1924 methods, modified by the restriction on current engines which could be run at full throttle for only five minutes. Even though the Establishments resumed testing and reporting of endurance of some new types in about 1932, RAF Commands were still, in 1936, making flights to establish the range of types already in service. Much discussion ensued after the Commands complained that their results were significantly inferior to what AAEE reports had led them to expect. The Establishment countered by specifying the techniques it used in tests, which differed from those used by Command crews. The range question was but one of several which led to misunderstanding, and which eventually led to the restriction on circulation of Martlesham reports.

Report Distribution

In late 1929 Martlesham (and Felixstowe) reports on aeroplanes had a limited routine distribution within the Air Ministry and sister Establishments; the Air Ministry's representatives at the manufacturers (known as Resident Technical Officers) were also sent copies of relevant reports for the information of the company concerned. RAF formations were excluded but in spite of entreaties from Commands, the Air Ministry decided not to broaden distribution on the grounds that there would be endless complaints. A review was, however, initiated, but in October 1931, the existing restricted circulation was retained. The reasons

given are instructive, and were as follows; the performance was reduced to standard atmospheric conditions, tests were flown by specially trained pilots with special instruments, changes to prototype aircraft before Service use were almost invariably introduced after AAEE trials, and finally, the documents were bulky and difficult to reproduce. There the matter rested until mid-1938, when circumstances and trials reporting procedures changed. Reports on civil aircraft for C of A trials were similarly treated, with the introduction in January 1932 of a second part to the report giving criticisms and recommendations for the grant or withholding of the Certificate. In 1933, it was decided not to send the second part to contractors.

Flutter

AAEE's concern with speed was limited, until the mid-1920s, to establishing accurately how fast a machine would travel in level flight at various heights. In a dive the speed would be exceeded, but only to the extent necessary to perform aerobatics or other less adventurous manoeuvres, and no formal recording of maximum speed achieved appears to have been made. Comments were confined to stability, ease of handling, and steadiness for gunfiring. Vibration was a term often used after high-speed dives, variously attributed to engine/propeller effects, and flutter. The last phenomenon first became a serious hazard on the Gloster Gamecock. Early Martlesham flying had excited mild flutter (attributed by pilots to the tailplane), but in service higher diving speeds were evidently obtained and wing failures soon led to serious and fatal crashes. Among RAF pilots to survive flutter was Sqn Ldr Pongo Brooks of No.43 Squadron who in July 1926 reported experiencing violent lateral kicking of the control column at 170mph. At the Central Flying School Flt Lt D'Arcy Greig (later a wartime Commandant of AAEE) undertook dives in the Gamecock, and he confirmed that the ailerons received violent and rapid buffeting. Evidence from Service crashes indicated that failure started at the ailerons which were wrenched off, followed by the failure of the outer and then the inner wings.

Scientific investigation of the Gamecock's flutter was put in hand at the RAE; one of the pilots Flt Lt Junor, was killed in the process. Meanwhile, at AAEE a Gamecock which had been flown for some time by several pilots for type experience was ordered by the Air Minsitry to be modified by balancing the ailerons. The work took some weeks under the direction of the Chief Engineer Flt Lt McKenna assisted by a pilot of 'C' Flight No.22 Squadron, Flg Off G Wheatley. After a careful check of the aircraft, Wheatly took off on 8 December, 1926, for a test flight having received specific instructions to undertake straight flying only. The Gamecock was in the air for 10 to 15 minutes in the vicinity of the aerodrome when airmen were attracted by the terrific whine of the engine and saw the wings and bits of the aircraft floating away and the fuselage diving to earth. Examination of the wreckage revealed that Wheatley had released his Sutton harness, as in the case of Junor of RAE, obviously when the flutter started, but was stunned or killed outright by the gravity tank structure before he could escape by parachute. Guards were immediately placed on the wreckage which was strewn in a line over a mile long. RAE stress experts soon arrived and all bits and pieces of the wreckage were carefully collected, tabulated and assembled in a hangar. From the result of this investigation, and subsequent wind-tunnel tests, the RAE was able to find the cause of flutter and design a relatively simple modification to brace the outer section of the upper wing. This modification was incorporated in new and existing Gamecocks, and also some earlier Grebes which had a similar wing design.

During consideration of the flutter question, it was decided to include dives as part of normal tests, and on 22 October, 1926, DTD issued an instruction to AAEE which stated, '..... all single-seat Fighters to include flying tests in a dive at speeds attainable under Service conditions'. Thus was the requirement for the so-called 'Terminal Velocity' or TV dive formalized. The technique used for achieving the highest possible speed was to climb to high altitude, close the throttle, switch off the engine and dive as nearly vertical as possible. On recovery the engine was switched on and level flight regained.

While TV dives became an established part of the testing routine, occasionally with alarming results, there were no fatal accidents. However, flutter remained a potential and actual hazard, even at relatively low speeds. In September 1928 the prototype Parnall Pipit, built to meet a naval fighter requirement, was being flown by Sqn Ldr Jack Noakes who had commanded No.22 Squadron since mid-1927. He was at 2,000ft in a slight dive at 140mph (naval aircraft had recently been specified to have the airspeed calibrated in mph in place of the earlier knots) when there was a bang and the tailplane folded. He was just able to keep control by pushing the stick fully forward and he attempted a landing during which the aircraft crashed and he was thrown out, breaking his neck. He spent several months in hospital at RAF Halton while the cause of the tail breakage was established as flutter. One of his visitors was Sqn Ldr E S Goodwin, a flying-boat pilot with No.480 Flight who, shortly after the visit was appointed to the Command of No.22 Squadron at Martlesham, a post he held for nearly four years. The second Pipit was extensively modified and made ready at the maker's aerodrome in February 1929. After two promising flights early in the month Flt Lt S L G 'Poppy' Pope went to Yate near Bristol to continue tests. On the initial climb at 2,500ft he used rudder to steer away from cloud, and immediately the rudder broke away and the aircraft rolled onto its back. Pope baled out and landed unharmed, although severely shaken; the aircraft was a write off. The cause was found to be lack of torsional stiffness in the rear fuselage.

The People

Early in 1929, the Secretary of State for Air, Sir Samuel Hoare, paid tribute during a debate in the House of Commons to the work at the Establishments when he said, 'The brilliant work of experimental pilots at Farnborough and Martlesham....[is] increasing our knowledge of wing flutter and stresses.....'. The scientific staff no doubt accepted that public credit should be given to the pilots, but probably felt that their salaries, at least, should reflect their contribution. Later, the press, in the person of C G Grey editor of *The Aeroplane* took up the scientists' case, pointing out the higher financial rewards in 'The Trade'. It is clear, however, that considerations of pay did not in any way curb the enthusiasm and achievements of the civilian staff at Martlesham.

Reference has already been made to the friendly atmosphere existing at Martlesham from the earliest postwar years. Writing many years after their service at Martlesham, all, whether pilots, engineering officers or NCOs, scientific staff or firms' representatives, comment on the harmonious relations. The improvements to the physical conditions made from 1925 added to the attractions of serving at a station whose role of testing the newest of the country's fighting aeroplanes lent excitement to the daily routine. Among those who enjoyed and contributed to life there are a few whose names occur frequently in the memories contributed in later years by their colleagues. 'Happy' C E Horrex first arrived as a Flying Officer in 1921 and finally left as a Squadron Leader in 1939; he served elsewhere from 1924 to 1933. A prewar acrobat, he is remembered for his one handed cartwheels in best uniform alongside airmen marching to church. His favourite trick, of many, was wiring a starting magneto to the brass door handle to give his unwary visitors an almighty electric shock as they grasped the handle on the outside.

An earlier Flight Commander was Flt Lt 'Poppy' Pope, whose height of 6ft 8in, gave him a unique view from the cockpit of many of the fighter types he flew; as mentioned he baled out of the second Parnall Pipit. Flg Off Duncan Menzies often seemed to be in trouble, but later became Prime Minister of Australia. Sgt George E Lowdell, whose flick rolls at 50ft in the Avro 504 were spectacular and long remembered by those who saw them, was often forestalled by the officers of his Flight. Flt Lt T A Tom Langford-Sainsbury, for six years on No.15 Squadron and latterly a Flight Commander, was unrivalled for his tatty uniform and battered hat; he also had the experience of an uncontrolled dive in a Vickers Virginia when an early autopilot 'ran away' and could not be disconnected before reaching a speed which threatened to shake him and the aeroplane to pieces. He was later an Air Vice-Marshal – presumably having bought a new uniform. Flt Lt P J R Pat King, a flight commander of No.22 Squadron in 1928 demonstrated his musical prowess on many occasions by playing the piano accompanied by his two pet dogs singing in time; he also was later an Air Vice-Marshal. Flt Lt N H Jenks Jenkins, whose party trick was consumption of wine-glass bowls, served on No.15

The Officers in 1931.

Back row left to right: Flg Off A E Groom, Flg Off G L G Richmond, unknown, Flg Off R C Greenhalgh, unknown, Flg Off M C Head and Flg Off T H Moon

Centre row: Flt Lt C B Wincott, Flt Lt E D Barnes, Flt Lt J R Addams, Flt Lt D M Fleming, Flt Lt B C Blofield, Flt Lt J Bradbury, Flt Lt R J Ford, Flt Lt T A Langford-Sainsbury, Flt Lt K A Meek, Flg Off P G Lucas and Flt Lt R L McK Barbour

Front row: Flt Lt T S Horry, Flt Lt D S Earp, Sqn Ldr E S Goodwin, Mr H L Stevens, Wg Cdr V O Rees, Lt-Col W Plummer (ret), Sqn Ldr G H Martingell, Sqn Ldr F R Wilkins and Flt Lt F G Griffin

and then No.22 Squadron before he left to fly the Fairey Long-range Monoplane and was killed when it crashed in 1931. Flt Lt C B Cyril Wincott of No.22 Squadron claimed he could move a piano with his ear; when his bluff was called during a Dining-in night, his ear was left hanging by a thread. The piano did not move. The doctor was rudely awakened and after much washing sewed the ear back into place. The following morning was very windy, but nothing daunted, a Viastra was soon bumping and bouncing its way to the RAF Hospital at Halton with Wincott and friends to give moral support. On arrival, the doctors found treatment was necessary – but only for the very sick friends – the ear required no further attention. Wincott retired as an Air Commodore. These stories illustrate that Martlesham had more than its share of extrovert young men, an unusually large proportion of whom reached senior rank. Between the World Wars, the station amply justified its reputation as one of the liveliest in the Service.

Among the more serious pilots were three who were subsequently knighted as Air Marshals – Flt Lt John W Jones (No.15 Squadron), Sqn Ldr Robert M Foster, Commanding Officer of No.15 Squadron from May

1933, and Flg Off Charles E N Guest (No.15 then No.22 Squadron).

Awards for outstanding flying at Martlesham were very rare; an exception was an Air Force Cross for Flt Lt Eric D Barnes in 1933 at the end of a tour of four years on No.22 Squadron.

Two officers, Flt Lts J N Boothman and R S Sorley went on to distinguished careers, frequently connected with the Establishment. Boothman joined No.22 Squadron after flying in the 1931 Schneider Trophy Team, and later became Commandant of AAEE. Sorley left No.22 Squadron in 1927 and played a key role at the Air Ministry in establishing the case for the eight gun fighter before also becoming Commandant.

Other pilots, perhaps of a more demure disposition, were enticed to leave the RAF and join Industry where their skill and experience gained at Martlesham was highly valued. Among the first was Sqn Ldr Tom Harry England who joined Handley Page early in 1927 after two years in command of No.22 Squadron. In 1929, the same squadron lost Flg Off Joseph 'Mutt' Summers to Vickers where he enjoyed a long career with his new employers. Flg Off Philip E G Sayer left No.22 Squadron in 1929 for Hawker and

later joined Gloster where he made the country's first jet-powered flight in 1941; he was killed the same year. Flg Off Philip G Lucas left for Hawker in 1931 where he was awarded the George Medal in 1940 for saving the company's new Typhoon. Flg Off Charles B Wilson left No.22 Squadron in 1929 to fly for Associated Newspapers.

At the RAF Displays at Hendon new military types as well as civil were shown to the public for the first time, usually by AAEE pilots. From 1929 another regular feature was formation aerobatics by No.22 Squadron pilots. Each year three or four single-seat fighters were sent to Martlesham well beforehand for practice; Gloster Grebes were the initial mounts, changing to Bristol Bulldogs for 1932 and 1933. An innovation was the fitting of canisters to the aircraft; the firm of Skywriting supplied the equipment which produced smoke in three colours – one for each aircraft. The results were spectacular, although the apparatus led to the need for much cleaning after use.

For 1931, the same firm painted the three aerobatic Grebes a vivid scarlet, and the following year the Bulldogs were similarly adorned. For the 1933 Display, rain and low cloud prevented aerobatics, but the orange, green and white smoke was used to good effect as the aircraft made interweaving patterns over the crowd. During practice for the 1933 event, on 19 May, tragedy struck when Flt Lt George E Campbell was killed; he was on his first aerobatic flight in forma-

tion, and was standing in for Flg Off H H Leach. The aircraft flown by Campbell collided with that of Flt Lt J W Moir; the latter escaped by parachute. When the doctor arrived at the crash Campbell was still conscious and his first question was 'Are the other pilots alright?'. The third member of the formation, Pilot Off A J Bill Pegg, landed safely. Two months previously Pegg had had another traumatic experience when testing an Avro Tutor in a dive the wings collapsed, and he took to his parachute landing heavily near a farmhouse. After borrowing a bicycle to ride back to the aerodrome, he presented himself to the doctor who was busy with paperwork. After a few minutes Pegg said quietly, 'I have just torn my wings off'. The doctor was galvanised into action, but could find nothing wrong with the pilot. Pegg joined the Bristol Aeroplane Company in 1935, and became chief test pilot – making the first flight, inter alia, of the Brabazon.

Throughout this middle period (1924-34), there were four senior civilian posts – the Chief Technical Officer (CTO), Senior Scientific Officer (SSO) grade, Scientific Officer (SO) and two Technical Officers (TO). Mention has been made of Capon and his contribution to the scientific advances in aeroplane testing. He was the Chief Technical Officer and was succeeded in 1927 by H L Stevens, in 1931 briefly by F W Meredith and in 1932 by E J H Lynam. The list of those filling the other posts is at Appendix C.

All made regular flights, but

Pilots, groundcrew and Gloster Grebes before the RAF Display at Hendon in 1929. Flt Lt C E N Guest (left) and Flt Lt J Bradbury (right) are the pilots; both were members of No.15 Squadron. The aircraft have anti-flutter bracing for the outer wings.

Stevens was alone in being a qualified pilot. However, their primary work was on the ground and concerned with problems of performance, handling, measurement, presentation of results, reduction methods and improvements in techniques of testing; the scientific aspects of armament tests were generally the responsibility of the Technical Officers. The M/Res series of reports give an insight into the work of those officers.

Of those listed in the Annex, N E Rowe and later Stuart Scott-Hall combined scientific duties at Martlesham with supervision of the trials at Orfordness, spending much of their time at the latter site. Both are remembered as exceptionally energetic and capable, and both returned in more senior positions at Martlesham – Rowe as Chief Technical Officer in 1935 and Scott-Hall as his deputy from 1937. Rowe eventually reached the highest level in the Scientific Civil Service while Scott-Hall contributed to the science of aircraft assessment as co-author of the reference book *Aircraft Performance Testing*.

Several junior civilian posts were created, starting in Capon's time, and the first four civilian mechanics were employed in 1932, a number rising to fifteen by 1938.

The Last Years of Peace 1934-1939

The Establishment

In the middle of 1934 the designation of the two Martlesham squadrons was changed without in any way disturbing their work. The change marks a suitable point to start consideration of the period leading to the start of the war in 1939, a period dominated by the Expansion of the RAF and corresponding changes at Martlesham. On 1 May, 1934, No.22 Squadron was renamed Performance Testing Squadron (PTS or Per T), followed a month later by No.15 Squadron becoming Armament Testing Squadron (ATS or ArmT); on 30 June, 1934 the Squadrons were renamed Sections. Flights within the sections became known as APerT or BArmT until the next reorganisation during the war. A new No.22 Squadron was formed at Donibristle, and a new No.15 Squadron at Abingdon.

Group Captain A C 'Cissy' Maund had command from 1933; he had previously had the same appointment as a Squadron Leader some twelve years earlier. In the intervening period he had not become any easier to deal with at the personal level, although he apparently had his favourites who found no difficulty in their work with him. On promotion, he was succeeded by Grp Capt H G 'Reggie' Smart, who soon became known for his bad temper early in the morning. By the time Grp Capt B McEntegart took over in December 1938 the average number of aeroplanes had, since 1928, more than doubled to eighty. Flying hours for 1938 totalled over 4,000 compared with 2,369 in 1929. These two statistics give some indication of the general increase in the work of the Establishment, particularly from mid-1937. In the same ten year period, the officer strength increased from thirty-seven to a total of forty-five, with a corresponding increase in NCOs and airmen. Thus while the work expanded by some 70 percent, the number of servicemen grew by only some 20 per-

cent, assisted by a handful of civilians. The changing tempo of activity is shown partly by the flying statistics; less easy to measure but equally necessary for the functioning of the Establishment, were the increasing demands on all the supporting elements. More flying demanded more servicing, more motor transport, more workshop assistance, more trials planning and reporting, more drawing office output and, above all, more working time from everybody. The minimum time possible was devoted to Service requirements such as parades; however, certain routines were sacrosanct. The station closed for two weeks every summer for the annual leave period, the last being from 8 to 21 August, 1939, only a few days before the war. Administration, however, followed strict Service practice, and to cope with the increasing task, a post of Squadron Leader Administrative was established, filled from late 1935 by Sqn Ldr W E Swann, the first regular officer in the post.

Among the duties of the new post was that of finding accommodation for the growing population of both servicemen and civilians. Airmen were found homes in the old wooden huts, unoccupied once the brick barrack blocks were completed, at the southern end of the station. Other unused but old buildings were found for the officers, NCOs and some civilians; the scientists working at Orfordness lived in Ipswich. Swann and his successors also had a major responsibility for three Royal visits – the first on 8 July, 1936, by King Edward VIII, accompanied by the Chief of the Air Staff. The royal party had already visited several RAF stations, and Martlesham, where the latest aircraft were lined up, provided a fitting climax; the visit lasted just under two hours and included tea. The second royal visitor a year later was The Duke of Kent in transit to a private function in Woodbridge, and the third in August 1937 when the King was on his way to Southwold.

In four of the five years before the war (1936 was the exception) the Establishment was open to the public as part of the Empire Air Day scheme which had as one of its aims making the public air-minded. The lure of the work at Martlesham, normally and increasingly of a secret nature, attract-

ed large numbers. Fourteen thousand came in May 1935 and there were 3,000 motor cars; a cheque for £289 was sent to the Memorial Fund (later the Benevolent Fund). The sum was the highest of any station. By the 1939 Air Day the number of the public attending reached 20,000 and receipts were £890. Determined and often youthful members of the public could on any other day watch the activities on the aerodrome from the public road running through the station. This pastime became increasingly difficult from 1937 when an attempt was made to improve security, at least to the extent of 'moving-on' those tempted to linger on the road.

By 1934 the Martlesham tie, a registered design and greatly prized by those entitled to wear it (restricted to test pilots of AAEE initially), had been available for some years. The timing of its design is difficult to establish. Air Chief Marshal Ivelaw-Chapman remembers the selection of the design taking place at the end of his tour of duty in 1926. F H B Kelson who was in charge of the drawing office and did not arrive at Martlesham until early 1928, remembers using his talent with the paint brush to produce several designs for consideration. Whatever the exact date, the tie remains available today only to those serving at AAEE.

No doubt attaches to the date of the presentation of the Unit Badge on 20 June, 1939, during the annual inspection by the Air Officer Commanding. It is said that the presentation was delayed so that an unnecessary parade could be avoided. The meaning of the badge, as given in Martlesham's official record, Form 540, is: 'The armoured gauntlet and airman's glove are intended to convey the spirit of co-operation existing between the flying and armament departments at Martlesham; the arrow being symbolic of true flight'. One widespread belief was that the gauntlet and glove symbolized the Service and civilian elements and their joint endeavours; another belief was that the symbolism was between Service testing and the civilian manufacturers. Both beliefs are mistaken, but are equally as apt as the official version.

During the years 1934 to 1939 some extra construction took place, and included additional petrol storage tanks, for the new 87 Octane fuel, some Bessonneaux canvas hangars and the works associated with the new speed course. The last was opened in 1938 and used huts five miles apart connected by Post Office landline and aligned with the Ipswich to Woodbridge railway line. Using co-ordinated stop watches, aircraft were timed in each direction as they passed exactly over the calibrated vertical of the huts. The new speed course had been surveyed in 1935 and an accuracy within one mph predicted at 200mph, providing the wind was not too strong. To measure the latter a second aircraft was proposed to make a smoke trail over the huts at the test height.

At the fourteenth annual Contractor's Dinner in December 1935, Grp Capt Maund announced the new speed course and the acquisition of the extra land to the west of the existing airfield for low level manoeuvring. These remarks were received in silence; his next remark, that new smooth runways had been prepared, was greeted with laughter by his audience. No doubt the evening deteriorated thereafter into another reputedly memorable occasion. The dinners, so much a feature of the Establishment life in the 1920s and 1930s, continue to the present day but are now combined with the annual ETPS prize-giving ceremony. Sport in the late 1930s continued at the high standards set in the earlier years, and Martlesham won and held many of the cups awarded for individual events and games. In 1936, for example, the station light – and heavy – tug of war teams won the trophies at both weights and the latter represented the RAF at the inter-Service games at Olympia that year.

It is hardly surprising that the Establishment's achievements and its reputation at work, socially and at sport led to the highest of that indefinable quality; 'esprit de corps' – Martlesham was *the* posting for Servicemen and the growing number of civilians. Of the latter, the scientific staff were mostly concerned with performance testing, while specialist RAF officers managed the armament trials. On the other hand, the Chief Engineer had responsibilities extending to all Establishment aeroplanes. From 1936 the post was held by F Rowarth, assisted by W Dancy. In

The Station Badge adopted in 1934.

addition to their duties at Martlesham, which included technical appraisal of new and modified aeroplanes and determination of weights and CG, Rowarth and Dancy found time to assist in handicapping sporting events under Royal Aero Club rules and became very well known as a team. Probably the most notable event they helped organize was the Mac.Robertson Race from England to Australia late in 1934.

Armament Testing

At the end of the First World War guns and bombs were plentiful, and in the years that followed, the RAF, in which economy was the watchword, made do largely with existing stocks and designs of equipment. Indeed, the Fairey Battle went to war in 1939 with the same basic defensive armament (one fixed forward-firing gun and one free gun) as the D.H.9A of 1918, and with much the same bomb load. Among the policy changes of the various Expansion plans from 1934 was a very marked acceleration in the pace of armament development. The effects were soon felt and led, in 1937, to a wide ranging investigation into the organization which then existed in the Service for research and development in armament. The effects at AAEE were significant. As early as 1935 the post of Senior Armament Officer had been upgraded to Sqn Ldr reporting directly to the Commanding Officer; previously, the senior arma-

The Unit Badge of the Aeroplane and Armament Experimental Establishment, Royal Air Force; it was presented on 20 June, 1939.

ment officer, of Flight Lieutenant rank, had been responsible to the Chief Technical Officer. As a result of the 1937 investigation, the post was again upgraded, and filled initially by Wg Cdr R St H Clarke, appointed in September on promotion from Officer Commanding the Armament Testing Section. He worked directly for the newly created Directorate of Armament Development at the Air Ministry. His Section had a wide responsibility to determine whether an air weapon could be safely and efficiently carried in the air, secondly whether the weapon could be released accurately and, thirdly whether the weapon would be effective on reaching its target. These terms of reference were not greatly changed from the previous arrangements, when new bombs, guns, sights and other warlike impedimenta were few.

By 1937, testing requirements for air armament were increasing rapidly from three separate but related causes. First, many types of new munitions, both offensive and defensive, were appearing. Secondly the aircraft on which the munitions were to be tested were proliferating and thirdly, the new types of aeroplanes, particularly bombers and fighters, had vastly increased armament capabilities.

To meet these demands funds were made available for testing equipment, previously denied on grounds of expense, and included high-speed cine cameras for observing the stability of bombs and the trajectory of tracer ammunition, rate of fire recorders, and thermo couples with appropriate recorders for measuring barrel temperatures.

Perhaps of more significance was the increased priority given to armament tests at the Establishment. In the pre-Expansion period, a single new or modified aeroplane would be tested first for performance and handling frequently leaving limited time for the armament trials. In 1935, for example, the contenders for the G.4/31 competition were transferred to the Armament Section only eight days before the date set by the Air Staff for the selection meeting. This arrangement was a constant source of irritation to the armament staff, who also observed that time was sometimes wasted by completing performance tests before any armament trials, as occurred in the prototype Gloster Gladiator. The preliminary armament inspection of the aeroplane, made only after full performance trials with a new type of engine, revealed that the guns could not be fired as they pointed straight at the cylinders! Gradually, however, more time and resources were made available, and the importance of armament was finally recognized by the Air Staff in 1938 when it decided to allocate four of the first six production aircraft to AAEE, of which two were for armament work as part of increased emphasis on operational assessment.

Until the large increase in manpower in 1938-9 for armament trials, the extra work of testing the new developments fell on the small number of specialists, predominantly Service officers. Outstanding among them was Sqn Ldr E D 'Dizzy' Davis, from January 1935, the first in the recently upgraded post. His pet subject was aircraft turrets, assessing first the Boulton Paul Sidestrand/Over-strand nose turrets, and then the development of the powered turret for the Hawker Demon. Many were sceptical about the controlling of a gun by turning hydraulic taps, but Davis persisted and his efforts over many months resulted in acceptable power operation. A particularly significant event was his convincing the turret designer, A Frazer-Nash that the three hydraulic controls were unmanageable in the air. By simplifying the controls to provide only rotation of the turret and elevation of the gun, operation was rendered simple and effective. The designer commented later that successful control of subsequent turrets, used throughout the war, followed that early modification insisted upon by Davis.

The role of the Establishment as arbiter between acceptable and unacceptable, and between the best and the rest, was in the case of the turret considerably exceeded, to the benefit of the wider Service interest. Davis retired after the war as an Air Vice-Marshal.

The turret also provides a good example of the increase in complexity of testing needed to match the progress in armament development. New methods and techniques were needed, and new standards set for acceptable technical achievement.

The Officers – 1933.
Back row left to right: Flg Off C R Crow, Flt Lt M V Ward, three unknown, Flg Off E G Ambridge, unknown, Flt Lt C Feather
Centre row: Flt Lt T H Carr, Flt Lt J N Boothman, Flt Lt J F Moir, Flt Lt A E Paish, Flg Off A J Pegg, Flg Off E M Morriss, Flt Lt F Simpson, remainder unknown
Front row: two unknown, Sqn Ldr J K McDonald, two unknown, Mr E J H Lynam, Grp Capt H L Reilly, Lt-Col Plummer, Sqn Ldr H O Long, Sqn Ldr R M Foster, unknown, Flt Lt D M Fleming and Flt Lt A J Warwick

Time honoured procedures were not good enough.

The contrast between the old methods and the new is well illustrated by the tests on the first multi-gun fighter, the Gloster Gladiator, and those needed later by the Hawker Hurricane and Supermarine Spitfire. The prototype Gladiator had, in addition to the two standard Vickers guns, four extra Lewis guns carried two under the top wing and two under the lower; each Lewis gun had a single ammunition drum. On the ground the installation was inspected, the harmonization and synchronization checked and re-arming times measured. In the air, guns were fired under the various loads imposed during manoeuvring. The Gladiator, including the novelty of extra guns, was conventional and amenable to well tried methods of assessment, methods which did not match the demands of the eight-gun Hurricane and Spitfire.

Among new problems were extreme cold, the need to reduce firing delay and the measurement of dispersion of bullets in the air. The extent of the extreme cold at the previously unusual firing altitudes around 30,000ft was measured on the prototype Spitfire and Hurricane by recording thermometers developed by AAEE. Having established exactly how cold the guns became (one unexpected finding was that the guns continued to cool on initial descent), it was possible to estimate the amount of heating required to prevent the oil of the Browning guns freezing and jamming them. Flt Lt E S 'Dru' Drury was largely responsible for the various palliatives tried, including graphite lubrication, electrical heaters and hot-air ducts. The last method was eventually adopted and successfully combined with dividing the internal wing structure into compartments to concentrate the available heat. Also, the unreliable Browning Mk 1 guns were replaced by the Mk 2 version. By the end of 1938 the firing of the machine-guns in the two key types of fighter was assessed as acceptable.

The original concept of the eight-gun fighter evolved from the need to concentrate firepower in the very short time, measured in the few seconds that the target was expected to be in the sights of the high-speed fighters. It was fundamental that firing should begin the instant that the pilot squeezed the firing trigger. When the prototypes of the Hurricane and Spitfire were first fitted with guns, the conventional operation by Bowden cable was fitted to link the pilot's firing lever to the eight guns. Martlesham trials soon revealed that firing was delayed and erratic, and much thought was given to devising an improvement; once again 'Dru' Drury put in many hours of work in finding and testing a successful answer to the problem. At first compressed air, piped to the eight guns was tried; the source of the air was the bottle, charged before take off, used originally solely for the brakes. Even a modest amount of taxying and use of brakes depleted the pressure sufficiently to render gun operation unreliable – although it was concluded that firing delays were reduced to an acceptable level. The next, and acceptable source of pressure was the use of oxygen from the cylinder charged to 1,800 psi (compared to 350 psi of the air bottle) but reduced to 180 psi for gun firing. The reduction in oxygen available to the pilot was insignificant.

The third illustration of the increased scope of armament testing necessary for the new aircraft concerns the determination of bullet dispersion in flight. It was considered that, however accurately the guns were aligned on the ground, it was probable that wing flexing and other factors would result in some scatter when the eight guns were fired in the air. A ground target, although easy to arrange, would not be suitable, so a simple device for air-to-air firing was devised, largely at the instigation of Flt Lt N C 'Hetty' Hyde (Officer Commanding 'A' Flight of ATS). It consisted of a large cloth target suspended under a free balloon to be launched under wind conditions that would take it over the sea air-firing range. The problem was retrieval after firing. The first idea, involving a drogue under the balloon attached by cord to a ripping panel for deflating the balloon was not a success. This method involved the attacking aircraft flying into the cord to operate the rip-panel; unfortunately the cord was liable to cut through the wing leading edge up to the main spar. The next idea was to fix a time-fused explosive charge to the balloon; the explosive fired either too early or too late and the system was abandoned. The idea adopted in the end was for the balloon to be shot down and the debris, including the cloth target to be retrieved by the duty motor launch. Even this method was not entirely free from snags as some targets were destroyed in mid-air by the burning balloon. However, after much time and effort had been expended, the dispersion pattern was determined.

Of a more routine nature were tests by the Armament Section for electrical efficiency, including suitability of the engine-driven generators then becoming standard, gun sights, pyrotechnics (usually on fighters restricted to a signal gun) and radio where the TR9a was rapidly superseded by the 9b and 9c models. AAEE insisted on rubber mountings for radio to reduce the effects of vibration on the valves and thus performance.

The increasing complexity of fighter armament in the five years before the Second World War was matched by the increasing size, bomb loads and sophistication of the bombers; aircraft for other roles made far less demands on ATS aircrew, groundcrew and specialist staff. In addition the development of new types of bombs and other devices led to a great deal of both ground assessment to check handling, loading and safety, and also flying. The last included carriage trials, often on the older aircraft, and then dropping trials to observe the release from the aircraft, the behaviour during free fall and an assessment of the effect of the explosion (of bombs) on the shingle at Orfordness. Meanwhile, the team at the ballistic hut recorded the trajectory of the weapon from the moment of release to impact. However, this simple statement hides the many vicissitudes besetting the attempts for the recording, and success was an occasion for celebration. Chief among the difficulties was communication, and even after the introduction of radios, comprehensible two-way conversations were more the exception than the rule. Cloud, fickle wind, and the sun combined with recalcitrant release gear in the aeroplane, tested the patience of all concerned. In the five years before the war some thirty ballistic reports were written on subjects ranging from four-pound practice bombs to 1,000 pounders, and from smoke floats to reconnaissance flares.

Orfordness was under S Scott-Hall from early 1937 and G J Richards a year later, followed in 1939 by A Daniels all of whose names appear as authors on the ballistics reports as they were issued in the Research series. The reason for inclusion in this series is unclear, although the ballistics reports are generally, but not invariably, more scholarly than the routine Armament reports of which some 170 topics were covered in the same period. Among subjects in the routine series are reports on tests made to assess the vulnerability of modern aircraft to hostile fire. The tests were done by a separate section at Orfordness formed early in 1938, also under A Daniels, to provide data urgently required by the Air Ministry to assess the need for armour in Service aircraft. By the end of 1938 definite conclusions had been reached based on the firing of 0.303in calibre bullets against the target aircraft. It is not clear whether higher calibre ammunition was used later.

Bombing trials were undertaken by 'B' Flight ATS which had responsibility both for assessing new aircraft and for tests of new weapons, bombsights and release gear. These last tests used a variety of usually older aircraft, ranging from the venerable Virginia to the Heyford and, later, Blenheims and others; the nature of the flying was usually routine. Among exceptions is the flight on 3 April, 1935, by Flt Lt W R Beaman (a member of the RAF boxing team) flying a Heyford; Flt Lt A E Groom was on board to conduct the icing trials of the electrical fusing gear. At 15,000ft in heavy snow the airspeed indicator froze and the controls jammed. With confusing indications from the bank indicator and the turn indicator, control was lost and the aircraft eventually came out of cloud at 3,000ft, with Beaman unable to rotate the control wheel to the right. After landing, damage was found to the fabric of the top wing, and the ailerons and the fins were bent; it was concluded that the aircraft had achieved its TV in the dive. Although considerably shaken by the experience, Groom immediately tried to operate the frozen release mechanism. It did not work and he commented that the flight was after all a success.

As part of the Establishment's remit to test the effectiveness of weapons, a number of trials were held away from Orfordness, arranged where possible in conjunction with the other two Services. Late in 1935 the Royal Navy was interested in determining how armour plating withstood armour piercing bombs, and had specially built a section of a warship with various thicknesses of plate. A diving attack was required for the 500lb bombs; the only aircraft suitable were the Armstrong Whitworth and Hawker contenders from the G.4/31 competition. The desired number of hits was soon obtained, and the pilots, including Flt Lt G Bearne, were invited to see the effects which, even without an explosive charge, were impressive where the thinner gauges of plating had been penetrated. The following year the Army ran a scheme for the Home Office to see how far Semi-Armour piercing bombs would penetrate into soil of the type found above the underground stations of London. Similar soil was found a mile from Canterbury, and the Army Commander refused to take responsibility for the safety of the city as he was unable to believe that the necessary accuracy could be guaranteed. Eighteen bombs were dropped from a Heyford flown by Flt Sgt Shippobotham from between 3,000 and 10,000ft; the least accurate bomb fell only 150yd from the aiming point. The results were not divulged to Martlesham.

New types of bomber, particularly the Vickers-Armstrongs Wellington and Armstrong Whitworth Whitley, had a capacity for bombs at least triple that of earlier types, as well as such complications as bomb doors, turrets, intercommunicating radio and increased navigation equipment. These developments coupled with the extended selection of weapons available increased testing requirements fivefold compared with the types being replaced. It was not until 1939 that sufficient extra manpower was made available to cope with the work of the ATS, which also had the responsibility for the Operational flights, introduced in 1938. For these flights, usually three production aircraft were prepared with representative loads of operational equipment and flown on a long cross country flight in formation at low, medium and high altitudes, releasing bombs and/or firing guns at appropriate times. Types assessed included the Handley Page Harrow, Bristol Blenheim, Lockheed Hudson, Supermarine Spitfire, Hawker Hurricane and Westland Lysander. Existing reports indicate how valuable the long flights were in revealing shortcomings – inadquate heating, carbon monoxide poisoning, noise and unacceptable periodic roll/yaw motion being typical problems.

Carbon monoxide contamination in crew areas had become a potential problem with the advent of enclosed cabins, but it was April 1939 before the Air Ministry formally directed specific tests to be made, the instruction forming No.1 of a regular series of DTD Instructions to Experimental Establishments; the sequence replaced the earlier unnumbered series. This direction followed the experience of severe and debilitating airsickness during the long flights from Martlesham.

Some of the people involved in incidents in ATS have already been mentioned. Others, remembered by colleagues, made their contribution on a continuing basis, and included Flt Sgt R H Garner whose practical flair and extensive experience led to many improvements in armaments under test. Others were Sqn Ldr C N H Bilney (later Air Vice-Marshal), Flt Lt R H A Emson (later Air Marshal Sir Reginald), Flt Lt C L 'Charles' Dann, Flt Lt A H 'Uncle' Fear and Sqn Ldr D W F 'David' Bonham-Carter (later Air Commodore).

Performance Testing Section (PerT)

During the RAF Expansion period leading up to 1939 the number of new types, both Service and civilian grew dramatically, and the widespread introduction of innovations such as retractable undercarriages, flaps and variable-pitch propellers together with dramatic increases in top speed gave test pilots, scientists and technical staff in PerT an interesting and busy time. As with the sister section ArmT, advances in aeroplane design and equipment created the need for improvements in testing techniques, instrumentation and analysis. However, while the increase in the work of

'PerT' was not so marked as in 'ArmT', the new problems being encountered led, inter alia, to the establishment in late 1937 of a scientific post, filled initially by A S Hartshorn, devoted to improving methods of performance testing and analysis. His first report, in February 1938, analysed the accuracy of reduction laws for aeroplanes with constant-speed propellers. He found that the existing 'half and half' method (ie combined half the correction using the pressure basis and half the correction from the density) gave small errors; for simplicity, the existing method was retained. Later in 1938, a more scientific method of measuring longitudinal stability was investigated using a Handley Page Harrow. Two positions of CG (fore and aft) were used and the displacement of the control column and trimmer noted at various speeds to determine the so-called stick fixed and stick free stabilities. Another test, on the Wellington, indicated that the production type of elevator horn balance would require heavy stick forces at all normal CGs. In 1939 the investigation was widened to include five other types to determine the effect of propeller slipstream on stability; the somewhat prosaic result was that the effect could be predicted merely by studying the side elevation of the aircraft. The effect of flap setting on the take-off performance of single- and twin-engined aeroplanes was measured. It was found that the optimum setting was 25deg to 30deg, but that take-off speed was the same irrespective of flap setting. The pilots' opinions were largely used in framing the report, and one conclusion, incidental to the flap setting investigation, sheds light on the developing concensus on handling multi-engined machines on take-off. The report says 'In fact, experienced pilots are seriously suggesting that the normal take off for a twin-engined aeroplane should take account of the possibility of one engine cutting out – relegating the minimum distance technique to special circumstances'. This conclusion was revolutionary. Previously engine failure on take off had been handled by closing both throttles and landing straight ahead.

Even in cruising flight, it was accepted in earlier years that an engine failure could result in a forced landing if the dead engine continued to rotate, giving rise to considerable drag. A trial in 1932 on the twin-engine Virginia had concluded, 'Any reasonably good pilot could slow up enough to stop a broken down engine without fear of stalling'. The report made no mention of the ease or otherwise of restarting during the trial. The case of Bristol Blenheims overseas, which had a longer run than the biplanes they were replacing, fequently needed to climb steeply to clear obstacles with disastrous results if an engine failed. The new thinking emanating from AAEE was not lost on the newly created Air Registration Board where the formulation of airworthiness requirements for civil aircraft was interrupted by the outbreak of war. Undoubtedly Martlesham's views in 1939 were a significant advance in the promotion of safety and were in marked contrast to the more conservative outlook of the 1920s. In 1921 the enclosed cabin of the Bristol Tramp had been condemned by pilots used to open cockpits, and in 1925 the ability of the Gloster Gamecock to pull out of dives was criticised because the machine sank bodily – the possibility of the stalling angle of attack being reached at high speed by the application of g was apparently not considered. Whatever the reluctance of pilots to accept new ideas, their skill and determination was never in doubt, and the long list of those who reached high rank or were enticed into industry has been related previously. No evidence has been discovered where a manufacturer presented a well-founded case to alter an Establishment recommendation – indeed the existing evidence is of the assistance and even enlightenment received by Industry.

Throughout the interim period standards of acceptable handling steadily rose. Two types illustrate the point. The Westland Wallace and Vickers Vildebeest were stated to have good handling when first tested in 1930; five years later, the Wallace and the Vincent (essentially the Vildebeest renamed) both virtually unchanged were assessed as possessing poor handling.

By the mid-1930s the reputation of AAEE in both Service and civilian circles was well established. Contemporary aeronautical publications, carrying advertisements to the effect that the product had been passed by Martlesham bear witness that the Establishment was widely accepted as the arbiter of good aeroplanes and equipment. In addition to its primary role of assessing new designs, Martlesham was frequently called upon to investigate problems which occurred in service, such as the serious erosion of performance of the Bulldog after several years; the degradation was found to be due largely to modifications made by the RAF after earlier trials. Civil machines were less demanding once in service, but in 1937 unexplained crashes of the de Havilland D.H.86 were referred to AAEE for investigation. The likely cause of the crashes was discovered, and again, attributed to modifications not previously assessed. The fund of knowledge acquired in assessing both new and older aeroplanes was assembled into the *AAEE Flight Test Handbook* issued formally as an Air Publication and replacing the series of notes entitled *Instructions for Routine Performance Tests*. The Establishment also produced a Technical guide and a handbook on armament testing. These three volumes, the first of their kind, amended to keep pace with developments received wide distribution both at home and overseas. Copies are known to have been eagerly received in the USA, where flight testing was rapidly expanding after years of slow development in military and naval aviation. It is probable that F Rowarth and Sqn Ldr C E Horrex took the handbooks with them when they joined the aircraft Purchasing Mission in April 1938. From these early contacts, the Establishment's influence on testing methods in America grew considerably during the war.

Other innovations in 1939, were pilots' notes for individual aeroplane types, which warned pilots of the idiosynchracies of the new monoplanes. The notes were produced by the CFS, but initially relied heavily on AAEE experience. The need for CFS to have early information was added to the more pressing pleas of Commanders-in-Chief for speedier availability from test Establishments of data on the many types rapidly entering service. As a result, the Air Ministry agreed in April 1938 that Commands could receive some reports, but insisted that no corre-

spondence on the contents could be made. To meet this requirement the Martlesham reporting system was changed so that various aspects, *eg* radio, armament, were reported in parts as the item was completed; the original procedure of producing a single, complete (and delayed) volume was abandoned for Service aeroplanes. One unforeseen consequence of the part-by-part issue of reports was the concentration on the more pressing operational aspects which needed urgent testing. An example is the Whitley where full performance was measured only on the unrepresentative first prototype, while such items as turrets, engines, cooling and handling on production aeroplanes were of greater priority. Indeed, the traditional comprehensive tests were sometimes abandoned altogether in the early stages, as was the case with the de Havilland Don and the Miles Master. Access to the Don was awk-

ward, and could have been the subject of the comment, possibly apocryphal, 'Entry to this aeroplane is difficult; it should be made impossible'! It could equally have been said of the Blackburn Botha and some other types. Criticism of the Master in its early form was extensive, and yet its characteristic high speed g stall which was very easy to induce and also occurred without natural warning, escaped adverse comment – a surprising omission from a report on a trainer. On the other hand the vicious level stall of the first North American Harvard for the same role led to immediate condemnation and rapid and effective modification action.

The heather-clad surface at Martlesham was becoming distinctly dated by 1939, and could not meet the requirements of new bombers. It was considered unsafe to make tests from the aerodrome involving take off at maximum overload weights. Watti-

HM King Edward VIII inspecting a Bristol Bombay at Martlesham Heath on 8 July, 1936; this was the first time that the King had worn RAF uniform since his accession.

sham with a long grass runway was used on at least one occasion, but Cranwell was ultimately chosen as it had both a grass and a tarmac runway permitting comparisons to be made between the two surfaces. A further implication of the longer take off and landing requirements of new machines was the need to use the longest run available, and not necessarily use a run directly into wind. At AAEE trials were instituted to assess handling in crosswind take offs and landings. The Battle and Blenheim were the first types to be landed across the wind.

The changes in the reporting system and the extra breadth and depth of testing added to the intensity and challenge of work in PerT; nevertheless the work in the Section was predominantly business as usual at an increased tempo. Flying was from first light to dusk and beyond when the weather was suitable and increasingly seven days a week. When the weather was 'dud', relaxation was equally vigorous, at least for that band of officers and NCOs whose profession was flying. In this heady atmosphere it is hardly surprising that postings to Martlesham were greatly coveted in the 1930s. Those selected were often accused of using unfair influence – Sgt 'Sammy' Wroath was asked who his father was on being given news of his new appointment. Retiring from the RAF as Grp Capt S Wroath after over 20 years of test flying, including the formation and command of the Empire Test Pilots' School, his original selection was certainly inspired by ability and needed no 'pull' from relatives. Similarly, others chosen were identified by outstanding flying assessments or by personal acquaintance of those already at the Establishment. The skill and judgment required is illustrated time and again both in personal reminiscence and in official reports as a few examples show. In April 1935, an Osprey was making high-speed dives when the dinghy in the top wing inflated, burst out of its housing and severely damaged the tailplane; despite the loss of much elevator control a safe landing was made. On 20 May, 1937, the second prototype Lysander, similarly engaged on high-speed dives, shed much of the fabric on the upper surface of the wing. Control could only be maintained at a speed well above that for a normal approach. The pilot, Flt Lt R W P Collings, decided to attempt a landing which he successfully completed; he was awarded the Air Force Cross for this feat. Another of these medals, rarely given, was won by Flt Lt J W McGuire at the end of his Short Service Commission in 1938 for his work at Martlesham. Within a period of a few days McGuire was granted a Permanent Commission, became engaged to be married, and was the subject of an embarrassing misunderstanding involving a Miss Lemon. This lady telephoned him to say that she was the secretary of the Bird Society and wished to discuss his terns. Convinced that the call was a

practical joke, McGuire entered into a lively conversation during which Miss Lemon informed him that she never drank and was going to church. Needless to say, Miss Lemon proved later to be entirely genuine, and McGuire had a red-face to complement his earlier red letter days!

A rather more serious incident concerns the Spitfire, which was due to arrive for the first time at 16.30hr on 26 May, 1936. Sqn Ldr E G 'Ted' Hilton, commanding PerT, told Flt Lt J H 'EJ' Edwardes-Jones that the Air Ministry wanted the Spitfire flown immediately on arrival, contrary to the normal lengthy acceptance procedure involving dismantling and weighing. Edwardes-Jones, who had previously only flown a retractable undercarriage on the Courier, made a 20 minute flight in the pale blue prototype, describing the experience as 'delightful' in spite of forgetting to lower the wheels until the last minute. On landing, Edwardes-Jones telephoned Air Marshal Sir Wilfrid R Freeman, the Air Member for Development and Production, and assured his listener that the Spitfire could be flown by new pilots, providing they had suitable training. Eight days later 300 Spitfires were ordered; it is probable that a Flight Lieutenant's opinion was a significant factor in the decision for the order. The opinion of Martlesham pilots was always given due consideration, but never so directly or dramatically as in this instance. Air Marshal Sir Humphrey Edwardes-Jones died early in 1987, shortly after relating the foregoing to the author.

The following year, Sqn Ldr J F X McKenna, who had recently taken over flying the Spitfire, had an engine failure some distance from the airfield, and, rather than bale out, he made a forced landing on Woodbridge Heath with only minor damage resulting. The fault was traced to a fractured oil pipe, one of many components contributing to unreliability in the early Merlin engines. McKenna later commanded PerT and was awarded the AFC in the New Year's List 1939; his memory is honoured every year at the Empire Test Pilots' School by the award bearing his name being presented to the best student.

Other notable pilots included Lt-Cmdr S W D 'Stacey' Colls, the first naval test pilot at AAEE (and shown

in the Air Force List as Sqn Ldr (Lt-Cmdr RN)), Flg Off C E 'Charlie' Slee, Flt Lt R G Slade (who flew the record-breaking Fairey F.D.2), and Flt Lt W H 'Bill' Markham. Markham was, according to all who met him, unforgettable; he spent some time on both ArmT and PerT. He was almost the most senior Flight Lieutenant on retirement and stories about him abound. The Air Ministry sent a team to Martlesham to find if there was excessive manpower in the critical skilled trades. Markham in his hospitable way, laid on a sumptious 'elevenses' for the team – prepared by a Fitter Aero who, Markham remarked, was very good at his job and had made such 'elevenses' for the previous twelve months. Within a week the posts in that trade were reduced by one! On a later occasion in the small hours of the morning, Markham was convinced that he had seen spies about the station. Lacking a sympathetic ear locally, he decided that the King should be aware of what was going on, and telephoned Buckingham Palace at about 4am. The repercussions were widespread, but entirely unexpected by Markham, whose notoriety throughout the RAF rose even higher as a result of the ensuing Inquiry.

Life at AAEE was marred in 1937 by three fatal accidents, including one to a crew of No 64 Squadron. Particularly tragic was the accident to Flt Lt E W Simonds on 22 July when he baled out of the first Miles Magister when it failed to recover from a spin. He descended into the water near a ferry which had seen the RAF launch approaching and consequently failed to stop. The crew of the launch assumed that the ferry, being nearer, would pick up Simonds and turned about. As a result of this grievous misunderstanding Simonds drowned; he is buried in the Ipswich cemetery.

One result of Simond's accident was the issuing of two orders intended to prevent a recurrence. With effect from 5 August, 1937, tail parachutes were to be fitted to experimental aircraft for spinning, and all test flights of land aeroplanes were to be made over land. History was fatally repeated in 1959 when a Handley Page Victor from Boscombe Down crashed in the Irish Sea; another order was then issued, again restricting tests to flight over land. On 10 September, 1937, Wg Cdr E G Hilton, until recently the very popular Commanding Officer of PerT and Wg Cdr P C Sherren, the first Commanding Officer of No.15 Squadron at AAEE, were killed when they were thrown out of their Miles Falcon Major in extreme turbulence off Flamborough Head during the Kings Cup air race. They are also buried at Ipswich. On 23 August, 1939, Flt Sgt Higgins, and Aircraftmen Machin and Treadwell were killed when the first Bristol Bombay crashed near the aerodrome.

The tragic loss of life should be considered in the context of the work being undertaken to test to the limits the country's fastest and most modern aeroplanes. Indeed, it is surprising in view of the proportionally greater number of fatalities in the Service as a whole that more accidents did not occur at Martlesham. Some of the reasons have already been summarised. It is also clear that in the five years before the war, the skill of the pilots had improved, as related, and there was progressively more understanding of the fundamentals of aviation testing which helped overcome problems as each new advance was made. Improved test instrumentation played a significant part, and the results of a flight at one speed, loading or altitude were analysed before proceeding to a more demanding condition, ie the step-by-step approach. Responsibility

for trials flying rested largely on the civilian scientists under H B Howard, N E Rowe in 1938 and E T Jones the following year. They maintained a close and cordial working relationship with their uniformed colleagues and the continuous exchange of views provided a stimulating and rewarding atmosphere.

Nevertheless by the end of 1938, an interesting divergence of view developed with protagonists both within the Establishment and outside. It arose from the increasing amount of quantitative data being gathered on handling flights as a consequence of the more scientific methods being evolved, coupled with the large number of different aeroplanes going through their trials. One body of opinion, largely represented by the scientists, held that the extra knowledge gained was of the greatest value, while the other view, largely held by the Service element, was that the pilots' opinions on handling qualities were sufficient, and that the latter could be obtained more rapidly. The argument was settled by Air Vice-Marshal Tedder, the Director-General of Research and Development at the Air Minsitry, who decided in favour of the scientific, quantitative approach as giving the Services the best possible information. In this way, the standards of the Establishment were maintained at the highest level, and in any case, still preserved the benefit of the expert, qualitative, opinions of the test pilots.

Demons and Radio Location

Between 1936 and the war, Martlesham was the temporary home for two units whose functions were unconnected in one case and loosely connected in the other case to the business of AAEE.

12 September, 1936, was the official date that Sqn Ldr P J R King (the ex-AAEE test pilot) and his Squadron took up residence in the western end of the Performance Testing Squadron. The airmen of No.64 Squadron were housed in temporary hutments at the southern end of the domestic area, while their Hawker Demons (which did not arrive until November) were housed in three temporary hangars at the northern end of the station. When a permanent station, Church Fenton, was ready the Squadron moved there in May 1938. Incidents were few, but included the untimely deaths of Flg Off P C Vickery and his passenger AC1 J Hutchinson when their Demon crashed on the aerodrome during formation flying on 28 May, 1937.

Such was the secrecy surrounding the early development of radar (radio location as it was then known) at Orfordness and, from May 1936, at Bawdsey that few at AAEE were

Spitfire K9788 in October 1938, suitably restrained for ground firing to develop a method of harmonizing the guns.

Fig.5

9534.E

aware of the part played by the Establishment in the provision of aeroplanes as targets, and later, other aircraft carrying their own sets. Those involved were not, at first, told of the purpose of their routine flights over East Anglia and the North Sea. Two Avro Ansons of No.220 Squadron from Bircham Newton, but flying from Martlesham, were also used as targets. Meanwhile a Heyford modified by the RAE with specially designed engine ignition harness (to reduce electro magnetic interference) and a generator, arrived at Martlesham in November 1936. Two Establishment pilots, one of whom was Sgt Shippobotham, were confidentially briefed on the work on airborne radar to be undertaken in the Heyford. In early 1937 the need for further aircraft to be modified for airborne work, and for them to be based near to Bawdsey led to two Ansons arriving in June under Pilot Off 'Blood-Orange' C D G Smith, as Officer Commanding the Radio Direction Finding Flight. By late 1937 the first airborne reception of RDF (radar) signals reflected from another aircraft using ground transmissions had been made on the Heyford. The first airborne transmission and reception of signals reflected from a target aircraft had been made in one Anson, and of signals from a target ship had been made in the second of the Ansons. All three events occurred in flights from Martlesham. The work on radar expanded as aircraft could be made available. By April 1938, following complaints of lack of progress by the Bawdsey scientists, the position was reviewed by the Assistant Chief of the Air Staff, and it was agreed that an enlarged flying unit should be established, using the accommodation to be vacated by No.64 Squadron. The unit was to be known as the Experimental Co-operation Unit, a title changed in August 1938 to 'D' Flight, Perform-ance Testing Section. By early in the following year 'D' Flight had a Harrow, three Ansons, three Battles, and a Magister; six Blenhiems followed in March 1939. The flying was under the supervision of the Officer Commanding PerT, but the work was controlled by Bawdsey, and not part of the business of the Establishment. On 4 September, 1939, 'D' Flight moved to Perth and ceased to be associated with AAEE.

Move of AAEE in War

Within a few months of the formation of No.15 Squadron in 1923, the Air Staff was considering the move of the Establishment in the event of war. By 1932 it had been decided that the two Squadrons should become operational No.15 with its Horsleys and No.22 with whatever weird machines it had at the time at Martlesham, and that the Establishment should move to Waddington for continued testing; how this was to be undertaken when all the Squadron personnel remained at Martlesham is not clear. However the plan was not put to the test and in 1933 the decision was taken to make the squadrons normal peacetime units, and for the Establishment to move as a going concern to a venue less vulnerable to attack from the east. The search for a suitable site with good weather, near London and the aircraft industry, and also with easy access to bombing and gunnery ranges was protracted. After a fruitless, and not very urgent, examination of the possibilities, the Chief of the Air Staff ruled in February 1936 that AAEE should remain in situ in the event of hostilities. The increasing threat from Germany led in 1938 to a re-examination of the need for relocation, made more urgent by the exposure of the increasing importance of Orfordness, particularly as a night bombing range. During consideration of the question it was suggested that two airfields would be required – one with a long runway of at least 1,000yd for prototype testing and a second, for armament testing, near a good bombing range. In the event, on 30 April, 1939, the Air Council decided to move both parts to Boscombe Down as the only possible aerodrome; the existing squadrons at Boscombe were already scheduled to move overseas on the outbreak of war.

Towards the end of August 1939 frantic efforts were made at Martlesham to fill sandbags and to camouflage the roads and aerodrome by copious use of soot, and, at night, to reduce visibility by the use of blue lamps. Capes were introduced for routine wear out of doors as a precaution against gas attack. Inevitably, the wearer perspired under the cape, and soon became engrimed with the soot with comic if unwelcome results. On 1 September, 1939, mobilization was ordered, the aeroplanes made serviceable and the equipment and furniture packed. Special trains were loaded at Woodbridge for the journey to Amesbury, the nearest station to Boscombe. On 3 and 4 September, a total of seventy aeroplanes was flown to their new home, by pilots of AAEE and also from local units – the latter needed to bolster the small number of Establishment pilots.

The main parties of personnel remained at Martlesham for a few days, and travelled by road and rail on 8 and 9 September arriving in time to see the last of the resident Battle squadrons departing for France. Temporary accommodation was found in a hangar for the new arrivals and their equipment – but it was to be a long time before order and efficiency were restored to the Aeroplane and Armament Experimental Establishment, after its official opening at Boscombe Down on 20 September, 1939.

Part II

This part forms the bulk of the work, and is devoted to the aircraft, the tests made on them, their armament and equipment and the results found at Martlesham Heath 1920-39.

In the twenty-year period between the World Wars, about 1,580 aeroplanes and autogiros of some 400 distinct types were flown and tested at Martlesham. A total of about 2,900 reports resulted of which about 65 percent survive; to the total must be added the reports devoted exclusively to armament (90 percent survive) and a few hundred on miscellaneous subjects. All known surviving reports have been consulted to prepare this part, which is based almost exclusively on their content, with occasional elaboration from Air Ministry files where considered necessary for clarification.

The aircraft have been categorised under nineteen headings, allocation being determined by the purpose for which a type was originally tested. Thus in general all tests of a type as its development progressed will be found in one category. However, there are several instances of types appearing in more than one category where developments of the original model were designed for new roles *eg* Vickers Vildebeest – mainly under Coastal but examples under General Purpose and Night Bomber categories.

In some cases the distinction between one type and another is not clear cut, *eg* some multi-seat civil types could be used by private owners and also used commercially; an arbitrary allocation of category has been made in these cases (The index will show the location).

The aim has been to give a brief comment on the opinion of AAEE as to the handling and suitability of an aeroplane, together with extracts of the performance found, and as far as possible a photograph. The mid- and late-1920s are not so well covered due to lack of existing source material.

Designations and identity markings are generally as given in the reports. Service Mark numbers therefore are frequently omitted.

Notes to Tables of Performance

The tables are presented in abbreviated form and based on the annual Record of Performances prepared by the Air Ministry (DTD) up to 1931. From that date figures have been taken from aeroplane reports. There are many anomolies, summarised below.

Line
A number corresponding to the cross reference in the text.

Type and Identity
Usually the name and identity appearing in the report.

Engine
Number and type as appearing in the report or in the Record. The power is as quoted in the Record or the maximum normal power given in the report. Supercharged engines are not treated consistently in reports, when the sea level (or gated) output was given; later the maximum power at full throttle height was given. Where possible, the latter is quoted in the tables.

The combined output of two or more engines is quoted where appropriate.

Seats
Normal crew seating.

Wing Area
The total wing lifting area (*ie* including ailerons and with flaps-retracted).

Maximum Speed
The maximum true air speed and the height at which this speed occurred. With supercharged engines maximum true air speed was achieved at full throttle height; unsupercharged engines gave maximum speed at sea level but speed was measured at the lowest practical height.

Take-Off Run
These figures must be treated with great caution.

Landing Speed
The true air speed as derived from camera records.

Climb
The time taken from rest to achieve the quoted standard height, together with corrected rate of climb at that height.

Service Ceiling
The standard height at which rate of climb fell to 100ft/min.

Fuel Capacity
Reports sometimes give only the fuel carried for the performance tests; the capacity where known, is quoted in Imperial gallons.

Weight
Weight empty includes cooling water where appropriate, but not usually fixed fittings for military equipment. Gross weight is the weight at start up for the performance measurements.

Report
M number and one suffix letter with date. The units used are those at the period – *ie* Imperial and were, of course, the figures used for comparison and selection of winners of competitions.

Night Bombers

Vickers Vimy

Wartime Vimy aircraft were stored until the reformation of Night Bombing Squadrons in 1923. Martlesham's postwar involvement with the Vimy started in March 1923, with F9158 fitted with wheelbrakes, and tested during eight hours of flying by the following June. Soon to follow were tests on squadron aircraft, which were suffering from three or four years of storage. The best of No.7 Squadron's five machines, F9176 arrived in October 1923 for official performance measurements *(line 1)*; although the Eagle VIII engines gave nearly full power, speed and particularly ceiling were considerably worse than those found during the war. The worst of No.7 Squadron's Vimys, F9180 was judged to be unairworthy on arrival in December 1923. On relegation of the type to the training role, dual controls and new engines were briefly tested at AAEE in late 1927 on F8634 with Jupiters and in mid-1928 on another machine with Jaguar engines. Shortly after the formation of No.15 Squadron, the two Vimys dedicated to armament were J7442 (in use between at least December 1924 and December 1926) and J7451 (at least early 1925); they were used for a variety of bombing duties.

Vickers Virginia

The Virginia (like its transport versions, the Victoria and Valentia), remained in front-line squadron service for over thirteen years, a longer period than any other type between the wars. Longevity was the more surprising in view of the type's poor performance from the very first Martlesham assessments *(line 2)*. Unfortunately, of about 50 AAEE reports written on the Virginia, only two appear to have survived.

The first prototype, J6856 with Lion I engines, was handed over in December 1922 for official trials following Vickers' flying at maximum weight from Martlesham during which a tailskid broke. The Establishment made standard performance measurements, and criticised the pilot's view (he had to stand for taxying) and the extreme vibration from the engines causing continual breakages to the cowling and exhausts. The Air Ministry were very disappointed at the low ceiling and speed, inferior to the single-engined Avro Aldershot, and computed range

of only 1,050 miles. Vickers modified the second aircraft J6857 to include a strengthened undercarriage, Lion II engines and a slanting decking in front of the pilot, apparently with results acceptable to Martlesham. Further modifications, and Lion IIs, were incorporated in the development Virginia J6992, which was subjected to performance measurements *(line 3)* early in 1924. (Note – the Mark numbers used by Vickers for differentiating the modification states of Virginias appear to have no echo in official documents until the Mk VII).

J6856, the original aircraft, made three further visits; first at the end of 1923 with Lion Is, and so called fighting tops, then at the beginning of 1925 with Condor III engines but without tops *(line 4)* and finally at the end of the year with both Condors and tops. The more powerful engines improved top speed, climb and ceiling *(line 5)*, but at the expense of estimated range, down to 780 miles in still air.

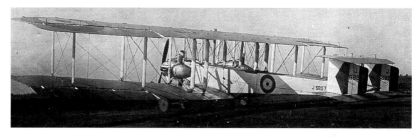

Virginia J6857 in mid-1923 with Napier Lion II engines closely cowled. (British Crown Copyright/MOD)

Vickers Virginia J6856 in original form in February 1923 with straight-sided engine cowlings, subject to excessive vibration and breakage. (British Crown Copyright/MOD)

Over the next five years, the various attempts to improve the Virginia were reflected in trials at Martlesham, but details of results are sparse. J7558, the first of the so-called Mk VI production type with the addition of a centre fin and dihedral on both wings arrived early in 1925, and was passed to No.15 Squadron for armament

work later in the year. J6993 was received with sweepback on the wings, Frise ailerons and a lengthened fuselage and known as Mk VII; the modifications improved both longitudinal and lateral stability, but reduced performance *(line 6)*. Performance was not materially altered by changing propellers on J7130 *(line 7)*. A further Mk VII, probably J7432, performed *(line 8)*, but retained the earlier Lion IIB engines. It was followed in July 1927 by J7439 with the wing (and possibly rear fuselage) in metal; the resulting saving of nearly 2,000lb in structural weight produced a disappointing increase in performance *(line 9)*. J7439 was inadvertently spun and apparently survived with unknown results to its metal members.

Next in the Virginia development came the Mk IX with rear turret aft of the tailplane represented in mid-1928 by J7715 *(line 10)* as a standard machine, followed immediately by J7720 with slotted wings. The latter is remarkable for the lowest service ceiling, 5,750ft, of any Virginia tested

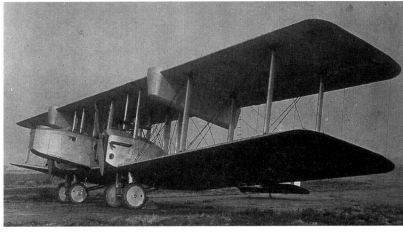

Virginia J6856 late in 1923 with early form of 'fighting tops' on the upper wing; just visible at the rear of the left 'top' is the ladder for access – apparently used while airborne. (British Crown Copyright/MOD)

Virginia J6856 late in 1925 with Rolls-Royce Condors and redesigned 'tops'; the fuselage has been lengthened since 1923, and a third fin added. (British Crown Copyright/MOD)

early aircraft coupled with gyro precession caused a divergent phugoid which led to the pilot cutting out the automatic control as the stall was approached. Later the same year, J7424 with swept wings and longer fuselage and thus greater stability led to more encouraging flights. Later the same year J7424 had two-axis control (the ailerons were not powered), but excessive rolling in bumps rendered the autopilot unsuitable for bombing but acceptable for cruising. In 1929, the Air Ministry ordered modification sets for thirteen Mk X aircraft for one squadron to be equipped with autopilots. Martlesham trials on J7558 in 1929 and J7275 in 1930 appear to have led to acceptable results, as by mid-1930 No.7 Squadron had twelve machines in Service (three with three-axes and nine with two-axes controls).

Experimental engines were tested at AAEE on Virginias. J8236 had French-built Jupiter VIIIs, but at least three failures delayed progress

(line 11), but it no doubt had the lowest landing speed. J7720 later had Suazedde wheel brakes; its landing run must have been measured in inches but no report to substantiate this assertion has been found. Finally, a Mk X, J7717 completed trials of the standard types of Virginia in 1928; the Mk X remained in squadron service until 1938 while J7717 itself remained droning over the Suffolk countryside, frequently en route to Orfordness, engaged on a multitude of flare and bombing trials until 1937.

Experimental work on autopilots was entrusted to the RAE at Farnborough as a major subject for investigation. Several Virginias were used for this work, and four were passed to Martlesham for comment and assessment for Service use. The first, early in 1927, (J7717 in its original form

with straight wing and short fuselage) had the three gyros and three servo motors mounted in the front gunner's compartment, a wind-driven generator under the wing and a Bristol gas starter in the rear gunner's compartment. The basic instability of this

Virginia J7421 in late 1930 with Bristol-built Jupiters. (Royal Air Force Museum)

between September 1928 and March 1929; Palmer brakes were later tested on J8236. Bristol-built engines were then tried at the end of 1930 in J7421 *(line 12)* which also had revised toilet arrangements and brakes; results were applicable to later Victorias in the Middle East. Engines for earlier Victorias had been tried in 1929 on J8238 fitted with the Lion XIA. Finally, the Pegasus engine, intended at one time for the B.19/27 type, were fitted in J7130 *(line 13)* on arrival in January 1934; this aircraft eventually left Martlesham in July 1939 after proof dropping hundreds of bombs, sea markers and other devices, and also posing as a target for the prototype Bawdsey radar station.

The last group of Virginias was used for armament trials; it included J7432 1929-33, J7562 1927-8, J7275 1930, J7130 1934-9, J7558 1929-31 and J7717 1928-1937.

Handley Page Hyderabad and Hinaidi

To complement the long-range Virginia, the Air Ministry required a medium-range night bomber (Specification 31/22) and ordered from Handley Page a single machine based on the existing W.8 airliner. Briefly flown at Cricklewood, the bomber, known as the Hyderabad, went to Martlesham for contractor's heavy weight trials in October 1923; the tail-skid succumbed to the vagaries of the aerodrome surface and J6994 was then unserviceable for over three months. AEE type trials followed in February 1924 with unknown results. However, by the end of 1924 the Specification (15/24) for the development version was agreed, incorporating modifications to the controls, rudder, bombsight and engine installation as a result of the trials. J6994 *(line 14)* with the modifications completed was tested by a Service pilot – probably from Martlesham; further fin and rudder alterations were found necessary to overcome a tendency to yaw. One Hyderabad, J8813, was tested at AAEE in the summer of 1928 with Handley Page slots for application to the similar Hinaidi.

The first Hinaidi, J7745, *(line 15)*, was converted from a wooden Hyderabad by fitting geared Jupiter IX

Handley Page Hyderabad J6994 in March 1924. It has the original fin and rudder shape; just visible under the fuselage roundel is the opening of the lower gun position. (R C Sturtivant)

engines – French made. It flew well, with outstanding stability and manoeuvrability, on trials in the summer of 1927; the front pilot had a good view, and the rear slightly less so. The persistent problems of noise and vibration on the Hinaidi first became manifest on J7745. In 1930 two further Hinaidis J9299 (wooden) and J9301 *(line 16)* (metal fuselage frame) were used to assess various propellers in an attempt to minimize vibration. First smaller diameter airscrews were tried, and then pairs of standard diameter, one set made from two separate blades and the other pair made from solid four bladed laminates. The separate blades were best and, together with heater muffs on the intakes, produced acceptable results, although in service vibration continued to plague the type – to the extent that the compass was rendered useless by continually rotating at cruising, *ie* maximum revolutions.

Handley Page Hinaidi J7745 in July 1927, showing clearly the lower Lewis gun. (British Crown Copyright/MOD)

Another problem in service was resolved by sweeping the wings back by 2½deg to overcome reported tail heaviness. Late in 1928 J9033 *(line 17)* was assessed with swept wings and found to be longitudinally stable up to 103mph, and neutrally stable at higher speeds; results were similar with automatic slots fitted. J9033 returned in April 1929 with modified propellers; fuselage panting was cured.

Late in 1929, after a 50hr endurance test by Handley Page, the first metal Hinaidi, J9478 *(line 18)*, completed full test including single-engine performance; at 55mph 2,300ft could be maintained on the starboard engine. The effectiveness of a third Lewis gun, under the pilot, was no doubt reduced by the need to communicate by touch. Main criticisms were the impossibility of the pilot leaving his seat with his parachute on, and a heavy rudder prone to snatching. J9301 followed for propeller and bombsight assessments; the latter device had to be used with the front window open producing considerable draught. Brief tests were made at Radlett on K1070 with modified ailerons (heavy but effective) and K1072 with a single mushroom head throttle lever for the two engines. In mid-1932, K1064 at Martlesham was found to be longitudinally stable at all

speeds with wing sweep increased to 5deg. Two years later, K1064 was subjected to 110 take-offs and landings fitted with low-pressure tyres intended for the Clive transports in India. Finally, the same machine had experimental hydraulic throttle controls to each engine; results were partially inconclusive as part of the old mechanical linkage remained in the system.

Vickers Vildebeest

During the International Disarmament Conference, one proposal seriously debated was the banning of large bombers. Consequently, early in 1932, the Air Staff considered the tactic of a small bomber approaching its target at night on a prolonged glide. A Vildebeest was modified to assess this idea – conceived probably as a result of improvements in sound location. The aircraft modified, S1715, was assessed by AAEE in the summer of 1933 for handling only; no performance or oil cooling trials on its Pegasus IM3 engine were done. Slow flying in prolonged glides was easy and stability good with slots free and fixed; stall behaviour was very good, and the elevators were light and effec-

tive. Night flying posed no problems. S1715 was passed to No.7 Squadron for Service trials but the single-engined night bomber was not adopted.

Specification B.22/27

Among the various attempts to provide an effective night bomber with a ceiling of over 15,000ft, *ie* twice what the Virginia was achieving, was a 1927 specification (B.22/27) for a three-engined aeroplane. De Havilland and Boulton and Paul each received an order for a single aeroplane. The latter, Type P.32 numbered J9950, flew first and arrived for testing late in 1931 – a year after its first flight. The delay was caused by overheating of the engines. Apart from stability, the official report was uniformly adverse. All three controls were heavy at all speeds – the elevator exceedingly so and also very slow acting particularly with the centre engine (alone on the top wing) throttled. The tail actuator (trimmer) was also heavy and required large adjustments for small

Boulton and Paul Type 32 J9950 in the summer of 1931. This view emphasises the large wing span. (Philip Jarrett)

Metal-framed Hinaidi K1064 in early 1932 with sweepback of the wings increased to 5 deg. (Philip Jarrett)

speed and power changes making landings dangerous. Finally, the cockpit was too narrow, some controls were poorly placed and the plate glass windscreen, susceptible to splintering in an accident, rendered pilots almost speechless. No performance was measured, and the machine returned to its makers for many modifications – including replacing its early type Pegasus engines with Mk X FBMs. The de Havilland D.H.72, J9184, was also delayed in construction having been completed by the Gloster Aircraft Company, and arrived at Martlesham in November 1931 for full load trials by the manufacturer. It is doubtful whether these tests were completed and no AAEE trials were made although at least one Service pilot flew the aircraft – his log book contains no comment on his experience.

Both B.22/27 types were weighed – the P.32 being used to assess two methods of calculating weight; the more accurate method indicated a maximum of 22,803lb. By the autumn of 1932 the requirement was cancelled.

Specification B.19/27

Although improvements to the Virginia's poor performance were expected from metalization, a replacement was specified in 1927 (ceiling over 17,000ft) and six companies tendered designs, of which four were built. The £50,000 available in the Air Estimates

for prototype development of night bombers was split between Vickers' proposal and that of Handley Page; Fairey financed its own type as did Vickers with a second, four-engined, machine (although two engines were specified). Among many factors causing delay was the 1929 decision by the Air Ministry that the pilot should sit on the left instead of on the right in side-by-side cockpits. The Vickers official entry was Type 150 J9131 which flew first, arrived at Martlesham on 28 August 1930, flew a little *(line 19)* but crashed on 9 October, 1930, when an engine cut on take-off. In addition to minor criticisms, the lateral stability was poor and the fuselage twisted alarmingly in flight. During rebuilding at Weybridge the weight was significantly reduced and the Rolls-Royce F.XIVS were replaced by production type engines (Kestrel IIIs); the steam cooling of the latter gave trouble both before and after redelivery to Martlesham in the late summer of 1931. As previously, lateral stability was severely criticised – the report stated 'The aircraft was

Vickers B.19/27 J9131 in November 1931 with Rolls-Royce Kestrel III engines and steam condensers behind the engine struts. (British Crown Copyright/MOD)

unstable and very unpleasant during flight if the air was at all disturbed owing to a continuous yawing and rolling motion'; bombing, night flying and instrument flying characteristics were unsatisfactory – as were the very stiff elevator and rudder controls. The motion experienced was much later known as 'Dutch roll' – caused probably by the wing sweep and insufficient directional stability. Moving the CG forward and downwards reduced the effect. Performance was not measured until the third visit to AAEE in the summer of 1932 *(line 20)* by which

de Havilland 72 J9184 in the winter of 1931/2. No official photographs appear to have been taken, and this private picture was taken from the corner of a hangar. (G Kinsey)

time Pegasus IM3 radial engines had been fitted, together with a steel fuselage and duralumin wing structure. Although the controls were lighter, the fundamental yawing and rolling remained though sweep-back had been reduced. A final attempt to cure the problem with new wings was evaluated and the performance measured *(line 21)*. The rudder was much improved and handling generally good with particular praise for steadiness as a bombing platform. The aircraft was written off after a fire on 18 July, 1934, when excessive fuel leaked and caught fire on start up.

Although the Vickers four-engined Type 163 visited Martlesham Heath in early 1932, flying was restricted to the company's own heavy weight trial and no official assessment was made. The type was withdrawn from consideration for selection to meet the B.19/27 Specification.

The Handley Page design, the H.P.38 J9130, arrived at Martlesham in November 1931 and stayed four months. The troubles and subsequent delays attending Vickers' design had allowed Handley Page time to incorporate many improvements in J9130

Vickers B.19/27 J9131 in July 1932 with Pegasus engines and reduced sweep-back on the wings. (British Crown Copyright/MOD)

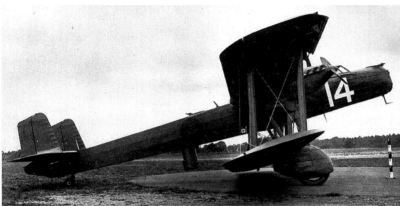

Handley Page Heyford K4029 in July 1935 with Kestrel VI engines and four-bladed propellers. The pilot had an enclosed cockpit; the front gunner was not so fortunate. (British Crown Copyright/MOD)

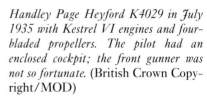

latest standard including Kestrel VIS engines. The exposed front gunner/bomb aimer became numb after 30 seconds at the operating height of 15,000ft, and the report concluded that this Heyford (produced as the Mk II) was of limited military value. Final handling of the Heyford type was completed in March 1934 when K3503 (with a covered cockpit and no front gunner's position) flew well with the CG range extended. Armament development on Heyfords involved K3489 in March 1935 with electrical fuzing of bombs; trials apparently came to an abrupt halt the following month when the aircraft iced up and was damaged following loss of control. K6902, a Mk III, in 1937 and K4029 in 1938, were used for a variety of bomb and other trials, while K3489 in 1936 and K3503 in 1937 had experimental nose turrets – neither of which was successful.

Elimination of Fairey's monoplane contender for the B.19/27 competition was decided in mid-1932, before AAEE's full assessment starting later in the year. K1695 had various modifications incorporated since earlier trials, including revised mass balances in all three controls and Flettner servo tabs for elevator and rudders. Controllability was improved and stability good. The AAEE report comments that the design was totally different from any in the Service, but that attention to detail in the design made maintenance particularly easy. Criticisms concerned the irregular longitudinal stability at high speed, a cold cockpit and exposed front gunner whose position was rendered ineffective above 100mph. The AAEE 1933

during protracted company flying with the result that official tests went very smoothly. Construction and handling were good and the performance *(line 22)* met the original requirements. Lack of oxygen equipment and high altitude (15,000ft) combined to make lengthy flights very unpleasant; oxygen was later fitted to the type. Maintenance was easy for so large an aeroplane – an engine could be changed in 4.3 man/hours although the 28 Fairey fasteners and 86 screws on each leg fairing were time consuming for oleo removal. No.15 Squadron in its assessment of the armament said, 'no position (for an attacking fighter) over 100 yards range was not covered by at least one (of three) guns'; J9130 was a particularly good bombing platform, and easy to fly, although the bomb aimer was cramped and the gunners' positions draughty.

Meanwhile, official funds had been found to purchase the Fairey B.19/27 which was numbered K1695 by the time it was briefly tested at Martlesham in May 1932, before joining Vickers J9131 and Handley Page J9130 for Service evaluation by squadrons in Wessex Bombing Area. The result was the choice of the Handley Page, named Heyford for the Service.

Heyford K3503 in early 1934. Just visible is the cover for the pilot; the slots are open and the under-turret extended. (Royal Air Force Museum)

The first production Heyford Mk I K3489 was found unacceptable by AAEE in late 1933 on grounds of poor view when taxying, restricted stick movement with the pilot's seat raised and, most important, shuddering of the elevator in all conditions of flight; performance was not measured. Nevertheless, fourteen similar production aircraft entered service late in 1933, over six years after issue of the Specification. Full type trials had to wait another two years until K4029 *(line 23)* was modified to the

Fairey B.19/27 K1695 in January 1933, displaying to advantage its very deep wing section. (British Crown Copyright/MOD)

Fairey Hendon K1695 in May 1935, with enclosed cockpit for pilot and cupola for the front gunner; it is not clear where the front gun was mounted. Other items of interest in this photograph are the venturi (under the cockpit) the windmill (under the fuselage), two brackets for Holt flares (under the port wing) and four small bombs (behind the left trouser). (British Crown Copyright/MOD)

Report *(line 24)* coupled with the Service opinions led the following year to a small production order for the advanced looking Fairey Night Bomber as the Hendon. The prototype, K1695 returned to Martlesham *(line 25)* in November 1934 with take-off boost increased and full armament and autopilot fitted. The latter was constrained to perform turns by rudder application while keeping the wings level. The exposed gunners' and bomb aimer's positions rendered fighting and bombing impractical. All these crew positions were given protection by the time of the third visit of K1695 at the end of 1935 *(line 26)* but although the nose cupola had severe shortcomings it was considered to be a great advance; both front and rear gunners were still subjected to severe draughts. The flying controls and lateral stability were criticised; above 180mph (indicated) the ailerons were immovable. Single-engined control was easy. The limitations discovered

were not rectified for Service use and a large part of the production contract was cancelled, although the first two production machines K5085 and K5086 underwent full load and structural tests respectively in 1937.

Vickers Wellington

In 1932, the Air Ministry began the process of replacing the daylight Boulton Paul Sidestrand; Vickers and Handley Page tendered successfully and each built single prototypes to Specification B.9/32. They flew in mid-1936 by which time both had been ordered into production to meet the demands of Royal Air Force Expansion. Thus there was no competition, and both were assessed at AAEE as medium bombers and subsequently equipped night squadrons. Following the usual contractor's heavyweight trials starting at Martlesham on 13 November, 1936, the

Vickers Wellington, K4049, was officially tested *(line 27)*. Initial reports criticised inter alia poor workmanship of the petrol tanks, the eight similar 'T' handles grouped together (two each for engine cut-out, variable-pitch control, fuel cocks and engine cooling), the 21 reflections in the cockpit perspex and excessively heavy rudder. Thirteen modifications were recommended for the navigation facilities. Ailerons, elevators and brakes were satisfactory, but the trim change on overshoot with undercarriage and flaps down was excessive and only controllable by immediately winding the trimmer nose down. Performance and much handling was incomplete when K4049 crashed on 19 April, 1937, and was destroyed; it was established that the large horn balance on the elevator had failed and thrown the machine onto its back. The first production Wellington, L4212 without horn balances and incorporating many other modifications was hastened ahead of its siblings and reached Martlesham one year later. Emphasis was on handling; the aircraft tended to tighten and stall in turns, the throttles vibrated closed and, even after modification, the aircraft was longitudinally unstable, stick free. From September 1938 the operational equipment of L4212 was assessed; the report on the early nose and tail turrets (Frazer-Nash) commented that the gunners (in both nose and tail) did not rotate with the turret. Improvements made the two turrets acceptable, as was the under turret which could be lowered

Vickers Wellington L4212 in April 1938, without armament but having non-rotating gunner's turrets in nose and tail. Large mass balances are visible on the port elevator. (British Crown Copyright/MOD)

in 6 seconds and raised in 15. Opinion in the Air Staff was divided about the usefulness of under turrets which completely blocked the fuselage in all types when retracted.

Wellington equipment testing continued on L4212 and L4221 and included pyrotechnics, electrical system, radio (rendered almost inaudible by unacceptable ambient noise) and bombing. The bomb load of 4,500lb involved reducing the fuel load but represented a three-fold increase over the Heyford and gave greatly increased flexibility in selection of bomb type, and, of course, a significant expansion of the tests to be completed by AAEE. Brief tests of dual controls were made on an otherwise standard aircraft, L4217; lack of dual operation of the wheel brakes was the only major comment. In mid-1939, L4223 incorporating modified longitudinal controls including re-introduction of a redesigned horn balance on the elevators was subject to comprehensive handling assessment at

Handley Page Hampden K4240 in July 1936. Features are the large area of Perspex on the nose, the pitot head some three feet above the fuselage (the pitot mast apparently has the thermometer sensor attached to it) and the variable-pitch propellers. (British Crown Copyright/MOD)

24,825lb take-off weight; the tightening in turns was absent, and the only criticism concerned 'kicking' of the elevator near the stall. Meanwhile, L4213 completed its lengthy performance, consumption and oil cooling trials *(line 28)*, and another Wellington made heavy weight take-offs at 27,000lb using Cranwell and Wattisham which had tarmac and grass surfaces respectively, both considerably more suitable than Martlesham for heavily laden aircraft.

In May 1939, L4298 started trials of the soundproofing, fitted in an attempt to reduce the unacceptable noise experienced earlier on L4221. Finally, L4335 spent eight weeks at AAEE before joining No.38 Squadron in July 1939.

Handley Page Hampden/Hereford

The Hampden, also to B.9/32, reached Martlesham in prototype form as K4240 in June 1936 when a brief assessment *(line 29)* was made during the firm's trials; there were ten points of criticism, including some of flimsy construction. Following heavy weight tests at Martlesham by Handley Page in the autumn of 1937 K4240 started offical trials, and many comments were similar to those made about the Wellington – viz – flaps

produced too large a trim change, the elevator was heavy and gave poor response at forward CG and various engine and fuel controls were too close together and similar in appearance and operation. After minor modifications, K4240 returned for further trials *(line 30)*; the variable-pitch propellers and slats were liked, but the lack of heating made a long flight at operational height very uncomfortable, intercommunication between the three crew was difficult, and, worst of all, the aircraft was longitudinally unstable making it unacceptably tiring to fly.

Four of the first six production Hampdens, L4032, L4033, L4035 and L4037 shared the extensive testing *(line 31)* from August 1938. Engine response was poor on L4032 but the flaps were improved. Intercommunicating remained a problem, and, on L4035, the type's inadequate field of fire was revealed by the inability to fire the guns to the beam. The maximum bomb load of 5,000lb was, however, impressive although carried at the expense of a reduced fuel load; great versatility in the load carried was demonstrated. The results of tests were not reported until March 1940 although the flying was largely completed before the war.

As a second source of production for the Hampden, Shorts at Belfast received a contract for the type, to be powered by Napier Dagger engines; the first of Short's machines (actually a re-engined Handley Page built aircraft, L7271, with the new engines), renamed the Hereford, reached Martlesham by May 1939 and the first two production aircraft, L6002 and L6003, in August. Very little flying was done prewar due to persistent engine cooling trouble, and no reports were issued.

Armstrong Whitworth Whitley

Classified as a heavy bomber, Specification B.3/34 required the ability to carry a bomb load of 1,500lb for 1,250 miles; Armstrong Whitworth built the prototype to meet this Specification,

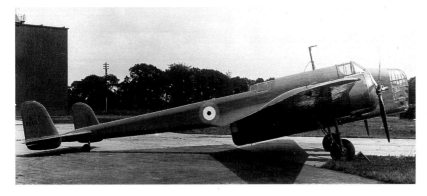

Hampden L4033 in January 1939 with dihedral on the outer wings, a new nose section and pitot head under the fuselage. (British Crown Copyright/MOD)

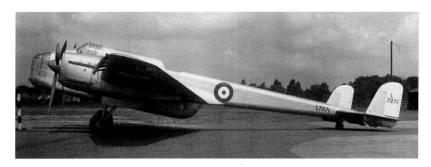

Handley Page Hereford L7271 in June 1939 in pristine condition, with Napier Dagger engines, straight wing incorporating slots and a third version of nose windows. (British Crown Copyright/ MOD)

and a second to B.21/35, similar to the original Specification but without the alternative load of ten troops. The first aircraft K4586 spent seven months at Martlesham from 20 August, 1936, *(line 32)*, and was assessed as unsuitable as a bomber, due to excessive directional stability. Full rudder at 160mph yawed the nose through 5-10deg where it remained on centralising the rudder; the phenomenon of the resulting steady sideslip was fully investigated, including fitting a flag on the nose to visualise the relative airflow. Bombing under autopilot (in which the steering command was fed to the rudders only) was almost impossible – a turn through 17deg of heading taking 35 seconds; verbal instructions from the bomb aimer to the pilot when manually flying the aircraft produced acceptable results. However, all controls were heavy; the ailerons produced delayed response making landings dangerous and the elevators were sluggish in response. Fortunately the elevator trimmer was effective and rapid – and its continuous use enabled the pilot to maintain control on overshooting with full flaps when large nose up change of trim occurred. During trials the pitot head was moved from the top of the fuselage (where 20mph overreading occurred at 200mph on the ASI) to the wing (when 15mph had to be added at 160mph ASI to correct the reading). There were many other less damning criticisms, including the excessive time taken to change an engine – 30hr 13min using two men.

The main report detailing the Establishment's finding on K4586 was dated 28 June, 1937; interim reports had been sent to the Air Ministry progressively from September 1936. Thus the shortcomings were known in time to incorporate major changes on the second prototype K4587 before reaching Martlesham in June 1937. Primarily the changes were aerodynamic by introducing increased dihedral on the wings and modified fins and rudders. Results of trials on K4587 are not known as no reports appear to have been written, possibly because the first production Whitley, K7183, preceded the second prototype at Martlesham by three months.

K7183 was camouflaged, had turrets and Trinity engine fairing rings; performance *(line 33)* and handling were similar to K4586 and an engine change took even longer. A hydraulic pump on the starboard engine provided power for the turrets in the nose (single Vickers gas operated gun) and under the fuselage (two Browning guns). Modifications tested in K8936 in October 1938 provided a cure for earlier hydraulic cavitation and for the 23 shortcomings in the turrets. K8936 had the first Whitley tail turret at AAEE, an A.W.38 type manually balanced and exceedingly draughty. The powered Frazer-Nash FN4A tail tur-

Armstrong Whitworth Whitley K7208 in May 1938 with Rolls-Royce Merlin engines and no armament. The pitot head is on the port wing. (British Crown Copyright/MOD)

ret flown in K7183 in early 1939 proved generally superior with its four guns, and was adopted. The new 2,000lb bomb could be fitted with great difficulty into the Whitley's narrow bomb bay; an air swing of the new aid to navigation, the direction finding loop gave accurate results.

No turrets were fitted to K7208 with Merlin engines and the maximum speed *(line 34)* greatly exceeded that of the Tiger variants. However, even with constant-speed propellers the noise inside the aircraft was unendurable, and it was very cold. These shortcomings made lengthy flights unattractive; such flights were, however, necessary for fuel consumption measurements. At 15,000ft the prototype Merlin-engined Whitley achieved 2.32 air miles per gallon in early 1939. In mid-1939, the Whitley III K8936 achieved a take-off weight of 24,500lb at Martlesham, and 26,500lb *(line 35)* at Wattisham and Cranwell; experimentation indicated an optimum flap setting of 15deg for these heavy take-offs. A Mk V Whitley, N1345, arrived on 28 August, 1939, incorporating most improvements recommended from earlier tests. Finally, Whitley Mk I K7202 and K7205 arrived in July 1939 for Bawdsey's requirements with D Flight.

Handley Page Harrow

Of the quartet of bombers which arrived at Martlesham in 1936 the Harrow was the last, and the least advanced with its non-retractable undercarriage. Ordered into production only in 1935 to Specification B.29/35, the Harrow, derived from the Handley Page C.26/31, was always seen as a stop-gap. Such was the rush that squadrons received the type almost before trials had begun on K6933 and K6934. Between 30 November, 1936, and 25 March, 1937, the former completed full perfor-

Night bombers

Line	Type	Identity	Engines No.	Type	Total Power (bhp/rpm)	Seats	Wing area (sq ft)	Max speed (mph/ft)	Take-off run (yd)	Landing speed (mph)
1	Vimy	F9176	2	Eagle VIII	704/1,800	3		106/6,500 98/5,000		
2	Virginia	J6856	2	Lion IC	936/2,000	4	2,174	92/6,500	300	
3	Virginia	J6992	2	Lion II	957/2,000	4		100/5,000		
4	Virginia	J6856	2	Condor III	1,356/1,900	4		106/6,500		
5	Virginia	J6856	2	Condor III	1,356/1,900	4	2,128	109/6,500		
6	Virginia	J6993	2	Lion II	942/2,000	4	2,164	95/6,500		
7	Virginia	J7130	2	Lion VB		4	2,164	88/6,500		
8	Virginia	J7432	2	Lion IIB	951/2,000	4	2,164	93/6,500		54
9	Virginia	J7439	2	Lion VA	1,010/2,000	4	2,164	92/6,500		
10	Virginia IX	J7715	2	Lion V	944/2,000	4	2,183	83/6,500		
11	Virginia IX	J7720	2	Lion V	955/2,000	4		85/6,500		
12	Virginia	J7421	2	Jupiter IX	970/2,000		2,174	99/6,500		43
13	Virginia	J7130	2	Pegasus IIM3	1,142/2,000		2,194	117/5,000		
14	Hyderabad	J6994	2	Lion	991/2,100	4	1,427	108/10,000		
15	Hinaidi	J7745	2	Jupiter IXAF	1,013/2,000	4	1,467	110/6,500	258	46
16	Hinaidi	J9301	2	Jupiter VIII	880/2,000	4	1,476	110/6,500	236	52
17	Hinaidi	J9033	2	Jupiter VIII	1,091/2,000	4	1,467	115/6,500		58
18	Hinaidi	J9478	2	Jupiter VIII	880/2,000	4	1,480	113/6,500	225	55
19	Vickers B.19/27	J9131	2	FXIVS	1,140/		1,367	125/11,000		
20	Vickers B.19/27	J9131	2	Pegasus IM3	1,175/2,000	4	1,386	135/5,000	296	
21	Vickers B.19/27	J9131	2	Pegasus IM3	1,175/2,000	4	1,593	139/6,500	228	
22	H.P. B.19/27	J9130	2	Kestrel IIIS	1,138/2,700	4	1,472	109/13,000	266	
23	Heyford	K4029	2	Kestrel VI	1,215/2,500	4		140/13,000	244	57
24	Fairey B.19/27	K1695	2	Kestrel IIIS	1,156/2,700	4	1,447	143/10,000	218	
25	Fairey B.19/27	K1695	2	Kestrel IIIS	1,126/2,700	4		137/10,000	207	55
26	Fairey B.19/27	K1695	2	Kestrel VI	1,180/2,500	4		152/15,000	193	
27	Wellington	K4049	2	Pegasus X	1,656/2,250	3		243/6,400	305	69
28	Wellington	L4213	2	Pegasus XVIII	1,540/2,250	5	753	245/15,000	340	62
29	Hampden	K4240	2	Pegasus PEVSA	/2,250			245/10,000	256	
30	Hampden	K4240	2	Pegasus PE5S (A)	1,457/2,250			250/15,000		
31	Hampden	Various	2	Pegasus XVIII	1,639/2,250	3	718	254/15,000	425	68
32	Whitley	K4586	2	Tiger IX	1,454/2,150	5	1,232	189/7,000	285	70
33	Whitley	K7183	2	Tiger IX	1,445/2,150			178/6,500		
34	Whitley	K7208	2	Merlin II	1,681/2,400			239/16,000		
35	Whitley	K8936	2	Tiger VIII					580	
36	Harrow	K6933	2	Pegasus X	1,666/2,250	5	1,092	187/10,000	300	66
37	Harrow	K6934	2	Pegasus XX	1,596/2,250	5		197/11,000	270	70

Line	Climb to 6,500ft Time (min-sec)	Rate (ft/min)	Service ceiling (ft)	Fuel† (Imp gal)	Weight Empty (lb)	Gross (lb)	Report No	Date	Endur (hr)	Remarks
1	16–15	300	11,900	372	7,547	10,000)				No bombs, 250 gal fuel
	26–05 to 5,000ft		5,170	372	7,547	12,500)	M353	10/23		1,560lb bombs
2	25–00	170	8,700	545	9,277	16,662	M326	3/23	8½	1,000lb bombs capacity
3	14–50 to 5,000ft		9,450	545		16,691	M372	3/24		1,000lb bombs capacity
4	14–00	315	10,530		11,208	18,450	M405	3/25		1,008lb bombs; same performance, new propellers
5	13–30	337	11,650	545	11,640	18,780	M436	11/25		With fighting tops
6	29–51	117	6,800	545	10,293	17,839	M443	1/26		2,076lb bombs capacity
7	27–00	133	7,500	538	10,195	18,448	M443A	12/26		2,240lb bombs capacity
8	26–36	135	7,600	538	10,247	18,460	M443B	3/27		2,240lb bombs capacity
9	20–12	220	9,400		8,271	17,205	M443C	2/28		Metal wings
10	32–29	90	6,200		9,691	18,460	M443D	5/28		Loaded to compare with J7432
11	38–36	70	5,750		9,833	18,460	M443E	10/28		Automatic slots
12	17–00	265	11,500	500	9,493	17,177	M443J	1/31		2,016lb bombs
13	658ft/min at 5,000ft		17,300			16,927	M443K	4/34		Power at rated altitude (5,000ft)
14	10–20	495	14,050	380	7,719	12,982	M358A	3/24	6¼	1,168lb bombs capacity
15	12–00	370	12,050	380	7,592	14,396	M490	11/27		1,500lb bombs capacity
16	15–06	475	15,400		8,136	13,120	M490D	5/30		Reduced diameter airscrew
17	20–00	220	14,750	380	8,054	14,396	M490B	6/28		1,500lb bombs capacity
18	16–05	490	14,900	380	7,799	12,692	M490C	1/30		1,448lb bombs capacity
19	19–45	320			10,435	16,170	M573	11/30		Aircraft crashed 9 Oct 30
20	7–29	610	15,000	336	10,238	16,252	M573/3	9/32		1,500lb bombs; capacity 2,200lb
21	8–00	715	19,000	442	10,130	16,122	M573/4	7/33		360 gal for trials 1,700lb bombs
22	14–45	440	19,000	384	9,757	15,534	M597	3/32		1,230lb bombs
23	9–00	550	20,400*	400	10,915	17,176	M597B	1/36		1,600lb bombs
24	15–45	410	17,500	540	12,997	19,259	M607	6/33		400 gal fuel for tests; 1,500lb bombs
25	14–54	380	17,200	540	13,090	19,317	M607/2	11/34		400 gal fuel for tests; 1,500lb bombs
26	9–12	555	22,800*	540	13,468	19,779	M607/3	1/36		400 gal fuel for tests; 1,550 lb bombs
27	6–30	885	20,900	270	12,262	21,014	M703	7/37		2,000 lb bombs plus 3,800 lb ballast
28	10–12	485	21,600	747	16,693	24,804	M703A	12/39	10	2,000 lb bombs plus 551 gal fuel for tests
29	11–00 to 15,000ft					14,896	M697	7/36		Range estimated at 1,000 miles
30						16,000	M697/2	7/38		
31	6–18	900	24,300	423	11,761	18,750	M697A	1/39		Range 1,460 miles - 2,100lb bombs
32	9–24	690	19,200	522	13,989	21,060	M699	6/37		431 gals on trials
33						22,300	M699A	7/38		Under turret extended
34						20,000	M699B	6/38		
35						26,500	M699D	10/39		
36	8–00	760	19,200	722	14,820	23,000	M706A	7/37		K6934 also used
37	9–30	720	21,000	722	14,824	24,518	M706	4/38	9½	Endurance found on range flight

* Absolute
† Capacity

Whitley K8936, with Armstrong Siddeley Tiger engines, in July 1939. Heavy-weight trials were deemed unsafe at Martlesham, and took place at Wattisham and Cranwell. (British Crown Copyright/MOD)

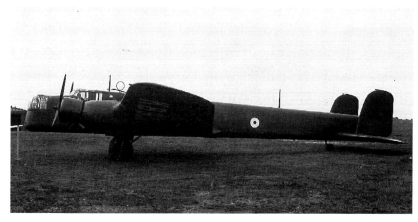

mance *(line 36)*, W/T and electrical tests. The spacious cockpit was unheated but otherwise satisfactory; of the controls, the elevator was extremely heavy and the aircraft was reported to be unstable throughout the speed range. The pitot head, some 4ft 4in above the fuselage gave good results. The instability was more fully investigated on K6934 in 1938; two CGs were tested both well aft (31 percent and 40 percent of mean chord) which may explain the lack of longitudinal stability. Useful data were recorded on control column and trimmer positions to achieve hands-off flight at various speed – only the second time this method of assessing stability had been used at AAEE. After arrival in December 1936 K6934 which had Nash and Thompson nose and tail turrets and an Armstrong Whitworth design in the mid position, was used for armament trials. A total of only four Lewis guns was fitted (one each nose and mid positions and two in the tail), and there were considerable blind areas which made the defences unacceptable. The nose position was cold and cramped, and the rear too small for a human gunner, it was reported. In March 1937 a long-distance flight at heights up to 15,000ft was generally favourably commented upon, but the tail gunner was violently ill for 10hr after landing. Ven-

Harrow K6934 in November 1937 with redesigned nose incorporating Nash and Thompson turret for a single Lewis gun. (British Crown Copyright/MOD)

tilation was improved, and successfully tested in September 1937 on K6983; other modifications included an increase in hydraulic pressure from the single pump to improve turret rotational speed, and modification (on K6998) to eradicate cavitation and improve turret smoothness of operation. Meanwhile K6934 came near to disaster following a dive to 225mph when it was discovered that the aircraft was almost uncontrollable in pitch. A safe landing was made with all the crew in the nose and the trimmer used to round out. The starboard elevator spar was found to have failed, attributed to an earlier, inadvertant dive to 250mph. During repairs Peg-

Handley Page Harrow K6933 in December 1936, with Blenheim K7033 in the background. The pitot head is over four feet above the fuselage, well clear of any disturbance from the fuselage; pressure errors were small throughout the speed range. (British Crown Copyright/MOD)

asus XXs replaced the Pegasus Xs, and testing resumed *(line 37)* including extensive single-engine investigation. At 20,000lb (some 4,500lb lighter than maximum take-off weight) height could be maintained at 7,300ft with either engine failed; stability was also better on K6934.

Short Stirling

In October 1938 the first of the four-engined night bombers was briefly assessed, albeit in model size. Known as the Half Scale Short B.12/36 (later the Short Stirling), three pilots made a few flights to look at stability, trim and stall. Full power (456hp from four Pobjoys) required more than full trim, the stall and the controls were normal, but stability and lateral trim poor. All up weight was 5,370lb and wing area 350sq ft.

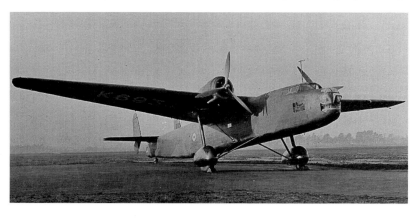

Day Bombers – Multi-Engined

Bristol Braemar and Sopwith Cobham

Designed for daylight raids over Germany, the four-engined Braemar C4297, was at Martlesham at the beginning of 1920 and completed its trials in spite of being kept outside during the preceding winter. Performance *(line 1)* was adequate with a load of 1,750lb of bombs while the handling and stability were good, although the elevator response was poor and slow; it could be kept straight with any three engines operating. Even with the control column fully back it was difficult to stall the Braemar, which had a speed range of 49mph to 122mph (true). After strengthening the landing wires, C4297 seems to have languished until mid-1921 when flying resumed; after a few flights it crashed fatally on take off in August 1921. Another wartime design, the Cobham, was represented at AEE by all three machines made. H671 (two Siddeley Puma engines) and H673 (two ABC Dragonfly engines) did little if any flying until struck off charge in July 1920. H672

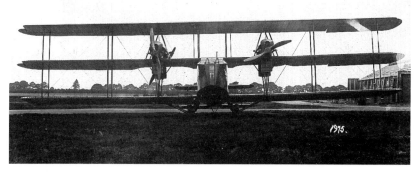

Bristol Braemar C4297 in mid-1919, showing the tandem pairs of Napier Lion engines, and the pilots' open cockpit. (British Crown Copyright/MOD)

(two Dragonfly engines) arrived in March 1920, and crashed three months later when the undercarriage collapsed on take off due, it was decided, to poor workmanship. Performance trials were not completed.

Boulton and Paul Bugle

Originally specified as a three- or four-seat night bomber, the Bugle (Specification 30/22) was tested as a day bomber. The first, J6984 *(line 2)*, with metal fuselage and wooden wing structure, was inspected in mock-up form in February 1923 and flown to Martlesham the following September. The propeller shaft of the early

Jupiters gave trouble, and the control loads were too heavy on the stick; a change to wheel control and horn-balancing of the ailerons only partially cured lateral heaviness. Jupiter IV engines were tried before the machine went to the RAE in April 1924, by which time J6985, with metal wings appeared briefly at Martlesham before No.22 Squadron flew it to the Hendon Pageant in June. Third of the type was J7235, arriving in May 1924 fitted with inboard fuel tanks, and an extra tank for ceiling climbs in mid-1924. Performance of J7235 was improved by fitting special propellers

Boulton Paul Bugle J6984 in late 1923; the test thermometer is visible in the front gunner's cockpit. The underwing fuel tank can just be seen behind the port engine. (British Crown Copyright /MOD)

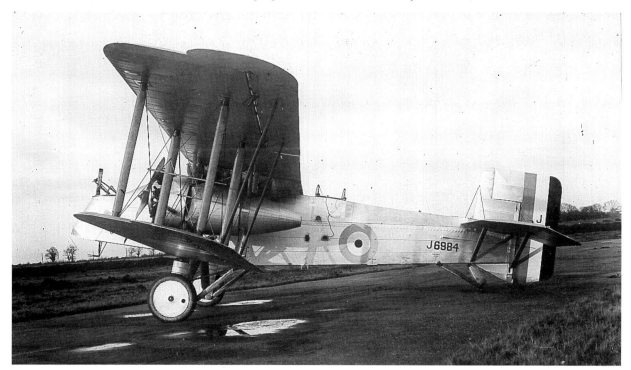

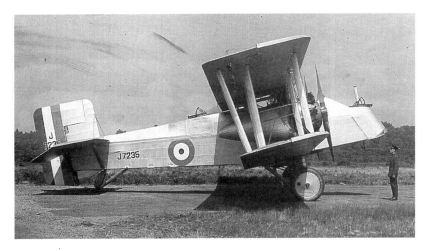

Bugle J7235 in the summer of 1924, with internal fuel tanks and steamlined inter-aileron struts. (British Crown Copyright/MOD)

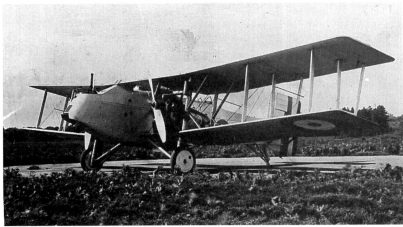

Bugle II J7266 late in 1925, with Lion engines and many minor changes. (British Crown Copyright/MOD)

(line 3); this aeroplane moved to No.15 Squadron for some months on armament trials. The next Bugle to reach AAEE in March 1925 was J7266 *(line 4)* with modifications to the wings, undercarriage, tailplane and elevators but apparently retaining Jupiters although Lions were originally planned and were fitted subsequently. Handling was good, but marred by a heavy rudder. J7266, with internal stowage for bombs spent two years with No.15 Squadron from October 1926. Finally, J7267 was flown by a Martlesham pilot in January 1927 for a purpose long forgotten.

Boulton Paul Sidestrand J9186 in November 1929, with Bristol Jupiter VIIIF engines which produced excessive vibration initially. The Flettner balance tab was one attempt to lighten the rudder forces. (British Crown Copyright/ MOD)

Boulton and Paul Sidestrand and Overstrand

The Air Staff decided against producing the Bugle, but kept alive the three-seat twin-engined day bomber class by contracting Boulton and Paul to build a slightly bigger all-metal design to Specification 9/24. Appearing at Martlesham by December 1926, the first Sidestrand, J7938, spent over six months on full type trials *(line 5)*; stability in all three planes was exceptional, making it an excellent bombing platform. However, the ailerons were poor, the rudder very heavy and manoeuvrability poor. A year later, J7939 was tested for a few months – possibly with changes to the balance of the flying controls. At the beginning of 1929 the first development Sidestrand J9176 completed full trials, *(line 6)*, remarkable only for high cylinder temperatures on the climb. Handling was apparently acceptable as no further modifications were made before entry into service, where at least the stronger pilots could loop and roll the type.

Later in 1929, J9186 was flown with the geared (ratio 2:1) Jupiter VIIIF giving more power above 4,000ft. On arrival at AAEE on 8 October, 1929, J9186 produced a marginally higher maximum speed at 6,500ft *(line 7)* but at the expense of severe vibration which resulted in the original ungeared Jupiter VI being fitted before the aircraft was handed to No.101 Squadron in the spring of 1930. Jupiter VIII vibration was evidently considered acceptable later as this engine was fitted to production aircraft – possibly as an interim measure pending delivery of the Jupiter XF. The latter was tested at Martlesham (probably in J7939) from mid-1931, but this advanced type of Jupiter was also far from satisfactory in spite of trying stub exhausts, then a Bristol exhaust ring inside a Townend ring cowling. The makers were instructed to continue trying various forms of cowling and exhaust, and to

fit the newer and more powerful Pegasus engine. Meanwhile, J7938 returned with the pneumatic Bambridge brakes; results of trials between September 1931 and September 1932 are not known, but the machine appears to have remained with No.15 Squadron until its demise in an accident in August 1934. Last of the Jupiter-engined Sidestrands to arrive at Martlesham was J9186 in early 1932 and again in the summer. At the latter date a comparison was made between standard and polygonal exhaust rings; in both cases the engines had polygonal Townend cowlings. At all heights, the polygonal exhaust gave an increase of 5mph to 6mph in top speed, although the climb rate and the noise were the same.

The improvements realised with the new engine arrangements were retained when J9186, was fitted with Pegasus I engines and tested in early 1933. Carburation, control flutter and re-rigged ailerons were among features tested. A year later the same aeroplane was assessed with the new pneumatically-powered nose turret fitted; many improvements were recommended. Essentially similar to J9186 was J9770, renamed Overstrand; type trials *(line 8)* were completed early in 1935, but with a larger

Bristol Blenheim K7033 in November 1936. Only 30 months separate this photograph and that of the Overstrand; the aerodynamic advances of the Blenheim are evident. (British Crown Copyright/MOD)

Boulton Paul Overstrand J9186 in March 1934, with an early pneumatically-powered nose turret; the pilot has a cockpit cover. The Bristol Pegasus engines have polygonal Townend rings. (British Crown Copyright/MOD)

turret, uprated engines and two-piece four-bladed propellers and minor control modifications. Normal practice on type trials was to dive to 50 percent above maximum level speed – J9770 reached only 170mph (15 percent) before a fin fitting failed in severe vibration. The first production Overstrand, K4546, was flown by No.22 Squadron pilots, and the vibration in dives was significantly less; it is not clear whether K4546 was at Martlesham for the trials. In spite of the severe speed limitation, the RAF received some twenty-five Overstrands for front line service until 1938. Almost the last of the type, K8175, was flown by B Flight, Armament Section on turret trials – in mid-1937 with the Boulton Paul SAMM version, and in mid-1938 with the hydraulically-driven version armed with 20mm cannon.

Bristol 142 and Blenheim

Hardly had the Overstrand finished its trials and demonstrated a top speed of 148mph, than the Air Ministry sent the monoplane Bristol 142 K7557 named *Britain First* for official assessment as a medium bomber. The result confirmed the top speed of 280mph at 16,500ft *(line 9)*, with Hamilton variable-pitch propellers. After only a few weeks at AAEE, further trials were brought to an abrupt halt when the undercarriage failed to lock down and the aircraft was extensively damaged on 17 July, 1935. Official embarrassment at this mishap to such an advanced machine, given by Lord Rothermere was offset by the Air Ministry insisting on paying its donor £18,000.

The promise of high speed and the pressure of the re-armament programme led the Air Staff to order the Blenheim (Type 142M) into production in 1935. The first aeroplane, K7033, arrived at Martlesham on 27 October, 1936, after only 22hr flying at Filton; it lacked many operational

items but representative weights and CG were achieved with ballast *(line 10)*. Stability and handling met with approval, but the cockpit was noisy and draughty, there was a vicious wing drop at the stall and the pressure correction at 100mph was plus 16mph, an unusually large figure. Operational and armament trials were done on K7034 which arrived in April 1937, after later but incomplete Blenheims had entered Squadron service. K7034 *(line 11)* had a Bristol turret, hydraulically-powered from a pump on the port engine; operation of its Lewis Mk III was considered ineffective due to jerky and imprecise movement of the turret. In November a modified turret (Mk II) proved better, but draughty with an unacceptable trigger mechanism; many faults persisted even after further modification. In May 1938 a Mk III turret with a Vickers K gun proved acceptable until subjected to extended flight at operational altitude when the hydraulic firing mechanism failed. The single fixed Vickers V gun in the port wing was inaccessible and difficult to rearm, taking two men 20 minutes; replacement by a Browning reduced the time to eight minutes. Bombing trials were more successful and culminated in a 3hr 52min Operational Flight on 14 July, 1937, on which very uncomfortable oxygen masks were worn throughout. Radio and electrics were generally accept-

Blenheim K7072 in July 1938 with the production form of lengthened nose. (British Crown Copyright/MOD)

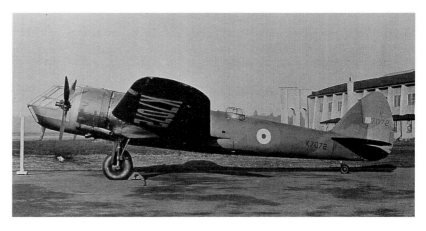

Blenheim K7072 in November 1937 with the original but unsatisfactory long nose. (British Crown Copyright/ MOD)

able. After nearly 120hr of testing, take-off and landing distances were measured on K7034; the still air take-off run of 360yd at maximum weight was disappointing, and attributed in part to the need for overhaul. After servicing, crosswind take offs were made to ensure satisfactory handling in cases where the required distance was not available into wind. Further take-off handling was assessed early in 1939 on the first Avro-built Blenheim I, L6594; the AAEE recommendation was to achieve 110mph as soon as possible after leaving the ground so that sufficient rudder control was available in the event of an engine failing at this critical phase. Although built to identical drawings as the Bristol machines, the Avro produce was found to have measurably inferior performance *(line 12)* and handling.

In November 1937 a flying assessment lasting only three and a half hours was made on K7072, with a long extension to the forward fuselage and intended for the Bolingbroke. Distortions and reflections were unacceptable, and the nose modified for a further assessment in July 1938; the modification was acceptable and adopted as standard on the long nose Blenheim (Mk IV in Service), with improved lighting and rain-proofing for the navigator. The first production Mk IV, L4835 arrived in July 1939 and trials had just started when war was declared. This machine had previously been in service with No.53 Squadron since January 1939.

L1424 arrived on 28 November, 1938, fitted with a pack of four Browning guns under the fuselage; heating and improvements to ammunition feed arrangements were found to be necessary in the course of firing 7,305 rounds. In early 1939 an interesting trial on two Blenheims, one with both propellers rotating in the

same direction and the second with one propeller rotating to the right and the other to the left, concluded that symmetric rotation gave greater longitudinal stability.

Other Blenheims used by AAEE included K7109 with the first opening direct vision panel (a feature of most later Service aeroplanes for quarter of a century), L1253, L1495 and L8662 for general armament development trials, and, for D Flight's work with Bawdsey, K7044, L1113, L1201, L4931, L4932, L6595, and L6622 to L6627 inclusive.

Day bombers – multi-engined

Line	Type	Identity	Engines No.	Type	Total power (bhp/rpm)	Crew seats	Wing area (sq ft)	Max speed (mph/ft)	Take-off run (yd)	Landing speed (mph)
1	Braemar	C4297	4	Liberty	1,680/1,750	4	1,905	122/5,650		
2	Bugle	J6984	2	Jupiter	805/1,580	3	947	116/6,500		
3	Bugle	J7235	2	Jupiter	794/1,575	3	947	109/6,500		
4	Bugle	J7266	2	Jupiter	795/1,575	3	947	118/6,500		
5	Sidestrand	J7938	2	Jupiter VI	916/1,700	3	965	130/6,500		50
6	Sidestrand	J9176	2	Jupiter VI	967/1,700		980	132/6,500		
7	Sidestrand	J9186	2	Jupiter VIII	880/1,700		957	139/6,500		
8	Overstrand	J9770	2	Pegasus IIM3	1,170/2,000	3		148/6,500		
9	Bristol 142	K7557	2	Mercury VIS2	1,200/2,400			280/16,500		
10	Blenheim	K7033	2	Mercury VIII	1,406/2,400		420	279/15,000	330	78
11	Blenheim	K7034	2	Mercury VIII	1,413/2,400		420	253/15,000		
12	Blenheim	L6594	2	Mercury VIII	1,418/2,400	3		265/15,000	340	

Line	Climb to 6,500ft Time (min-sec)	Rate (ft/min)	Service ceiling (ft)	Fuel capacity (Imp gal)	Weight Empty (lb)	Gross (lb)	Report No	Date	Remarks
1	15-5 to 10,000 ft		15,300	428		16,512	271C	2/20	
2	11-00	445	13,500	260	5,229	8,910	360A	1/24	5½ hr endurance
3	8-20	535	14,300	260	5,300	8,300	386	5/24	1,700lb military load
4	9-00	560	14,350		5,300	8,300	386A	4/25	
5	6-30	970	21,500	260	5,275	8,852	471	6/27	
6	7-15	815	18,300		5,865	9,232	471B	3/29	Servo rudder
7	6-42	1,070	20,800		6,370	9,963	471C	12/29	
8	5-24	1,010	21,300	261	8,004	11,923	667	12/35	1,100lb bombs
9							677	9/35	
10	3-36	1,890	31,400	278		11,776	707	5/37	
11	5-18	1,330				12,500	707A	1/39	No bomb doors
12	4-24	1,595	26,600	278	8,483	12,500	707C	6/39	Avro built

Day Bombers – Single-Engined

de Havilland D.H.9A

Selected in 1919 as the standard Royal Air Force day bomber, the D.H.9A (Liberty engine), of which 1,262 were officially on strength in November 1919, required little further testing at Martlesham. H3629 had an increased fuel tankage, but was destroyed before flying began by the crash of the Braemar in August 1921. H3567 spent most of 1922 riding on a Westland-designed oleo undercarriage of various widths and positions; after 250 landings, the coil spring broke through the structure and the aeroplane was written off. As an alternative to the American Liberty engine, some D.H.9As had British Napier Lions. Performance and consumption of the Lion were tested on the three-seat E753, which was also being considered for coastal work, between April and October 1920; two passenger seats made the CG too far aft but the Lion engine ran well. In mid-1923 the Establishment reported on Lion radiator suitability and the differences between two types of propellers on J6957.

Other D.H.9As for trials work included J597 in 1921 for parachute development, and E8627 from 1924 for many armament trials until replaced by J7864 in 1927; J7864 was finally burned to test a new fire extinguisher. J7316 may also have been used in 1929 for armament work.

No.15 Squadron appears to have received its full complement of D.H.9As, although relatively little flying was done on them. The first Flight received *E797* (Dual Control), E869, E8722, J7009, J7038 and J7057 on formation in 1924, while J7307, J7328, J7605, J7607, J7797 had arrived by 1925. Other D.H.9As of No.15 Squadron before full re-equipment with the Hawker Horsley in 1927 were E957, E8696, F1611, F2796, H3478 and J7805; there may have been others. Finally, in at least 1928, the dual control D.H.9A J8492 remained at Martlesham after use by the Training Flight of No.15 Squadron.

de Havilland D.H.14 Okapi

Designed during the war to replace the D.H.9A, the Okapi was used at Martlesham for endurance testing of the new Rolls-Royce Condor engine. Both J1938 and J1939 arrived in the spring of 1921. After 40 hours in the air the engine of J1938 was changed in October and the aircraft struck off charge in May 1922; J1939 crashed in August 1921, and was not repaired.

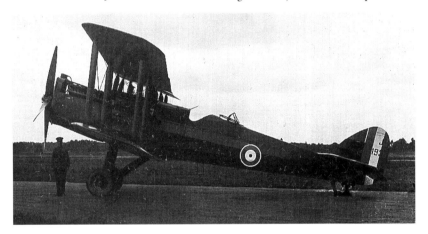

de Havilland D.H.14 Okapi J1939 in August 1921. It was used for endurance flying of the new Rolls-Royce Condor engine. (British Crown Copyright /MOD)

de Havilland D.H.9A J6957 in mid-1923 with Napier Lion engine and its large radiator, just visible between the front undercarriage struts. (British Crown Copyright/MOD)

de Havilland D.H.29 Doncaster

The Doncaster was designed to meet the requirements of the Director of Research Type 4B (modified) – later renamed Specification 10/20. Type 4B was a long-range bomber; the word 'modified' indicated a deep chord cantilever monoplane wing. The first Doncaster, J6849 arrived on 21 September, 1921, and crashed, still in the hands of a company pilot, on 7 November due to loss of elevator control at slow speed and low engine power. The second, G-EAYO, fitted out for passengers, languished virtually unflown at Martlesham for eighteen months from September 1922. The firm's full load trials on the extensively modified and lengthened first prototype resumed in September 1923 at Martlesham. Serious vibration (probably rudder flutter) was not cured by fitting a four-bladed propeller, and only brief trials were made by AAEE in January 1924. The inadequate control led to five pilots condemning the Doncaster and the type being abandoned; the wing escaped criticism.

de Havilland D.H.29 Doncaster J6849 in late 1923 in its lengthened form, but still lacking acceptable handling. Above the port wheel is a platform for the engine starting mechanic to stand and wind up the engine – the cranking handle is visible. (British Crown Copyright/MOD)

Specification 2/20

D of R Type 4B (renamed Specification 2/20) led to the construction of two types, both tested officially. First to arrive was the Avro Aldershot J6852; testing was delayed by the type's introduction to the public at the Hendon Pageant in June 1922. A trap door under the fuselage held the packed parachute which was attached by external wire to the occupant of the rear seat; results were encouraging but only dummies were used. Brief consumption measurements indicated a range of 240 miles – insufficient to meet the 'long-range' requirement. In August 1922 the second and lengthened Aldershot, J6853, arrived; stability was improved, but the machine was still neutrally stable at high speed. Airflow measurements on the tailplane failed to indicate a possible improvement. A calibrated fuel tank permitted accurate consumption measurements; at 6,000ft full power propelled the aircraft 81 statute miles in one hour using 41 gallons; the type

Aldershot J6952 in the summer of 1924, in production form with horn-balances to the elevators and struts between the ailerons. (British Crown Copyright /MOD)

needed greater fuel capacity. After modification by the makers J6853 returned with additional fuel tanks over the wings, differential ailerons operated by a stick in place of a wheel and other changes. Trials indicated that further alterations to the ailerons and undercarriage were needed, and the increased range led to a decision to fit a seat for a second pilot. With these improvements and a Condor III in place of the Condor I, J6853 made a final visit to Martlesham in early 1925; the all up weight increase to 11,200lb was approved. Meanwhile the

first production Aldershot, J6942, arrived in October 1924 for armament trials, preceded in July 1924 by J6952 *(line 3)*, for type trials which were completed satisfactorily in three months. Finally, late in 1925, J6953 visited AAEE for an unknown reason.

Avro 549 Aldershot J6853 in the autumn of 1922, with lengthened fuselage and changes to the fuel tankage, undercarriage, tailplane bracing and elevators (British Crown Copyright /MOD).

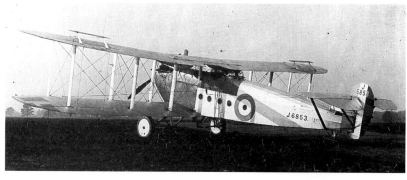

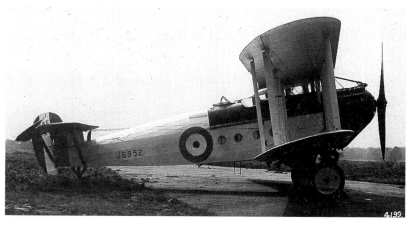

The Aldershot's rival, the de Havilland D.H.27 Derby J6894, spent five months at AAEE from November 1922; it was mostly unserviceable, but performance *(line 4)* trials were completed in the 11hr 50min spent airborne. The only report extant criticised many points of design including poor view, inability to use full wheel control, inaccessibility of rudder trim in flight and need for an electric starter for the engine mounted high above the ground.

Specification 5/21

Built initially to a reconnaissance specification (5/21), the Fairey Fawn was mostly tested as a day bomber; no reports have been found. The first two Fawns J6907, *(line 5)*, and J6908 *(line 6)*, arrived in April 1923 and completed initial trials rapidly in spite of engine misbehaviour. Both were ready for delivery back to Northolt in June although J6908 had a minor crash on arrival; J6907's return was delayed until September. Production followed, and J7184 completed short performance checks *(line 7)*, with

Fairey Fawn J6907 in April 1923, with short fuselage and only the gravity feed fuel tank above the wing. (British Crown Copyright/MOD)

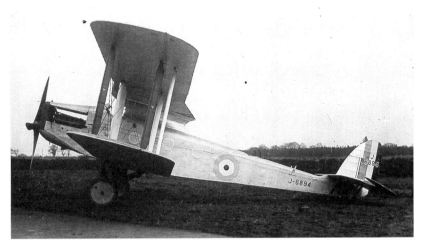

de Havilland D.H.27 Derby J6894 early in 1923. The slim lines of this aeroplane belie its size; it was four feet longer and over two feet taller than its rival, the Aldershot. (British Crown Copyright/MOD)

original and modified propellers *(line 8)*, within six weeks; Martlesham's expertise was used, from May 1924, to modify it for parachute development work. After the dummy and live drops J7184 toured Service stations giving practical experience in the use of parachutes about to be introduced into the RAF. From May 1925 J7187 spent several months on bombing and W/T work; in 1926 J7224 flew with revised

armament and, for a period, a flowmeter for calibration. J7786 with a Lion V in place of the Lion II spent some months from May 1925 at Martlesham. Finally, J7978 with a supercharged Lion VI may have been tested, probably early in 1926.

Vickers Vixen

Vickers modified their Vixen private venture prototype G-EBEC, and submitted it late in 1923 for AAEE assessment as a light bomber. Performance *(line 9)*, was superior to the Fawn; the report is lost but one pilot's log book comments cryptically 'not bad'.

Specification 26/23

The first Specification to be entitled 'Single-engine Day Bomber' was 26/23; four companies received contracts for prototypes. All four types reached Martlesham, powered, as required, by the Condor III engine. First to arrive in January 1925 was the Handley Page Handcross J7498: then, in May 1925, the Hawker Horsley J7511 *(line 10)* (which had been badly damaged on its first flight in December 1924), the Bristol Berkeley J7403 *(line 11)*; and the Westland Yeovil J7508 *(line 12)*. The basis of the selection of the winning design is obscure; the Berkeley had the worst performance and was eliminated by

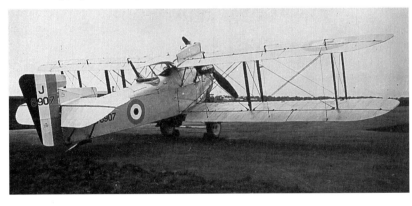

Fawn J6908 in 1923, with lengthened fuselage, main fuel tanks above the wings and increased fin area. Well shown in this view are the kingposts for operation of the unique Fairey camber changing flaps inboard of the ailerons. (British Crown Copyright/MOD)

Handley Page Handcross J7498 early in 1925. Under the starboard wing is a finless 230lb bomb. (British Crown Copyright/MOD)

July 1925; the Horsley to one pilot was 'a sloppy old cow' and the Handcross led another pilot to remark in his log book '7 furniture vans equal one Handcross'. The choice of the Horsley, in the absence of the relevant reports, is an enigma particularly as coincident with the production order (to Specification 22/25) was the issue of another Specification (23/25)* for its replacement. Of the unsuccessful types, Yeovil J7508 returned in late 1926 for armament trials, Handcross J7499 *(line 13)* made a short visit to Martlesham in mid-1925, before joining its sister J7500 as a general purpose armament machine for over two years with No.15 Squadron.

Details of production Horsleys are sparse. J7511, returned briefly in September 1926 by which time J7721 had arrived for type trials lasting a year, with several improvements including the repositioning of the radiator under the fuselage; performance is at *line 14*. The first production Horsley, J7987, spent four months with AAEE, with performance *(line 15)* very similar to the prototype. Meanwhile the first torpedo version had arrived (it is described under Coastal Types), and J7997 (probably the first metal-framed version) paid a short visit until January, 1927. In May of the same year, one

Hawker Horsley J7511 in mid-1925. The barrel of a Lewis gun can be seen under the roundel. (British Crown Copyright/MOD)

Bristol Berkeley J7403 in mid-1925. Unique of the four contenders to Specification 26/23, the Berkeley has ailerons on top and bottom wings. (British Crown Copyright/MOD)

---

* A third Specification (24/25), for a coastal torpedo carrier, was issued at the same time. Aircraft types for 24/25 were suitable for 23/25 also. When tested at AAEE the torpedo requirement predominated; details are given under Coastal Types.

Westland Yeovil J7508. The single 230lb bomb under the port wing has fins in this view. The various arrangements of cowling on the Condor engines of the four 26/23 contenders is interesting. (British Crown Copyright/MOD)

attempt to improve the performance of the torpedo version, the Armstrong Siddeley Leopard engine was fitted to J8620 and tested with disappointing results in 1928. With a later Leopard III, J8620 completed performance measurements in 1930/1 with bomber load *(line 17)*. Similarly, improved performance was expected from the Rolls-Royce H engine in J8932; results are at *line 18*, from flying starting in April 1930.

Horsleys replaced D.H.9As as the equipment of No.15 Squadron starting with J8007 and J8008 in August, 1926, followed by J8015, J8018, J8019, J8604, J8610, J8613, and J8619; all but J8008 had gone by September 1928 when several were transferred to No.504 Squadron. A second batch of Horsleys for No.15 Squadron arrived during 1928, including J8611, J8612 and J8617 and these were in frequent use for a variety of armament and associated tests until the last, J8611, left in mid-1933. Among items investigated on the latter batch were Constantinesco interrupter gear, experimental practice and other bombs, magnetic bomb release gear, electro-magnetic gear, windscreen heating, electric camera control, BSA gun and target towing.

Hawker Horsley J8620 in mid-1928 has an Armstrong Siddeley Leopard engine and a single 500lb bomb between the undercarriage legs, mounted on the torpedo release unit. (British Crown Copyright/MOD)

Horsley J8932 in the summer of 1930, with Rolls-Royce H engine enclosed in a cowling little different from that of the Condor. (R C Sturtivant)

pilot flew J8608 immediately before the long-range record attempt; no report appears to have been written. The Horsley was fitted with the popular slots, and J8606 was assessed with and without these aids to safety from May 1928. The slots started to open at 90mph, were half open at 66mph and fully open at 44mph. Performance is at *line 16*. Further handling on J8606 took place in 1930 and 1931. In an

Fairey Fox

The courageous decision by Fairey to design and build the best aeroplane possible based on the American Curtiss D-12 engine, resulted in the Fox – unencumbered by the usual official Specification for incorporation of Service impedimenta into the design. In August 1925 Martlesham found the unmarked Fox to be very fast *(line 19)* (one pilot said 159mph at 18,000ft, but officially 135mph true at that height), but with a long take-off run and fast landing; handling was summed up succinctly by another pilot as 'damn good'. The same pilot was spun at least twice by Fairey's pilot – an unheard of antic for a bomber. Returning early in 1926, the aircraft had increased span *(line 20)* and thus wing area giving a decrease of 10mph in stalling speed and concomitant reduction in take-off and landing distances.

The Establishment's favourable view of the Fox was supported in squadron trials, and sufficient machines to equip one squadron were ordered – the only changes required were strengthening of the wing and the provision of greater space for kit in the cockpit. In early 1926 the Air Ministry issued a new day bomber Specification (12/26), using as a criterion a top speed of 180mph at 15,000ft, *ie* greater than that of the Fox.

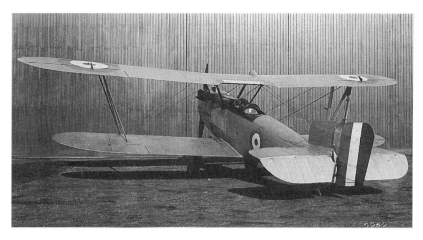

The private venture Fairey Fox in February 1926. The clean lines, unencumbered by Service equipment, set a new standard in light bombers. It is seen after having the wing area increased by 40sq ft. (British Crown Copyright/MOD)

J8427 with dual controls was briefly flown from August 1927; it returned late in 1930 and spent several periods at Martlesham until well into 1934 acting as a fast target tug for other types and guns undergoing testing.

The Fox was the natural choice for Service trials of the new Rolls-Royce Kestrel engine (previously FXI and FXII). The Fox prototype, *(line 21)* still unnumbered, but with an FXIB completed the performance schedule in the summer of 1928; in June it was taken by No.22 Squadron to the RAF

Display. Starting in June 1929 J9026 *(line 22)* with an FXII was subjected to full trials, including consumption, cockpit heating, oil heating (for cold weather engine starting), in addition to handling and performance. In 1931 J9026 completed its research programme with drag measurements with various bombs fitted. Late in 1931 J7945 flew at AAEE for an unknown purpose.

Specification 12/26

Replacement of the ubiquitous D.H.9A was the aim of Specification 12/26. Three types were in contention at Martlesham in the last

Fox J9026 early in 1931, with radiator extended and four bomb carriers. (British Crown Copyright/MOD)

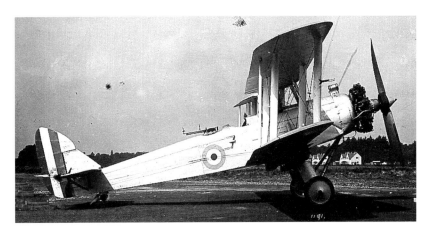

months of 1928 – the de Havilland
Hound (which was bought by the Air
Ministry for the purpose), the Avro
Antelope and the Hawker Hart; the
Antelope and the Hart had FXI
engines, the Hound had a Lion. Two
designs to 12/26 by Fairey were tested
later, (see later) but well after the decision in favour of the Hart.

On 11 September, 1928, the
Hound J9127 arrived; a year earlier it
had outperformed the other General
Purpose candidates (see General
Purpose Types). On this later occasion, the Hound's performance was
slightly inferior to the other two types,
but it was soon eliminated when the
rear fuselage plywood was found to be
delaminating. Another, redesigned,
Hound (line 23) was tested later in
1928 as a light bomber; powered by a
Jupiter radial its performance was
slightly lower than the Lion version.
This unmarked aeroplane was easy to

*Hawker Hart K2424 in June 1932, was
the first produced by Vickers and is virtually indistinguishable from the prototype J9052. (British Crown Copy-
right/MOD)*

fly with good view, but floated on
landing; the cockpit was cramped. No
RAF or overseas interest followed
these trials. Next of the 12/26 types to
arrive, on 13 September, was the
Antelope, J9183 (line 24); the aeroplane handled extemely well and easily met the critical top speed requirement. It went for Service trials before
returning to Martlesham in the spring
of 1929 to complete armament assessment. The Hart J9052 (line 25), was
an immediate success on arrival on 8
September, 1928, with well harmonized controls and excellent performance which did not compromise the

stringent landing requirements.
Construction, said the initial report,
was excellent – rigid and simple. The
only criticism was the cramped gunner's compartment which required
enlargement. On return from Squadron trials J9052 was dived vertically
from 16,000ft to 2,000ft, reaching
282mph (328mph true); bombs and
guns were removed. Spins were
acceptable, although the propeller
always stopped (and, presumably,
always restarted). The Hart was
selected by the Chief of the Air staff in
April 1929 on the basis of AAEE's recommendation, confirmed by Squadron opinion, largely on the grounds of
the ease of maintenance. The Antelope was disliked because it made

*Avro 604 Antelope J9183 in the autumn
of 1928. The prominent chin radiator
was a feature of this design. (British
Crown Copyright/MOD)*

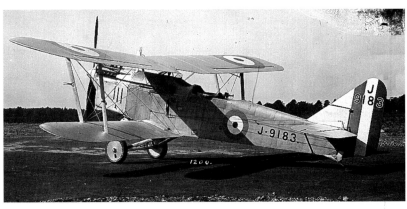

excessive use of unusual metal components. The decision was amply justified over the next ten years by the production of over 3,300 Harts and Hart
developments for eight distinct roles.

Over the next ten years Harts continued to be tested; they are described
in four groups: bomber developments,
special versions, trainers and engine
test-beds. The first development Hart
J9933 (line 26) differed only superfi-
cially from J9052 (in contrast to earlier
types), and the report reiterates many
of the earlier comments – well co-
ordinated controls, good view, easy
take off and landing, even but fast spin

Hart K3027 in April 1935, with blind-flying hood over the front cockpit. The absence of gun in the rear seat and the presence of a windscreen indicate that the aircraft was modified for the station flight at Andover (whose badge is on the fin). The station was the home of many staff officers. (British Crown Copyright/MOD)

(only one stoppage of the propeller), and the undramatic dive to high speed. Extending the radiator to contain the rise in water temperature reduced top speed by 7mph; the only criticism concerned the lack of hand holds for baling out. Later in 1930 J9933 *(line 27)* returned with an FXIIB engine (replacing the FXIB with low gear ratio); the new engine suffered four breakages to the cylinder block. Early in 1931, Hart K1416 *(line 28)* quickly completed its trials, including satisfactory bombing with the high-level bombsight. K1416 initially had a production Kestrel IB (FXIB renamed) with an increased gear ratio, and in 1931 *(line 29)* a Kestrel IIB; performance remained unchanged. In August 1932 a Fairey-

Reed metal propeller gave a slightly better rate of climb at low altitude, and made a spin more difficult to enter due to the greater moment of inertia compared to the wooden type. In late 1938 K1416 was used to test a dive-bombing sight. In 1932 the first Vickers-built Hart, K2424, exhibited no significant differences; in 1933 K2968 (Kestrel IB) demonstrated a better climb from a one degree reduction in propeller pitch allowing higher engine revolutions. With a supercharged engine, extra fuel and Palmer hydraulic brakes, K2915 had a superior performance *(line 30)* in mid-1933; this machine later became the Hind prototype. The evolving technique of

dive-bombing was successfully tested on K2466 and K2967 early in 1934; worries about control flutter were allayed by satisfactory dives on K2967 with 6lb mass balances in each aileron, and 3lb in the rudder. K2967 and K2968 returned to AAEE late in 1933 and remained in use for general work until August 1938 and August 1939 respectively; among trials on K2968 was an assessment of a magnesium propeller in 1937-8. Fitting new W/T equipment to K3012 in 1934 gave AAEE several months of work – both on the ground and in the air.

Of the variants, the first, early in 1932, was the Hart (India) K2083 *(line 31)* with larger radiator and 100lb of

Hart Trainer K3153 in June 1934, with blind-flying hood (here shown stowed) fitted to the rear seat. (British Crown Copyright/MOD)

extra equipment; the radiator was assessed as suitable for a hot climate, but the reduction in performance was greater than expected. In the winter 1932-3 two communications versions, K2455 and K2456 were handled and spun; cockpit heating was ineffective, but the wheelbrakes reduced the landing run by 42 percent, to a mere 127yd. An interesting modification to K3027, originally built as a standard aircraft with gunner/bomb airmer's position in the rear, was a blind flying hood for the pilot; handling and spinning were normal for a Hart – the report does not indicate whether the rear seat occupant had blind faith as well. The final AAEE tests on a standard Hart were made in late 1938 when K3031 arrived, modernized for the rapidly expanding Elementary and Reserve Flying Training Schools; it had brakes, night flying equipment, a tailwheel and radios. K3031 appears to have been as delightful to fly in 1938 as the prototype Hart of ten years earlier.

The Hart's potential as an advanced trainer was recognised early, and K1996 *(line 32)* was modified at the company's expense by Hawker, and flown at Martlesham in mid-1932. The only recommendations were for the fitting of brakes, a smaller rear windscreen and access to the main petrol cock by the instructor. Brakes were tested on K1996 in late 1933, and dual brakes in 1935, K3153 was assessed in mid-1934 with a blind flying hood over the rear seat. For use in Singapore, Hart Trainer K6426 had additional equipment; it was weighed by AAEE in 1936.

Of the re-engined Harts the first

Hart K2434 in February 1932 with Napier Dagger engine – later used in the Hector Army Co-operation type. (British Crown Copyright/MOD)

was a private venture submission to the single-engined day bomber Specification 20/30. The unmarked machine had a Panther IIa engine and after disappointing performance trials *(line 33)*, it failed to recover from a right spin in October 1931; the pilot escaped by parachute. Five previous spinning programmes on Harts and Hart Variants had all been satisfactory; the airflow round the large cowl and the change to a radial engine were blamed for the crash. Next, in mid-1932 came the company's own G-ABTN *(line 34)*, with a Jupiter XFAM; it handled well, performed better, and was dived to 340mph (true); civil C of A tests were done at the same time and resulted in a restricted CG range of 3.2in (but still greater than the 1.2in allowed on Hart Trainers). Later in 1934, comparisons were made between K3020, *(line 35)*

with Pegasus IIIM2 and K2434 *(line 36)* with Dagger II. The former had a combined exhaust collector in the shape of a Townend ring which produced low cylinder temperatures, and the latter was initially prone to faults – no fewer than fourteen being reported. The Dagger was returned for modification by Napier, and trials the following year were completed. No conclusions were drawn by AAEE on the relative merits of the two engines. Hart K3036 had the first Merlin (then known as PV12) installed for a brief eight-day visit to Martlesham in 1935 – probably for weighing.

Long after Hawker had won the 12/26 competition, Fairey's design, the Fox II J9834 arrived at Martlesham in March 1930. Handling was good, aided by Frise ailerons; spins of up to ten turns and dives to 240mph (indicated) presented no problems. Performance with the FXI engine *(line 37)* was disappointing; when J9834 returned the following year with the supercharged FXII, performance was improved *(line 38)*. Also on the second visit the Palmer brakes were approved for use, but were only partially effective due to awkward operation by the heels. Trials terminated in March 1931 when the engine cut out at 50ft and the undercarriage collapsed; no adequate reason for the failure was found. G-ACKH, another Fox II was submitted for extended C of A trials in late 1933; it had an Armstrong Siddeley Serval engine – but the report is missing.

Fairey Fox II J9834 in April 1930; it arrived too late for the Competition. (British Crown Copyright/MOD)

Fairey Fox II G-ACKH in November 1933 with Serval engine. Tests were made at the maker's request and included those for the C of A. (British Crown Copyright/MOD)

ing schools formed during the RAF's expansion period, the Hind Trainer was represented at Martlesham by K5387, *(line 41)*, with derated Kestrel V engine, in mid-1938. Handling, including dives to 270mph (indicated) and eight turn spins were satisfactory, but the blind flying hood flapped against the heads of tall pilots; other minor criticisms were made.

Hawker Hind

The Hawker Hind was developed by way of standard Hart K2915 , fitted with a supercharged Kestrel II which was tested by AAEE late in 1933. Returning eighteen months later, K2915 was representative of the Hind with Kestrel V engine, tailwheel and brakes; performance *(line 39)* was superior to the Hart in spite of a 10 percent increase in weight, and handling received the accolade 'Just like the Hart'. K4636, *(line 40)* the first production Hind to Specification 7/34 produced no surprises but the Ramshorn type of exhausts fitted to reduce flames for night landing reduced performance. There were crude but acceptable dual controls in the rear seat. Steep dives to 282mph (indicated) during which bombs were released resulted in fuel flow irregularities; an engine-driven fuel pump provided a cure. In mid-1937, an eleven-element Potts oil cooler proved adequate for the ambient temperatures expected in the tropics. Destined to see widespread use in fly-

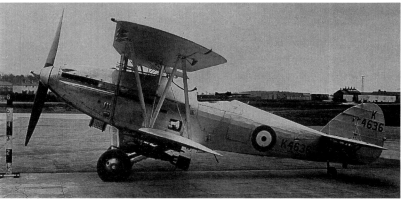

Hawker Hind K4636 in January 1936, with ramshorn exhausts which reduced performance. Two 250lb bombs are fitted. (British Crown Copyright/ MOD)

Vickers Wellesley K7556 in April 1936. In this original form it was tested by AAEE. The bomb containers under the wings are dummies; no armament was fitted, but the rear seat windscreen is raised and can be seen above the starboard mainwheel. (British Crown Copyright/MOD)

Vickers Wellesley

Vickers' ingenuity in designing and selling their monoplane to the Air Ministry to meet the G.4/31 Specification was rewarded by orders for the Wellesley. The prototype K7556 (modified private venture) eventually reached Martlesham in March 1936 when the performance *(line 42)* achieved as a day bomber was good. Aileron heaviness was criticised, as were the horn and lights for indicating the position of the undercarriage; also, at full throttle the gaps in the KLG sparking plugs opened. Visible flexing was a new and disconcerting phenomenon of the high aspect ratio, geodetically constructed monoplane wing. K7556 was progressively modified at Vickers works; a stronger elevator was fitted and then a rear mounting with a single Lewis Mk 3 gun. Both were satifactory but the gunner had no oxygen when moving between prone to firing positions. A production wing with improved undercarriage features was also satisfactory in 1937. Initial assessment of the under-wing bomb nacelles and the bomb

Wellesley K7729 in September 1937 during lengthy and comprehensive trials at Martlesham Heath. The unique bomb carriers gave much trouble before being made acceptable. (British Crown Copyright/MOD)

aimer's position resulted in many unsatisfactory features of both being reported. The prototype was joined by K7713 (Pegasus X) in March 1937 for type trials – but no report appears to have been written, possibly on account of the unrepresentative engine as later aircraft had the Pegasus XX. K7724 and K7729 *(line 43)*, with the latter powerplant completed type trials in 1937/8 and demonstrated the Wellesley's outstanding range achievable in 13½ hours' flying. Remarkable flights were later achieved in Service with a special Long Range Unit equipped with modified aircraft. At Martlesham, diving trials with strengthened wings were satisfactory up to a maximum of 245mph (indicated) when the aircraft rolled left; as a result the maximum speed permitted

Fairey Battle K7558 in November 1937, with only two seats and a Holt flare bracket in spite of the presence of two landing lamps. Just behind the exhaust is the venturi for gyro instruments. (British Crown Copyright/MOD)

in service was raised from 220mph to 240mph. Lack of effective cockpit heating in the prototype was evident again in K7729 where pilots became completely numb after only three hours . The unique bomb carriers required much diving and modification before becoming satisfactory in K7754 *(line 44)* in 1939. K7791 completed gunnery and dive-bombing trials early in 1938. A Mk IXA bombsight in K7740 was acceptable, but not the Potts oil cooler in K7724 even when increased to eleven elements for tropical flying. Consequently a new type of cooler, the Serck, was specified. A modification (provision of seating for a third crew member to meet the needs of the Middle East Command) was designed and installed by Rollason, but appears not to have been tried out at AAEE.

Specification P.27/32

Two major companies, Armstrong Whitworth and Fairey, each received contracts for single prototypes to meet the medium bomber Specification P.27/32. The former was delayed, largely on account of engine trouble and then suffered a minor crash; it did not reach Martlesham. The latter type, named Battle, arrived in prototype form as K4303 *(line 45)* in July 1936 with an early Merlin F engine. A wide speed range (58mph to 308mph indicated) was complemented by docile handling – although the rudder was sluggish at slow speed. Range was estimated at 980 miles. Flat turns for bombing were difficult as the aircraft tended to bank – interestingly the straight wing of the prototype was given a slight dihedral in production which would have increased the tendency. The main criticism was levelled at the unsatisfactory bomb loading arrangements – there was no way of checking positively that bombs were secure. A Merlin I engine was fitted for production trials on K7558 *(line 46)*, fitted with only two seats. The wing-mounted Vickers gun was replaced by a Browning which remained inaccessible; in the rear the Lewis gun was replaced by a Vickers on a rocking pillar. Engine changing was hampered by lack of suitable slings and took an unacceptable 20 man/hours. K7558 spent nine months from July 1937 on trials – much of the time engaged on various improve-

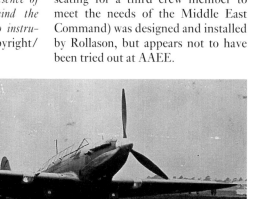

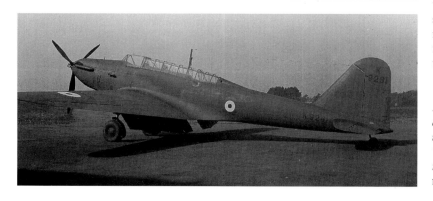

Battle K9281 in September 1938; the camouflage paint was held partly responsible for a decrease in top speed. The test thermometer is taped to the wireless mast. (British Crown Copyright/MOD)

ments to the exhausts and propeller. Ejector exhausts were preferred for night flying, but performance suffered slightly until an improved air intake and propeller boss more than restored top speed .at the expense of take-off distance. K9281 had a Merlin II and reached no less than 3,600 rpm in dives to 320mph with bomb doors open; on take off 2,600rpm were the maximum. K9281 repeated tests with various exhausts *(lines 47 and 48)*, but performance was inferior to K7558 and attributed to camouflage finish and other minor differences. Two wing-mounted lamps (each of 350 watts) for landing at night were well liked – undoubtedly a great advance on the short burning Holt flares previously standard on RAF aeroplanes. A brief check late in 1938 of the performance of the first Austin-built Battle , L4935 *(line 49)*, revealed no significant differences. Standard performance was also maintained on K7605 when fitted with Goodrich inflatable de-icing boots on the leading edges of the wing. The Austin aircraft was used for crosswind landing trials using the wing-down technique; a cross component of up to 20mph was found to be acceptable.

The armament type trials were largely completed on K7577 between September 1937 and August 1939; special bombsight trials for Scatter-bombing were completed on K9221 and K9231 from June 1938 and gun firing on K9227. Two Battles, K7682 and K9223, were allocated for armament development from early 1938; the former was written off after a forced landing at Orfordness on 8 June, 1938, when the pilot was caught out by the fuel selector which required to be turned to the left to select the right tank. Before this event there had been no comment on this misleading

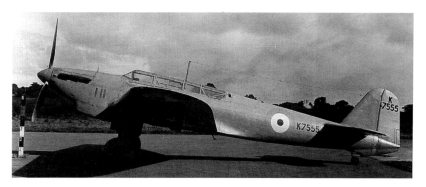

Fairey P.4/34 K7555 in September 1937 – a view emphasizing the sleek lines and similarity to the Battle. (Imperial War Museum)

arrangement. The Experimental Co-operation Unit used K9207, K9208 and K9230 from mid-1938 until after the outbreak of war.

Specification P.4/34

In 1934 Fairey and Hawker successfully tendered for the light bomber Specification P.4/34. During design and construction dive-bombing became a popular tactic for which both were assessed. Before AAEE trials were concluded, Air Staff thinking had changed, and the Henley, already in production, became a target tower. Fairey's own trials on their P.4/34 K5099 included a period at Martlesham in mid-1937, but AAEE's trials took place on the second machine, K7555 *(line 50)*, from June, 1937. It was extremely stable directionally and the rudder very heavy rendering impossible the flat turns required for level bombing. The aircraft was otherwise pleasant to fly, but distortion through the perspex wind-

Hawker Henley L4243 in August 1939 in production form. (Imperial War Museum)

screen was thought to be the cause of tailwheel-first landings. After modification K7555 returned in April 1938 with its wing span and aileron area reduced. Handling remained similar to previous experience, but it was found more difficult to stall. Various combinations of 250lb and 112lb bombs were carried and released satisfactorily.

The Establishment took the opportunity of flying briefly the Hawker Henley K5115 during company flying at Martlesham in July 1937. AAEE trials began in January 1938 when K5115 *(line 51)*, had a production Merlin I fitted in place of the early Merlin F and metal covered wings in place of fabric. Apart from slight longitudinal instability at extreme aft CG in dives up to 380mph (indicated), handling was good although the rudder was heavy. The following comment, 'very little change of trim occurs as the flaps and undercarriage are raised. This is fortunate, as the operation of the flap and undercarriage requires the full attention of the pilot' was made since the operating lever was on the right. This arrangement was strongly criticised, as were the nine-inch flames from the exhausts at full power at night; poor lighting and cockpit distortion aggravated the situation. Oil cooling was not considered sufficient for tropical operations. Production Henleys, to Specification 42/36 for target towing were presumably not required to fly at night, and the type attracted no adverse comment on trials beginning in November 1938 on L3243, *(line 52)*. The target winch appears to have worked satisfactorily. L3247 arrived in November 1938 for general armament (probably target towing) work and L3313 in May 1939 for handling (including diving) trials. L3247 and L3313 were in use at the start of the war.

Day bombers – single-engined

Line	Type	Identity	Engine Type	Power (bhp/rpm)	Seats	Wing area (sq ft)	Max speed (mph/ft)	Take-off run (yd)	Landing speed (mph)
1	D.H.9A	E753	Lion	460/2,000	3	485	136/6,500		
2	Aldershot	J6852	Condor IA	679/1,575	3	1,064	100/6,500		
3	Aldershot	J6952	Condor	660/1,900	3		93/6,500		
4	Derby	J6894	Condor IA	652/1,900	3	1,108	90/6,500		
5	Fawn	J6907	Lion	482/2,100	2		113/10,000		
6	Fawn	J6908	Lion	494/2,100	2		112/10,000		
7	Fawn	J7184	Lion II	502/2,100	3		104/12,000		
8	Fawn	J7184	Lion II	502/2,100	3		104/12,000		
9	Vixen II	G-EBEC	Lion II	496/2,100	2	525	123/6,500		
10	Horsley	J7511	Condor III	689/1,900	2	696	113/6,500		
11	Berkeley	J7403	Condor	690/1,900	2	985	110/6,500		
12	Yeovil	J7508	Condor III	693/1,900	2	813	123/6,500		
13	Handcross	J7499	Condor III	691/1,900	2	785	117/6,500		
14	Horsley	J7721	Condor III	673/1,900	2	696	122/6,500		
15	Horsley	J7987	Condor III	671/1,900	2	696	122/6,500		61
16	Horsley	J8606	Condor III	701/1,900	2	696	126/6,500		
17	Horsley	J8620	Leopard III	873/1,700	2		128/3,000	153	58
18	Horsley	J8932	R-R H	812/2,000	2	693	126/10,000		
19	Fox	-	Curtiss D-12		2	326	155/6,500		
20	Fox	-	Curtiss D-12		2	364	153/6,500		
21	Fox		FXI B		2		167/5,000		70
22	Fox	J9026	FXIIA	490/2,250	2	362	157/6,500		
23	Hound	-	Jupiter VIII	537/2,000	2		156/6,500		
24	Antelope	J9183	FXI B	538/2,250	2	377	171/6,500	165	64
25	Hart	J9052	FXI B	531/2,250	2	346	176/6,500	147	61
26	Hart	J9933	FXI B	480/2,250	2	347	170/2,000	107	47
27	Hart	J9933	FXII B	480/2,250	2	347	167/5,000	112	
28	Hart	K1416	Kestrel IB	480/2,250	2	347	168/5,000	187	51
29	Hart	K1416	Kestrel IIB	480/2,250			166/5,000		
30	Hart	K2915	Kestrel IIS	480/2,250	2	347	185/13,000	218	
31	Hart (I)	K2083	Kestrel IB	480/2,250	2	347	164/5,000	182	51
32	Hart T	K1996	Kestrel IB	480/2,250	2	347	179/6,500		
33	Hart PV 20/30	-	Panther IIA	525/2,000	2	347	164/5,000		
34	Hart	G-ABTN	Jupiter XFAM	545/2,000	2	347	173/8,000		
35	Hart	K3020	Pegasus IIIM2	682/2,200	2	347	188/6,500	110	
36	Hart	K2434	Dagger II	650/3,500	2		191/11,900	133	
37	Fairey B.12/26	J9834	FXIB	480/2,250	2	370	157/5,000	182	48
38	Fairey B.12/26	J9834	FXIIS	474/2,250	2	370	177/10,000	214	54
39	Hind	K2915	Kestrel V	619/2,500	2		190/14,300	175	50
40	Hind	K4636	Kestrel V	607/2,500	2		188/15,000		50

Line	Climb to 10,000ft		Service ceiling (ft)	Fuel capacity (Imp gal)	Weight Empty (lb)	Gross (lb)	Report No	Date	Remarks
	Time (min-sec)	Rate (ft/min)							
1	6-00 to 6,500 ft		19,700	108		4,660	277	7/20	Float gear
2	43-00	90	9,700	214	6,027	10,880	309	8/22	1,500lb bombs
3	37-00 to 6,500 ft		6,350		6,425	11,200	397	12/24	1,500lb bombs
4	29-30 to 6,500 ft		8,300	210	7,033	11,888	322A	3/23	1,500lb bombs
5	16-30	372	14,750	115	3,237	5,548	337	6/23	336lb bombs
6	17-11	350	14,600	124	3,478	5,789	340	6/23	336lb bombs
7	17-30	323	13,850	124	3,529	5,870	373	3/24	336lb bombs
8	16-24	380	15,140			3,635	373A	5/24	No bombs
9	22-40	242	13,200	133	3,267	5,554	368	2/24	396lb bombs
10	11-20	610	18,200	230	4,901	7,810	418	7/25	520lb bombs
11	16-06	382	14,800	228	5,188	8,078	438	1/26	520lb bombs
12	12-24	545	17,700	300	5,191	8,121	419	7/25	520lb bombs
13	10-33	680	19,250	230	4,615	7,500	406	6/25	520lb bombs
14	14-54	430	15,800	226	5,062	7,906	418B	3/27	520lb bombs
15	11-45	665	18,000	230	4,798	7,773	418C	3/27	520lb bombs
16		535	17,000		4,654	8,030	418G	11/28	
17	6-48	735	17,750	230	5,358	8,230	418F	1/31	
18	10-27	655	19,000	180	5,510	8,227	418I	4/31	1,500lb bombs
19	11-25	570	17,000	78	2,383	4,018	428	10/25	460lb bombs
20	11-15	550	19,350	78	2,518	4,117	448	5/26	Larger wing
21	7-48		21,000	78	2,960	4,200	428A	10/28	36 gal on trials
22	10-00	685	18,600	74	3,075	4,639	428B	4/30	500lb bombs
23	8-32	935	19,200			4,626	485A	7/28	
24	8-09	900	20,700	90	2,867	4,538	513	10/28	500lb bombs
25	8-36	890	20,700	87	2,649	4,320	512	10/28	500lb bombs
26	7-37	1,000	21,300	81	2,861	4,314	512B	7/30	500lb bombs
27	7-43	970	21,400		2,677	4,310	512B	11/30	500lb bombs
28	8-55	910	21,600	83	2,786	4,596	512C	4/31	500lb bombs
29	9-22	800	20,600	83	2,780	4,592	512C	7/31	500lb bombs
30	9-30		25,400	100	3,086	5,010	512J	10/33	500lb bombs
31	10-24	760	20,000		2,896	4,700	512E	2/32	460lb bombs
32	6-50	1,190	23,400	83	2,798	3,911	610	8/32	
33	9-45	690	20,000	83	2,720	4,708	512D	12/31	
34	7-54	975	22,000	88	2,818	4,781	512F	7/32	500lb bombs
35	5-04	1,490	26,000		2,932	4,635	512N	7/34	500lb bombs
36	4-24	1,840				4,635	512O	5/35	500lb bombs
37	8-33	865	20,200	80	3,045	4,665	563	7/30	500lb bombs
38	8-38	1,370	28,000		3,191	4,806	563/2	3/31	340lb bombs
39	7-30	1,350	27,000	100	3,178	5,217	668	6/35	
40	6-42	1,330	26,400	100	3,260	5,296	668A	5/36	Stub exhausts

Line	Type	Identity	Engine Type	Power (bhp/rpm)	Seats	Wing area (sq ft)	Max speed (mph/ft)	Take-off run (yd)	Landing speed (mph)
41	Hind T	K5387	Kestrel VDR	575/2,500	2	348	185/15,500	240	47
42	Wellesley	K7556	Pegasus X	/2,250	2		202/8,000	228	
43	Wellesley	K7729	Pegasus XX	821/2,250	2	586	207/10,400	330	62
44	Wellesley	K7754	Pegasus XX	834/2,250	2		204/9,400		
45	Battle	K4303	Merlin F	970/2,600			258/16,800	280	53
46	Battle	K7558	Merlin I	980/2,600	2		252/15,000	436	69
47	Battle	K9281	Merlin II	967/2,600			241/16,800		
48	Battle	K9281	Merlin II	967/2,600			232/15,800		
49	Battle	L4935	Merlin II	970/2,600	2		233/17,200		
50	Fairey P.4/34	K7555	Merlin I	980/2,600	2	346	284/17,200	370	65
51	Henley	K5115	Merlin I	955/2,600	2		292/17,100		
52	Henley	L3243	Merlin II		2		259/16,400		

Line	Climb to 10,000ft		Service ceiling (ft)	Fuel capacity (Imp gal)	Weight Empty (lb)	Gross (lb)	Report		Remarks
	Time (min-sec)	Rate (ft/min)					No	Date	
41	8-24	1,365	27,450	103	3,382	4,657	724	5/38	
42	9-30	880	26,200	184	5,440	9,254	695	8/36	
43	10-48	860	25,500	414	6,812	11,128	695A	1/38	271 gal on trials
44	11-18	830				11,128	695C	2/39	Bomb doors removed
45					8,032	10,540	700	12/36	Ejector manifold
46	10-48	1,010	26,500	208	7,410	10,898	700A	2/38	Ejector manifold
47	25-48 to 20,000 ft		25,200			10,900	700C	1/39	With spinner
48	30-00 to 20,000 ft		24,600			10,900	700C	1/39	No spinner
49	10-48	980	25,100		7,504	10,992	700B	12/38	Old exhausts
50	8-06	1,330	29,600	216	6,405	8,787	715	12/37	500lb bombs
51				193	6,434	9,400	723	4/38	
52	8-00	1,295	26,000		6,030	8,499	723A	6/40	Target tower

Ambulances and Troop Carriers

Vickers Vimy Ambulance and Vernon

The success of the Vickers Vimy Commercial in the 1920 Competition at Martlesham led naturally to a derivative, known as the Vimy Ambulance, being ordered for the new role of the RAF. The first, J6855, arrived on 8 March, 1921; trials were protracted until August by the need continually to adjust the carburettors of the two Lion engines, a broken tailskid and persistent loss of cooling water. The last fault was attributed to the propellers being too close to the radiator shutters preventing the latter's remaining open to keep the engine cool. The controls had poor response, particularly the elevator which became ineffective on landing, and taxying was difficult. Increasing the elevator gearing and moving the undercarriage forward six inches cured two problems, but even after modification 72 percent of the cooling water was lost after running at high power for three minutes. Red crosses on the sides were lit by battery operated lamps inside the fuselage. In spite of ponderous handling and poor performance *(line 1)* for hot

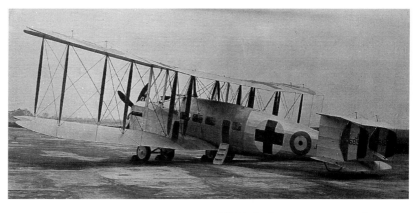

Vickers Vimy Ambulance J6855 in March 1921. The Red Cross on the fuselage was mounted on a transparent panel and lit by lamps inside the cabin. (British Crown Copyright/MOD)

climates, another four Ambulances, with strengthened undercarriages, were ordered for the Service.

To complement the Ambulances overseas, a similar type, the Vernon, was ordered for troop carrying. Reverting to the earlier Eagle engines,

J6864, had such a poor performance when tested in September 1921 *(line 2)*, that take off and initial climb in hot climates was estimated to be marginal when fully loaded. In addition, the radiator shutters could not be opened at high speed. In February 1922 J6884 with Lion engines had a somewhat better performance *(line 3)* but 'uncertain' lateral stability – ill defined because of the difficulty of setting the rudders for straight flight. A continuous turning flight path resulted from

Vickers Vernon J6884 in February 1922 with unsatisfactory slab sided cowlings for the Napier Lion engines. (British Crown Copyright/MOD)

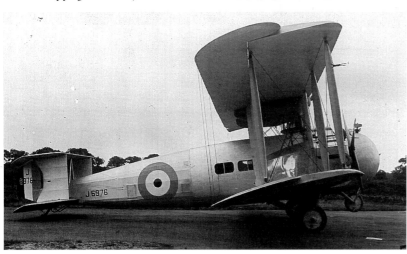

single-engine flying as the rudders were insufficiently powerful. Among other Establishment criticisms were the need for a man to enter the engine nacelle to engage the starter dogs, and the paucity of the petrol supply. Also in early 1922, J6879 was flown with a complicated oleo undercarriage which had poor shock absorbing characteris-

Vernon J6976 in July 1923, with new propellers and a box fitted above the nose; the purpose of the latter is unknown. (British Crown Copyright/MOD)

Armstrong Whitworth Awana J6897 in mid-1923. The span of over 105ft made this aeroplane too large for Service use. (British Crown Copyright/MOD)

tics, and also needed topping up after every flight. To remedy the Vernon's lack of fuel J6976, *(lines 4 and 5)* was tested in mid-1923 with an additional pair of tanks under the top wings; a full fuel load could be carried only at the expense of leaving out all but two of the troops.

Specification 5/20

Early in 1920 the first specification for an aeroplane to carry twenty-five troops was issued (initially Director of Research Type 12 later known as 5/20); Armstrong Whitworth with the Awana and Vickers with the Victoria each received orders for two prototypes. After much reasearch into steel tubing for construction of the fuse-

Vickers Victoria J6861, the second prototype, in June 1924, has dihedral only on the lower wings. (British Crown Copyright/MOD)

lage, the Awana J6897 with its 105ft wings reached Martlesham on 12 June, 1923. After the firm's trials, during which a strengthened tailskid and modified exhausts were fitted, the normal official trials were completed *(line 6)*. The latter revealed generally satisfactory handling, although the aircraft hunted directionally in the cruise and the elevator was poor at low

Victoria K2340 in November 1931. The Jupiter X engines were unsatisfactory. There are two Holt flares under the left wing. (Royal Air Force Museum)

speed; a second elevator on the upper tailplane was suggested. The chief complaints were the constant re-rigging required to keep the flexible fuselage in shape and the poor seating arrangements. J6898 arrived at Martlesham in November 1923, but the Lion engines were condemned the following month before the firm had completed its flying and the Awanas were stored at Grain and the RAE pending a decision on ordering the Victoria, which was by early 1924 on Service trials in Iraq. The Awana was too flexible and too large for RAF use.

After arrival on 12 October, 1922, the first Victoria, J6860, spent several

months undergoing modifications to the engine arrangements in an attempt to cure excessive vibration and oil leaks. At least one complete failure of the early Lion IA engines occurred, further delaying progress. Eventually, by May 1923, the second aircraft, J6861, had arrived (also requiring engine mounting modifications), the firm had finished its trials, and, with the original flat sided cowlings, removed, both aircraft underwent official testing *(line 7)*. It appears that in eight months at Martlesham J6860 flew a total of only ten and a half hours. Handling was 'ponderous' in the words of one pilot, and the performance *(line 8)*, poor, even with the slightly more powerful Lion IIs of J6861. Many modifications were suggested, including sweeping back the wings and increasing the fuel capacity. The changes were incorporated in the production aircraft, J7921, flown in March 1926. Results were disappointing *(line 9)*, particularly when the degradation of performance likely in the heat of Iraq was considered. Re-engining and metalization offered improvements, and consequently air-cooled radial Jupiters were fitted and

Vickers Valentia K3599, in mid-1934, is virtually identical to Victoria K2807. (British Crown Copyright/MOD)

the airframe lightened by 1,000lb; trials *(line 10)* were conducted in late 1928 with J9250. Pending results from Iraq on J9250, the more powerful Lion XIs were fitted to production machines, and J9766 was tested *(line 11)* for two months at the end of 1929 with these engines, strengthened undercarriage and automatic slots; all three features were accepted for Service use. The radial Jupiter XFBM was the next engine tried in K2340 at the end of 1931; this powerplant was unsatisfactory and was not adopted. Finally, the Pegasus was fitted, and K2808 was tested, initially with Mk IM3 at the end of 1932, and six months later with Mk IIL3. The latter improved take off and low altitude performance and was satisfactory. The Pegaus IIL3 became the standard engine of the type, and the subsequent development, the Valentia. To increase the payload, the Victoria K2807 was strengthened to increase all up weight by 1,000lb to 19,500lb, and tested, with wheelbrakes and a tailwheel, between August and October 1933. Revisions to the fuel system were flown at Martlesham in early 1934 in K3168, which also had an auxiliary engine for the compressor to power the autopilot.

With all the improvements incorporated production aircraft were known as the Valentia – but only pro-

peller and handling trials were done at AAEE. K3599 was variously fitted with standard two-blade, four-blade and the so-called Aboukir two-blade propellers from May 1934; all gave similar results but the four-blade type produced less vibration. The brakes of K3599 were improved and gave progressive and thus acceptable application. K3603 appeared in December 1934 and was loaded with the CG four inches forward of the existing limit. Handling was unaffected by the movement of the CG, but criticism of the sluggish controls, particularly the ailerons, was probably prompted by the higher handling standards then being achieved on other large aircraft. In 1936 K3603 was modified with the neutral position of the rudders offset; this arrangement was satisfactory in normal cruise but the rudder bias was insufficient to trim out foot loads with only one engine operating. After this brief trial K3603 joined the Armament Testing Section and spent most of its time flying between Martlesham and Orfordness; there is no record of engine failure, or of pilots with tired

legs from the three years of routine droning over the Suffolk countryside. The aircraft went to Cranwell at the end of 1939, after assisting with the move to Boscombe Down in September.

Avro Andover and Bristol Brandon

Nearly contemporary with the original requirement for the Victoria was Specification 29/23 for ambulance duties; the Andover was the result. J7261 *(line 12)* was flown for seven months from December 1924 – delays were caused by burning of the fuselage by the engine exhaust, propeller bolts shearing and defective magnetoes. Handling was described by one pilot as 'very nice, unstable fore/aft' and 'quite gentlemanly' by another. While the Andover was adapted from Avro's

Avro 561 Andover J7261 early in 1925. The overwing fuel tanks are typical of the period. (British Crown Copyright/ MOD)

Bristol Brandon J6997 in mid-1925, before official testing began. (British Crown Copyright/MOD

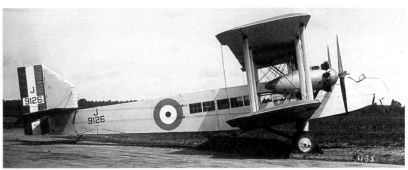

Handley Page Clive J9126 in July 1928. The straight wing was replaced by sweepback on the two production aircraft. (British Crown Copyright/ MOD)

Aldershot, the civil Bristol Ten-seater was adapted into an ambulance as the Brandon. J6997, eventually arrived late in 1925 after much redesigning by the manufacturers – but without success as, it appears, no formal official trials were completed.

Handley Page Clive

The Clive J9126 paid for by the Indian Government, arrived at Martlesham in prototype form with wooden airframe and two Jupiter VIII engines in June 1928 for handling assessment; it was found to be excessively unstable longitudinally throughout the speed range. Consequently, the two metal Clives had five degreees of wing sweep; J9948 was at AAEE for under

Gloster C.16/28 J9832 in May 1933, with four Rolls-Royce Kestrel engines with radiators above the cowling for the front pair and below the cowling for the rear pair. (British Crown Copyright/ MOD)

two days *(line 13)* (17/18 March, 1930) and found acceptable aerodynamically although the whole aircraft vibrated continuously at cruising (*ie* full) power. The mechanical throttle control was however, unsatisfactory. Ten days later a No.22 Squadron pilot flew the aircraft at Cricklewood; the modified throttle control was pronounced satisfactory. Hydraulic brakes (by Lockheed) were tested on J9126 in February 1930, but the production aircraft reverted to the Palmer air-operated system, although containing many rubber pipes considered unsuitable for use in a hot climate.

Specifications C.16/28 and C.26/31

In the hope of obtaining an aircraft to carry a 1 ton load over 1,200 miles (twice the range of the Victoria), the Air Ministry produced Specification C.16/28. Prototypes were ordered from Handley Page and Gloster; a Private Venture by Vickers, the Type 163, was made but not tested against this Specification. The Handley Page, J9833, was flown at Cricklewood for a few flights before the RAF Display in June 1933. The brief handling report was severely critical – the controls

were not harmonized – the elevators were exceptionally heavy and the rudders even heavier and also ineffective. Round out for landing required Herculean effort, and there were excessive trim changes with change of engine power; the brakes and engine starting were very bad. The type was not tested at Martlesham.

The Gloster C.16/28 J9832 was tested *(line 14)* at light weight; although not measured, the take-off run was considered to be excessive and unsuitable for Service use. Handling was simple with light control forces, but there was pronounced adverse aileron yaw; the undercarriage was harsh on Martlesham's infamous surface at light weight. The C.16/28 requirement had been dropped as being too heavy (the Gloster was 29,000lb) and unwieldy even before

Bristol Bombay L5808 in June 1939, with three-bladed propellers, flaps lowered, and radio masts and D/F loop in evidence. This aircraft crashed in the following August. (British Crown Copyright/MOD)

Handley Page Harrow J9833 in August 1935, clearly showing its transport origins for the C.26/31 Specification, but used for trails in connection with the bomber version. (British Crown Copyright/MOD)

the two types designed for it had reached AAEE; the new Bomber/Transport Specification, C.26/31 included a limit of 18,000lb on maximum all up weight. The Handley Page aircraft, J9833 (the same fuselage as the C.16/28 aeroplane but with monoplane wing) was withdrawn from the C.26/31 competition but visited Martlesham later in connection with the Harrow programme. The Armstrong Whitworth C.26/31 (A.W.23) K3585 had many vicissitudes during the maker's flying, and was only briefly at AAEE for take-off and landing measurements from October 1936. Distance to unstick was 274yd and the landing roll 289yd; lowering the flaps reduced the landing run to 169yd. Bristol's contender, the eventual winner of the C.26/31 and later named the Bombay, was K3583 *(line 15)* and arrived late in 1935. The ailerons were

good, the elevator heavy but responsive and the rudders very heavy – the last attributed in part to excessive friction in the control runs. The rear gunner's position was a mock-up, while the front turret was in need of further development particularly regarding the power operation of lateral movement; the guns were elevated manually. It was also difficult to move from the turret down to the bomb-aiming position and vice-versa. Engine changes were accomplished in 24.3 man/hours by two men with great difficulty due to lack of specialist equipment. The type had prodigious potential for carrying bombs; in additon to external stowage, no fewer than 168 20lb bombs could be carried internally. However, loading difficulties rendered the practical total somewhat less than the maximum. In mid-1936 K3583 returned with its Pegasus III engines replaced by the more powerful Pegasus X; only three hours of flying were needed to check the oil cooling and cylinder temperatures of the new engines. In 1937/8 K3583, was subject to a longitudinal stability investigation. Three production Bombays, built by Short Brothers at Belfast, arrived in 1939, L5808 in May, L5809 in August, and L5812 in June. L5808 crashed near the aerodrome on 23 August, 1939; the only prewar report of the type concerned the bombing assessment of L5812, which had the new Mk IXA bombsight. A marked periodic yaw at the optimum speed of 130mph to 140mph spoilt the bombardier's aim; his ability was further degraded by a lack of heating. L5809 continued testing at Boscombe Down.

Ambulances and troop carriers

Line	Type	Identity	Engines No.	Type	Total power (bhp/rpm)	Crew seats	Wing area (sq ft)	Max speed (mph/ft)	Take-off run (yd)	Landing speed (mph)
1	Vimy Ambulance	J6855	2	Lion II	944/2,000	2	1,329	105/5,000	300 #	
2	Vernon	J6864	2	Eagle VIII	740/1,800	2	1329	93/2,000	284	
3	Vernon	J6884	2	Lion II	940/2,000	2	1329	101/6,500	299	
4	Vernon	J6976	2	Lion	970/2,100	3	1253	108/6,500		
5	Vernon	J6976	2	Lion	970/2,100	3	1253	112/6,500		
6	Awana	J6897	2	Lion IA	966/2,100	2	2309	91/6,500	295	
7	Victoria	J6860	2	Lion I	934/2,000	2	2184	92/6,500		
8	Victoria	J6861	2	Lion II	991/2,100	2		89/6,500		
9	Victoria	J7921	2	Lion V	949/2,000	2	2164	90/6,500		
10	Victoria	J9250	2	Jupiter IX	981/2,000	2		105/,6,500	245	53
11	Victoria	J9766	2	Lion XIA	1,060/2,350	2	2194	93/6,500		
12	Andover	J7261	1	Condor III	693/1,900	2	1062	105/6,500		
13	Clive	J9948	2	Jupiter VIII					176 #	
14	Gloster C.16/28	J9832	4	Kestrel IIS+IIIS	1,506/2,250	2	2493	141/13,000		
15	Bombay	K3583	2	Pegasus IIIMS	1,386/2,200	2	1345	172/5,000	267	46

Into 10mph wind

Line	Climb to 6,500ft Time (min-sec)	Rate (ft/min)	Service ceiling (ft)	Fuel capacity (Imp gal)	Weight Empty (lb)	Gross (lb)	Report No	Date	Remarks
1	10-48 to 5,000 ft		12,600	167	8,635	12,500	282B	7/21	8 stretchers
2	35-14 to 6,000 ft		5,800	164	7,567	12,800	287	9/21	12 passengers
3	14-36	308	10,600	167	7,850	12,500	295	3/22	2½ hr endurance
4	16-00	270	9,900	406	7,981	12,500	348	9/23	
5	16-30	260	9,675	406	7,981	12,500	348A	9/23	New propellers
6	28-30	145	8,000	310	10,228	18,458	352	9/23	4¼ hr endurance
7	33-00	100	6,550	215	10,154	18,169	319A	5/23	3¾ hr endurance
8	38-18	77	5,350		10,376	18,471	393	9/24	
9	44-00	64	5,450	405	10,981	18,460	446	4/26	
10	19-12	220	9,550		9,862	17,760	446A	1/29	200 gal on trials
11	14-46 to 5,000 ft		8,800		10,933	18,000	446B	12/29	
12	18-15	235	9,550	300	6,987	11,800	404	5/25	
13					8,218	14,110	552A	3/30	
14	16-26	395	19,100	774	19,063	29,004	618	10/33	10 troops
15	6-24	850	20,600	360	12,696	18,740	684	2/36	11 troops

Fighters – Single-Seat

1920–1927 – Non-Competition Types

Four wartime types of single-seat fighter were in use at Martlesham for short periods in the very early 1920s; all four were at the end of their useful lives. Sopwith Snipe E8137 was soon replaced, in March 1921, by E7534 for a year's general parachute work. The Royal Aircraft Factory S.E.5A F9097

Martinsyde F.4 H7781 in 1921. (Philip Jarrett)

was similarly employed for two years from December 1920; it also undertook fuel consumption measurements. Sopwith Dragon F2917 flew but little throughout 1920; some performance work was completed, but its unreliable ABC Dragonfly engine prevented conclusive tests. Martinsyde F.4 H7781 produced performance figures *(line 1)* in 1920-21 well below those achieved by the type two years previously, but handling remained satisfactory. Oxygen tests were followed by fuel consumption measurements. At 8.9 air miles per gallon, the figure was similar to the Spitfire (8.3) of nineteen years later; the latter aircraft was over twice as heavy as the F.4, and cruised over twice as fast at a greater altitude. A second F.4, H6542, was used in 1921-2 for general equipment trials, including radiator temperature measurements and five types of revolution indicator.

Several fighter designs originating during the war escaped the widespread cancellation of production

contracts, and were assessed at Martlesham for suitability as Service types to meet the 1920 requirements. For the Type IA, Long Distance High Altitude Single-Seat Fighter, there were two contenders, the British Aerial Transport Company's Bantam and the Westland Wagtail. The ninth prototype Bantam, F1661, was tested early in 1920 *(line 2)* for civil purposes at the request of its makers; controllability and manoeuvrability were better than any existing fighter, and handling approached the ideal. Severe vibration was cured by attaching two substantial stay rods to the engine. The two Bantams ordered in 1920, J6579 and J6580, appeared briefly at

Westland Wagtail J6582, probably in 1921. The two engine ignition switches are outside the cockpit. (Philip Jarrett)

AAEE in 1921 for comparison with the Wagtail, but persistent problems with their Wasp engines prevented all but the briefest of flying on J6579. No type reports were written.

The Wasp I engine of the first Wagtails was replaced by the modified Wasp II (from ABC Motors Ltd). J6581 spent January 1921 on trials of what was intended to be an improved version of the Wasp; from November 1921, 15hr were flown in eight weeks with an experimental Armstrong Siddeley Lynx before J6581 was despatched to the Experimental Establishment at Grain.

Wagtail J6582 also had its Wasp II replaced by the new Lynx engine (No.3) by November 1921 and then flew over 51hr in eight weeks during which type trials were completed. The report states that the controls were 'excellent and could not be improved'. The lack of a gravity fuel tank, the cramped cockpit and poor performance *(line 3)* were, however, criticised.

For the RAF Type 1, four types were considered – the Sopwith Snapper and Snark, the BAT Basilisk and the Siddeley Siskin. The Snapper, F7031, left Martlesham in January 1920. All three Snarks reached the Establishment; top speed was low *(line 4)* and replacement of the recalcitrant Dragonfly was not considered worthwhile. Incomplete type trials included diving to 120mph (indicated) with the engine off (a somewhat strange trial as the level top speed of 130mph (true) at 3,000ft was higher), manoeuvring (worse than Siskin and Nighthawk) and handling

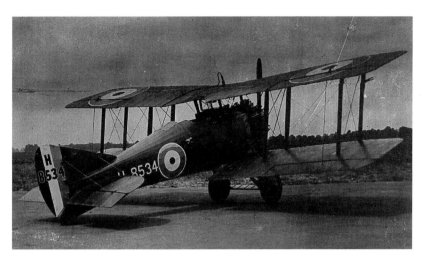

Nieuport Nighthawk H8534 with probably the first Armstrong Siddeley Jaguar engine; June 1921. (British Crown Copyright/MOD)

(heavy ailerons). The triplane configuration restricted the pilot's view and the monocoque construction was expected to give trouble in Service. F4069, in use March to July 1920 was the subject of the type report while F4068 (1919 to July 1920) did a little flying on engine development and F4070 (October 1920 to March 1921) achieved little, if any, time in the air. Two Basilisks, F2907 and F2908 suffered from weak undercarriages, their Dragonfly engines and the demise of their makers; few, if any, tests were completed by mid-1920. The first Siskin, C4541, apparently had a Dragonfly engine of sufficient durability to demonstrate the type's outstanding handling characteristics and performance figures in 1919 *(line 5)*; the Siddeley Company's new engine, the Jaguar was officially sponsored for the Siskin's further development. Meanwhile C4541 languished in a dismantled state until returned to the makers in August 1921, and C4542, after flying the 120 miles from Coventry to Martlesham in 50 minutes in January 1920, was found to have suffered such damage from the shaking, caused by the Dragonfly engine, that it was scrapped. C4543 was used for endurance trials of a modified type of Dragonfly between March 1920 and mid-1921. With a new metal frame and the Jaguar engine, the later Siskins had a long association with AAEE.

The final Dragonfly-powered type, the Nieuport Nighthawk, had finished

type trials by the end of 1919; F2910 and F2911 disappeared early in 1920, F2911 after its undercarriage collapsed. J2403 was used for endurance flying of the modified Dragonfly and achieved 43hr in the air between February and May 1920, while H8533, J2405 and J2416 were employed on general equipment and parachute tests from the end of 1920 to early 1922. The Nighthawk was selected for development flying of the new Jaguar and Jupiter radial engines, and H8534, with probably the first Jaguar made, arrived in May 1921 and by August had flown 50hr; with the fourth Jaguar a further 34hr were completed by early in 1922. Two metal-framed Nighthawks, J6925 (Jaguar) and J6927 (Jupiter), were briefly assessed early in 1923 before

Armstrong Whitworth Siskin J6998 in 1924, revealing the reduced size lower wing, additional flying wires, redesigned struts and fin and raised tailplane. (British Crown Copyright/MOD)

being packed for hot weather trials in the Middle East; performance is at *lines 6 and 7*. Martlesham's view on these early versions of the two engines was that both had poor response at high altitude and were excessively noisy; but both were considerably more reliable than the Dragonfly. With the exception of the re-engined Siskin, all wartime fighter designs had gone by early 1923.

The RAE fitted Jaguars to Siskins C4541 and C4543 early in 1922. The former was grounded at Martlesham by excessive vibration in August after six weeks, and the latter was destroyed by the hangar fire in October 1922 after six months of intermittent flying. When J6583 arrived in January 1923 tests resumed on the new Jaguar II, but type trials were soon abandoned because the fore and aft trim and the Remy ignition were unsatisfactory and the machine was sent back to Coventry. Specification 14/22 was written for three new Siskins incorporating new Jaguar engines and the lessons of the original types; the first, J6981, arrived in May 1923 and completed type trials *(line 8)* before crashing on landing in a gale the following month. The next machine, J6982 with modified ailerons and wing structure, reached AEE in December 1923 for aerobatic, *ie* structural, tests and left the following February for RAE. Martlesham's efforts established the need, inter alia, for stronger wing flying wires, already fitted to J6998 on arrival in May 1924 for further type trials *(line 9)*. Flying resumed in 1925 with a new fin, skid, exhaust ring and a Bamburger Statoscope. Similar to J6998 in its original form but fitted

with armament of two Vickers guns was J7148; tests, including armament, occupied June and July 1924 *(line 10)*. Four further Siskins flew at Martlesham in 1925; between February and July J7172 was assessed with full Service equipment fitted, and incorporating current modifications. J7163, the first with the supercharged Jaguar IV (and thus most nearly meeting the requirements of Specification 19/23) completed flying in June *(line 11)*, while J7000, the first dual control version, but with an unsupercharged engine and to Specification 33/23, underwent similar trials, finishing in August, *(line 12)*; it was very draughty and the collector ring suffered from vibration. At the end of 1926, a similar dual aircraft, J7550, had seats modified to accept parachutes. The fourth Siskin in 1925 was the Mk V No.S10 for Romania.

By February 1926 a strengthened and improved version (unnumbered) (known in service as the Mk IIIA, compared with the Mk III of the earlier machines) had been subjected to normal type trials *(line 13)*. It reached 24,000ft in 19½ min, and the heated goggles frequently froze over,

A Siskin in early 1926 with deepened fuselage and strengthened frame; prototype of the version which became the Mk IIIA in service. (British Crown Copyright/MOD)

Siskin DC J7000 in mid-1925. The troublesome exhaust collector ring is behind the cylinders. (Royal Air Force Museum)

even at temperatures as warm as minus 29 deg C; the outside air was on occasions recorded as minus 49 deg C.

As a private venture, Armstrong Whitworth produced another Mk V version of the Siskin and had it tested at Martlesham as G-EBLQ in mid-1926. It was generally cleaned up aerodynamically and had a redesigned empennage; top speed and rate of climb were impressive *(line 14)*, and a pilot commented, 'master climber, very nice to handle'. The Mk V was not adopted for the Service. Contemporary with G-EBLQ at AAEE was another Siskin (probably J8428)

(line 15); J8428 later spent the last six months of 1928 on trials *(line 16)*, including a cockpit heater drawing warm air from a muff around the exhaust. For over a year from September 1928, J8391 completed various armament trials, including an investigation into an ammunition box designed to operate in inverted flight; the aircraft returned in 1931 with RAE-designed automatic slots. Cockpit heating was the subject of an investigation on J7001 in the winter of 1931-2, and J9880 had in 1934 an intercomm system designed by Herr Blattner. There were probably other Siskins in use for short periods, plus J8627 in 1928-9 for later competitions.

Another single-seat fighter (later used as a night fighter) was the Woodcock, the new Hawker compa-

ny's first essay into a class for which it was to become pre-eminent. Officially tested from August 1923, the first prototype, J6987 was not a success, with its modest performance *(lines 17 and 18)* reduced further by the fitting of a modified propeller at the end of the year. Handling was 'rotten' in the word of one pilot, and rigging soon became slack, requiring some redesign late in 1923, included a new cantilever tailplane and modified controls. The second aircraft, J6988, was delayed by the incorporation of changes found necessary on J6987, and the fitting of a Jupiter engine in place of the earlier Jaguar. After protracted flying by Hawker, J6988 arrived in July 1924 fitted with wing flaps, soon abandoned, and single-bay wings. Performance was a little better *(line 19)*, and after Service trials at Biggin Hill the aircraft was fitted with a Jupiter V with variable timing, giving, inter alia, a slight increase in ceiling during AAEE trials in mid-1925 *(line 20)*. Slots were fitted for the latter trials which included engine cooling with

Hawker Woodcock J6987 in mid-1923 in original form. (British Crown Copyright/MOD)

Woodcock J6988 has single-bay wings and its Jupiter engine well hidden by cylinder helmets in late 1924. The externally mounted Vickers gun is noteworthy. (British Crown Copyright/MOD)

cylinder helmets, and armament; controls remained unsatisfactory.

Meanwhile, Martlesham type trials were under way between May and November 1925 on the first production Woodcock, J7512; performance is at line 21. One pilot found it 'nicer than the original', while another said it was 'flabby'. In October 1925 the fully-equipped version, J7733, but without an exhaust ring started inconclusive trials which terminated in June 1926 when the propeller became detached in the air. After tests early in 1927 of wing slots, J7974 returned for assessment of a reflector gun sight and a new Constantinesco gun firing gear in 1928. J8312, with cylinder helmets, concluded Woodcock flying at Martlesham in the summer of 1927.

The Hawker Heron J6989 was a Woodcock with a metal frame and Jupiter VI engine. Several short visits were made to AAEE between late-1925 and mid-1927 for performance measurements *(line 22)*, investigations into the strength of the wings, and, probably, a metal propeller. The only comment from a pilot was that the Heron 'climbed steeply' – but the rate of climb was slightly lower than the Woodcock's.

Third of the post-war fighters to enter Service was the Gloster Grebe, for which Specification 3/23 was written just before the first flight; work had started on the Grebe to Specification 25/22 – the same as the Woodcock. J6969 and J6970 arrived in

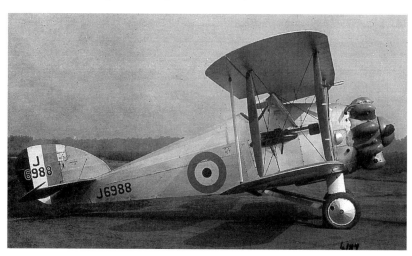

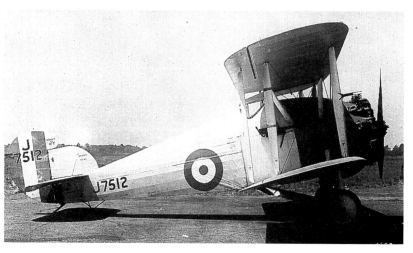

Production Woodcock J7512 in mid-1925, with revised fin and unshielded horn-balance to the fin. (British Crown Copyright/MOD)

Hawker Heron J6989 with Jupiter VI and original wooden propeller. Ailerons are fitted only to the top wing. (British Crown Copyright/MOD)

July 1923 and were initially virtually identical. The former performed *(line 23)* 'delightfully' according to one pilot, and soon left. J6970 required a new propeller to overcome a problem of low revolutions before performance tests in September *(line 24)*; comparative trials with the Siskin were followed by oil temperature measurements which revealed unsatisfactory cooling – a problem never completely solved in the Grebe. A German Seppeler Flowmeter was briefly assessed before a modified engine was fitted in June 1924; in the following months extensive damage led to the eventual removal by road early in 1925. J6970 returned in late-1925 for a stay of eighteen months, possibly for general equipment tests. The arrival of the production J7283, in June 1924, powered with the unsupercharged

Jaguar III had a performance similar to the prototypes *(line 25)*, and completed standard gun tests. Another persistent and more serious problem with the Grebe appears to have been first found during flying on J7283, namely wing flutter; strengthening the wing wires was not a successful cure. The oleo undercarriage was, however, liked. When the super-

charged Jaguar IV became available, J7402 completed performance and handling trials within four weeks from February 1925; top speed was increased, but not, surprisingly, service ceiling *(line 26)*. Redesigned ailerons on J7400, flown in February 1925, were heavier and more responsive but did not cure the tendency to wing flutter. J7400 left for RAE and, eventually, experiments in being dropped from an airship. 1925 also included assessment of the first two-seat Grebe, J7519; handling appears to have been adversely effected – 'even more under ruddered' in the words of one pilot, 'dithers' commented another.

Returning in September 1926, J7519 continued tests, possibly with a new fin and rudder. By early 1927, J7519 had RAE-designed bracing struts to the outer portion of the upper wing and was dived to 204mph (indicated) with no sign of flutter. J7574 visited for the final three months of 1926. Armament trials, including a slightly refined Constantinesco interrupter gear occupied J7396 for eighteen months from

Gloster Grebe J6970 in the summer of 1923 – unarmed but otherwise similar to the prototype J6969. For the official photographs, chocks were often placed behind the wheels. (British Crown Copyright/MOD)

Grebe J7402 in February 1925, with oleo undercarriage and modified fuel tanks protruding under the wings. The supercharger exhaust is visible above the port wheel. (British Crown Copyright/MOD)

December 1929. A feature of several Hendon Displays was formation aerobatics by AAEE pilots, first performed in 1929 on three Grebes – J7413, J7568 and J7581 – using coloured smoke.

The Gloster Gamecock J7497 (originally known as the Grebe-Jupiter) was flown between March and July 1925 at Martlesham and, with a horn-balanced rudder introduced midway through the trials, was preferred to the Martinsyde A.D.C.1 G-EBKL with which it was compared. One pilot found the speed range to be 49-153mph (true), and he reached 26,000ft, although the official performance figures *(line 27)* omit a service ceiling. In May 1925 the Chief of the Air Staff agreed to the production of the Gamecock. The second Gamecock, J7756 similarly powered with a Jupiter IV but with an exhaust ring to eliminate glare, arrived after the RAF Display at Hendon in June 1925. Described by pilots as 'snappy' and having 'good controls', it nevertheless exhibited flutter – attributed to the tailplane at the time, although later wing flutter was the scourge of the type. Performance of J7756 *(line 28)* was similar to that of the first machine. With the availability of the more powerful Jupiter VI, J7757 spent four months from November 1925 at AAEE. The new engine was generally liked, but at least one engine failure, at 19,500ft, occurred. J7891 spent nearly all of 1926 on type trials which ended in a fatal crash on 8 December when the wings came off. Previously another pilot had reported that the ailerons were loose – probably caused by the incipient onset of wing flutter. J8075, apparently identical to J7891, continued the trials until mid-1927,

Two-seat Grebe J7519 probably in 1927; an exhaust ring is fitted, as are the bracing struts to the outer upper wing to reduce flutter. The extensive lettering on the side is an exhortation to use ballast to keep the CG within acceptable limits. (British Crown Copyright/ MOD)

although the engine of the former had produced some ten per cent more power than J7891 when tested on the ground before installation *(lines 29 and 30)*. Spinning of the Gamecock was an interesting exercise, but little documentary evidence has been found describing the work of AAEE. J8047 completed a spinning experiment at RAE in 1927 with the wings moved rearwards, and later Martlesham pilots flew the aircraft to investigate performance *(line 31)* and flutter as well as spinning characteristics. With

Gloster Gamecock J7910 in June 1927, with narrow-chord ailerons. (British Crown Copyright/MOD)

bracing struts and a recording airspeed indicator, J8047 was put into increasingly steep dives, culminating in a vertical descent with the throttle closed from 17,000ft to 4,000ft. 230mph (indicated) was held for some time and there was no flutter, although some engine vibration was felt between 160mph and 220mph. Also in mid-1927, J7910, with narrow-chord ailerons aimed at improving the flutter speed without bracing struts, was subjected to a series of dives at increasing speed; the maximum reached is not known. All the improvements indicated by the results of earlier trials were incorporated in an experimental Gamecock, J8804, tested at AAEE in mid-1927; the performance is at *line 32*. In late 1928, J8804 returned for further handling and diving tests up to 250mph (indicated); there was no flutter and only the characteristic vibration at lower speed.

Gloster received an order for prototypes of a single-seat high-speed fighter to Specification 24/23. With Lion engines and metal frame fuselages, all three Gorcocks built flew at Martlesham, but no performance report was written. J7501, with a geared engine, was tested in the summer of 1925 – and criticised by one pilot because the stick was too short and the aeroplane lacked sufficient rudder response. J7502 with a direct-drive engine, arrived in November 1925 and stayed until after the 1926 Hendon Display the following June. Although it reached 156mph and the engine was smoother, one pilot said, 'not fast enough, bad on rudder – no good'. Trials on the metal-framed

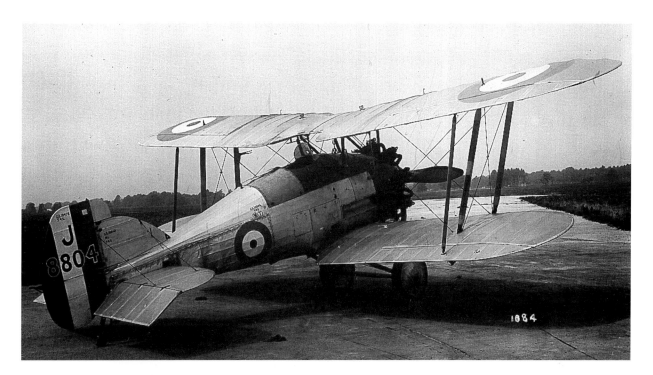

Gamecock J8804 in July 1927; it has struts inclined outwards to the top wing and other minor modifications. (British Crown Copyright/MOD)

Gloster Gorcock J7502 in winter 1925-6 with direct-drive Napier Lion and radio aerials. (British Crown Copyright/ MOD)

J7503 terminated in mid-1927, shortly after arrival, when a piston failed.

The Hawker Hornbill J7782 was built to meet the Specification 7/24 for an experimental high-speed fighter, or Interceptor as the class became known. It appeared at Martlesham late in 1925 and left early in 1927. Armed with a single Vickers gun, the

Hawker Hornbill J7782 late in 1926, with a metal propeller. (British Crown Copyright/MOD)

Hornbill possessed an impressive top speed of 181mph (true) at 6,500ft, but had a poor high level performance *(line 33)* and low ceiling. It was directionally unstable at high speed even

after a larger fin and rudder were fitted, lateral control was poor under 80mph and the landing run long. Although the view was good, the cockpit was very cramped. These were serious shortcomings, but the type was not developed further as the existing Siskin had a 5,000ft higher ceiling and better performance above 15,000ft. One pilot, no doubt with unintentional humour in view of the date of its arrival (5 November), commented that the Hornbill 'climbed like a rocket' after take off; he did not mention that the cooling water boiled in consequence.

For three months starting in October 1926, Martlesham pilots flew

the Lion-engined Avro Avenger G-EBND, a private venture design tested at the request of the makers. The performance *(line 34)* at low level was good, but the engine gave trouble and the type did not find official favour. The Fox with a Falcon XI was considered in 1927 for this role, but not tested at AAEE.

Fighters in 1927 and 1928, and the Specification 9/26 Competition

Between the summer of 1927 and the spring of 1928 seven new types of single-seat fighter arrived at Martlesham, each representing the aspirations of its maker for largescale orders. The seven were competitors, yet although the Air Ministry requirement (Specification 9/26) for which some were designed, was met by the winning design in 1928, the specification in modified form was used again in 1933 for a day and night fighter in a further competition involving another four designs.

The original seven were the Bristol Bulldog, Hawker Hawfinch, Gloster Goldfinch, Armstrong Whitworth Starling, Boulton and Paul Partridge, Westland Wizard and Vickers Type 141. The unmarked Bulldog prototype and the Hawfinch (both private ventures at conception but the latter recently purchased by the Air Ministry as J8776) arrived first in August and July 1927 respectively, well before their competitors. The Goldfinch J7940, ordered by the Air Ministry to encourage Glosters to

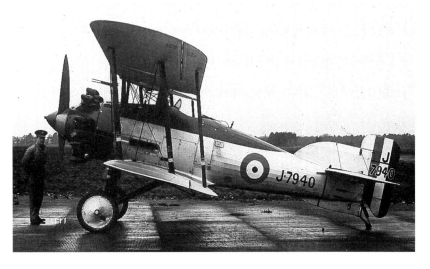

learn metal airframes, and tested from December 1927 *(line 35)* was pleasant to fly but heavy on the controls, particularly at altitude when they froze solid. Spinning to the right was easy but recovery difficult, the view was poor, taxying bad and the guns impossible to load. The Starling, J8027, flown early in 1928 *(line 36)* had a symmetrical wing section with stall characteristics so bad as to make Service use out of the question; the outstanding take off of 81yds (into a

light wind) was consequently of no account. The Starling was originally designed to meet a 1924 Specification (No.28/24), but the type was not assessed at Martlesham against that requirement; with a new wing, the Starling was entered for the F.20/27 competition.

Powered, like the Goldfinch, with a Jupiter VII, the Partridge J8459 *(line 37)*, was warm and comfortable and the Frise ailerons gave light and effective control in roll. Elevator control

Armstrong Whitworth Starling J8027 early in 1928 in its original form with symmetrical wing section. (British Crown Copyright/MOD)

spin characteristics and weak tailplane attachment points, although the Bulldog was exceptionally stable longitudinally *(line 41)*. By February 1928 a second private venture Bulldog had arrived at Martlesham with a longer fuselage, a new tailplane and a Jupiter VIII in place of the earlier Jupiter VIIs. This second aircraft was submitted to meet the requirements of Specification 9/26; spins of up to eight turns were eventually satisfacto-

was, however, poor throughout the speed range and produced difficulties in aerobatics and landing; the undercarriage was spongy and the structure complicated. Westland's private venture Wizard monoplane (unmarked in 1928) had an in-line FXI engine and suffered three breakages of the undercarriage before a more substantial crash in May 1928 interrupted completion of tests *(line 38)*. The landing run of over 300yds was excessive, the view poor for fighting and the controls indifferent. With an engine similar to the Wizard's, the private venture Vickers Type 141 appears to have featured only briefly at Martlesham (possibly on Company trials) in 1928, and no official performance figures were taken.

The five foregoing types, all of which had metal frames, were eliminated, leaving the Bulldog and the Hawfinch well ahead by the spring of 1928. The extra time available to the latter pair was well used by their makers. The Hawfinch had its 1927 Jupiter VI replaced in early 1928 by the Jupiter VII with higher full throttle height, conferring a better all round performance at operating heights *(lines 39 and 40)*. Martlesham was very enthusiastic over the Hawfinch, 'Exceptionally pleasant with no vices'. Spins up to fourteen turns were satisfactory and landing was particularly easy and slow

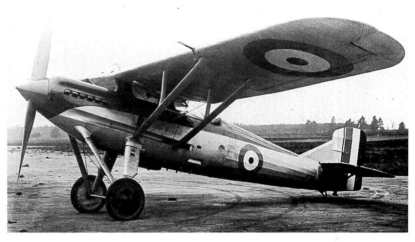

The Westland Wizard in its original form for the 9/26 competition, in which it was the only monoplane. (British Crown Copyright/MOD)

(44½mph indicated or 57½mph true); construction was especially good. Minor comments included the need to place the trimmer for the left hand, and the desirability of more heating. Against the Hawfinch, the first, short fuselage, Bulldog did not show up particularly well with poor

ry and the cockpit warm and free from draughts. Top speed at 10,000ft was seven mph faster than the Hawfinch *(line 42)* and Service pilots in the Fighting Area confirmed the test pilots' opinion that both were good fighters but that the Bulldog had the edge with larger tankage and more accessible guns. After selection in July 1928 for Service use, the second Bulldog, fully equipped, returned in mid-1928. The aircraft was nearly lost in September when an uncontrolled dive from 28,000ft followed the loss of

The Hawker Hawfinch J8776 in the winter of 1927-8 and a Jupiter VII engine. With a Jupiter VI it was the first of the 9/26 contenders to arrive at Martlesham Heath. (British Crown Copyright/MOD)

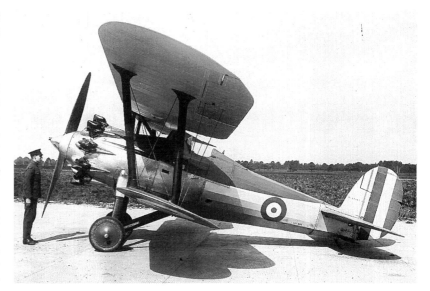

The Bristol Bulldog short fuselage first prototype in August 1927. (British Crown Copyright/MOD)

consciousness of the pilot; he came-to at 19,000ft with the only damage being to the propeller which split as the engine raced above maximum permitted revolutions. The cause was traced to the oxygen knob being inadvertently knocked off and the flow indicator being poorly placed and thus out of the pilot's normal scan.

Arriving on 8 May, 1929, J9567, the first development Bulldog, did not at first achieve the marginally acceptable spin characteristics of the second prototype but was otherwise satisfactory although the ailerons were slightly heavier. In June a larger fin enabled normal recoveries to be effected from even a flat spin, and with a strengthened sternpost the type was assessed as suitable for the Service *(line 43)*.

J9567 returned in 1931 and 1932 with various improvements. First was a plate-type Townend ring, which conferred an 8 mph increase in top speed when compared to the speed without it; the higher speed was still below the maximum achieved by the same aircraft two years previosly, *(line 44)*. Modified ailerons were satisfactory, as were Bendix brakes if adjusted properly but the toe pedals were judged to be too close to the rudder bar. Extensive spinning with the Townend ring and, later, brakes were eventually acceptable after two increases in fin area; the first increase merely offset the effect of the fin area forward created by the ring.

Bulldog J9567 in May 1929 in production form but without navigation lights or flare brackets. (British Crown Copyright/MOD)

The second Bulldog, with lengthened fuselage, in the spring of 1928, equipped for service. (British Crown Copyright/ MOD)

Meanwhile in early 1931, the production Bulldog K1603, with a larger propeller, taller undercarriage, Potts oil cooler, radio, aerials and generator windmill was 289lb heavier than J9567 and had a disappointing performance

(line 45). K1691, with minor changes, was 98lb lighter than K1603 but achieved an even worse performance *(line 46)*, and suffered two engine failures later in 1931, both due to No.6 piston seizing, and both resulting in safe forced landing on the airfield.

G-ABBB, a Bulldog built privately by Bristol, had, among other improvements a wider undercarriage track and improved cable-operated wheel-brakes; both features were liked by Martlesham pilots.

In early 1933, K2476 with mass-balanced rudder demonstrated steady diving characteristics and a year later K2221 with mass-balance additionally in the ailerons was dived to 260mph (indicated). K3513 had a parking brake and a tailwheel which had no adverse effects on handling or spinning in mid-1934. The last tests on a standard single-seat Bulldog were completed in 1935 on K2226 after several years in service with No.56 Squadron. The table *(line 47)*, shows the decrease in top speed due largely,

Bulldog K1603 in March 1931 with full Service equipment and a disappointing performance. The large windmill/generator on the port lower wing is noteworthy. (Royal Air Force Museum)

it was discovered, to the Service modifications including a non-standard windmill, a snow trap by the engine intake and heater muff; with these items removed top speed was only 5 mph less than earlier machines.

The dual control Bulldog, K2188, arrived on 30 December, 1931, with its lighter Jupiter VI engine mounted six inches further forward than on the single-seater and a yet larger fin and rudder, *(line 48)*. No problems were encountered then, or later, in 1933 with mass-balanced ailerons and rudder, nor in 1935 with dual controlled wheelbrakes and tailwheel.

A contemporary at AAEE of the original F.9/26 contenders was the Blackburn Lincock G-EBVO – a private venture lightweight fighter tested at the request of the makers. While the view was good, handling sensitive and

Blackburn Lincock G-EBVO in 1928 – a light fighter with good handling but poor performance. (British Crown Copyright/MOD)

twelve-turn spins satisfactory, the performance *(line 49)* was too low for a fighter in the Establishment's opinion but it was suitable as an advanced trainer. No armament was fitted during trials from February to May 1928 during which larger wheels and cylinder head helmets were fitted.

The F.20/27 Competitors

A new type of fighter for the RAF was conceived in the early 1920s and by 1927 Specification F.20/27 was produced for a Single-Seat Interceptor for use against opposing bombers; a

new engine, the Mercury, held early promise as the powerplant for this fast climbing type. Twelve designs from nine constructors were considered. Initially five of them, all with the Mercury IIA, were ordered for prototype construction from Bristol (Bullpup J9051), Vickers (Type 151 J9122), Hawker J9123, Westland J9124, and Gloster (S.S.18 J9125). Private venture designs were submitted from Hawker (FXI engine), Fairey (FXI), Westland (FXI), Saunders-Roe (FXI), de Havilland (Rapier) and Armstrong Whitworth (Panther); the Armstrong Whitworth Siskin was also evaluated.

Bristol Bullpup J9051 was the first F.20/27 contender to arrive in mid-1928. It is seen here in 1933 – long after the competition – with a short stroke Bristol Mercury engine. (British Crown Copyright/MOD)

Engine problems eliminated the Gloster from this competition but it was ultimately successful in meeting the fighter requirement F.9/26 (Mod). The remainder reached AAEE.

First to arrive in mid-1928 was the Bullpup J9051; the engine was probably a Jupiter VI and trials if any were brief. On return to Martlesham in 1929 with an early Mercury engine, unacceptable vibration, failure of an engine mounting and high oil temperatures prevented serious performance measurements. In 1933, J9051 with a short-stroke Mercury engine completed performance and engine tests satisfactorily *(line 50)*. High oil temperatures and other faults characterised the Mercury in 1929 and led to delays in all five officially sponsored types. In December 1929 the Air Ministry told firms that trials for the F.20/27 would finish by 31 January, 1930. Gloster

Armstrong Whitworth Siskin J8627 as submitted for evaluation against the requirements of Specification F.20/27; handling and performance were out-of-date. (British Crown Copyright/ MOD)

withdrew to concentrate on the multi-gun requirements, and the Saunders-Roe exhibited serious handling shortcomings in mid-1929, and was not considered for this or the multi-gun specification.

A Siskin, J8627, with a geared supercharged Jaguar engine had arrived in January 1929, and was later tested for suitability to meet the 20/27 Specification. The performance *(line 51)* was good for a Siskin, but handling only fair with ailerons being heavy with slow response. The engine was assessed as excellent, but the type was out of date as an interceptor due to handling and a badly arranged, cramped and uncomfortable cockpit. Trials continued later in 1929 to assess

the effect of the Townend ring; as performance was degraded on removal it was concluded that all radial types should have the ring. The view was acceptable. At the end of the year minor improvements improved lateral control. In 1930, J8627 with night flying impedimenta and an exhaust ring was briefly flown in comparison with the Bulldog (Specification 9/26) but the performance *(line 52)* was worse than as an interceptor. The Siskin was not considered further.

The Vickers Type 151 Jockey, J9122, flew at Martlesham in the spring of 1929 in the hands of pilots from the firm and from the Establishment. The main conclusion from the brief trials was that the type

lacked torsional rigidity, and that major alterations were necessary. There was no comment on the Mercury engine, but the monoplane Jockey was eliminated from the 20/27 competition. After three years at Vickers' factory J9122, with a Jupiter VII engine, found its way back to Martlesham. Performance is at *line 53*. Handling, taxying and the brakes were good and the cockpit roomy and comfortable; maintenance was praised largely on account of the novel engine mounting which could be swung completely to one side. Take off and landing from the approach at 100mph were too long. Spinning trials by the firm in the summer of 1932 were followed by the AAEE's trials during which the aeroplane failed to recover and crashed. The pilot baled out.

Hawker's Mercury-powered Interceptor J9123, was plagued by high oil temperatures and, early in 1930 at Martlesham, suffered failure of the oil tank; it was withdrawn.

Westland's low-wing monoplane J9124 exhibited alarming handling characteristics. The elevator became ineffective in sustained steep turns, resulting in a spiral dive or spin from which recovery could only be made by pushing the stick fully forward. On one such dive the wing covering partially failed on one side. The test pilots showed no enthusiasm for this aircraft and it was withdrawn; high oil temperatures on the Mercury engine also helped to eliminate this type.

Westland Interceptor J9124, in late 1929, suffered from alarming handling behaviour and high oil temperatures. (British Crown Copyright/MOD)

Persistent unreliability in early 1930 of the novel high revving Napier engine of the unnumbered low-wing de Havilland D.H.77 forced withdrawal from consideration at the decision date at the end of January 1930. However, further trials were warranted, and in the summer and autumn the

lightweight aircraft of simple design completed various trials, including full performance *(line 55)* which nearly matched that of the winning Hornet. Control harmony was spoilt by heavy ailerons and extremely light longitudinal control resulting from the all-moving tail hinged on the centre of pressure. Petrol fumes and long take-off run spoilt the first report; the second praised the steadiness in the dive to 353mph true but criticised the

Hawker Interceptor J9123 was plagued by high oil temperatures in its early Mercury engine in 1930 and did not complete its trials. (British Crown Copyright/MOD)

de Havilland D.H.77 J9771. The unreliability of the novel Napier engine eliminated this type from the F.20/27 competition. (British Crown Copyright/ MOD)

reluctance to recover from a lefthand spin when over 7,000ft were needed for recovery.

Arriving in the summer of 1930, the Armstrong Whitworth, F.20/27, A-2, was too late for consideration; its heavy elevator and ailerons reduced its fighting capabilities below the current standards. However, with unintentional humour, the report praises the type's ladylike behaviour, but later, in the maintenance section, states 'the fuselage can easily and quickly be

The Fairey Firefly II in early 1932. Its lines are strikingly similar to those of the Hornet. (British Crown Copyright/ MOD)

unlaced' – rather less ladylike perhaps. Its performance was mediocre *(line 56)*, but the dive to 300mph was steady. While A-2 was at Martlesham, a test pilot visited Coventry to fly the similar J8028, with modified ailerons; a considerable improvement was reported.

With the elimination or absence of the foregoing contenders, the F.20/27 competition was reduced in January 1930 to three types, all private ventures, by Westland, Hawker and Fairey. All three had the FXIS engine and a top speed of about 195mph (true) at the operational height of 20,000ft, but the Wizard took significantly longer to reach that altitude.

The Wizard, purchased by the Air Ministry as J9252, had a poor view and was uncomfortable; more significantly it was unstable longitudinally and was easily out-manoeuvred by the other two. It had a flat glide, was difficult to land and thus eliminated; the performance is at *line 52*.

Arriving just in time early in 1930, the unnumbered Firefly II, with its metal frame and metal propeller, met the Specification at all points. It was particularly robust dived to 380mph (true), the controls beautifully harmonised at all speeds, the view good and the landing, although slightly fast, was easy. Armament (two Vickers Mk II) and maintenance were praised. Performance is at *line 57*. The only fault of this paragon was the failure of the undercarriage on 27 February, 1930, but this could have been due to the Heath's capricious surface.

The Hawker Hornet officially purchased during the period of the F.20/27 trials as J9682 had the advantage of early arrival on 4 April, 1929, when it immediately set the standard for the competition by being light and easy to fly and well constructed; per-

Hawker Hornet J9682, in May 1929, set new standards of handling for single-seat fighters, won the F.20/27 competition and was renamed Fury. (British Crown Copyright/MOD)

formance was also outstanding *(line 58)*. After incorporation of several modifications, some to remedy minor failures at Martlesham, the Hornet returned at the end of 1929 nearly 100lb heavier and marginally slower *(line 59)*. Handling was unchanged and pilots particularly liked the draught-free cockpit permitting flight without goggles. Maintenance was found to be easy, and the type complied very well with the Specification with the exception of its wooden propeller and lack of wheelbrakes.

The Establishment thought that the Firefly was marginally the best fighter, but after Service trials, the Hornet was chosen in April 1930 and renamed the Fury.

After brief trials in J9682 to prove Hawker's performance guarantees to Yugoslavia, the production Fury K1927, completed type trials starting in mid-1931, demonstrating a better performance *(line 60)* than the prototype while retaining the delightful handling qualities. Minor modification (using radiator water to heat the air intake) cured earlier engine failures at low temperatures. These tests were followed by a comparison in the summer of 1932 between the standard wooden and a Fairey-Reed metal pro-

Production Fury K1927, May 1931, virtually unchanged from prototype form and showing the gleaming cowling - a feature used by fighter squadrons to achieve reflected glory. (British Crown Copyright/MOD)

peller; performance was almost identical. Armament trials followed; there were minor criticisms of the Vickers Mk III gun installation. After several years at the RAE, K1927 returned in March 1936 with powered ailerons. Six Martlesham pilots flew a total of 11hr; after engaging the hydraulic power, the ailerons lost all feel and there was considerable backlash and friction. This was the first aircraft with powered flying controls at AAEE.

Hawker's private development Fury, G-ABSE with a Kestrel IIS engine, completed brief performance trials in May 1933 but, the firm's other development aircraft, K3586 suffered undercarriage failure at Martlesham in September 1933 before flight measurements started and the aircraft returned to Brooklands.

In early 1934 Fury K2082 with a 4½lb mass-balance in the ailerons and 6lb in the rudder, handled normally. The same aircraft was used to compare standard and interceptor propellers; the trials were restricted to 20,000ft as oxygen was not fitted, and the top speed and time to that height were the same with both propellers. Performance is at *line 61*. K2082 with a tailwheel needed a slightly longer landing run when tested in 1936.

Foreign Furies (*see* British Aircraft for Overseas) were followed at the end of 1935 by K2876, with adjustable gaps ahead of the ailerons for lateral trimming; the idea was not successful. Following the crash at Martlesham in

March 1935 of K2077 with a full power Kestrel VI, it was replaced by K1935, at the end of the year. The performance *(line 62)* was sufficiently improved for the Service to order similar aircraft as the Fury II. The only modification necessary was increased cockpit heating to counter the extremes of temperature at the ceiling of over 30,000ft.

Gloster F.10/27 (J9125) as it was known at Martlesham when this photograph was taken in December 1932. It has a Jupiter VIIF engine and provision for wireless. (Philip Jarrett)

Three Furies, K2082, K2876 and K1935, remained in use in 1938 on general duties for armament trials and as targets; K2082 was at Martlesham until the outbreak of war.

The 10/27 Competitors

The first multi-gun Specification (10/27) called, inter-alia, for two fixed Vickers guns in the fuselage plus four Lewis or Vickers guns to fire outside the propeller disc, the latter with only a single drum each. Two types were proposed, the Saunders A.10 and the Gloster S.S.18; both were also entered for the 20/27 competition – the Gloster type being one of those selected by the Air Ministry for prototype construction as J9125. The unmarked Saunders's machine arrived in August 1929 armed initially with only two guns, but it immediately revealed serious handling deficiencies – full rudder was insufficient to prevent a swing on landing, it was longitudinally unstable above 75mph, the elevator lacked authority on landing and taxying was difficult. After returning to Saunders for modifications, including lengthening the fuselage, further tests (bearing the 'B conditions' number L2) from July 1930, indicated no improvement in longitudinal stability and thus tracking a target was impossible. No official performance trials were done. It was rejected for Service use, but was nevertheless purchased by the Air Ministry as K1949 and continued on gun trials both on the ground and in the air; the latter apparently ceased following failure in 1931 of the radiator of its FXIS engine.

The Gloster aeroplane, J9125, arrived in September 1930, long after the Martlesham trials for the 20/27; it

had the required six-gun armament for F.10/27, with a total of 1,588 rounds of ammunition. After changes to the rudder profile, a horn-balance and a new fin, the type made in the words of the report 'an excellent fighter' *(line 63)*. It was robust, was stable in a dive from 20,000ft with the engine stopped and achieved 320mph (true), had excellent spin characteristics and yet the Deputy Chief of Air Staff said it was unsuitable as a fighter, a view repeated later even after some minor criticisms of fuel system, brakes and cockpit had been rectified. Trials continued until mid-1932 on its unique armament; late in 1931 it was concluded that the six guns of the Gloster gave a proportionally far greater probability of hitting the target at long range than the four guns of the Saunders design. After removal of the four wing-mounted Lewis guns, fitting Palmer instead of Bendix brakes and incorporating full night flying equipment (Martlesham pilots had previously completed many hours flying in darkness without the benefit of this new luxury), J9125 returned for a brief performance and handling assessment – apparently at the request of Glosters. Performance was slightly improved *(line 64)*. Afterwards, the company once again modified the aeroplane by fitting a Mercury IVS in place of the Jupiter VIIF, and J9125 re-entered the fray to compete in the second F.9/26 competition.

The Second F.9/26 Competition 1932 – 33

Two private venture fighter designs, the Armstrong Whitworth A.W.XVI,

Armstrong Whitworth A.W.XVI A-2 in September 1932. Changing the Panther III engine took an excessive time and performance was inferior to the Gloster in the F.9/26 (mod) competition. (British Crown Copyright/MOD)

A-2, and the Bristol Bulldog IIIA, R-5, were together at Martlesham in the summer of 1932 and were joined in September by the Gloster S.S.19, J9125. Called initially the Private Venture Fighter competition, it became, for reasons unknown, the F.9/26 (Mod) Competition in April 1933 for a Zone Day and Night Fighter.

After a brief visit in April 1932, the A.W. XVI had its fin, rudder and elevator modified before return to AAEE in August. It was pleasant and easy to

Bulldog IIIA R-7 in May 1933. (British Crown Copyright/MOD)

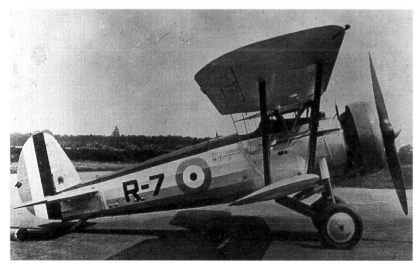

fly, although the controls were somewhat out of harmony; the spin and diving (to 350mph true) characteristics were good, performance *(line 65)* was inferior to the Gloster. Changing the Panther III engine took two men 14½hr – a time considered excessive. After Service trials in Fighting Area, a Panther VII was fitted, the structure strengthened and tankage increased, but engine failure on 30 June, 1933, ended the A.W. XVI's trials at Martlesham *(line 66)*; the failure was attributed to the engine requiring fuel of a higher octane than that available. The A.W. XVI was also a poor gun platform over 250mph (indicated).

The Bulldog IIIA R-5, possessed improved handling compared to earlier versions, but the Townend ring round the Mercury IVS engine restricted the view, although the cockpit was roomy and comfortable; the armament of two Vickers Mk III guns was not fitted. An engine change took under five hours. After returning from trials with Fighting Area, the aircraft was extensively damaged early in March 1933, but flying continued on a replacement Bulldog, R-7, after rebuilding to repair damage sustained in a forced landing on the way to Martlesham from the SBAC Display at Hendon in July 1933. R-7 had four ailerons – the top pair of which bent in a high speed dive at 265mph (indicated) in September. Performance *(lines 67 and 68)* of R-5 and R-7 was similar – but inferior to the Gloster S.S.19.

Referred to as the Gloster F.10/27 in January 1933, J9125 returned in the following summer as the Gloster F.9/26. The metamorphosis included a longer fuselage, Mercury IVS engine, rudder mass-balance and other changes – all combined to improve the type's performance *(line 69)* (top speed increased by 24mph, true) while retaining the pleasant handling previously achieved. Maintenance of the Gloster was slightly easier than the other two types and it was selected by the Chief of the Air Staff in October 1933 for Service use where it was known as the Gauntlet. After 16 months J9125 returned for type trials, complete with a new exhaust, Mercury VIS, radio, cameragun, compressor (to charge cylinders for starting and for brakes), but the spats were removed. Handling and performance *(line 70)*, remained very good. Armament trials included firing 24,000 rounds from the pair of the new type Vickers Mk V guns; the Gauntlet was an excellent gun platform. The RAE-designed oxygen and microphone mask gave a range of 35 miles (transmission) via the newly introduced TR9 radio. Brief trials in spring 1935 on the first production Gauntlet, K4081 confirmed the performance *(line 71)* of J9125, although the former was slightly slower, probably on account of the lower power of its engine and changes to the Townend ring and wheels. Small flaps on all four wings were assessed late in 1936 on K4103; hydraulic operation by a hand pump was too slow, but pneumatic operation (from the starter

Gloster F.9/26 J9125 in May 1933 in the form in which it entered the F.9/26 (mod) competition; it was named Gauntlet. (British Crown Copyright/ MOD)

bottle) took a quarter of a second. Both versions of the flap improved the view for landing, particularly useful for night flying. Oil on the windscreen was a persistent problem on the Gauntlet; K5271 was tested late in 1936 with ineffectual oil deflectors. A spray of petrol was later partially effective on K5271, but in 1937, a new type of deflector, also on K5271, appears to have been successful. This aeroplane with a three-bladed metal propeller demonstrated reduced vibration compared with the standard two-bladed wooden variety, but at the expense of performance *(line 72)* in combat manoeuvres.

The F.7/30 Competitors

A great deal of staff effort went into drafting the requirements for the Bulldog replacement, Specification F.7/30 issued in definitive form on 1 October, 1931. Known as a Zone Fighter, features of the Specification (subject to no fewer than seventeen corrigenda by July 1932) were extended endurance at 15,000ft, low landing speed for night flying, fast climb and four guns, and a preference for the steam-cooled Rolls-Royce Goshawk engine. Seven types were officially notified to the Air Ministry for the competition – three were bought by the Air Ministry from Blackburn, Supermarine and Westland, and four were private ventures from Bristol (two types) Hawker and Gloster. Other manufacturers briefly considered entering, but did not pursue their proposals. All seven competitors completed their maiden flights between February and September 1934; every Goshawk type (except one Bristol and the Gloster) suffered severe cooling problems and the competition at AAEE was consequently delayed until mid-1935. By that time the Blackburn K2892 had been withdrawn, as had both Bristol F.7/30 machines (the monoplane with Mercury engine had crashed); the Supermarine K2890 was not officially tested although it visited Martlesham in May 1937 on its way to destruction at Orfordness as a target. Of the remaining three types the first to arrive was the Mercury-engined Gloster G.37 in early April 1935. Official trials were soon completed. Controls were light with quick

Gloster Gauntlet J9125 in September 1934 in production form with Service equipment. (British Crown Copyright/ MOD)

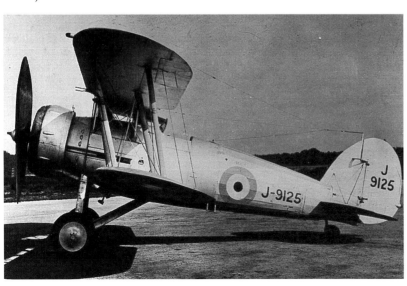

Gloster F.7/30 G37 in April 1935 – a private venture without the handicap of the Rolls-Royce Goshawk engine; its Bristol Mercury engine gave a top speed of 242mph. It was ordered into production as the Gladiator. (British Crown Copyright/MOD)

response at all speeds and CGs and sideslips up to 40deg could be held, while the performance *(line 73)* met the specification. Continuous trouble was experienced with the exhaust ring, the cockpit was too cold necessitating electric clothing on ceiling climbs, and the undercarriage needed damping. The Hawker F.7/30 type, 1-PV3, paid a brief visit to Martlesham in 1935; details are sparse, but, it seems its steam-cooled Goshawk engine was unacceptable for Service use, and trials minimal. The Hawker PV3 appears to have had a better performance than the Westland K2891. Trials of the latter were abandoned in mid-1935 when its performance was so woeful *(line 74)*. The Gloster was selected in July 1935, named the Gladiator and the prototype purchased, as K5200, by the Air Ministry. Thus the RAF acquired its last biplane fighter after what was, to AAEE, a non-competition.

K5200 with a more powerful Mercury and three-bladed propeller

crashed on arrival on 23 October, 1935, when the undercarriage collapsed. After repairs and the fitting of Vickers V machine-guns in the wings and a cockpit cover, trials continued. At 30,000ft the cockpit was warm, and handling was unaffected by the new cover. No radio telephone was fitted – only an intercom tested by the pilot talking to himself; no doubt many

Westland F.7/30 K2891 in April 1935 – one of only two competitors (of an original seven) to reach the stage of performance measurement; this aircraft was 100mph slower than the winner. (British Crown Copyright/MOD)

pilots were well qualified for this task. The armament gave satisfactory results, but the interim two-bladed wooden propeller produced excessive vibration. In October 1936 a three-bladed Fairey-Reed metal propeller cured the vibration and raised top speed at full throttle height of 14,000ft from 248mph to 253mph, but at the expense of longer runs for both take off and landing. The first production Gladiator, K6129, arrived in February 1937, but had to be sent after a few days to RAE for investigation into continuing vibration. With propeller reduction ratio increased from 0.5:1 to 0.572:1, K7964 displayed similar vibration with a two-bladed propeller

Gloster Gladiator K5200 (G37, after purchase by the Air Ministry) on 23 October, 1935, after an undercarriage collapsed on arrival from Glosters. (British Crown Copyright/MOD)

but the new ratio was satisfactory with three blades; performance trials were completed with the latter *(line 75)*. At the end of 1937, the Establishment visited No.3 and No.72 Squadrons; in both cases vibration was less on three-bladed machines. Similar results were observed at Martlesham on K8049 with Mercury VIII in January 1938. Work at the RAE produced the first standard blind flying layout in 1936, and the 'Instrument Flying Panel Mk I' was flown at AAEE in early 1938 in K7919. The large venturi soon had the gyroscopic instruments erect after take off and, apart from the vertical speed indicator, the panel was satisfactory although the artificial horizon and direction indicator were easily toppled. K7919 also completed tests on the four-gun armament on the lower wing. Tests on the Naval

Gladiator K7964 in the summer 1937, with the three-bladed propeller which cured vibration. A cockpit cover is fitted. (British Crown Copyright/MOD)

Gladiator are covered under Deck Landing Fighters.

The Monoplane Fighters

The Hawker company, convinced that only a monoplane could significantly improve fighter performance, persuaded the Air Ministry that their design, later named the Hurricane, was a worthy type for official sponsorship, and obtained an order for one prototype. Specification 36/34 was prepared but never issued. In Feb-

ruary 1936, K5083 reached Martlesham with retractable undercarriage (45 seconds to raise and 20 seconds to lower), flaps (10-15 seconds for full travel) and an enclosed cockpit among other novel features. The stall was viceless, dives to 310mph (indicated) steady and the elevators light and responsive; performance was good, *(line 76)*. Ailerons and the rudder were too heavy at high speed and during aerobatics but the overall impression was of an aeroplane that was simple and easy to fly. Three different Merlin engines were needed to complete these early trials. After fitting armament and other military equipment K5083 returned early in 1937. High power settings made radio reception and transmission poor (the TR9b was fitted), cockpit heating was satisfactory, but the first set of eight Browning guns needed replacing and both sets suffered from excessive cooling. By January 1938, measurements of temperature in the port wing fitted with hot air indicated that the gun bay cooled to minus 16 deg C with an outside temperature of minus 43 deg C. Two months later, the production Hurricane L1562 with heating in both wings fired 5,831 rounds in the air; the heating was effective but seventeen stoppages occurred due to lack of compressed air for firing. The air bottle also supplied the brakes; taxying before take off often depleted the pressure. Four more Hurricanes (all with Merlin II engines) arrived in 1938 (L1547 June, L1574 March, L1695 and L1696 November) and completed the full performance *(lines 77 and 78)*, handling and radio trials of

Hawker Hurricane K5083 as originally tested in March 1936. The purpose of the fixture on the inboard wing is unknown. (British Crown Copyright/ MOD)

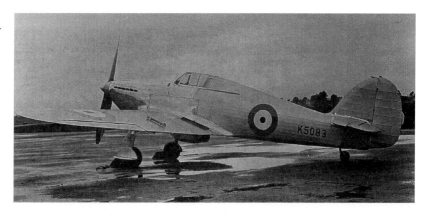

the type. L1547 later had a two-pitch, three-blade, metal propeller (the others had the standard two-blade wooden model), maximum speed at 18,000ft was 319mph (true) and unstick distance reduced to 230yd with 30 deg of flap. L1547 also had a tail parachute for spinning trials. Spins with both types of propeller were normal at both forward and extended aft CG; however, stick position on recovery was critical as it was found to be easy to induce a secondary stall with subsequent flick into another spin. L1547 was stable in a dive, and apparently it was easy to exceed the maximum authorised speed of 380mph (indicated) as 395mph (indicated) was inadvertently achieved, but without adverse effect. Hood opening at 380mph was reported without comment. For night flying the streamlined exhausts of L1696 were preferred as they were well below the pilot's line of sight, and the flames experienced from the ejector exhausts were absent. However, cockpit lighting was poor, battery life marginal for the landing lamp, and the undercarriage lights too bright at night. By May 1939, L1547 had an engine driven generator and a more modern Type 9c radio less prone to the adverse effects of engine and airspeed. L1702 and L1750 arrived in February 1939; the former had been prepared at RAE for work with Bawdsey, and the latter for a temporary purpose unknown before the fitting of 20mm armament by Hawkers. Brief tests were made in the summer of 1939 on L1669 with an air filter;

Hurricane L1696 in November 1938 with streamlined exhausts and in camouflage. (British Crown Copyright/ MOD)

this aeroplane was later sent to the Middle East.

Supermarine's progressive thinking resulted in the Spitfire, for which Specification F.37/34 was written after the main features of the design had been established. The prototype, K5054, with an early Merlin C engine

Supermarine Spitfire K5054 in June 1936, displaying its narrow-track undercarriage and generous flaps. It has no guns. (British Crown Copyright/ MOD)

and ballast in place of guns, arrived in May 1936. Performance *(line 79)* was exceptional and the type simple and easy to fly although headroom was cramped; more flap was needed to reduce the length of the landing run, and increased gearing was needed between stick and elevator. Early in 1937 with eight Browning guns fitted, K5054 fired 8,600 rounds with mixed success. On one flight, after a period at 32,000ft (minus 54 deg C) only three guns fired, and three others fired one round each on landing as the frozen mechanism was jerked free; the GD5 gun sight was unsuitable. Handling trials at this stage (with Merlin F and modified elevator controls) came to an abrupt halt in March 1937 when engine failure resulted in a wheels-up forced landing. Returning in October 1937 with a Merlin II and gun heating, trials included night flying and revealed unacceptable internal reflections; the flat approach made landing difficult, a situation made worse when blister-type exhausts blocked the pilot's view. Ejector-type exhausts were acceptable, but, once again, trials were curtailed when the port undercarriage collapsed on landing in March 1938. Repairs and improved gun heating were followed by Martlesham trials in October; heating was

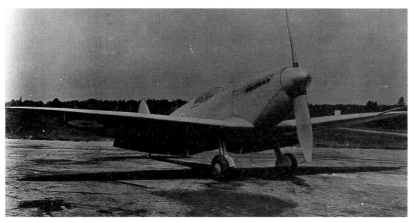

satisfactory but the stoppages of the guns occurred due to faulty firing mechanism. Fitting Browning Mk II guns cured the fault.

Three production Spitfires K9787, K9788 and K9793 arrived within a six-week period from mid-July 1938. All three were fairly intensively flown during the first three months of 1939 on the recently instituted operational trial; only minor comments resulted. K9788 was flown by the Armament Section on trials such as pyrotechnics and armament. With the radio mounted on a rubber susupension, K9793 achieved acceptable results, and also completed satisfactorily electrical tests before returning to Supermarine's. Tests at AAEE resumed in January 1939 when K9793 had a two-pitch propeller. Take-off distance and top speed were improved *(line 80)*, at the expense of rate of climb. A technique for optimum climbing was evolved and resulted in the pitch being changed to coarse at 2,000ft and 170mph (indicated). Spins and dives to 450mph (indicated) were satisfactory, except for the ailerons which were immovable above 300mph even after strengthening and fitting string to the trailing edge. K9787 was wholly devoted to performance *(line 81)*, and handling, including the measurement of the effects of various exhaust arrangements. A tail parachute was fitted for early spinning trials late in 1938; various recovery techniques

were tried – all eventually successful but the best was the application of full opposite rudder followed by down elevator. Early dives to 450mph (indicated) caused the engine to cut (cured in 1939 on K9793) and the hood could not be opened above 300mph (indicated). Night take offs required the lengthening of the flarepath to 800yds (double the standard distance). By mid-1939, K9787 had completed most of its tests (all with fixed-pitch wooden propeller) including consumption – 8.3 air miles per gallon were achieved at 7,000ft and 184mph (indicated).

Two months before the start of the war L1007 was received with two 20mm cannon, a Merlin III and two-pitch propeller. Handling and performance *(line 82)*, were unchanged. Armament trials were starting in late-August 1939.

Spitfire K9793 in early 1939 with the two-pitch, three-bladed propeller which improved take-off run and top speed. The oil cooling flap is shown fully open. (British Crown Copyright/MOD)

The Hawker Fury replacement Specification, F.5/34, produced two officially sponsored designs by Gloster and Bristol and private ventures by Vickers and Martin-Baker. The two official types were not sent to Martlesham Heath for type trials as both revealed deficiencies during contractors' flying, although the first of two Gloster F.5/34s, K5603, arrived

The second Gloster F.5/34, K5604, in mid-1939. No report was issued for this type. (Imperial War Museum)

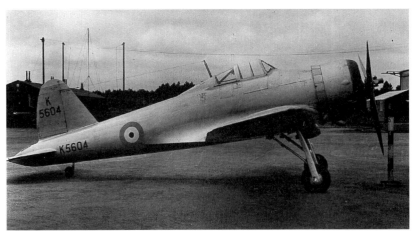

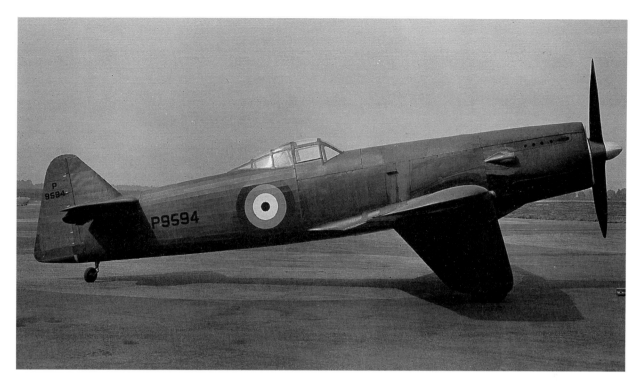

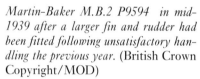

in May 1939 for unspecified trials; no armament is visible in photographs. The Vickers Venom (numbered PVO-10) with its battery of eight machine-guns and a Bristol Aquila engine spent eight weeks from early October 1937 at AAEE. Official trials began, but were not completed, and the aeroplane returned to Vickers for investigation of the wrinkling of the skin on the wings. No report was written and the Air Ministry took no further interest. Late in 1938, Martin-Baker's F.5/34, M.B.2, arrived and soon revealed unsatisfactory handling characteris-

Westland Whirlwind L6845 on 28 August, 1939; clearly visible are the four cannon demanded by Specification F.37/35. The aircraft was at Martlesham for only 24hr prewar. (British Crown Copyright/MOD)

tics; at low speed the rudder was ineffective in preventing the nose yawing right, and at high speed application of rudder swung the nose rapidly – the swing continuing after centralization of the rudder. The ailerons were too heavy and the aeroplane generally unpleasant to fly, especially during aerobatics. No performance measurements were made. However, the equipment assessment concludes, 'Many features are excellent and seem hardly capable of improvement'. In particular the eight Browning guns were readily accessible, and two men re-armed all guns in only six minutes – a remarkably short time. Over 11,000 rounds were fired in early trials. After modification, the M.B.2 returned in mid-1939 having been bought by the Air Ministry as P9594. Handling trials with the larger

Martin-Baker M.B.2 P9594 in mid-1939 after a larger fin and rudder had been fitted following unsatisfactory handling the previous year. (British Crown Copyright/MOD)

fin and rudder were satisfactory, but the ailerons remained too heavy. Test flying continued into the wartime period.

Four cannon were the unique features of Specification F.37/35; prototypes were ordered from Boulton Paul, Hawker and Westland. The former two with single-engine were cancelled early in development, but the Westland Whirlwind, L6844, was flown by AAEE pilots at Boscombe Down on 30 December, 1938. The throttles of the two Rolls-Royce Peregrine engines (which rotated in opposite directions) were too stiff, but handling was satisfactory; there were twelve points of criticism including uneven brake operation and the flap control lever which was considered to operate in the wrong sense. The latter was changed to an up/down lever in the natural sense. In April 1939, the second prototype, L6845, (also flown at Boscombe Down) had the engines changed to rotate in the same direction. Take off and handling remained easy and pleasant; L6845 reached Martlesham shortly before the war and stayed less than 24 hours.

Fighters – single-seat

Line	Type	Identity	Engine Type	Total power (bhp/rpm)	Wing area (sq ft)	Max speed (mph/ft)	Take-Off run (yd)	Landing speed (mph)
1	Martinsyde F.4	H7781	Hispano-Suiza	319/1,800	334	132/3,000		
2	Bantam	F1661	Wasp II	200/2,000		146/10,000		
3	Wagtail	J6582	Lynx	162/1,700	185	119/6,500		
4	Snark	F4069	Dragonfly	340/1,650	322	130/3,000		
5	Siskin	C4541	Dragonfly	320/1,650	247	146/3,000		
6	Nighthawk	J6925	Jaguar	336/1,500	270	139/15,000		
7	Nighthawk	J6927	Jupiter	391/1,580	270	140/15,000		
8	Siskin	J6981	Jaguar	356/1,500	296	137/6,500		
9	Siskin	J6998	Jaguar III	349/1,500	296	136/6,500		
10	Siskin	J7148	Jaguar III	331/1,500	296	139/6,500		
11	Siskin	J7163	Jaguar IV	400/1,700		146/6,500		
12	Siskin DC	J7000	Jaguar III	340/1,500	291	134/6,500		
13	Siskin IIIA	Nil	Jaguar IV	394/1,700	293	154/6,500		
14	Siskin V	G-EBLQ	Jaguar		252	169/10,000		
15	Siskin IIIA	J8428	Jaguar IV	400/1,700	292	138/6,500		
16	Siskin IIIA	J8428	Jaguar	376/1,700	292	153/10,000		
17	Woodcock	J6987	Jaguar II	358/1,500	356	139/6,500		
18	Woodcock	J6987	Jaguar II	358/1,500	356	134/6,500		
19	Woodcock	J6988	Jupiter IV	402/1,575	346	141/6,500		
20	Woodcock	J6988	Jupiter	416/1,650	346	136/6,500		
21	Woodcock	J7512	Jupiter IV	399/1,575	346	134/6,500		
22	Heron	J6989	Jupiter VI	431/1,700	291	151/6,500		
23	Grebe	J6969	Jaguar	357/1,500	251	147/6,500		
24	Grebe	J6970	Jaguar III	354/1,500	251	145/10,000		
25	Grebe	J7283	Jaguar III	339/1,500		145/6,500		
26	Grebe	J7402	Jaguar IV	397/1,700		150/6,500		
27	Gamecock	J7497	Jupiter IV	428/1,650	264	153/6,500		
28	Gamecock	J7756	Jupiter IV	408/1,700		152/10,000		
29	Gamecock	J7891	Jupiter VI	426/1,700	264	147/6,500		
30	Gamecock	J8075	Jupiter VI	474/1,700	264	150/6,500		55
31	Gamecock II	J8047	Jupiter VI	470/1,700		157/5,000		
32	Gamecock	J8804	Jupiter VI	470/1,700	261	146/6,500		
33	Hornbill	J7782	Condor IV	698/1,900	317	181/6,500		69
34	Avenger	G-EBND	Lion VIII	542/2,350	336	170/6,500		
35	Goldfinch	J7940	Jupiter VII	400/1,775	274	171/10,000		61
36	Starling	J8027	Jaguar V	416/1,820	239	168/10,000		64
37	Partridge	J8459	Jupiter VII	382/1,775	317	167/10,000		61
38	Wizard	Nil	F XI	552/2,250	222	188/10,000		72
39	Hawfinch	J8776	Jupiter VI	475/1,700	293	160/6,500		57
40	Hawfinch	J8776	Jupiter VII	364/1,775	293	171/10,000		59
41	Bulldog	Nil	Jupiter VII	440/1,750	306	166/10,000		62
42	Bulldog	Nil	Jupiter VII	414/1,775	306	178/10,000		61
43	Bulldog	J9567	Jupiter VII	427/1,775	306	174/11,000		62
44	Bulldog	J9567	Jupiter VII		306	171/10,000		
45	Bulldog IIA	K1603	Jupiter VIIF	480/1,775	306	166/10,000		59

| Line | Climb to 15,000ft | | Service ceiling (ft) | Fuel capacity (Imp gal) | Weight Empty (lb) | Gross (lb) | Report | | Remarks |
	Time (min-sec)	Rate at 15,000ft (ft/min)					No	Date	
1	15-42	476	19,800	36		2,440	278	/20	Range 285 miles
2	16-18 to 17,000 ft		23,450	32	1,220	1,618	272	5/20	
3	21-36	305	18,600	22	1,073	1,476	289	1/22	
4	17-00	540	23,500	37	1,555	2,283	276	7/20	
5	24-15 to 20,000 ft		23,800	40	1,463	2,181	260	7/19	
6	11-03	700	20,600	40	1,820	2,270	324	2/23	
7	10-03	960	25,700	40	1,810	2,270	323	2/23	
8	14-23	585	22,050	46	1,853	2,758	339	6/23	
9	14-54	525	20,200			2,758	367	2/24	
10	13-24	656	22,600			2,800	384	6/24	
11	12-30	1,080	28,700	46	2,060	2,820	423C	7/25	Supercharged
12	16-20	480	20,350	46	2,084	2,740	426	9/26	
13	10-36	1,000	27,100	48	2,015	2,946	444	2/26	Supercharged
14	7-56	1,330	28,600	60	1,724	2,464	457	9/26	
15	16-06	520	21,600		1,923	2,777	384A	3/28	Supercharged
16	11-06	980	26,400		2,007	2,861	384B	9/28	Supercharged
17	16-01	500	20,550	48	2,083	3,023	344	8/23	3½ hr endurance
18	21-00	280	17,300			3,036	369	2/24	New propeller
19	15-00	590	22,500	50	2,014	2,979	390	8/24	
20	12-19	781	24,300	50	2,008	2,973	430	10/25	
21	16-10	530	21,500	54	2,075	3,040	420	8/25	
22	11-30	880	25,000	46	1,881	2,688	451	8/26	Wood propeller
23	14-49	550	20,950	52	1,690	2,574	343	7/23	3½ hr endurance
24	12-25	680	21,875	52	1,690	2,574	351	10/23	
25	14-24	610	22,000	52	1,740	2,622	388	7/24	
26	12-58	660	22,000		1,805	2,622	410	4/25	Supercharged
27	10-30	920			1,887	2,757	407	4/25	
28	12-00	795	24,300	60		2,757	431	10/25	
29	13-48	612	21,500	60	1,927	2,960	415	4/26	
30	13-09	740	23,000	60	1,927	2,960	415B	3/27	
31	13-18	660	21,600			3,082	415C	5/27	Anti-flutter wings
32	14-40	585	21,500		1,999	2,960	415G	9/27	New control surfaces
33	11-42	750	22,700	57	2,913	3,769	449	1/27	
34	10-30	870	24,700	62	2,495	3,301	475	3/27	
35	10-18	1,085	26,900	57	2,154	3,236	503	4/28	
36	10-30	1,100	26,600	52	2,088	2,990	496	5/28	
37	10-05	1,215	28,950	62	2,194	3,160	497	5/28	
38		1,245		50	2,467	3,326	502	6/28	Crashed on trials
39	9-42	1,060	26,300	54	1,768	2,775	493	11/27	
40	8-15	1,470	30,500	54	1,822	2,908	493A	4/28	Power at sea level
41	9-30	1,240	28,800	70	1,965	3,114	494	2/28	1st prototype
42	9-12	1,380	30,500	70	1,999	3,067	494A	4/29	2nd prototype
43	9-48	1,305	28,800	62	2,276	3,254	494B	7/29	
44	9-48	1,130	26,600				494B	11/31	Townend ring
45	12-06	895	26,400	68	2,438	3,543	494C	3/31	

Line	Type	Identity	Engine Type	Total power (bhp/rpm)	Wing area (sq ft)	Max speed (mph/ft)	Take-off run (yd)	Landing speed (mph)
46	Bulldog IIA	K1691	Jupiter VII			160/13,000		
47	Bulldog IIA	K2226	Jupiter VII			141/10,000		
48	Bulldog TM	K2188	Jupiter VI	477/1,700	305	149/5,000		
49	Lincock	G-EBVO	Lynx IV	192/1,620	177	134/6,500		64
50	Bullpup	J9051	Mercury	393/2,500	230	173/13,000		
51	Siskin IIIB	J8627	Jaguar IV	405/2,000	282	175/15,000		50
52	Siskin IIIB	J8627	Jaguar E	405/2,000	290	164/15,000		
53	Jockey	J9122	Jupiter VIIF	490/1,775	150	205/16,500		
54	Wizard	J9252	FXIS	487/2,250	231	197/15,000		
55	D.H.77	J9771	Napier	301/3,500	156	204/10,000		
56	Starling	A-2	Panther III	510/2,000	256	195/15,000		
57	Firefly II	Nil	FXI	480/2,250	237	199/13,000		
58	Hornet	J9682	FXI	494/2,250	251	214/10,000		68
59	Hornet	J9682	FXI	480/2,250	251	203/15,000		
60	Fury	K1927	Kestrel IIS	480/2,250	251	207/13,000		56
61	Fury	K2082	Kestrel IIS					
62	Fury II	K1935	Kestrel VI	604/2,500		223/14,000		
63	Gloster F.10/27	J9125	Jupiter VIIF	480/1,775	304	188/13,000	128	
64	Gloster F.10/27	J9125	Jupiter VIIF	496/1,775	304	191/13,000		
65	Arm Whit 9/26	A-2	Panther IIIA	501/2,000	261	195/14,500		
66	Arm Whit 9/26	A-2	Panther VII	565/2,100	261	195/15,000		
67	Bulldog IIIA	R-5	Mercury IVS2	515/2,250	291	201/15,000		
68	Bulldog IV	R-7	Mercury IVS2	507/2,250	294	200/16,000		
69	Gloster F.9/26	J9125	Mercury IVS2	517/2,250	315	215/16,500		
70	Gauntlet	J9125	Mercury VIS2	643/2,400		230/15,000		
71	Gauntlet	K4081	Mercury VIS2	619/2,400		223/14,000		
72	Gauntlet II	K5271	Mercury VIS2	605/2,400		227/14,500	185	
73	Gladiator	G37	Mercury VIS2	648/2,800		242/13,800	123	58
74	Westland F.7/30	K2891	Goshawk IIS	602/2,600		146/10,000		
75	Gladiator	K7964	Mercury IX	706/2,400		245/14,200	150	68
76	Hurricane	K5083	Merlin C	1,029/2,600	256	315/16,500	265	59
77	Hurricane	Various	Merlin II	979/2,600	258	301/17,200	410	62
78	Hurricane	Various	Merlin II	979/2,600		310/17,000	350	
79	Spitfire	K5054	Merlin C		242	349/16,800	235	
80	Spitfire	K9787	Merlin II	966/2,600	242	362/18,500	420	60
81	Spitfire	K9793	Merlin II	998/2,600		367/18,600	320	
82	Spitfire	L1007	Merlin III	953/2,600		364/18,500		

Line	Climb to 15,000ft		Service ceiling (ft)	Fuel capacity (Imp gal)	Weight Empty (lb)	Gross (lb)	Report No	Date	Remarks
	Time (min-sec)	Rate at 15,000ft (ft/min)							
46	12-54	880	25,500	68	2,364	3,445	494D	6/32	
47	18-38	440				3,610	494K	3/35	Squadron aircraft
48	16-17	505	20,700	66	2,415	3,426	604	5/32	
49	33-20	155	16,070	26	1,211	1,878	507	8/28	
50	10-50	1,025	25,100			3,040	506/2	/33	Engine tests only
51	9-12	1,550	31,300		2,288	3,118	523	5/29	Geared engine
52	11-36	1,155	28,500	52	2,387	3,375	523/2	5/30	
53	8-57	1,345		55	2,409	3,246	525/2	7/32	
54	9-58	1,335		53	2,623	3,444	502/2	2/30	
55	7-24	1,550			1,655	2,279	551	10/30	Normal climb speeds
56	11-44	1,500		61	2,375	3,337	496A	9/30	
57	7-22	1,855		46	2,435	3,259	556	2/30	
58	7-12	1,540	27,300		2,338	3,148	527	7/29	
59	7-37	1,702		50	2,409	3,232	527/2	2/30	
60	7-12	1,800	29,200	50	2,528	3,317	527B	10/31	
61	7-41	1,615	29,000				527G	6/33	Interceptor propeller
62	5-49	1,910	32,000	49	2,752	3,620	527K	3/36	Slower without spats
63	9-30	1,125	26,100	60	2,562	3,468	572	1/31	Six guns
64	9-53	1,035	26,000	58	2,661	3,726	572/2	1/33	Two guns
65	12-36	1,120	28,650	60	2,889	4,067	598	4/32	
66	9-15		29,000	74	2,933	4,056	598/2	7/33	Townend ring
67	9-40	1,515	29,000	70	2,785	3,956	606	9/32	
68	9-10	1,425	30,550	80	2,912	4,067	606A	8/33	
69	8-12	1,640	33,350	79	2,704	3,858	572/3	7/33	
70	6-25	2,040	34,000	80	2,790	3,910	654	4/35	
71	6-18	1,970	33,200	80	2,823	3,937	654A	7/35	
72	6-30	1,870	32,200	80	2,944	4,070	654C	10/36	Two-blade propeller
73	6-30	1,900	33,500	94	3,050	4,390	666	5/35	
74	12-06	1,000		82	3,861	5,207	676	7/35	
75	6-48	1,800	32,900	72	3,502	4,646	666B	7/37	
76	5-42	2,150	34,500	107		5,672	689	4/36	Two-blade wood propeller
77				97	4,743	6,068	689A	3/39	Two-blade wood propeller
78	6-30	2,080	32,200	97	4,743	6,040	689A	10/39	Two-pitch propeller
79	5-42	2,300	35,400			5,332	692	7/36	Two-blade wood propeller
80	6-30	2,065	31,900	84	4,482	5,819	692A	1/39	Ejector exhausts
81	8-06	1,725	34,400	84	4,598	5,935	692B	7/39	Two-pitch propeller
82	7-30	1,750	34,500		4,599	5,925	692C	7/39	Two-cannon

Fighters – Multi-Seat

Martlesham Heath's involvement with two-seat fighters was in two distinct periods – 1923 to 1926 and 1931 to 1939. Before 1923 the Bristol Badger and Westland Weasel were officially classified as fighters, but as they were tested for reconnaissance, details are under Army Co-operation.

In the first period, three types are included: the Bristol Bullfinch, the de Havilland D.H.42 Dormouse, and the Bristol Bloodhound.

Bristol Bullfinch

Specification 2/21 was for an alternative single- and two-seat fighter, and the Bullfinch, J6901, duly appeared in March 1924 after lengthy trials at Filton involving several structual and aerodynamic changes. The performance is at *line 1*; J6901 as a single-seater was described as a 'clumsy beast' by a pilot. It was permanently

de Havilland D.H.42 Dormouse J7006 in April 1924, with Jupiter IV engine. The fuel tanks above the wing are typical of the period. (British Crown Copyright/MOD)

grounded in June 1924 after bowed fuselage longerons were found, and struck off charge. J6903 was tested as a two-seater between May and September 1924, but little flying was done after similar, but less severe bowing was found; a brave soul flew the aircraft to the RAE in September. Both Bullfinches had early Jupiter engines, and the type was unsuitable for Service use.

Bristol Bullfinch J6901 as a single-seat monoplane, in the spring of 1924. (British Crown Copyright/MOD)

Bullfinch J6903 as a two-seat biplane, mid-1924. The Jupiter engine has a collector ring and exhaust pipe. The mounting step has been removed from the starboard side. (British Crown Copyright/MOD)

Specification 22/22

The requirement for a two-seat High Performance Fighter (Specification 22/22) attracted two contenders, each company being rewarded with contracts for three aeroplanes (the third being of metal in each case). First to arrive at Martlesham was the de Havilland Dormouse J7005 in November 1923; performance is at *line 2* while handling was described as 'rather heavy', but 'visibility good'. Type trials were soon completed, and trials with a Sperry turn indicator made before J7005 returned to de Havilland in March 1924 for conversion to an Army Co-operation type and subsequent renaming as Dingo. The second Dormouse, J7006 with a Jupiter in place of 7005's Jaguar, was briefly flown between April and June 1924; performance *(line 3)* and handling were found to be 'a great improvement'. J7006 was crashed early in Service trials by No.41 Squadron.

Before the availability of the official Bristol Bloodhound, the company's privately-owned aircraft, G-EBGG, was modified and flown to AAEE in February 1924 for type trials lasting until the following May. Performance is at *line 4*. J7248, the metal-framed machine suffered undercarriage failure within a month of arriving in March 1925; repairs at Bristol were followed by further tests in the first three months of 1926; breakage of the centre section at Henlow terminated further Martlesham flying. Performance is at *line 5*; one pilot commented, 'rudder heavy, NOT a good 2 str fighter'. Between July and September 1925, J7236 powered by a Jupiter with variable timing, performed *(line 6)* but failed to impress by its handling

Bristol Bloodhound J7236 (formerly G-EBGG) in the summer of 1925. (British Crown Copyright/MOD)

Hawker Demon J9933 with the shield for the gunner, in July 1932. The unacceptable view for the pilot is readily apparent. (British Crown Copyright/MOD)

which was 'not nice, badly balanced controls' in the words of one pilot. No orders were forthcoming for either the Dormouse or the Bloodhound, and the class of aircraft disappeared from Martlesham until 1931.

Hawker Demon

The outstanding performance of the Hart bomber in 1929 led directly to the type being adapted into a fighter (specified in F.15/30). Minor modifications to a Hart, J9933, included a redesigned gunner's cockpit which slightly improved the field of fire, but the slipstream at speeds above 130mph (indicated) caused the gun-

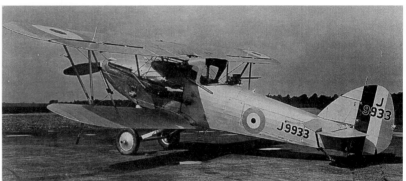

Hawker Demon K2857 (Kestrel VI) in July 1935; the Lewis gun is not fitted. (British Crown Copyright/MOD)

ner's goggles to flutter, and above 160mph (indicated) he could not train the Lewis gun to the sides. In spite of these rather serious shortcomings, the excellent performance *(line 7)* and handling led to production contracts. Initial trials lasted from July 1931 to February 1932, and included tests with stub exhausts which produced no

significant benefits. J9933 was thereafter used for development installations of the various schemes to improve the effectiveness of the gunner, and became an almost permanent resident at Martlesham until its demise in the summer of 1938. First to be tried were simple screens, followed in mid-1932 by a cumbrous enclosure

Demon K4496 in July 1937 with Frazer-Nash turret, and still bearing the badge of No.604 Squadron with which it served before the turret was fitted. (British Crown Copyright/ MOD)

over the pilot and providing a shield for the gunner. The enclosure did not effect spinning or handling characteristics, but the view of the pilot was so seriously restricted as to be unacceptable. Gun firing trials continued until April 1934 when J9933 was seriously damaged at Orfordness when it turned over on landing on soft ground; full braking and a forward CG were contributory factors. The aircraft was rebuilt with a Frazer Nash cupola turret, initially in mock-up form in 1935 when the motor was found to be inadequate to rotate the turret cross wind. In production form in 1936, the turret had a serious effect on handling due both to aerodynamic interference and rearward movement of the CG; full handling trials including diving and spin convinced the Establishment that this modification was unsuitable for Service.

Earlier, in early 1933, the first production Demon, K2842, underwent full type trials without a major hitch.

Boulton Paul Defiant K8310 in December 1937, with a non-operable turret. (British Crown Copyright/ MOD)

The following January K2857 with mass-balanced ailerons and rudder, two of the latest Vickers IIIN guns and a gunner's shield retained the type's excellent handling and performance *(line 8)*. The shield was inadequate, although some swivelling of the free gun was possible up to 200mph (indicated), and diving speed was limited to 260mph (indicated) when the engine reached its maximum permitted revolutions. In 1935 K2857 was flown with a Kestrel VI (performance is at *line 9*) and achieved a take-off run of only 135yd into a 5mph wind; a fault with engine cooling was attributed to ice blocking a pipe. After tests of modifications to the oil cooler (unsatisfactory on K2857), in August 1934 K3764 was used for radio tests, target towing and general duties; it moved to

Boscombe Down in 1939.

Notwithstanding earlier AAEE comments, improved FN turrets were fitted in Demons, initially by conversion of existing aircraft. K4496 was tested for six months from May 1937 – interest being focused on the CG, performance *(line 10)* with the derated Kestrel V, and the right handed propeller. After improvements to the turret, K4496 returned in March 1938 for weight and CG comparison with a production Demon (Turret), K8182; the latter had a CG 1.3in further aft at the same loading. K4496 was then ballasted to the same condition, and handled, spun (once a tail parachute was fitted) and dived with satisfactory results, the only comments concerned a tendency to swing on take off, and the limitations for night flying. Turret

movement was easy and precise at all speeds.

As the Hart bomber's performance in 1929 lead to the fighter Demon, so the remarkable speed of the Blenheim inspired the fighter derivative. Modifications for the Blenheim fighter were small, and Martlesham trials equally minimal.

Specification F.9/35

The first Specification (F.9/35) for a land-based turret fighter resulted in the Boulton Paul Defiant, and the Hawker Hotspur; the latter did not reach AAEE pre-war. The Defiant K8310 was found easy to fly, but the ailerons were too light at high speeds when tested in December 1937 (line 11). Comments from the brief assessment included the need for more effective flaps and details of improvements required to maintenance aspects; 308mph (indicated) was the maximum safe diving speed, limited by the sensitive ailerons. Returning in August 1938, K8310 had the mock up replaced by an electrically-powered turret, the Merlin F replaced by a production Merlin I, and the ailerons extended aft to increase hinge moment and reduce sensitivity. Turret fairings were automatically retracted by compressed air on rotation of the turret, but inadequate air supply prevented proper operation; when fairings were retracted, speed was reduced by 5mph to 6mph. Handling of the type was considered satisfactory, but performance was not comprehensively reported pre-war.

Fighters – multi-seat

Line	Type	Identity	Engine No.	Type	Power (bhp/rpm)	Seats	Wing area (sq ft)	Maximum speed (mph/ft)
1	Bullfinch	J6901	1	Jupiter III	396/1,585	1 or 2	272	137/6,500
2	Dormouse	J7005	1	Jaguar	338/1,500	2	397	123/6,500
3	Dingo	J7006	1	Jupiter IV	394/1,575	2	397	121/6,500
4	Bloodhound	G-EBGG	1	Jupiter IV	400/1,575	2	475	122/6,500
5	Bloodhound	J7248	1	Jupiter IV	404/1,575	2		117/6,500
6	Bloodhound	J7236	1	Jupiter	414/1,575	2	491	120/6,500
7	Demon	J9933	1	Kestrel IIS	480/2,250	2	347	185/13,000
8	Demon	K2857	1	Kestrel IIS	476/2,250	2	347	181/15,000
9	Demon	K2857	1	Kestrel VI	600/2,500	2		202/15,000
10	Demon	K4496	1	Kestrel V(Der)	584/2,500	2		186/15,000
11	Defiant	K8310	1	Merlin I		2		

Line	Climb to 10,000ft Time (min-sec)	Rate (ft/min)	Service ceiling (ft)	Fuel capacity (Imp gal)	Weight Empty (lb)	Gross (lb)	Report No	Date	Remarks
1	9-26	785	22,000	88	2,358	3,256	377	4/24	Test as single-seater
2	7-30	675	17,200	60	2,294	3,719	361	1/24	
3	12-14	580	18,900	60	2,397	3,719	376	5/24	
4	14-20	461	17,860	114	2,515	4,029	378	4/24	2½ hr endurance
5	17-35	365	15,450		2,552	4,263	414	6/25	All-metal frame
6	13-00	565	18,900	95		4,236	427	9/25	
7	10-56 to 15,000 ft		26,100	85	2,885	4,196	587	10/31	
8	7-24	1,390		82	3,067	4,464	587B	4/34	3⅓ hr endurance
9	5-36	1,830	28,850	82	3,209	4,576	587B	6/35	
10	9-42	1,235		82	3,336	4,668	587C	12/37	Turret Demon
11	13-8 to 20,000 ft				5,702	7,100	720	1/38	

Fighters – Heavy Armament

This small group of aeroplanes is characterised by its armament - all but one with the Coventry Ordnance Works (COW) 37mm gun firing a one and a half pound shell. Two of these mighty weapons with a recoil of some 2,000lb were specified for each of two types of three-seat fighter ordered in 1924. The Westland Westbury, J7765, with its large 68ft wingspan underwent normal performance tests starting in October 1926; the results were not spectacular *(line 1)* , but at least one pilot reported very good handling. The second Westbury, J7766, with a metal-covered centre-section joined in armament assessment in mid-1927 and both machines enjoyed relatively long and useful lives at AAEE firing many hundreds of shells at both air and ground targets. No fewer than thirteen reports of breakages to the airframes were written between 1927 and 1930 - many no doubt attributable to the effects of the guns. The contemporary Bristol Bagshot did not reach Martlesham due to structural problems with the 70ft monoplane wing.

Specification F.29/27 defined a new requirement for the heavy fire power of a single COW gun (weighing 227lb with mounting) fixed in a single-seat fighter and aimed by the 'no allowance' method as the fighter passed under its quarry. Two types were ordered; the first to arrive was the Westland type, J9565 *(line 2)*, in April 1931, J9565 was not successful as a fighter in spite of various aerodynamic fixes; as first delivered it required full left stick on take off

which only just prevented the starboard wing from striking the ground; giving the port wing wash-out and the starboard wing wash-in, resulted in flying extemely port wing low. Tabs were then tried on the ailerons with mixed results. No rolling tendency was apparent until speed was increased to about 100mph; at 200mph the aircraft rolled inverted without the pilot being able to stop it. In addition the whole tail shuddered alarmingly, summed up as follows '...unusual and disquieting characteristics and oscillations of the tail organs have been observed'. The makers stiffened the wings, fitted mass-balance to the rudder and connected controls to the pilot's stick and pedals with tubes in place of cables. At Martlesham again in late 1932 the tail still oscillated and

the ailerons were heavy and response sluggish; a great deal of firing of the Mk III COW gun was, however, completed using an ingenious target suspended between two balloons at Orfordness at one period. The other design, by Vickers (Type 161), J9566 *(line 3)*, had complicated control runs for its unique pusher configuration but it handled well, if a bit sensitively. The sighting position required the pilot's head to be lowered within the cockpit which was low, cramped and draughty – the take off was long and

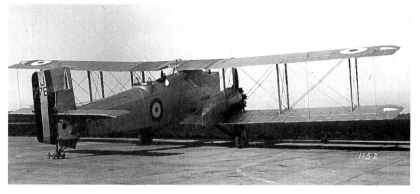

Westland Westbury J7765 in late 1927. The fixed fittings for the COW gun are visible in the middle cockpit. Under the skid is the handling trolley with four castoring wheels. (British Crown Copyright/MOD)

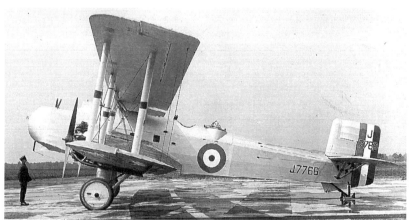

Westbury J7766 in May 1927. The nose has been redesigned and the front fittings for the COW gun are well shown in this metal-framed version. (British Crown Copyright/MOD)

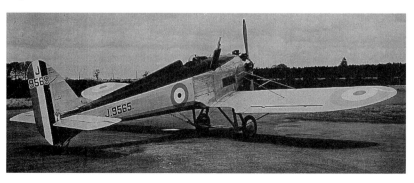

Westland F.29/27 J9565 in March 1932, with COW gun in evidence on the starboard side of the cockpit. (British Crown Copyright/MOD)

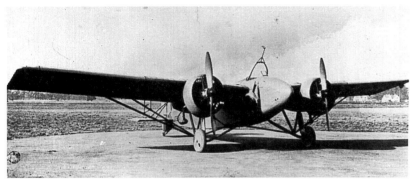

Boulton Paul Bittern J7937 in November 1931. The gunsight on a modified Scarff ring over the pilot's cockpit was linked to the two barbettes; the right one is visible below the cockpit. (British Crown Copyright/MOD)

Vickers F.29/27 J9566 in November 1932, also showing the COW gun. This unique and rigidly-built type displayed none of the oscillations of the tail sections evident in its Westland competitor. (British Crown Copyright/MOD)

the landing short thanks to the effective Vickers hydraulic wheelbrakes; Only 24 shells were fired, trials being delayed by an engine failure late in 1931.

The desire for great fire power in fighters was met later by increasing the standard armament of two machine-guns to four and then eight in later designs. The COW gun was developed for flying-boats.

The last type in this group was designed to meet Specification 27/24 for a bomber destroyer, employing swivelling machine-guns on the sides of the nose. The twin-engined monoplane was the Boulton and Paul Bittern, and the second machine of the type, J7937, reached AAEE by October 1931, probably for armament experiments as the type had been considerably delayed in maker's trials to cure wing and aileron flutter. The Heath at Martlesham claimed the Bittern as another victim in December 1931 when the undercarriage collapsed resulting in a write-off before trials were properly underway.

Fighters – heavy armament

| Line | Type | Identity | Engines | | Total power (bhp/rpm) | Crew seats | Wing area (sq ft) | Maximum speed (mph/ft) | Landing speed (mph) |
			No.	Type					
1	Westbury	J7765	2	Jupiter VI	860/1,700	3	917	118/6,500	56
2	Westland F.29/27	J9565	1	Mercury IIIA	480/2,250	1	221	184/13,000	
3	Vickers F.29/27	J9566	1	Jupiter VIIF	481/1,775	1	207	170/10,000	

| Line | Climb to 6,500ft | | Service ceiling (ft) | Fuel capacity (Imp gal) | Weight | | Report No | Date |
	Time (min-sec)	Rate (ft/min)			Empty (lb)	Gross (lb)		
1	7–06	885	19,500	160	5,221	8,318	479	9/28
2	4–02	1,630	28,100	64	2,737	3,856	580	9/33
3	5–04	1,475	22,400	54	2,529	3,546	588	1/33

Civil Aircraft – Public Transport

The role of the Establishment in the testing of large civil aeroplanes was discussed earlier and in 1920 the Air Ministry used Martlesham for the Civil Aircraft Competition and the Establishment closed for the duration, although practically all the facilities of aerodrome, hangars, test equipment and people were fully occupied.

Before the competition, Vickers sent their unmarked Vimy Commercial with two Rolls-Royce Eagle VIII engines *(line 1)* for standard trials; it later came second in the Competition. During the trial the aileron control failed at 300ft and only by rapidly closing the left throttle could control be maintained and a safe landing made. At the weight tested, 12,500lb, the aircraft wallowed and could not reach 6,000ft; a maximum weight of 10,000lb was recommended for airline use. There is no comment on the economy of operating without the intended ten passengers who could not be accommodated at the recommended weight if any fuel was carried. Bristol flew their four Liberty-engined Pullman C4298 to Martlesham in mid-1920; very little flying was done before it was grounded in

Handley Page W.8 G-EAPJ in 1920 during the Air Ministry Competition. (British Crown Copyright/MOD)

The Vickers Vimy Commercial – unmarked in mid-1920 at the time of AEE tests; later this aeroplane probably took part in the Air Ministry Competition for large Aircraft. (British Crown Copyright/MOD)

October after pilots rejected the enclosed seating arrangements. The winner of the Large Aircraft Competition, the Handley Page W.8 G-EAPJ, with two Napier Lion engines, was not subsequently official-

Bristol Pullman C4298 in November 1920. Not visible in this view is the enclosed pilots cabin – an arrangement disfavoured by the pilots. (British Crown Copyright/MOD)

ly tested; however, a development, the W.8b G-EBBG to Specification 16/21 with two Eagle VIII engines *(line 2)* went through full performance trials between 21 April and 2 May, 1922. The rudder control was very heavy and the aeroplane tiring to fly in rough air; below 80mph turns were unpleasant for an unspecified reason. Fire hazards were considered minimal on account of the fuel tanks being mounted on top of the wings. The Establishment recommended that weight should be restricted to 12,000lb unless the wind was over 10mph when take off could be made at 12,500lb.

To increase safety a third engine was fitted in Handley Page's next air-

liner, the W.8f Hamilton, built to an Air Ministry specification, initially 40/22 but later refined. With two Puma engines and an Eagle in the nose, total power of 767hp was only slightly greater than the power of the earlier W.8b, but performance *(line 3)* of the Hamilton was better. The report from September 1924 is lost; it would have made an interesting comparison with the 1930 report on the same aeroplane, G-EBIX, which was retested for C of A with two FXIIA engines *(line 18)*. On the latter occasion severe criticism was made of the type: elevators and ailerons were very heavy, the machine was extremely unstable in roll and yaw, the view poor in the climb and the throttles could not be pushed fully forward when the pilot was strapped in. In addition, even at 2,000ft and a low weight, height could not be maintained on one

de Havilland D.H.18B G-EAWX in about December 1921, with two-bladed propeller. This view of the aircraft illustrates the difficulty of the pilot in seeing past the wing. (British Crown Copyright/MOD)

Handley Page W.8b G-EBBG in April 1922, with fuel tanks on top of the upper wing. (British Crown Copyright/ MOD)

The Handley Page W.8f Hamilton G-EBIX in September 1924. (British Crown Copyright/MOD)

engine, and with two engines working there was excessive vibration. The Hamilton received a C of A, but crashed into high ground later in 1930 in the service of Imperial Airways.

The first of many de Havilland civil aeroplanes to be tested at Martlesham was the D.H.18, G-EAWW, in October 1921 *(line 4)* (G-EAWW was

the fifth D.H.18 – the first four were already in service by October 1922, having received their C of A before delivery). The top wing obscured a vital part of the pilot's view, and below 75mph control became marginal; however, the Air Ministry issued a C of A for this aeroplane in due course. In November 1921 D.H.18B G-EAWX *(line 5)* had a two-bladed propeller in place of the three-bladed unit of G-EAWW; fuel still leaked into the cabin and the report commented that the fire risk had not been given sufficient attention; a C of A was nevertheless issued in January 1922. G-EAWW ended its days by being ditched in the sea (by a pilot of the 'other' Establishment at Felixstowe) to see how long it would float. The Air Ministry drew up a specification (17/21) and de Havilland developed

the D.H.18 into the D.H.34 with fuel carried in external tanks. Two weeks after the first D.H.34, G-EBBQ, entered service, the second, G-EBBR with a three-bladed propeller, went to Martlesham on 18 April, 1922 *(line 6)*. The control response was slow and the lack of longitudinal trim a serious handicap. Worse than the handling

de Havilland D.H.34 G-EBBR in April 1922; the external fuel tanks are clearly visible. (British Crown Copyright/ MOD)

deficiencies was poor performance, particularly the take-off distance. Changing to a four-bladed propeller made matters worse still, and the Establishment recommended that even with the three-bladed propeller weight should be restricted to 7,000lb and then only in a wind favourable for take off. Another D.H.34, G-EBBV *(line 7)*, produced even more marginal take-off figures (reaching an altitude of only 11ft some 500yd after starting); however, if the CG was fully aft, it was found possible to reach the C of A requirement of 50ft after 466yd. Finally, a third D.H.34, G-EBBW with an adjustable tailplane, demonstrated an acceptable take off – but the wind of 15mph undoubtedly assisted results in the urgency of the situation. Consideration of the type's problems led to the conclusion that the unusual impression gained by the pilot, whose view forward was blocked by the water tank, caused him to hold too low a nose attitude during take off with the result that initial climb was too shallow. The Establishment recommended that all pilots should be warned of the false impression.

The conventional-looking D.H.50, G-EBFN *(line 8)*, with only four passenger seats arrived in August 1923 and quickly completed its trials. The

The de Havilland D.H.54 Highclere G-EBKI in November 1925. (British Crown Copyright/MOD)

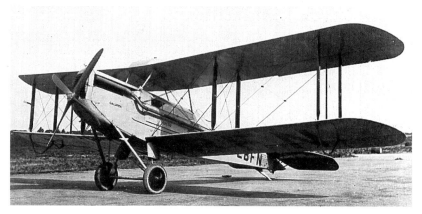

de Havilland D.H.50 G-EBFN in August 1923. The hoops under the lower wings were a feature of several light aeroplanes of the period. (British Crown Copyright/MOD)

second D.H.50, G-EBFO, had full-span variable-camber aileron/flaps. Most D.H.50 reports are lost, but one aircraft did climbs in mid-1924, also powered by a Puma. G-EBFO was the aeroplane flown by Alan Cobham on his epic flights to Australia and South Africa.

Last of the early single-engined de Havilland types to reach Martlesham was the D.H.54 Highclere built under Air Ministry sponsorship for a European Transport to Specification 40/22. The single machine built, G-EBKI, appears to have exhibited satisfactory performance *(line 9)* in late 1925 but at least one pilot found the controls, particularly the rudder, inferior to the D.H.50.

The only Bristol aeroplane between 1920 and 1939 to be built for public transport was known as the Ten-

Bristol Ten-Seater G-EAWY in the summer of 1921. Three fuel tanks are visible; on the lower fuselage just aft of the light-coloured cowling are two vane-type fittings – probably driving pumps for the fuel from the wing tanks. (British Crown Copyright/MOD)

Vickers Vulcan G-EBEK in late 1922 in its original freighter form. It had a Rolls-Royce Eagle engine. (British Crown Copyright/MOD)

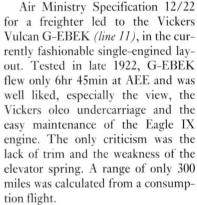

Seater. The prototype, G-EAWY (line 10), was tested for one month from 5 August, 1921, and again, after purchase by the Air Ministry, for a further two months from 30 November, 1921. Initial handling was spoilt by a tendency to wallow at low speed, and take-off distance was greatly affected by the propeller used; at least two were tried. Taxying was difficult, and the passengers' windows were made of plate glass and thus unacceptable.

Air Ministry Specification 12/22 for a freighter led to the Vickers Vulcan G-EBEK (line 11), in the currently fashionable single-engined layout. Tested in late 1922, G-EBEK flew only 6hr 45min at AEE and was well liked, especially the view, the Vickers oleo undercarriage and the easy maintenance of the Eagle IX engine. The only criticism was the lack of trim and the weakness of the elevator spring. A range of only 300 miles was calculated from a consumption flight.

G-EBES (line 12), a passenger version with Eagle VIII was at AEE also in late 1922, and G-EBFC (line 13), with a Lion engine in the spring of 1923; reports for these have not been found.

After the somewhat lengthy development flying period of two years, the 23 seat Vickers Vanguard, G-EBCP (line 14), arrived in time for No.22 Squadron to demonstrate the type at the RAF Pageant in June 1925. Pilots' log book comments include 'fine aircraft for such a size' and 'very good'. Two pilots record flying the Vanguard J6924 ; this was the same machine which had dual identity at the wish of its owners, the Air Ministry.

Armstrong Whitworth submitted their Argosy G-EBLF for AAEE assessment in June 1926; the machine suffered two serious failures of the tyres and petrol system and no tests

Vickers Vanguard G-EBCP in July 1924. Although a poor copy, this photograph clearly shows the heath-like nature of the aerodrome. (British Crown Copyright/MOD)

Armstrong Whitworth Argosy G-EBLF having just arrived from the 1926 RAF Pageant. (British Crown Copyright/ MOD)

were completed. A pilot recorded in his log book that the three Jaguar engines were good. By January 1927 the third of the type, G-EBOZ (owned by the Air Ministry) had completed full trials *(line 15)*. Pilots found the handling very satisfactory.

Vickers Vellore G-EBYX in November 1928 appears large in relation to its Jupiter engine. (British Crown Copyright/MOD)

In early 1929, Argosy II G-AACH, *(line 17)* with more powerful, geared, Jaguar IVA engines in place of the earlier direct drive Jaguars, completed C of A trials.

The Vellore, G-EBYX later J8906 *(line 16)*, built by Vickers to Air Minsitry Specification 34/24 for a civil mail carrier was praised in 1928 for its low structural weight, advanced controls and 10hr endurance. The single Jupiter was started by compressed air – the cylinder being charged by foot pump. G-EBYX was however, slow and in 1930 a twin-engined version, G-AASW *(line 19)*, was rushed through trials for the imminent King's

Cup Air Race. On one engine it could climb at 3,500ft and turn into the live engine, its handling was docile, but a C of A could not be recommended for passenger carriage as the door in the floor could be opened only from the outside. A further twin Vellore, K2133, spent three years until 1935 on general duties, largely ferrying to Orfordness. Early in 1934, a C of A was recommended for the Vellore's development, the Vellox O-8 later G-ABKY *(line 20)*, which was also easy to fly.

Vickers' monoplane airliner, the Viastra, using the all-metal Wilbault-type structure was first tested in its export version for Australia. Next, in late 1932, came the version with a single Jupiter VIIIF engine, numbered O-6, for performance tests. New engines, the Pegasus IM3, and special fittings characterised the Viastra G-ACCC for the Prince of Wales, tested in May and again in September 1933; no reports have been found. Its handling was again assessed three years later – the reason is unclear.

The Westland IV, G-EBXK *(line 21)* with Cirrus III engines, the company's second essay into passenger aircraft, was not initially a success, although it was manoevrable in spite of heavy controls. The two unacceptable faults were the breakage of engine bearers in three places, and the CG being seven inches behind the aft limit, in spite of the use of copious ballast in the nose. An extreme aft CG and great manoeuvrability would seem to be compatible. Seven months later, in October 1929, the version with

Vickers Vellox G-ABKY in February 1934. (British Crown Copyright/ MOD)

Vickers Viastra O-6 in June 1932. (British Crown Copyright/MOD)

three Cirrus Hermes Is, G-AAGW *(line 22)*, was successful in spite of fuselage vibration caused, it was thought, by the unsynchronised engines, and the landing run without brakes being too long. Had the brake lever been within the pilot's reach, the landing run would no doubt have been shorter! The landing run was acceptable on the radial-engined Wessex (renamed from Westland IV) P-1 in May 1930 *(line 23)*; although successfully flown at 5,742lb, the required performance on initial climb could only be achieved at 4,669lb. Fitting three Genet Majors appeared to cure the type's vibration and flying on two engines produced a speed of 65mph. The final machine of this type,

Westland Wessex G-ABVB in May 1932. (British Crown Copyright/MOD)

G-ABVB *(line 24)* with more powerful Genet Majors improved performance sufficiently for a C of A to be recommended at 6,300lb – which allowed full fuel and eight passengers to be carried.

Only brief trials appear to have been made of the Gloster Survey G-AADO (originally the de Havilland D.H.67B) *(line 25)* which was praised as a very good and stable survey aeroplane with an outstanding view; the petrol guage was, nevertheless, useless and the airspeed indicator over-read by 22mph at maximum speed.

Westland IV G-EBXK in January 1929, as originally powered with three Cirrus engines (British Crown Copyright/MOD)

Following successful appraisal by MAEE, the Saunders-Roe Cutty Sark flying-boat G-AAIP (also L1) *(line 26)* was made into an amphibian and the C of A extended to land operations, but only after a thinner rudder had been fitted to overcome directional sensitivity. Saunders-Roe's similar amphibian, the Cloud G-ABCJ *(line 27)*, was good on all major points but

Saunders-Roe Windover G-ABJP in the autumn of 1931. (British Crown Copyright/MOD)

raising the undercarriage was hard work, the control wheel too big and a single engine could not maintain the aircraft's height. Third of a trio of Saunders-Roe amphibians was the Windhover G-ABJP, *(line 28),* tested in early 1931 as a landplane first, when it was rejected on the basis of bad control at low speed, and bad take-off characteristics. A C of A was recommended in July 1931 after modifications, although the machine was very sensitive in bumps.

G-AAYR *(line 29),* an Avro Six, was the first of the company's high-wing monoplanes to be tested at Martlesham for a British C of A. It was criticised for having the pilot's seat on the right, contrary to the international civil agreement. The final Avro design derived from the Fokker high-wing layout was the Type 642 (twin Jaguar VID), represented by G-ACFV for its successful C of A trials in March 1934. Avro's speedy 627 Mailplane, G-ABJM, with its Panther IIA engine was quickly recommended for its C of A in August 1931. Somewhat slower was the Handley Page H.P.42 Hannibal, G-AAGX *(line 30),* but such was the urgency to get the type into Imperial Airways' service that top speed appears not to have been measured. Most of the five days that G-AAGX was at AAEE were spent in determining an accurate

Avro 642 G-ACFV in February 1934. (British Crown Copyright/MOD)

CG – both longitudinal and vertical; the latter moved down 10in as fuel was consumed. To simplify the controls of the four Jupiter XIF engines, final rearward movement of the throttles closed the petrol cocks. In Martle-

Avro 627 Mailplane G-ABJM in August 1931. (British Crown Copyright/MOD)

sham's view this was a serious defect as the accepted way of extinguishing an engine fire was by cutting off the petrol supply and opening the throttle – a procedure not possible in the Hannibal.

No fewer than seven Monospar cantilever wing monoplanes were tested with five different powerplants and two undercarriage systems. The first, ST-3 G-AARP, with two small Salmson A.D.9 engines, was built by Gloster, and tested first in March

The General Aircraft ST-4 Monospar G-ABUZ in August 1932, with two Pobjoy R engines which could be started from inside the cabin. (British Crown Copyright/MOD)

1931 for its C of A *(line 31)*, when it was rejected due to tail vibration. On return three months later with a fixed tailplane and slats, G-AARP was again rejected as the elevator was too sensitive at high speed, and lacked response at slow speed; also the tail vibrated badly with one engine throttled.

Testing took place a year later of the Pobjoy-engined, ST-4 G-ABUZ, built like the remainder by the new General Aircraft Limited. In 1935, comprehensive handling and diving trials were completed on the version with Gipsy Majors (possibly G-ADBN), followed in 1936 by C of A trials for the Niagara III- powered ST-25 G-AEGY. American Pratt & Whitney Wasp Juniors propelled the larger ST-18 Croydon G-AECB, the subject both of a full performance

Monospar ST-25 G-AEGY in May 1936. (British Crown Copyright/ MOD)

report and of a recommendation for C of A. Also in 1936, the ultimate standard version of the Monospar, the ST-25 G-AEMN performed with Niagara engines but was not subjected to assessment for C of A. Finally, as part of a programme into the suitabili-

ty of tricycle undercarriages (all the other Monospars had conventional tailwheels), an unmarked* ST-25 was flown by eight AAEE pilots on 4 November, 1937. Taxying was easy, but the uneven surface at Martlesham caused exaggerated pitching; landings required less judgment than usual and even non-pilots achieved passable touchdowns.

A C of A was not recommended initially for the Saunders-Roe Percival Mailplane (as it was known in late 1931) G-ABLI, *(line 32)*, due to the excessive vibration caused, it was believed, by the centre engine. The vibration was not cured by replacing the single rudder with twin rudders nor by strengthening the front fuse-

Monospar ST-18 Croydon G-AECB in June 1936. (British Crown Copyright/MOD)

---

* At some time it was T42.

Spartan Cruiser G-ACDW in March 1934; this was a development of the Mailplane G-ABLI. (British Crown Copyright/MOD)

Airspeed Ferry G-ABSI in May 1932. (British Crown Copyright/MOD)

Airspeed Envoy G-ACVI in October 1935 on its second visit, and re-engined with Wolseley Aries IIIs. (British Crown Copyright/MOD)

lage. A third attempt, in February 1932, with the centre section altered improved the vibration sufficiently for a C of A to be recommended. The

Mailplane was developed into the passenger-carrying Spartan Cruiser, and was successfully tested at Farnborough at 5,700lb all up weight. Martlesham extended the C of A of Cruiser G-ACDW to 6,200lb in April 1934.

The first of the new Airspeed Company's aircraft, the three-engined Ferry G-ABSI *(line 33)*, had good controls, view and layout in 1932 but a harsh undercarriage which, when

taxying, threw passengers against the cabin roof – a feature which apparently did not deter the joy-riding throng who tasted aviating first in this machine operating in its design role with Cobham's National Aviation Day Displays. Next of Airspeed's products tested was the special Viceroy G-ACMU assessed at Portsmouth in October 1934 for the England to Australia race. With two Cheetah VI engines, the handling of the Viceroy was normal even though all up weight had been increased by extra fuel tankage to 6,500lb from the normal 4,850lb. Airspeed's Envoy G-ACMT *(line 34)*, was plagued by recurrent trouble during trials with its two early Wolseley A.R.9 radial engines; Martlesham pilots were reassured, however, by its ability to fly on one engine and they liked the novel electric indicator for that innovation – the retracting undercarriage.

A second Envoy, G-ACVI *(line 35)*, had tankage increased to 159 gallons (and maximum weight to 5,500lb); full trials were not completed as G-ACVI was urgently required for a flight to Australia in February 1935. Sufficient work was done for a recommendation for C of A to be made in spite of continuing unreliability of its A.R.9 engines. On return G-ACVI *(line 36)* was fitted with Aries III motors and was fully tested in May 1936. Comments were generally favourable and the automatic mixture controls worked well; the pres-

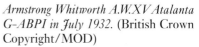

Armstrong Whitworth A.W.XV Atalanta G-ABPI in July 1932. (British Crown Copyright/MOD)

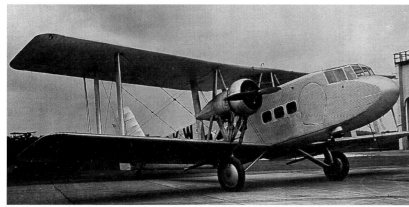

The Blackburn C.A.15C ten-seater bi-plane G-ABKW in July 1932. (British Crown Copyright/MOD)

sure correction was minus 13 at an indicated 190mph. Tests of Envoys for South Africa are noted under British Aircraft for Overseas. C of A trials on the Cheetah IX powered Envoy G-AEXX *(line 37)*, bought for the use of the monarch were limited to: weight, CG determination, handling and dives in April 1937. Martlesham weighing showed that if six passengers were to be carried, full fuel capacity could not be used and that the forward limit of CG was easily exceeded. Flaps and undercarriage took under 30 seconds to lower.

Armstrong Whitworth's second airliner (after the Argosy) was the

four-engined Atalanta of strikingly modern appearance. G-ABPI *(line 38)* was tested in July 1932 only four weeks after its first flight. The throttles had to be slammed closed to achieve idling of the engines for landing – unfortunately this action could cause complete stoppage of the engines but fortunately for the makers

the phenomenon was considered acceptable for its C of A, as was the extreme longitudinal instability with aft CG. The rudder was adequate for control with any two engines stopped.

Sponsorship of civil designs by the Air Ministry included Specification 6/29 and the Blackburn C.A.15C ten-seater – built in biplane, G-ABKW *(line 39)*, and monoplane, G-ABKV *(line 40)* versions for comparison. The former, tested in October 1932 had stiff ailerons, a heavy rudder and a disconcerting directional hunting aggravated by poor ventilation; the brakes were fierce. Full performance measurements were made to compare the benefits of each version. The monoplane was heavier structurally, had a

The Blackburn C.A.15C ten-seater monoplane G-ABKV in January 1933. (British Crown Copyright/MOD)

Short Valetta G-AAJY at the time of its AAEE trials in July 1932. (British Crown Copyright/MOD)

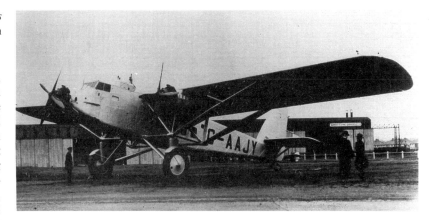

longer landing run without brakes, was faster, and carried more fuel; both were directionally poor, and the monoplane in particular, heavy and tiring to fly. The Bendix brakes in Dunlop wheels were not a success, but the Elsan toilet was passed with flying colours – quite a relief. The comparison appears to have been inconclusive, but the monoplane, as K4241, ended its days in a fire to test extinguishers; the fire was conclusive.

Specification 21/27 produced the Short Valetta floatplane in 1930; in June 1932 G-AAJY *(line 41)* was fitted with wheels and sent to Martlesham. Its extreme stability and heavy elevator with poor response made for a tricky high-speed landing requiring full nose-up trim to be applied during roundout. The landing run was extended by the unsuitability of the Palmer wheels. After these tests, it remained on radio trials at AAEE until written off late in 1933.

Specification 21/28 for a mail carrier led to the twin-engine Boulton Paul P.64 G-ABYK, first received at Martlesham Heath in June 1933 for the RAF Display at Hendon. The type was quickly sent back to its manufacturers as it was not only directionally unstable but divergent in yaw even with full correcting rudder; control was maintained only by differential use of the engines. On return to AAEE on 16 October, 1933, the auxiliary fins on the tailplane helped but did not cure the problems; at maximum weight (11,300lb) firm rudder was

Boulton Paul P.71A G-ACOX in August 1934. (British Crown Copyright/MOD)

needed constantly and sideslips were alarming. On 21 October, during a flight to corroborate the previous opinions, the aircraft crashed, killing the pilot. It was considered that the long, deep fuselage ahead of the CG was to blame. The following year, the same company's P.71A G-ACOX *(line 42)* was tested, devoid of cabin furnishings, a common condition with aircraft submitted for initial type certification. Generally similar to the ill-fated P.64 but with a slimmer and longer fuselage, the P.71A also was directionally unstable yet was recommended for C of A.

The flying-boat company, Short Brothers, submitted their landplane Scion and Scylla airliners. First, early in 1934, was Scion G-ACJI *(line 43)* with two 75hp Pobjoys both of which were needed to keep the aeroplane airborne. The undercarriage was harsh and the Dunlop brakes difficult to operate otherwise the Scion was pleasant to fly except in bumps. Scion G-ACUZ *(line 44)* successfully visited Martlesham for approval of an increase in maximum weight from 3,000lb to 3,200lb; the trial was in February 1935. Four engines in the Scion Senior G-AECU *(line 45)* gave better performance in 1936, and the ceiling with two engines failed was 6,000ft; the only criticism of the Senior was of the engine switches – so placed as to be easily knocked off. The Short L.17 G-ACJJ *(line 46)*, known at Martlesham by its airline name of Scylla displayed no vices, except that of the engines cutting out in damp weather, and attracted one comment which concerned the air bottle capacity for the brakes being sufficient for only a single take off and landing. The latter was an irritant during trials where performance measurements required repeated take offs and measured landings.

Short Scion G-ACUZ in February 1935. (British Crown Copyright/ MOD)

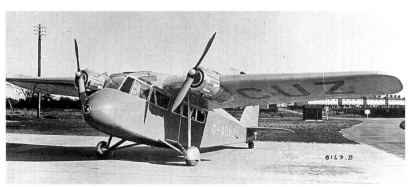

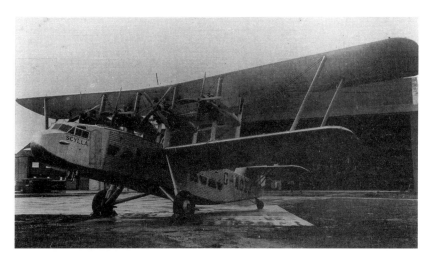

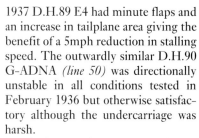

Dominating the small airliner market from 1932 were the four de Havilland biplane types – the twin D.H.84 Dragon, D.H.89 Dragon Rapide, D.H.90 Dragonfly and the four-engined D.H.86. AAEE pilots liked the handling of the D.H.84 E9 *(line 47)* when tested only a few days after its maiden flight in November 1932, and a C of A was recommended provided four minor modifications were incorporated; single-engined flying was easy in level flight at 1,000ft. Eighteen months later, with 130hp Gipsy Majors replaced by 200hp Gipsy Sixes, the D.H.89 E4 *(line 48)* was also pleasant, but the glide was flat – an interesting comtemporary comment at a time when pilots were becoming used to the benefit of flaps. In April 1936, D.H.89 G-ADWZ *(line 49)* had a 10 percent increase in

Short L.17 Scylla G-ACJJ in May 1934. (British Crown Copyright/ MOD)

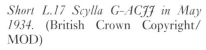

de Havilland D.H.89A Dragon Rapide E-4 in February 1937, with small flaps under the lower wing. (British Crown Copyright/MOD)

weight to 5,500lb which, coupled with a heavy elevator control led to a tendency to take off at too slow a speed with consequent wing drop. de Havilland then thickened the wingtip section; the problem was cured, and a C of A was recommended. In March

1937 D.H.89 E4 had minute flaps and an increase in tailplane area giving the benefit of a 5mph reduction in stalling speed. The outwardly similar D.H.90 G-ADNA *(line 50)* was directionally unstable in all conditions tested in February 1936 but otherwise satisfactory although the undercarriage was harsh.

The four-engined D.H.86, E2 *(line 51)* was very rapidly assessed in January 1934 to meet the customer's contractual time limit for certification. All controls were very heavy above 170mph but handling was otherwise good and ceiling adequate with three and two engines operating. The Martlesham report contains the uncritical phrase 'as good as the usual de Havilland'. Following two unexplained losses of D.H.86s in Australia, VH-USF was examined at Martlesham, with particular emphasis on the effect of the pilot delaying rudder application following engine failure; it was also found that rotating the

co-pilot's seat could foul the control column and that it was easy to exceed the forward and aft limits of the CG. However, no conclusions on the likely cause of the Australian crashes were drawn by AAEE. In December 1936 D.H.86A G-ADYH, *(line 52)* was flown after adverse criticism by its British Airways owners (who had also suffered a crash of a D.H.86A). It was found that in certain conditions rudder over-balance occurred, and, more alarming, that with the rudder fixed a small bank angle produced a slow turn in the opposite direction possibly due, it was thought, to wing twisting. The C of A was withdrawn, and D.H.86As in service at Gatwick and Croydon with five airlines were tested, including G-ACVY, resulting in eight of the sixteen being grounded. Rapid modifications including a spring in the elevator circuit and the fitting of auxil-

de Havilland D.H.86 G-ACVY of Railway Air Services late in 1936 during investigation of rudder overbalance and other phenomena. (British Crown Copyright/MOD)

iary fins were assessed on E2 *(line 53)* (later SU-ABV) resulting in satisfactory handling and reinstatement of the C of A. The final modification, increased tailplane chord on G-AENR, gave handling characteristics similar to E2.

The Avro 652 G-ACRM, required several minor modifications before a C of A could be recommended; the uncommanded swinging from side to side through 30 deg of heading was acceptable and 1,500ft could be maintained with either engine alone operating.

In September 1933 AAEE received for British civil certification the first transport aircraft made in the USA in the shape of the Ford 5AT-D trimotor monoplane G-ACAE *(line 55)*. Although stable, it had very large trim

Avro 642 G-ACRM in March 1935. (British Crown Copyright/MOD)

Percival Q.6 X-1 in January 1938. (British Crown Copyright/MOD)

changes with alteration of power on its two underslung engines; there were no adverse comments, and height could be maintained on any two engines.

Exceptionally well balanced controls characterised the British Aircraft Manufacturing Company's Double Eagle, Y-1, *(line 56)*, but the type had

no rudder trim nor heating and care was needed to keep the CG within limits. Performance was marginally improved by replacing the twin Gipsy Majors with Gipsy Sixes in G-AEIN, tested in November 1936. Gipsy Six engines also powered the Percival Q.6 *(line 57)* which had insufficient nose up trim at forward CG above 105mph,

although capable of 153mph in level flight; single-engine power was sufficient to maintain 3,000ft.

Of very modern appearance, the D.H.91 Albatross mail carrier G-AEVV *(line 58)* and passenger-carrying E.2 were nevertheless extensively criticised by AAEE during tests made in June to September 1938. At 28,500lb (1,000lb below maximum), G-AEVV just achieved the civil landing run requirement of 328 yards, and at the same weight could maintain 9,000ft on three engines. The similar E.2 *(line 59)* on trials needed over 328 yards to land and could only maintain 1,000ft on three engines at 29,500lb. G-AEVV (with double the fuel load of E.2) achieved 2.53 air miles per gallon, giving a calculated range of 2,500 miles against a 40mph headwind. This calculation was made to meet the new Airworthiness Board's requirements for the range of a civil aircraft to be calculated, and was an outstanding figure. Less

The de Havilland D.H.91 Albatross G-AEVV in July 1938. This was the mail carrier version. (British Crown Copyright/MOD)

Armstrong Whitworth A.W.27 Ensign G-ADSR in May 1938 – at 49,000lb easily the heaviest civil airliner tested at Martlesham before 1939. (British Crown Copyright/MOD)

The de Havilland D.H.95 Flamingo G-AFUE in July 1939. (British Crown Copyright/MOD)

praiseworthy were the controls – of which the elevator and rudder were very heavy, even after the fitting of geared balance tabs to the former. Severest comments were directed at the all-wood construction which required several modifications before a C of A could be recommended.

Easily the heaviest civil airliner tested before the war was the Armstrong Whitworth Ensign, eventually recommended for a C of A at 49,000lb. The all-metal stressed-skin construction of ultra modern appearance raised no comment; attracting adverse observations were the undercarriage (one and a half minutes to raise) and the ailerons (slow response at low speed). Many take-offs were made to determine the best flap angle, but even at optimum setting the type failed to meet the requirements. Brakes were good, but had no means of replenishment of the accumulators in flight. There were several minor failures, including the second pilot's controls, and minor modifications required before a C of A could be recommended. With some of the minor

Lockheed 14 G-AFGN in August, 1938. (British Crown Copyright/MOD)

changes incorporated G-ADSR *(line 60)* returned after two weeks in June 1938 and just met the new, relaxed, take-off criterion of reaching 66ft, 620yds after starting the take-off run. However, the major criticism of the possibility of taking off with the control locks engaged was not remedied until a third test of G-ADSR on 20 August, 1938, (at Coventry) when the C of A was finally recommended, and immediately issued by the recently constituted Air Registration Board. In 1939, the Ensign G-ADSW *(line 61)* named *Eddystone* by its owners,

Imperial Airways, was briefly assessed with the length of the control runs halved to rudder and elevator, a servo tab on the rudder and with constant-speed propellers. Controls were improved, but the ailerons remained heavy and tiring and the rudder bias required delicate setting; its C of A was recommended.

With two powerful Bristol Perseus engines, the de Havilland Flamingo G-AFUE *(line 62)* easily met all performance criteria in July 1939; it was exceptionally good on one engine. The dashboard-mounted control column was an innovation and was generally liked; the single instrument for revolutions, cylinder and oil temperature was, however, not liked – particularly as operation of a switch was required to make the instrument read. The novel Exactor engine cowl flaps were imprecise, and were included in the four items requiring improvement.

Following the Lockheed 10A and 12A into British airline service, the Lockheed 14, G-AFGN *(line 63)*, was the first to require flying tests for its type C of A. Martlesham was asked only to measure take-off performance in August, 1938.

Civil aircraft – public transport

Line	Type	Identity	Engines No. Type		Power (bhp/rpm)	Seats (crew – pass)	Wing area (sq ft)	Maximum speed (mph/ft)	Take-off run (yd)
1	Vimy Commercial	—	2	Eagle	700/1,800		1,334	94/3,000	
2	W.8b	G-EBBG	2	Eagle VIII	730/1,800	1 –	1,459	92/3,000	350
3	Hamilton	G-EBIX	2	Puma	424/1,400	2 –	1,458	103/3,000	
			1	Eagle	324/1,800				
4	D.H.18	G-EAWW	1	Lion LC	436/2,000	1 – 8	624	122/1,000	337
5	D.H.18	G-EAWX	1	Lion LC	436/2,000	1 – 8	624	118/3,000	
6	D.H.34	G-EBBR	1	Lion II	449/2,100	1 – 9	535	112/3,000	310
7	D.H.34	G-EBBV	1	Lion LC	459/2,100	1 –	535	112/3,000	
8	D.H.50	G-EBFN	1	Puma	230/1,400	1 –	445	112/3,000	
9	D.H.54	G-EBKI	1	Condor III	678/1,900	2 – 12	1,004	117/3,000	
10	Bristol 10-Seater	G-EAWY	1	Lion IB	465/2,000	1 – 9	681	113/3,000	375
11	Vulcan	G-EBEK	1	Eagle IX	370/2,000	1 –	837	102/3,000	200
12	Vulcan	G-EBES	1	Eagle VIII	354/1,800	1 –	840	95/3,000	
13	Vulcan	G-EBFC	1	Lion	463/2,026	1 –	840	113/3,000	
14	Vanguard	G-EBCP	2	CondorIII	1,360/1,900	2 –	2,164	112/3,000	
15	Argosy	G-EBOZ	3	Jaguar IV	1,263/1,700	2 –	1,857	107/3,000	
16	Vellore	J8906	1	Jupiter IX	437/2,000		1,419	111/1,000	275

Line	Type	Identity	Engines No. Type		Fuel capacity (Imp gal)	Seats (crew – pass)	All-up weight for C of A (lb)	Height after 3min (ft)
17	Argosy	G-AACH	3	Jaguar IV			19,200	2,340
18	Hamilton	G-EBIX	2	FXIIA	223	2 -14	13,999	1,850
19	Vellore	G-AASW	2	Jupiter XI			9,972	3,400
20	Vellox	G-ABKY	2	Pegasus IM3	255	3 – 8	13,500	3,250
21	Westland IV	G-EBXK	3	Cirrus III		1 – 5	4,900	1,480
22	Westland IV	G-AAGW	3	Hermes	100	1 – 5	5,400	1,550+
23	Wessex	P1	3	Genet Major	102	1 –	4,669	1,410
24	Wessex	G-ABVB	3	Genet Major IA		1 – 8	6,300	1,730
25	Gloster Survey	G-AADO	2	Jupiter XI	250	2 –	9,008	4,600
26	Cutty Sark	L1	2	Hermes		1 – 2	3,700	1,700
27	Cloud	G-ABCJ	2	Whirlwind J6	125	1 – 5	8,600	1,650
28	Windhover	G-ABJP	3	Gipsy II	68		5,700	1,200
29	Avro Six	G-AAYR	3	Genet Major	94	1 – 5	5,000	1,580
30	Hannibal	G-AAGX	4	Jupiter XIF	400	2 –	28,000	2,680
31	Monospar ST-3	G-AARP	2	Salmson A.D.9			1,704	1,235
32	Saro Percival	G-ABLI	3	Gipsy III	260		6,117	1,350
33	Ferry	G-ABSI	1	Gipsy III	58	1 -10	5,600	1,300
			2	Gipsy II				
34	Envoy	G-ACMT	2	A.R.9 IA	75	1 – 5	5,300	2,260
35	Envoy	G-ACVI	2	A.R.9	159	1 –	5,500	
36	Envoy	G-ACVI	2	Aries III	102	1 –	5,700	2,300
37	Envoy	G-AEXX	2	Cheetah IX	151	1 –	6,600	
38	Atalanta	G-ABPI	4	Dbl Mongoose III	317	2 –	20,000	1,600
39	Blackburn C.A.15C*	G-ABKW	2	Jaguar IVC	166	2 –	12,150	1,640
40	Blackburn C.A.15C†	G-ABKV	2	Jaguar IVC	304	2 -10	13,074	1,850

* Biplane   † Monoplane   + at 5,750lb

Line	Climb to 3,000ft		Service ceiling (ft)	Fuel capacity (Imp gal)	Weight Empty (lb)	Gross (lb)	Endur (hr)	Report		Remarks
	Time (min-sec)	Rate (ft/min)						No	Date	
1	16-00	165	5,850	168		12,500	4½	275A	6/20	Competition machine
2	9-36	260	7,350	200	7,209	12,500		302	5/22	
3	6-17	400	10,475	218	8,439	13,000		396	9/24	see line 18
4	5-00	415	10,650	105	4,310	7,000		288	11/21	Three-blade propeller
5	5-48	450	10,800	100	4,458	7,000	3¼	292	2/22	Two-blade propeller
6	7-36	300	6,400	82	4,453	7,000	2¾	301A	5/22	Three-blade propeller
7	7-12	374	8,800	82	4,613	7,200	2¾	307	7/22	
8	5-26	495	14,450	45	2,358	3,900	2¾	347	9/23	
9	6-21	410	10,500	150	6,768	11,000		440	11/25	
10	6-00	435	9,300	110	4,427	7,100	3½	290	1/22	
11	8-12	304	7,500	82	4,110	6,690	3	316	11/22	1,650lb freight
12	9-48	261	6,900	72	4,414	6,699		313	10/22	
13	5-45	460	12,100	72	4,390	6,750	3½	331	5/23	
14	4-55	535	14,000	260	12,462	18,460		432	9/25	
15	7-21	340	9,100	250	10,916	18,000		476	4/27	Landing speed 60mph
16	17-18 to 6,500 ft		12,900	164	4,780	9,500	10	514	2/29	Landing speed 52mph

Line	Height after distance travelled (ft/yd)	Landing run		Maximum speed		Report	
		with brakes (yd)	without brakes (yd)	Level (mph)	Dive (mph)	No	Date
17	95/546					476A	5/29
18	64/656					550	1/30
19	**218/546	64	206	132		514A	7/30
20	**255/507	181	288	142	164	638	3/34
21	123/546		240	103		524	3/29
22	116/546		263	108		524A	10/29
23	104/546	163	221	104		524C	5/30
24	110/546	182	413	115		524D	5/32
25	304/656			141		549	12/29
26	95/546		201			555	2/30
27	73/546		188			571	7/30
28	71/656		278			583	7/31
29	121/546	166	242			567	7/30
30						578	5/31
31	65/656	108	142			582	7/31
32	71/656	200	304			590	11/31
33	78/500	149	191	95		603	4/32
34	**100/656	272	543	138	204	658	11/34
35	**66/656	283				658A	12/34
36	** 60 /550	281	520	169		658A	5/36
37					230	658D	5/37
38	73 /656		330	147		609	7/32
39	84 /656	220**	380**	116		611	10/32
40	313 (run)	159**	416**	140		611A	8/33

** corrected to 5mph headwind

Line	Type	Identity	Engines No.	Type	Fuel capacity (Imp gal)	Seats (crew – pass)	All-up weight for C of A (lb)	Height after 3min (ft)
41	Valetta	G-AAJY	3	Jupiter XIFP	360	2 –16	23,500	1,600
42	P.71A	G-ACOX	2	Jaguar VIAA	186	1 – 7	9,400	2,500 (2min)
43	Scion	G-ACJT	2	Pobjoy R	30	1 – 4	3,000	1,650
44	Scion	G-ACUZ	2	Pobjoy R	31	1 –	3,200	
45	Scion Senior	G-AECU	4	Niagara III	58	1 – 9	5,750	2,350
46	Scylla	G-ACJJ	4	Jupiter X FBM	652	2–29	33,500	1,435
47	D.H.84	E9	2	Gipsy Major	57	1–6	4,200	1,850
48	D.H.89	E4	2	Gipsy Six	80	1–6	5,000	2,950
49	D.H.89	G-ADWZ	2	Gipsy Six	74	1–6	5,500	2,700
50	D.H.90	G-ADNA	2	Gipsy Major	86	2–3	4,000	2,170
51	D.H.86	E2	4	Gipsy Six	114	2–10	9,200	3,180
52	D.H.86A	G-ADYH	4	Gipsy Six Srs II	189	2–	10,250	3,100
53	D.H.86B	E2	4	Gipsy Six Srs I	191	2–8	10,250	
54	Avro 652	G-ACRM	2	Cheetah V	123		7,400	2,080
55	Ford 5AT-D	G-ACAE	3	Wasp C		2–8	14,000	
56	Double Eagle	Y-1	2	Gipsy Major	55	1–4	3,600	2,100
57	Percival Q.6	X1	2	Gipsy Six Srs II	80	1–5	5,252	1,850
58	Albatross	G-AEVV	4	Gipsy Twelve	860	3 (mail)	29,500	1,950
59	Frobisher	E.2	4	Gipsy Twelve	444	2–	29,500	2,100
60	Ensign	G-ADSR	4	Tiger IXC	675	2–32	49,000	1,600
61	Ensign	G-ADSW	4	Tiger IXC		2–	48,500	2,800
62	Flamingo	G-AFUE	2	Perseus XIIC			16,500	3,450
63	Lockhead 14	G-AFGN	2	Wright Cyclone			17,500	2,950

Line	Height after distance travelled (ft/yd)	Landing run with brakes (yd)	Landing run without brakes (yd)	Maximum speed Level (mph)	Maximum speed Dive (mph)	Report No	Date
41	314 (run)	280**		122		612	10/33
42	**128/656	270	560		172	655	10/34
43	**125/550	147**	212**	115	152	635	2/34
44					165	635A	2/35
45	**126/656	195	335		176	693	7/36
46	**66/640	234	465	126	135	641	5/34
47	**142/546	198	284			614	12/32
48	**200/656	265	500		195	643	6/34
49	**100/656	220	510		215	643B	4/36
50	**93/656	195			182	685	2/36
51	**140/656	260		171	194	636	2/34
52	**80/656	239				636B	12/36
53	**103/656	227			205	636D	12/36
54	100/656	210			210	663	4/35
55	**144/656	256		152		627	8/33
56	**110/656	172			240	698	11/36
57	**66/500	255			220	721	2/38
58	**66/730	380		213	230	728A	9/38
59	**64/656	over 328			225	728	9/38
60	**59/656	280			202	726	6/38
61	**80/656				197	726A	5/39
62	**66/525	310			250	745	7/39
63	**66/656	280				729	9/38

** corrected to 5mph headwind

Civil Aircraft – Non-Public Transport

English Electric Wren J6973 in September 1923; the engine is hidden behind the wing in this view. (British Crown Copyright/MOD)

This group comprises aeroplanes and autogiros for the private owner and for training; it includes some purchased by the Air Ministry.

Before about 1929, Martlesham tests of light types were made at the direction of the Air Ministry, or under the scheme for makers to have their products tested on payment of a fee of £20. From 1929, when the system of awarding Certificates of Airworthiness was changed, the Establishment made tests on light civil aeroplanes to assess their suitability for C of A.

There is a dearth of photographs for the period 1928-31; it may be that financial constraints were responsible and that none was taken.

Among the first postwar interests both of manufacturers and the Air Ministry was the challenge of producing the lightest practicable aeroplane. At least thirteen types with an all-up weight under 1,000lb reached Martlesham between August 1923 and September 1926, although four were not subject to the normal reporting action, possibly as the four were present only for weighing.

First, in August 1923, came the English Electric Wren J6973 with the

3hp engine (using the current RAC rating system) which used the tarmac apron to avoid the tailskid catching in the heather roots of the aerodrome; aileron reversal was suspected, but otherwise control was acceptable. One pilot commented that the Wren was 'priceless'. Next, eight months later, came the Gnosspelius Gull; a report

Hawker Cygnet with Anzani engine, early 1925. (British Crown Copyright/MOD)

was produced but no performance figures. Later in 1924 two Hawker Cygnets (Mk I with Anzani and Mk II with Scorpion) were photographed, handled but apparently neither reported on nor assessed. The Avro 560 J7322, two Parnall Pixies J7323 and J7324 *(line 2)*, and two D.H.53 Humming Birds J7325 and J7326 *(line 3)*, all single-seaters with Blackburne Tomtit engines of 700cc capacity appeared over New Year 1925. One pilot commented that the Pixie was 'very nose heavy – a nasty little brute'. Other comments were that the Avro 560 was 'inferior to the D.H.53', while the latter was 'delightful' and 'nice on all controls'. The consecutive num-

Avro Type 560 J7322 in January 1925. (British Crown Copyright/MOD)

bering of these three types indicates simultaneous purchase by the Air Ministry, logically with a view to comparing them; as the D.H.53 was already in Service, the object may have been to select the most suitable light aircraft for the planned airship hook-up trials (performed by the RAE later in 1925 using the D.H.53). A second Pixie, G-EBJG (line 4), was assessed some six months after the Light Aircraft Competition for which it was built. G-EBJG reappeared in August 1925 modified to be the only biplane of the very light aircraft tested, and thereby adding 50 per cent to its cciling (line 5), which nevertheless remained low.

In early 1925 two competitors from the previous years Light Aircraft Competition were purchased by the Air Ministry – the Air Navigation and Engineering Co ANEC I J7506 (line 6), and the Raynham Light Plane J7518. Contemporaneously tested

Parnall Pixie G-EBJG in February 1925 as a biplane. (British Crown Copyright/MOD)

Aerial Navigiation and Engineering Company's ANEC I light aircraft in mid-1924, apparently before purchase by the Air Ministry. (British Crown Copyright/MOD)

was the single-seat Avro 562 Avis, G-EBKP (line 7), and the Cranwell C.L.A.2; the latter is believed to have crashed while at Martlesham. The ANEC 'thoroughly frightened' one pilot who flew it, another pilot thought the Raynham 'not good'. While the ceiling of the Avis at 1,150ft was lamentable and the Cranwell C.L.A.2 found difficulty in taking off;

Pixie G-EBJG in the summer of 1925 as a monoplane. (British Crown Copyright/MOD)

Parnall Pixie J7323 in August 1924. (British Crown Copyright/MOD)

these four were hardly good practical machines.

Finally, three types of light machines were flown at Martlesham late in 1925 and 1926. The Bristol Brownie, G-EBJK (line 8), a two-seater with wooden wings and later steel wing structure, paid at least two visits; the performance quoted is for the wooden structure, and taken from the only report issued; it was found to

Raynham Light Plane J7518 in early 1925. (British Crown Copyright/ MOD)

be 'heavy laterally' by one pilot – and 'a curious little toy with too little rudder' by another. Earlier, another Brownie, G-EBJL with steel wing, was judged to have a 'lifeless aerofoil'; further comment is lacking. The Beardmore W.B.XXIV Wee Bee I G-EBJJ *(line 9)* had a bad take off and was too cramped. Finally, the Cranwell C.L.A.4 G-EBPB paid a short visit after the *Daily Mail* trials at

The Beardmore W.B.XXIV Wee Bee I G-EBJJ in early 1926. (British Crown Copyright/MOD)

Avro 562 Avis G-EBKP in early 1925. (British Crown Copyright/MOD)

Bristol Brownie G-EBJK in late 1925. (British Crown Copyright/MOD)

Lympne in 1926; nothing is known about the AAEE trials. Similarly, apart from the pilot's log book comments quoted, there is no information available on the behaviour in a significant wind of any of the light aircraft mentioned above; apart from the D.H.53 none appears to have been acceptable.

Of the remaining light civil types of aeroplane tested in the first ten years after the war all but the earliest, the Bristol Type 73 Taxiplane, were evaluated for training. In the event, the Taxiplane could not be recommended for its intended role as an air taxi with

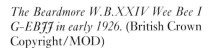

Cranwell C.L.A.4A G-EBPB in mid-1926. (British Crown Copyright/MOD)

Bristol Type 83A Trainer G-EBGE in late 1925. (British Crown Copyright/MOD)

two passengers as the performance was poor. G-EBEY tested in July 1924 *(line 11)* with the 111hp Bristol Lucifer was only marginally better than the earlier G-EBEW in mid-1923 *(line 10)*, with the original 100hp engine, and the type was restricted to one passenger plus the pilot. The slimmer and lighter version of the Taxiplane, the Bristol Type 83A Lucifer G-EBGE *(line 12)* achieved a performance in November 1925 satis-factory for training.

Two civil versions of the wartime Avro 504 at Martlesham were the Type 548A, G-EBKN *(line 13)* in April 1925 fitted with an 80hp Renault engine modernised by the Aircraft Disposal Co, and the Type 504R Gosport G-EBNE *(line 14)*, in September 1926. The latter was a refined 504, but with the wartime Gnome Monsoupape engine; perform-ance was inferior to the Service 504N, but met civil requirements. The same year, the Westland Widgeon G-EBRO appeared; the only report on the type extant describes a breakage in fuel tank restraint during a slow roll. No fewer than five Blackburn Bluebirds graced the Suffolk skies starting with G-EBKD, *(line 15)*, the Bluebird I, powered by the new Genet I in early 1927 some six

months after the Certificate of Airworthiness had been granted fol-lowing tests by RAE Farnborough. Next was the Bluebird IV G-AABV

Avro 504R Gosport G-EBNE in Oct-ober 1926. (British Crown Copyright/MOD)

for C of A trials early in 1929, shortly followed by two visits of G-AACC with a Cirrus III engine in place of the Gipsy I of G-AABV. Towards the end of the year the Saunders-Roe-built Bluebird IV G-AAIR (Cirrus III) was tested for its C of A. Contemporary with the Bluebird was the de

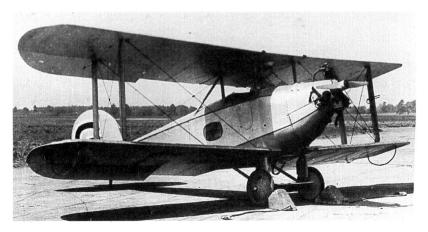

Blackburn Bluebird I G-EBKD in late 1925, with the original Blackburne Thrush 1,100cc engine; no record of any tests with this engine has been found. (British Crown Copyright/MOD)

de Havilland D.H.60T Moth Trainer E-3 in May 1931. (British Crown Copyright/MOD)

Havilland Moth which first appeared at Martlesham in RAF form, followed at the end of 1929 by the metal-framed Civil Moth (a D.H.60M temporarily identified as E.2). Moth Trainers G-ABKM and E.3 were flown in mid-1931; the former making the some-what sketchy tests for the C of A, and the latter extensive performance tests, probably in connection with an order for the Moth from the Swedish Air Force. Several other early D.H.60 Moths were flown at AAEE but no reports were written; they included G-EBUW, G-EBQX, G-AACD and G-EDCA, the last being the official aircraft of the Director of Civil Aviation. Both the Bluebird and the Moth saw widespread use at home and overseas, but several of their contemporaries in 1929 and 1930 were not so commercially successful, although the Hawker Tomtit both with Mongoose engine (G-AAS1) and Wolseley (G-ABOD) was robust, viceless and handled well.

At least three Simmonds Spartan aircraft were tested including G-EBYU and G-AAMH between

Hawker Tomtit G-AAS1 in late 1930. (British Crown Copyright/MOD)

December 1928 and October 1929. The latter was severely criticised on grounds of structural safety because the ailerons had excessive backlash and the wings (of 4ft greater span than the earlier models) were too flexible and thus liable to flutter; a C of A was withheld for G-AAMH although the earlier models appear to have been sat-isfactory as nearly fifty examples were produced and flown.

The only civil Avro Avian reported on by AAEE was the final version the Type 616 Avian IVM (G-AACV) *(line 16)* with Cirrus III engine; a C of A in the aerobatic category was recom-

Avro 621 Tutor G-AAKT in late 1929 – apparently considered worthy of a photograph on account of its testing for possible Service use. (British Crown Copyright/MOD)

The Cierva C.19 Mk III Autogiro G-AAYP early in 1932. (Imperial War Museum)

mended with a restricted forward limit to the CG as the type was very nose heavy. Earlier, the Type 581 Avian prototype G-EBOV in 1926 and Avian IV G-AACF in 1928 were flown but no reports issued; G-EBOV is preserved in Brisbane, Queensland.

The de Havilland D.H.83 Fox Moth G-ABUO in April 1932. (British Crown Copyright/MOD)

The Clarke Cheetah (later G-AAJK) with a 1,100cc Thrush engine and a civil D.H.9A G-AADU with extended aft CG were briefly flown, as was the Henderson Gadfly G-AAEY *(line 17)*. The Gadfly had ineffective Pearson rotary ailerons producing unpleasant handling – possibly also due to lack of structual stiffness, and its engine stopped in spins; a C of A was not recommended. Conversely, a

Cierva C.30P Autogiro G-ACKA in January 1934 – the third type of Autogiro to reach Martlesham Heath. (British Crown Copyright/MOD)

C of A was recommended for the Parnall Elf G-AAFH *(line 18)* following its second visit in 1930 *(line 19)* after the control slots had been sealed, but in spite of directional instability and lack of control co-ordination. Another Henderson design, the monoplane pusher H.S.F.1 G-EBVF *(line 20)* with twin fuselage booms was initially deemed too dangerous to fly in 1929; after strengthening in 1930 to the satisfaction of the RAE structural experts, AAEE pilots found the controls heavy and the ailerons sloppy and disconcerting in bumps. Two attempts, one in 1929 and the other in 1930, were needed to produce satisfactory handling, performance and structure of the Civilian Aircraft Company's Coupé monoplane G-AAIL *(lines 21 and 22)* after pilots initially criticised the apalling view and the dangerous take off and landing while the weak structure resulted in five engine bearers breaking and the undercarriage collapsing. Similar undercarriage disintegration attended the Desoutter G-AAPK, but the Southern Martlet G-AAII *(line 23)* appears to have had no major problems, nor did the amphibian Moth

de Havilland D.H.85 Leopard Moth E.1 in June 1933. (British Crown Copyright/MOD)

Blackburn B-2 G-ABWI. (British Crown Copyright/MOD)

G-AADV *(line 24)* which the AAEE endorsed for land operations, the C of A already recommended by MAEE, Felixstowe, for flying from water.

No fewer than ten types of British light aircraft were first tested at Martlesham in 1930 – a remarkable total in the light of the economic plight of the country. First, in January, was the Mongoose-powered Avro 621 Tutor G-AAKT *(line 25)*, for which the C of A report to DCA was based on the assessment already made for the RAF on its suitability as

Miles M.1 Satyr G-ABVG in November 1932. (British Crown Copyright/MOD)

aircraft appears to comply in every respect with the requirements for C of A.' Praise indeed, and coupled with the pilots' reort 'A most excellent aircraft – free from vibrations and drumming' – no wonder less than 48hr were

a military trainer. Another civil Tutor, G-AARZ with Lynx engine, was test flown later in 1930 but purely for its military training potential. Next was an ultra light, the A.B.C. Robin G-AAID *(line 26)*, with a gross weight of only 739lb but underpowered and difficult to land; the Chief Engineer made many criticisms of the construction, yet a C of A was recommended once the worst failings were rectified. Another ultra-light flown was the Comper Swift G-AARX. Much more practical were the three-seat de Havilland Puss Moth and five-seat Hawk Moth, the former with its inverted Gipsy III engine and metal airframe. The Puss Moth G-AATC *(line 27)* attracted the following comments from the Chief Engineer, 'The

R.A.E. Scarab G-ABOH in early 1933. (British Crown Copyright/MOD)

needed for the whole C of A tests. Four years later, G-ABMD *(line 28)*, with a high-compression engine, flaps and drooping ailerons, was briefly assessed before a competition in Poland, and it was praised, although pilots appear to have been wary of the aerodynamic innovations. The Hawk Moth G-AAUZ *(line 29)* attracted less enthusiastic comments due to a flat glide, fierce brakes, and sluggish ailerons; a C of A was recommended within a restricted CG range, and weight limited to meet the take-off requirements.

In June 1930 the first twin-engined aircraft in this category, the Segrave

Miles M.2 Hawk G-ACHJ in July 1933. (British Crown Copyright/MOD)

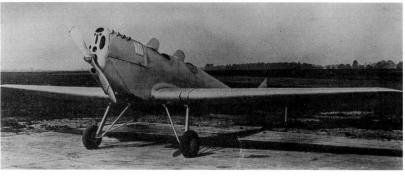

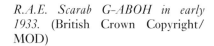

Spartan Clipper G-ACEG in June 1933. (British Crown Copyright/ MOD)

Meteor, G-AAXP *(line 30)*, built by Saunders-Roe, was tested. A limited C of A was recommended in spite of doubts about passenger safety, inability to fly on one engine due to excessive rudder forces and a propensity to enter an immediate spin at the stall. After three months G-AAXP *(line 31)* returned with aerodynamic improvements but was again extensively criticised, partly on the grounds that the pilot sat on the right. In March 1931, the Blackburn-built Segrave I G-ABFP *(line 32)* with metal fuselage frame, wings moved aft and better rudder was found to be much better, but asymmetric handling was still interesting.

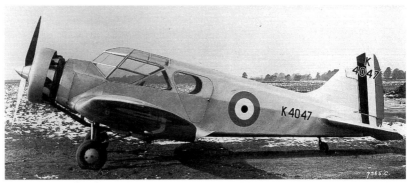

Airspeed Courier K4047 in February 1934, with exhaust manifold. (British Crown Copyright/MOD)

The final four light applicants for C of A in 1930 were the Hendy 302, the Spartan Arrow, Avro 625 Avian Monoplane, and Robinson Redwing. The Hendy 302 G-AAVT *(line 33)* had a disappointing view, a flat glide and a complicated fuel system, while the Arrow G-AAWY *(line 34)* was well liked, including the aerobatics, as was the single-seat Avian Monoplane G-AAYV *(line 35)*. Martlesham's reaction to the Redwing II (Genet IIA engine) G-ABDO is unknown. Similarly no 1931 report appears to exist for the interesting Arrow Active G-ABIX, a single-seater with the new inverted Hermes engine. A brief report on the de Havilland D.H.82 Tiger Moth G-ABPH says that the increase in sweepback and larger dihedral made no noticeable difference to the handling when compared with the earlier E5. So were settled the shape of the ubiquitous Tiger Moth and

Shackleton-Murray S.M.1 light aircraft G-ACBP in August 1933. (British Crown Copyright/MOD)

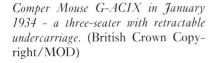

Comper Mouse G-ACIX in January 1934 - a three-seater with retractable undercarriage. (British Crown Copyright/ MOD)

de Havilland D.H.87A Hornet Moth E-1 in May 1935 illustrates the unfinished state in which many aircraft were submitted for C of A trials. (British Crown Copyright/MOD)

Martlesham's approval of the type. Reports for the Avro Cadet G-ABRS with the Genet Major engine, and the Avro Club Cadet G-ACAY with folding wings are missing, as are those for two versions of the civil Autogiro mentioned below.

In early 1932, the Cierva C.19 Mk IV Autogiro G-AAYP, with Genet Major IV power was the first rotary-wing aircraft to be tested at AAEE; its all up weight was 1,549lb. A somewhat tentative report includes comments on the low rotor speed of 140rpm

de Havilland T.K.1 E.3 in July 1934. (British Crown Copyright/MOD)

de Havilland T.K.2 E.3 in August 1935 in original form. (British Crown Copyright/MOD)

Avro 641 Commodore G-ACNT in May 1934 with Lynx engine. (British Crown Copyright/MOD)

achieved on take off (180rpm was normal), the easy landing and the susceptibility to gusts. The cockpit was uncomfortable and exceptionally difficult to enter. Maximum speed at 3,000ft was 95mph (true) and ceiling 8,800ft. A second Autogiro, the de Havilland-built C.24 G-ABLM followed in April 1932, and received its C of A the same month. Late the following year, the improved C.30P, G-ACKA, built by Airwork and powered with a 140hp Genet Major, quickly passed its tests for the Type C of A; many C.30s were built thereafter.

The de Havilland D.H.83 Fox Moth G-ABUO *(line 36)* needed replacement of an undercarriage leg after contending with the heath at Martlesham in April 1932, but was generally satisfactory in the air, as was the D.H.85 Leopard Moth E.1/ G-ACHD *(lines 37 and 38)* a year

later. The latter type was recommended in the aerobatic category once the passenger's seat had a seat harness, even though the ailerons were poor for slow rolls. Test pilots recommended that a cockpit notice should be fitted in the Leopard Moth to remind pilots of the special undercarriage leg fairings which could be rotated to act as airbrakes – a recommendation made as the result of experience, perhaps?

The Blackburn B-2 was tested in its production form, G-ABWI *(line 39)*, for C of A and found easy and pleasant to fly, if a little cramped. In late 1932 the first true Miles aircraft – the single-seat Satyr, G-ABVG *(line 40)*, was also cramped but otherwise satisfactory, provided that four minor

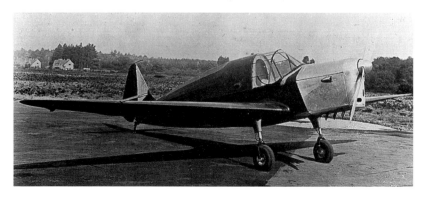

de Havilland T.K.2 E5 in May 1938 – is the same aircraft as E-3 in previous photograph but considerably modified with scant regard for appearance. (British Crown Copyright/MOD)

de Havilland T.K.4 E-4 in August 1937. (British Crown Copyright/ MOD)

Percival Mew Gull G-ACND in July 1934 was unstable. (British Crown Copyright/MOD)

modifications were incorporated. Only six months later the second Miles design, the monoplane M.2 Hawk, G-ACHJ *(line 41)*, appeared, it was tiring to fly and had a long landing run. No adverse comments were made on the Scarab, G-ABOH *(line 42)*, a diminutive single-seater by the sister Establishment at Farnborough. Six months later, in June 1933, catastrophe appears to have been close during tests of the Spartan Clipper

Miles M.4 Merlin U-8 in June 1935. (British Crown Copyright/MOD)

G-ACEG when there was 'serious wing oscillation in rectilinear flight at 100mph' – *ie* flutter. The type had large ailerons with servo tabs but no mass- or aerodynamic-balances; the modifications recommended were not subsequently tested at Martlesham.

Tests on the Airspeed Courier G-ABXN *(line 43)* were in two parts – undercarriage up and then down; such thorough examination of this novel item will have increased confidence – and decreased forgetfulness. Raising the wheels improved climb to 5,000ft by four minutes and top speed by 30mph. Initially a weight restriction was applied due to the long landing run. Wheelbrakes were fitted to Courier G-ACJL *(line 44)* and the permitted weight consequently increased, allowing five passengers to be carried. The RAF's sole Courier K4047 was another 100lb heavier, but still achieved a creditable 137½mph (true) at 5,000ft in spite of the reduced performance from fitting exhaust manifolds. The Courier was the Service's first aeroplane with retractable undercarriage.

Cs of A were recommended for the Hirth-engined Shackleton-Murray S.M.1 pusher G-ACBP *(line 45)*, provided two strengthening modifications were made; for the British Klemm Swallow G-ACMK *(line 46)* with its flat glide, and for the Klemm Eagle G-ACRG *(line 47)* with ineffective brakes on its retractable undercarriage.

The 1934 reports on the Comper Mouse G-ACIX (Gipsy Major) and Avro 641 G-ACNT (Lynx IV) are missing.

de Havilland continued to keep the Establishment busy with four versions

Hendy Heck G-AEGH in June 1936. (British Crown Copyright/MOD)

of the D.H.87 Hornet Moth. The first protoptye, E.6, *(line 48)*, and the slightly heavier D.H.87A E.1 *(line 49)* were passed without criticism, although in the hands of private owners the type displayed an unpleasant wing drop at the stall. G-ADMS *(line 37)* was tested in 1936 with square wingtips replacing the tapered design, and G-ADMT was assessed for training service in India; spinning was passed as acceptable provided only 50lb (7 Imp gal) of fuel was carried with two people. The workmanlike T.K.1 E.3 *(line 50)*, designed by de Havilland Technical School students had no difficulty in passing its tests for the C of A in July 1934. Some two years later the T.K.2 E.3 *(line 51)*, was assessed noisy and cramped with an extra fuel tank in the right seat; the T.K.2, as E.5, returned in June 1938 in modified form and was then found to be stable.

Flown for the normal and special categories of the C of A, the lethal

De Bruyne Snark G-ADDL, of novel construction and unpleasant handling, in mid-1935. (British Crown Copyright/MOD)

looking T.K.4 E-4 *(line 52)* handled well up to 235mph (indicated), but had the very high stalling speed of 95mph (indicated) with flaps up.

A glance at the performance table reveals the advance made by the Percival Mew Gull G-ACND *(line 53)*, in climb and top speed – but at the expense of landing distance; this

first aircraft was unstable longitudinally and neutrally stable in roll and yaw. Modifications, unspecified but taking over a year, rendered G-ACND *(line 54)*, stable but elevator sensitivity gave the impression of instability – a C of A was recommended with the caveat that only experienced pilots should fly the machine. In 1937, with a Series II Gipsy Six engine Mew Gull X2 *(line 55)* possessed a vicious stall at high weight – but controls were well harmonized.

The Comper Streak G-ACNC (line 56), possessed high speed characteristics similar to the Gull; the landing run was long, while the electrical system and aileron control arrangement were among other criticisms.

The Miles M.3 Falcon U3/G-ACTM *(line 57)*, was submitted for C of A trials in October 1934

Heston Phoenix G-ADAD in October 1935. (British Crown Copyright/MOD)

before its participation in the Mac.Robertson race to Australia. It was later fitted with extra fuel tanks, but normal fuel capacity was flown at Martlesham where the type was found to have good handling characteristics, but poor brakes and no emergency exit in the roof. The latter shortcomings were not considered as significant as the lack of a 'No Smoking' label in the cockpit. Eight months later the slightly larger five-seat Miles M.4 Merlin U8/G-ADFE *(line 58)* was also criticised for poor brakes with poor under-

Percival Vega Gull G-AEAD in February 1936 without spats. (British Crown Copyright/MOD)

Hillson Praga G-AEON in November 1936. (British Crown Copyright/ MOD)

carriage damping, but in spite of these shortcomings was recommended for a C of A.

In early 1935 favourable recommendations for Cs of A were made for two other types, which nevertheless had unsatisfactory handling characteristics. The Hendy Heck G-ACTC *(line 59)* had a very strong nose-down change of trim with lowering of the flaps which could only be held by retrimming – a situation aggravated by the position for the right hand of the trim control – together with flap and undercarriage controls; the throttle was placed for the left hand. G-ACTC was also unstable longitudinally with flaps down – a phenomenon cured by the time Heck IIC G-AEGH *(line 60)*, was tested in 1936 – but the latter retained unpleasant trim change with flap lowering which made landing difficult. A Heck, K8853, purchased by the Air Ministry for gunnery trials, had two old Browning guns in each wing; ground trials only were made, and they were also unsatisfactory due to stoppages caused by faulty hydraulic feeding of the ammunition.

The unpleasant and tiring de Bruyne Snark G-ADDL *(line 61)* (the

sole example built) with ineffective rudder and poor elevator controls did not use its restricted C of A for long as it was bought by the Air Ministry for the aerodynamicists at Farnborough to broaden their experience.

C.L.W. Curlew G-ADYU in November 1936. (British Crown Copyright/ MOD)

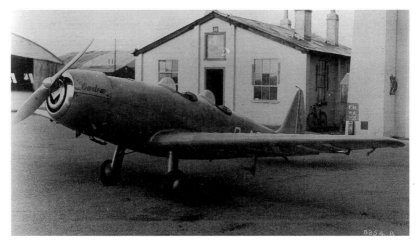

General Aircraft Cygnet I G-AEMA in June 1938. (British Crown Copyright/MOD)

Miles M.7A Nighthawk U-5 in February 1936. (British Crown Copyright/MOD)

Pilots and engineers at AAEE did not find fault with the Heston Phoenix G-ADAD *(line 62)*, or Percival Vega Gull G-AEAD *(line 63)*, tested in the winter of 1935-6. Both had Gipsy Six engines and yet the Vega Gull cruised some 25mph faster than the Phoenix, despite the latter having a retractable undercarriage. Percival may have hoped for an even faster cruising speed for his Vega Gull, as it was dived to 225mph *(ie* 150 percent expected cruising speed). A second Phoenix G-AEHJ was spun and dived to 208mph in September 1936, five months before trials on the long-range Vega Gull G-AEKE with a Series II

Moss Bros M.A.1 G-AEST in August 1937. (British Crown Copyright/ MOD)

Foster Wickner Wicko G-AEZZ in February 1938, with a trimmer, brakes and spats. (British Crown Copyright/MOD)

Gipsy Six.

Three two-seaters at the end of 1936 were the Hillson Praga G-AEON *(line 64)*, the C.L.W. Curlew G-ADYU *(line 65)*, and the Aeronca 100 G-AENW *(line 66)*. The Curlew was submitted for the aerobat-ic category and had light controls whereas the other types had heavy controls, suitable for the normal category; all three needed modifications before Cs of A could be granted.

Miles had its M.7 Nighthawk U5 (G-AEBP), M.2H Hawk Trainer G-AENT and M.11 Whitney Straight G-AECT tested within a few months. The Nighthawk was acceptable for C of A, but failed to meet Military standards; the Nighthawk and Hawk

Trainer are described under Trainers. The generally similar Whitney Straight was preferred although the new moulded Perspex windscreen was liable to scratching and visual distortion.

C.W. Aircraft sold out to General Aircraft Ltd during the year it took to remedy the lack of elevator authority

Aeronca Ely G-AEVE in October 1938. (British Crown Copyright/MOD)

and ineffective rudder plus other shortcomings of their metal-skinned Cygnet G-AEMA *(line 67)*. In July 1938 *(line 68)*, it was finally recommended for an aerobatic C of A, but approval was limited to three months or until some rivets were officially approved.

The British-made Foster Wikner Wicko G-AEZZ *(line 69)* was not liked initially, it had no elevator trimmer, was very tiring to fly and lacked

Tipsy B G-AFGF in July 1938. (British Crown Copyright/MOD)

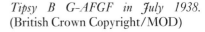

wheelbrakes. Some five months later, in February 1938, G-AEZZ *(line 70)*, re-engined with a Gipsy Major met with success in the normal categories subject to minor improvement, and G-AFKK was recommended for an aerobatic C of A in July 1938.

Moss Brothers, a name more normally associated with winged collars, submitted their first aeroplane, the M.A.1 G-AEST *(line 71)*. It was recommended for a C of A with restricted forward CG; lack of an elevator trimmer made assessment of stability difficult as the aeroplane was always nose heavy.

The first British built Tipsy, a model B, G-AFGF *(line 72)*, had insufficient rudder on its first visit in August 1938 for an aerobatic C of A; with greater rudder travel and 18 percent increase in area, aerobatics for the private owner were approved in December. Early in 1939 the Aeronca Ely, G-AEVE *(line 73)* was found to have poorly harmonized controls and a stalling speed of 53mph (indicated) – a cockpit placard said it was 40mph. The Reid and Sigrist R.S.1 Snargasher three-seater G-AEOD *(line 74)* had good handling in normal and aerobatic flight and a C of A was recommended once the tendency of the hood to jam was remedied.

Reid and Sigrist R.S.1 Snargasher G-AEOD in May 1939. (British Crown Copyright/MOD)

Civil aircraft – non-public transport (mostly single-engine)

Line	Type	Identity	Engine Type	Power (bhp/rpm)	Seats	Wing area (sq ft)	Maximum speed (mph/ft)
1	Wren	J6973	ABC	3/ –	1	166	49/
2	Pixie	J7323	Tomtit	23/3,250	1		66/3,000
3	D.H.53	J7325	Tomtit	22/3,250	1	121	70/3,000
4	Pixie III	G-EBJG	Cherub I	24/2,500	2	137	72/1,000
5	Pixie IIIA	G-EBJG	Cherub	24/2,500	2	237	65/1,000
6	ANEC I	J7506	Tomtit	23/3,250	1	138	72/3,000
7	Avis	G-EBKP	Cherub	24/2,500	1	246	62/1,000
8	Brownie	G-EBJK	Cherub	24/2,500	2	205	69/3,000
9	Wee Bee I	G-EBJJ	Cherub	24/2,500	2	185	85/3,000
10	Taxiplane	G-EBEW	Lucifer	100/1,600	3	292	86/3,000
11	Taxiplane	G-EBEY	Lucifer	111/1,600	3	292	84/3,000
12	Bristol Trainer	G-EBGE	Lucifer	128/1,700	2	268	87/6,500
13	Avro 548A	G-EBKN	ADC	110/1,800	2		83/3,000
14	Gosport	G-EBNE	Monosoupape	108/1,233	2	311	87/6,500
15	Bluebird	G-EBKD	Genet I	71/1,850	2	230	84/3,000

Line	Type	Identity	Engine/s Type	Fuel capacity (Imp gal)	Seats	All-up weight for C of A Normal (lb)	Aerobat (lb)	Height after 3min (ft)
16	Avian	G-AACV	Cirrus III	22	2	1,600	1,450	1,450
17	Gadfly	G-AAEY	Scorpion II	9		744		1,200
18	Elf	G-AAFH	Hermes	22	2	1,651	1,551	1,170
19	Elf	G-AAFH	Hermes			1,700	1,600	1,470
20	H.F.S.1	G-EBVF	Puma	32		4,112		915
21	Civilian Coupé	G-AAIL	Hornet	15	2	1,493		1,160
22	Civilian Coupé	G-AAIL	Hornet	16	2	1,505		1,400
23	Martlet	G-AAII	Hornet			1,030		2,500
24	Moth (amphib)	G-AADV	Gipsy	15	2	1,644		1,530
25	Tutor	G-AAKT	Mongoose	30	2		2,230	1,970
26	Robin	G-AAID	Scorpion II	9	1	739		1,175
27	Puss Moth	G-AATC	Gipsy III	21	3	1,900		1,850
28	Puss Moth	G-ABMD	Gipsy Major	35		2,050		
29	Hawk Moth	G-AAUZ	Lynx VIA	65	5	3,870*		2,130
30	Meteor	G-AAXP	2 Gipsy III	47	4	2,951		2,550
31	Segrave I	G-AAXP	2 Gipsy III	42	4	2,958		2,400
32	Meteor	G-ABFP	2 Gipsy III	52	4	3,296		
33	Hendy 302	G-AAVT	Hermes	25	2	1,700		2,430
34	Arrow	G-AAWY	Hermes	21	2	1,750	1,560	1,625
35	Avian Monoplane	G-AAYV	Genet Major	28	1	1,351		2,500
36	Fox Moth	G-ABUO	Gipsy III	25	4	2,100		1,100
37	Leopard Moth	E.1	Gipsy Major	35	3	2,150		1,530
38	Leopard Moth	G-ACHD	Gipsy Major	35	3	2,225	1,750	1,620
39	Blackburn B-2	G-ABWI	Gipsy III	22	2	1,770	1,547	1,960
40	Satyr	G-ABVG	Pobjoy R	7	1	900	900	2,700

*Reduced to 3,600lb for full C of A

Line	Climb to 3,000ft Time (min-sec)	Rate (ft/min)	Service ceiling (ft)	Fuel capacity (Imp gal)	Weight Empty (lb)	Gross (lb)	Report No	Date	Remarks
1						402	346	9/23	
2	13-48	180	6,250	5	301	529	392	12/24	Slower climb-mod rudder
3	16-22	155	5,700	2	349	551	401	1/25	
4	23-15	103	3,150	5½	486	825	408	7/25	Monoplane
5	19-00	130	4,550	5½	592	910	425	7/25	Biplane
6	11-50	235	8,700	2	384	583	411	4/25	
7	33-30	62	1,150	5	566	944	413	4/25	
8	14-52	176	7,450	4	542	915	433	10/25	Wooden structure
9	9-30	273	9,300	5½	509	890	442	12/25	
10	9-40	244	6,550	20	1,330	2,000	332	5/23	
11	9-16	255	6,950	24	1,369	2,000	387	7/24	
12	6-48	380	10,200	15	1,324	1,834	435	11/25	
13	8-30	285	7,050	17	1,459	2,114	412	4/25	
14	13-00 to 6,500ft	13,700	25	1,104	1,716	463	8/26		
15	7-54	332	10,100	12½	809	1,303	477	2/27	

Note: Line 14 reads "13-00 to 6,500ft" under Time, then 13,700 / 25 / 1,104 / 1,716 / 463 / 8/26.

Line	Height after distance travelled (ft/yd)	Landing Run with brakes (yd)	Landing Run without brakes (yd)	Maximum Speed Level (mph)	Maximum Speed Dive (mph)	Report No	Date
16	125yd run		155			519A	4/29
17			124			535/2	9/29
18	66/546		191			539	7/29
19	145yd run		136		200	539/2	6/30
20	278yd run		259			540/2	5/30
21	72/656		177			544	10/29
22	187yd run		258			544/2	6/30
23	66/265					542	9/29
24	118/656		145			547	10/29
25	138yd run		145	108		548	1/30
26	238yd run		197			559	5/30
27	106/546		146			564	5/30
28	71/656					564B	11/34
29	†227yd run	230	354			565	6/30
30	†141yd run		244	132		566	6/30
31	†130yd run	186	230			566/2	9/30
32						566A	3/31
33	†167yd run		193†			567	7/30
34	†168yd run		193†		170	568	7/30
35	153yd run		234			569	7/30
36	†80 /546	99	159†	106		605	5/32
37	†90 /656	198†	235†	108		620	7/33
38	†98/656	128†	258†		185	620/2	11/33
39	†120 /302		99†			613	11/32
40	†137/346		99†	108		615	12/32

† into 5mph wind

Line	Type	Identity	Engine/s Type	Fuel capacity (Imp gal)	Seats	All-up weight for C of A Normal (lb)	Aerobat (lb)	Height after 3min (ft)
41	Hawk	G-ACHJ	Cirrus III	23	2	1,800		1,510
42	Scarab	G-ABOH	Cherub III	4½	1	680		1,000
43	Courier	G-ABXN	Lynx IVC	131	2	3,700		1,475
44	Courier	G-ACJL	Lynx IVC	51	6	3,900		1,680
45	S.M.1	G-ACBP	Hirth HM 60	12	2	1,450		1,410
46	BK Swallow	G-ACMK	Salmson A.D.9R	19	2	1,550		1,740
47	BK Eagle	G-ACRG	Gipsy Major	38	3	2,300		1,550
48	D.H.87	E.6	Gipsy Major	26	2	1,800		2,000
49	D.H.87A	E.1	Gipsy Major	36	2	1,925		
50	T.K.1	E.3	Gipsy III	26	1	1,452		2,450
51	T.K.2	E.3	Gipsy Major HC	36	1	1,593		3,050
52	T.K.4	E.4	Gipsy Major	25	1	1,356		3,900
53	Mew Gull	G-ACND	Gipsy Six	24	1	1,520		4,200
54	Mew Gull	G-ACND	Gipsy Six	40	1	1,725		
55	Mew Gull	X.2	Gipsy Six srs II	50	1	1,875		
56	Streak	G-ACNC	Gipsy Major HC	46	1	1,260		3,450
57	Falcon	G-ACTM	Gipsy Major	32		2,000		2,200
58	Merlin	G-ADFE		51	5	3,000		1,780
59	Heck	G-ACTC	Gipsy Six	37		2,600		2,550
60	Heck IIC	G-AEGH	Gipsy Six	41	3	2,700		2650
61	Snark	G-ADDL		33	4	2,200		1,950
62	Phoenix	G-ADAD	Gipsy Six	51	5	3,313		1,705
63	Vega Gull	G-AEAD	Gipsy Six	41	4	2,775		2,650
64	Praga	G-AEON	Praga B		2	1,050		900
65	Curlew	G-ADYU	Niagara III		2	1,500	1,500	1,420
66	Aeronca 100	G-AENW	J AP		2	1,020		820
67	Cygnet	G-AEMA	Gipsy Major		2	1,596		2,060
68	Cygnet	G-AEMA	Gipsy Major		2	1,800		2,500
69	Wicko	G-AEZZ	Cirrus Major		2	1,520		2,900
70	Wicko	G-AEZZ	Gipsy Major		2	2,000	1,690	1,980
71	Moss M.A.1	G-AEST	Niagara III		1	1,400		1,850
72	Tipsy B	G-AFGF	Mikron II	10	2	1,073	1,045	1,300
73	Ely	G-AEVE	JAP	9	2	1,050		770
74	Reid & Sigrist R.S.1	G-AEOD	2 Gipsy Six	82	3	4,900	4,100	3,000

Line	Height after distance travelled (ft/yd)	Landing Run with brakes (yd)	without brakes (yd)	Maximum Speed Level (mph)	Dive (mph)	Report No	Date
41	†66/475		316†	111	180	622	7/33
42	†138/546		45†			616	2/33
43	†72/656		307	139		624	8/33
44	†84/656	137†	409†	148	213	624A	10/33
45	†160/656	97†	169†	80		626	9/33
46	†66/250		95	102		633	2/34
47	†114/656	252	332		180	633A	7/34
48	†124/400	135	235	117	174	649	7/34
49	†108/400	110	230		180	649A	6/35
50	†125/400		180		170	650	7/34
51	†150/450	260	347		195	683	1/36
52	†87/656		250		235	711	9/37
53	†144/656	354			240	651	7/34
54		240			245	651/2	10/35
55		250			230	651B	9/37
56	†143/656		300		210	652	7/34
57	†110/656	233			220	660	11/34
58	†73/656	270	420		210	671	6/35
59	†160/656	220	360		198	662	3/35
60	†85/550	162	276		220	662A	11/36
61	†175/656	135	190		158	670	6/35
62	†99/656	200	320		167	682	11/35
63	†118/656	135	325		225	687	2/36
64	†147yd run		70†		115	702	12/36
65	†290yd run		153†		180	701	2/37
66	†485yd run	125†			130	704	12/36
67	†143yd run	213†			174	712	9/37
68	†170yd run	140†			175	712/2	7/38
69	†145yd run		255†		185	714	9/37
70	†240yd run	195†			185	714/2	2/38
71	†160yd run	170†			180	713	9/37
72	†66/365		160		150	727	8/38
73	†66/254		180			731	1/39
74	†66/455	275†			203	744	7/39

† into 5mph wind

British Aircraft for Overseas

This section summarizes tests at AAEE on British aircraft for customers in twenty Colonial, Commonwealth and other Countries. In general, contracts for military aircraft were between the constructor and the purchasing government, and tests were made under arrangements between the former and the Air Ministry. At least until 1928, standard AAEE performance tests were completed in accordance with procedures agreed in 1920, and thus at the risk of the constructor.

Australia At the end of 1930, the all-metal Vickers Viastra VH-UOO with two geared Jupiter XIF engines completed the normal and brief British C of A trials before delivery to West Australian Airways. The Royal Australian Navy was to be the recipient of the Supermarine Seagull V, tested at Martlesham in prototype form as N-2 in September 1933; it was easy to fly with a take-off run of 155yd and landing in 156yd (with brakes) at maximum weight. Retested in February 1934, N-2 had satisfactory Vickers undercarriage legs replacing

Gloster Sparrowhawk J.N.400 in August 1921, for Japan. (British Crown Copyright/MOD)

Hawker Demon A1-1 in October 1935, for Australia.   The wheel chocks are marked APERT; the bombs are fitted for performance testing. (British Crown Copyright/MOD)

Avro Tutor E.59 in March 1936, for Greece. (British Crown Copyright/ MOD)

the earlier harsh and undamped Messier type. The four-engined de Havilland D.H.86 entered Australian service on the basis of C of A type trials for British airlines; the Australians, however, made several modifications including a seat for a second pilot. Following two unexplained fatal accidents to D.H.86s in the Dominion,

Panther-engined Hawker Fury 401 in December 1932, for Norway. (British Crown Copyright/MOD)

VH-USF was tested at the end of 1934, and included investigation into handling with one and two engines inoperative. It was found that the second pilot could foul the control column, as could rotating his movable seat; it was also found easy to exceed both the forward and aft CG limits. These findings were inconclusive but modifications to the D.H.86 were made before further service. In April 1936 the Australian version of the Hawker Demon A1-1 completed trials, following brief handling of Hart K2915 loaded to represent the Demon to Specification 1/34. The Demon A1-1 retained the type's delightful handling qualities, but had a great deal more equipment than its British counterpart; performance suffered accord-

Armstrong Whitworth Scimitar 405 in September 1935, for Norway. (British Crown Copyright/MOD)

ingly, with the time to climb to 15,000ft being nearly doubled.

Bolivia Vickers arranged for the last of six Type 143 Scouts for Bolivia to be flown at Martlesham with the Jupiter VIA engine; tests were restricted to the C of A requirements with 80gal of fuel, the all up weight of the Type 143 was 3,216lb and the Establishment commented that this

weight was the maximum authorised, and included no military equipment. Handling was good, spins satisfactory but very fast, and take off only 101yd.

Canada Some 2,400 rounds were fired from Blackburn Shark 525 in December 1938 to assess the Browning gun which replaced the armament of similar aircraft for the Fleet Air Arm.

Chile Vickers sent their Vixen V (Lion V) to Martlesham in early 1926 for independent assessment of the performance for their contract with Chile for eighteen of the type. Apparently the requirement was met, with a top speed of 130mph (true) at 6,500ft, and a ceiling of 15,750ft at the maximum weight of 5,552lb.

Eygpt Increased all up weight to 8,000lb, from the 7,400lb of the original Anson, necessitated further trials in October 1936 of the version for Egypt, SU-AAO. Performance with two Cheetah IX engines was similar to the lighter version and handling good although there was a large trim change with power adjustments. At Martlesham, over 8,000ft could be maintained on either engine alone.

Following criticisms of their D.H.86, de Havilland modified the type with revised controls and fins on the tailplane. The first with the improvements was tested in December 1936 as E.2, and was actually an Egyptian machine, SU-ABV.

Greece Four types for Greek service were tested at Martlesham Heath. In

Hawker Fury 204 in January 1935, for Persia with Bristol Mercury VI engine and variable-pitch propeller. (British Crown Copyright/MOD)

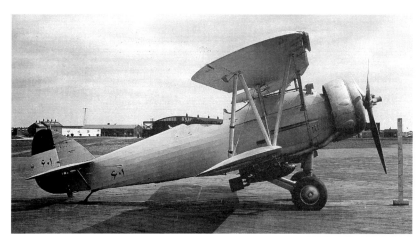

Hawker Hind 601 in April 1938, for Persia. The engine is a Bristol Mercury VIII. (British Crown Copyright/ MOD)

Hawker Fury 50 in June 1934, for Portugal. (British Crown Copyright/ MOD)

on the Cheetah V engined development of the Tutor known as the Avro 626. The Type 626, II8, established a top speed of 134mph and a service ceiling of 16,800ft. – typical of the type but tests insisted upon by the Greek authorities.

Hong Kong The Colonial postal authorities ordered a special Avro Avian, VR-HAC, with a mail compartment in place of the front cockpit, and extra fuel. Performance in August 1930 was similar to the Standard Avian, and aerobatics were easy. The reason for the latter is not clear.

India The Viceroy's special Avro 642/4m VT-AFM completed successfully normal C of A tests in November, 1934.

Iraq Early in 1931, a de Havilland Moth with Gipsy II engine was tested.

Japan A development of the Gloucestershire (later Gloster) Nighthawk was named Sparrowhawk for Japan, and the first, J.N.400, of fifty was fully tested in mid-1921.

Kenya Wilson Airways of Nairobi ordered a Westland IV with inline engines (probably Hermes) but the contract for VP-KAD was cancelled because engine-induced vibration on AAEE trials in late 1929 was so bad, in spite of rubber mountings, that C of A could not be recommended. The same operator ordered an Avro Five, VP-KAE, with three Genet Major engines which also did not meet the

1929, two Armstrong Whitworth Atlas with geared Jaguar engines were flown, the first in February and the second in April. In the same year, a Hawker Horsley for the Greek Navy completed standard performance measurements. Similar tests were made on Avro Tutor E.59 (Lynx IVC) in early 1936, and a little later,

Gloster Gladiator G5 in July 1938, for Portugal. (British Crown Copyright/ MOD)

Armstrong Whitworth Siskin S10 for Romania. The various weights have yet to be stencilled on the fin. (Royal Air Force Museum)

requirements for the C of A, this time on account of an excessive landing distance. The Avro, however, entered service in Kenya in late 1929.

New Zealand It is probable that the AAEE tested a Vickers Vildebeest for New Zealand in late 1934.

Norway The single Norwegian Hawker Fury, 401, was tested twice – in September 1932 and March 1933. With the Panther IIIA radial engine in place of the streamlined Kestrel the performance at altitude (201mph at 16,400ft, reached in 9min 55sec) was similar to the RAF version. Two of the four Norwegian Armstrong Whitworth Scimitar fighters (Panther IXA engine) were tested late in 1935. 407 was criticised for poor attention to detail, and 405, suitably cleaned-up aerodynamically achieved 217mph at 6,500ft and reached 20,000ft in 11min 36sec (compared with 201mph and 14min 48sec respectively on 407). 405 also completed British C of A tests; it

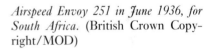

Airspeed Envoy 251 in June 1936, for South Africa. (British Crown Copyright/MOD)

was approved in the aerobatic category at 4,167lb.

Persia Hawker Fury 204 was tested with a Pratt & Whitney Hornet and a Watts wooden propeller in January 1934, and with a Mercury VI engine and a Hamilton variable-pitch version a year later. The latter was slightly faster at 211mph (true) at 15,000ft, but was less stable longitudinally than the former – both erect and inverted. The view was partially obstructed by the large Townend ring – a feature not liked by the test pilots. Persia ordered Hawker Audaxes with the Pratt & Whitney Hornet. In January 1934, Audax 407 was pleasant and easy to

fly, and climbed and flew slightly faster than the standard RAF model. In mid-1938 Hind 601 with a Mercury VIII and two-pitch de Havilland propeller had very good handling, and unusually docile stall with top speed and climb some 15 percent better than the RAF version of two years previously.

Portugal Hawker Fury 50 was generally similar to the RAF fighter with Kestrel IIS; extra equipment specified by the Portuguese added some 200lb and performance suffered slightly in consequence when tested in June 1934. Four years later the Gloster Gladiator with Mercury VIII had an almost identical performance to early RAF aircraft with the Mercury IX.

Hawker Hind No.1 was also almost the same as RAF machines but with

British Aircraft Double Eagle ZS-AIY in May 1937, for South Africa. (British Crown Copyright/MOD)

Pegasus-engined Hawker Hart 1301 in April 1934, for Sweden. (British Crown Copyright/MOD)

Marconi wireless and Handley Page bomb gear, and performed and handled in usual Hawker fashion in June 1937.

Romania In January 1925, Armstrong Whitworth Siskin V S10 was, in the words of one pilot, 'nice, poor visibility, cold'. S10 was lighter than the similarly powered (Jaguar III) Siskin for the RAF and the former had a significantly better performance. This aircraft, together with other Siskins for Romania, was apparently scrapped before delivery.

South Africa Percival Mew Gull ZS-AHM had retired from a race in

September 1936 before assessment at Martlesham in March 1937 fitted with a Gipsy Six Series II engine. Two Airspeed Envoys (two Cheetah IXs) featured in Martlesham reports – the Military 251 in mid-1936 and the civil ZS-AGD in January 1937. 251 was unarmed for its trials, although equipped with a manual turret, and completed the C of A tests at 6,400lb, reaching 4,100ft after 3min and 110ft in 656yd after starting its take off; a successful dive achieved 220mph (indicated). ZS-AGD was assessed following service reports of vibration; the Establishment found that vibra-

Hawker Fury 4 in December 1936, for Yugoslavia. (British Crown Copyright/MOD)

tion was eliminated by carefully synchronising the engine revolutions. In June 1937 the British Aircraft Double Eagle ZS-AIY, with two Gipsy Six Series II engines flew the normal C of A trials, including flights at three CG, and achieved 74ft in 656yd on take off and 2,700ft in 3min. The brakes were effective but awkward; the ailerons were required to be made lighter before C of A could be granted.

Sweden The first of four Hawker Harts for Sweden, 1301, passed tests easily in March 1934 with its Pegasus IM2 radial engine, becoming airborne after a run of 138yd and achieving 178mph (true) at 8,000ft – a performance significantly better than the standard RAF version.

Turkey The single Blackburn Turcock crashed on the speed course on 28 January, 1928, killing the pilot; no report was issued.

Yugoslavia Tested briefly at Martlesham even before the RAF production version, the Hawker Fury (Kestrel IIS) for Yugoslavia had a better performance than the prototype, especially above 13,000ft – thus substantiating Hawker's claim to their customer. With Darne machine-guns a second version of the Fury for Yugoslavia was flown in December 1936. Its Kestrel XVI was more powerful than the standard version, and gave the highest top speed, 242mph (true) at 15,800ft of any Fury.

Army Co-Operation Types

Wartime Types

Three new wartime designs for Army Co-operation (then called Corps Reconnaissance), all powered by the ill-fated ABC Dragonfly engine were at Martlesham Heath at the beginning of 1920 – the Austin Greyhounds H3417, H3418 and H3419, the Bristol Badgers F3495, F3496, and F3497 and Westland Weasels F2913 and F2914. The Greyhounds stopped flying about March 1920, the first and third Badgers flew until September 1920 on engine endurance trials but with limited success (F3497 achieved 16hr), while the two Weasels flew spasmodically until the summer of 1920. In November 1921 Weasel J6577 arrived with the Jupiter fitted, but the greater weight of the new engine so reduced structural safety factors that straight and level flight only was permitted. Fitting heater muffs to the induction pipes cured the cutting out of the engine after prolonged glides and the Jupiter was assessed as suitable for two-seater machines. The Weasel itself, however, required much modification for

Bristol Badger, probably F3496, in May 1920. In this view, the upper wing has dihedral, and the lower anhedral. (British Crown Copyright/MOD)

Westland Weasel J6577 in April 1922. Features are the fuel tank under the port wing, and horn-balances to the ailerons on both wings. (British Crown Copyright/MOD)

Service use, including improvement to elevator control on landing. A few days after the favourable report was submitted *(line 1)*, J6577 caught fire on 20 July, 1922, and was burnt out – the pilot escaping on landing; some 46hr in the air had been completed. The third Weasel, F2914, returned with a Jaguar engine and flew 50hr during the summer of 1922.

Meanwhile, the wartime Bristol Fighter continued to be developed, and the type was the subject of the first postwar production aeroplane contract. First however, trials continued on older machines. Bristol Fighter F4819 was used to test metal propellers, and a new Reid gyro turn instrument from mid-1921 to mid-1922 during which 40hr were flown; the venturi for the suction worked well. F4864 completed consumption trials from October 1920 before use on parachute work ending in a crash in about June 1921. The replacement for parachute work was H1436, still in use in March 1926. H1559, converted for dual control, was also used for parachute trials in mid-1921 and for assessment of the new F16 type of fuel with a specific gravity of 0.76 compared with 0.728 of the standard fuel. C4654 came from the RAE late in 1922 with the very latest in engine silencers. F4949 continued miscellaneous trials until it crashed in January 1925, while F4724 (1924-8), F4745 (1927-8) and H1490 (1927) were original-type Bristols with No.15 Squadron on armament work.

First of the new Bristol Fighters was J6586, arriving on 20 January, 1921, and completing full type trials *(line 2)*; the usual problem of radiator water boiling led to an increase in climbing speed from 60mph to 70mph (indicated). The finish and improved cable runs were praised. Later in 1921, other two-bladed and then three-bladed propellers of both wood and metal were fitted, the original two-bladed wooden version gave the

Bristol Fighter J6800 in January 1922; the long-range tank held 40gal and was successfully tested but little used in service. (British Crown Copyright/ MOD)

Short Springbok J6974 in August 1923, with fabric-covered wing and metal-covered fuselage. (British Crown Copyright/MOD)

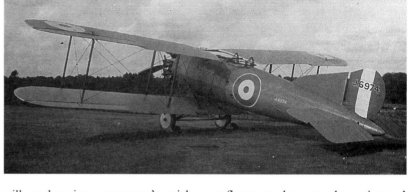

best climb and a two-bladed metal Leitner gave the longest take-off distance. Night flying trials of the new lighting on J6689, radiator suitability tests on J6753, and an extra 40gal tank which doubled endurance on J6800 appear to have been successful *(line 3)*. Perhaps the most significant trial at this period was on J6970 with an oleo undercarriage containing a heavy spring in place of rubber and intended for service in the East; the shocks of over one hundred landings were well absorbed and taxying smooth – praise indeed on the Martlesham Heath of the early 1920s. J7643, flown for two years on armament miscellanea, included the first British firing of the 0.5in Browning gun. Structural strengthening was introduced in production aircraft and J8251 was fully tested from 26 October, 1926, later joined by the similar J8242, J8263 and the rebuilt F4545 and F4618, all on various minor tasks up to 1931. Final type trials were completed on the Bristol Fighter with slots, using F4587 and F4675, the latter also possessing an enlarged rudder.

Short Springbok, Hawker Duiker and Armstrong Whitworth Wolf

The pioneering work of Shorts led to the first metal covered (as well as metal framed) British aeroplane at Martlesham – the Springbok. Although official interest centred mainly on the all-metal construction, the Specification, 19/21, was written for an Army Co-operation type, and it was tested as such at AEE. The first, J6974, suffered severe damage shortly after arrival in April 1923 when the metal wing covering came off while

still undergoing contractor's trials. After replacing the covering with conventional fabric, J6974 completed type trials in October 1923 *(line 5)*; the original metal covering, it had been noted, was 'sluggish' on the elevators. The performance table indicates that when comparably loaded both machines possessed similar performance. During November 1923 J6975 crashed, killing the pilot; rudder blanking during the spin was blamed.

The first true Corps Reconnaissance Specification, 7/22, produced the Duiker from the newly constituted Hawker company. It was not a success; the ailerons were prone

to flutter on the monoplane wing and the machine was directionally unstable. J6918 *(line 6)* left on 15 April, 1924, after four months for investigation by the RAE.

The following Specification 8/22, produced the Wolf; J6921 spent well over two years at Martlesham from May 1923 starting with eight months of firm's tests, repairs and modifications. One Establishment pilot found the Wolf unwieldy, but he said that it improved with acquaintance. Type

Hawker Duiker J6918 early in 1924; the Lewis gun has swivelled to an unusual angle. (British Crown Copyright/ MOD)

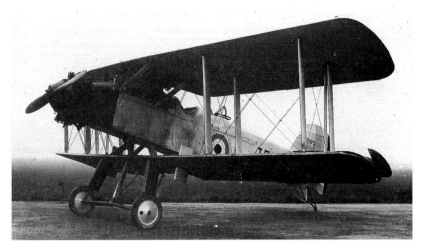

trials *(line 7)* were followed by oil cooling measurements and long periods of unserviceability and then some flying on research items such as a control column position indicator and a new type of statoscope.

Vickers Vixen and Venture

Following submission by Vickers of two versions of their Vixen, a small Air Ministry order was placed for the Venture to Specification 45/23. Vixen I G-EBEC flew at AAEE early in 1923 *(line 8)* and was immediately tested as an army co-operation type suitable for overseas. G-EBEC returned later in the year with a lengthened fuselage followed in mid-1924 by G-EBIP with various improvements – although an inferior performance *(line 9)*. Type trials *(line 10)* on the first Venture, J7277, occupied the latter months of 1924 and handling was found to be unremarkable and similar to the Vixen but with heavier controls. Venture J7282 was used for general research and armament work for at least two and a half years from May 1927. Other Vixens were tested for the

Vickers Venture J7277 in the autumn of 1924. Well shown in this view are the radiator header tank and the pilot's Aldis sight for the Vickers gun firing through the trough on the upper fuselage. (Royal Air Force Museum)

role of a light bomber for Chile and as a general purpose machine.

Specification 30/24

Another attempt was made early in 1925 to state the requirements (Specification 30/24) for a replacement of the Bristol Fighter, and five types reached Martlesham – de Havilland Hyena, Armstrong Whitworth Atlas,

Vickers Vixen G-EBEC in December 1923 with lengthened fuselage. (British Crown Copyright/MOD)

Short Chamois, Vickers Vespa and Bristol Boarhound. The Chamois (which arrived late) and the Hyena were owned by the Air Ministry at the time of their trials, the remainder were private ventures. The Hyena J7780 was tested in two periods, at

de Havilland D.H.56 Hyena J7780 in early 1926. Under the roundel is the message hook, and behind it a looped structure – purpose unknown. (British Crown Copyright/MOD)

Bristol Boarhound G-EBLG early in 1926, with Jupiter VI. The form of the exhaust collector ring is unusual. (British Crown Copyright/MOD)

the end of 1925 with Jaguar III and in mid-1926 with Jaguar IV *(line 11)*, it handled well with the exception of the differential ailerons which lacked effectiveness. The Boarhound, G-EBLG, was initially tested from August 1925 with a Jupiter VI *(line 13)* ; handling was its shortcoming, one pilot commenting, 'lumbering – pulls forward on turns', and another 'a bit countable fore and aft' – descriptions from log books and not official reports. Retaining its original Jupiter IV, the Vickers Vespa G-EBLD spent six months at AAEE from January 1926 *(line 14)*. It had an excellent view from the cockpit, but the mass-balanced ailerons gave poor response at slow speed and it was 'altogether nothing thrilling'. The Atlas, G-EBLK, performed *(line 15)* and handled well at the end of 1925 – and was assessed as 'admirably suited to army co-operation duties' – while one pilot went further 'Best 2-seater since BF'. Various aerodynamic changes were made to the Atlas in an attempt to meet minor criticisms, but on return to AAEE in April 1926, some of the pleasantness had gone from the handling. Nevertheless, it

went as a firm favourite, ahead of the other three types, for Service trials, and the Atlas was selected in late 1926 (Specification 33/26 covered initial production). Early in 1927 the Chamois J7295 *(line 16)*, (converted from the Springbok) flew, and reached Martlesham in April – too late for consideration. Its metal-covered fuselage had no longerons, but wings and control surfaces were fabric covered. Maintenance qualities were considered to be good, handling generally indifferent and directional qualities poor. Access and view for the pilot were bad, and the pronounced swing to the right was countered by fitting bungee cord to the left pedal.

In the words of one pilot it was 'A nasty machine'.

Armstrong Whitworth Atlas

On selection for the RAF, the Atlas prototype *(line 17)* (J8675 on purchase by the Air Ministry) travelled frequently between the makers at Coventry and the Establishment at Martlesham in attempts to achieve handling charactaristics acceptable to the latter. Various combinations of wing sweep angle, wash out, wing section and, most effectively, automatic slots were tried throughout 1927 and 1928. Late in 1927, the tailskid of J8675 was disconnected from the rudder, thus reducing pedal loads to an acceptable degree. During these developments production aircraft appeared – the first, J8777, in July 1927, apparently unmodified, and quickly sent to the RAE before type trials were completed on J8799 *(line 18)* from April 1928. Other standard Army Co-operation Atlas at Martlesham were J9563 for a check weighing in early 1931, K1035 for

Vickers Vespa G-EBLD early in 1926. The low setting of the upper wing afforded the pilot an excellent view. (British Crown Copyright/MOD)

extended cooling trials in the summer of 1934 following problems with the type in the Middle East, and J9041 briefly with No.15 Squadron in August 1933.

Following the decision to use the Atlas as a trainer, J8792 (a metal framed machine with early increased wing sweep angle and a fin) was tested in the summer of 1928; the main problem appears to have been incon-

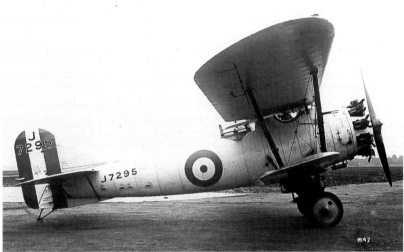

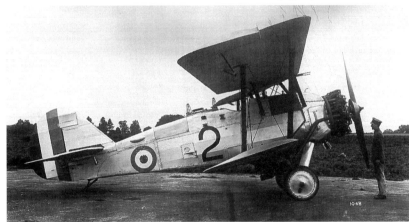

sistent spinning and recovery. The first production dual control Atlas, J9435, with a wood frame, reduced wing sweep and without a fin flew at the end of 1928. Thirty-seven pounds of ballast was fitted in the tail for early spinning tests, but was found to be unnecessary as satisfactory recoveries were made without the ballast fitted, and at all (forward, mid and aft) settings of the tail trimmer. Further handling and spinning trials were completed between May and November 1929 on J9453 without a fin, followed by an extended programme of spins in 1929 and 1930 on J9477 with a fin, probably at the instigation of the Aeronautical Research Council, and involving Professor Jones of Cambridge University. Both versions were satisfactory, but rudder forces for recovery were heavier without the fin. Further spins with the slots sealed took place in late 1929 on J9462, and in 1934 on J9458 – probably with a blind flying hood; the latter

Atlas, Dual Control, J8792 in mid-1928. (British Crown Copyright/ MOD)

machine made a further brief visit in May 1936. Low-pressure tyres characterised K1502 early in 1932, while in 1930 some unspecified handling tests were completed on K1457.

The Atlas Re-engined

Five re-engined Atlas had the benefit of assessment by AAEE. Known locally as the 'Super Atlas', G-EBNI completed standard tests in mid-1928 with a Jaguar S in place of the usual

Armstrong Whitworth Aries J9037 in December 1931. The slots are interconnected with the ailerons. (British Crown Copyright/MOD)

Jaguar IV, returning the following year as J9129 with a new propeller. J9516 was tested between May and November 1929 with a Jaguar V, and with a Jaguar VIC the following year; the increase in power of the latter engine appears to have had little impact on performance *(line 19)*. G-EBYF mounting a Panther III with horse-power slightly increased over the Jaguar VIC did achieve a significantly higher performance *(line 20)* late in 1930, probably attributable as much to aerodynamic improvements as to engine power. Late in 1931, G-ABIV (Panther IIA) underwent

Hawker Audax K1438 late in 1931. Under the wings are two Holt flares and two picketing rings, while between the wheels are the cables for brake operation and the message hook. (Imperial War Museum)

tests for a civil C of A, and the following year standard trials were completed on G-ABKE (Pather IIIA).

Armstrong Whitworth Aries, Hawker Audax and Westland PV.3

An improved Atlas, the Aries J9037, spent over a year at Martlesham from

November 1931; trials of the type's special features for ease of maintenance to meet Specification 20/25 and performance tests were reported at the end of 1931.

Compared with the lengthy series of trials of modifications to make the Atlas acceptable, the single Audax prototype K1438 sufficed to establish the type's characteristics in one visit to Martlesham *(line 21)*. It is surprising in view of the requirement later in the Expansion period to test the first machine made by a second manufacturer that the Audax aircraft built by the four other contractors were not deemed to require separate trials. Of course, the Audax represented in mid-1932 only relatively minor alterations from the Standard Hart; handling was similar in both types, but the Audax's Palmer brakes made taxying easier and the landing shorter.

Late in 1931, Westland submitted their PV.3 which was tested as a possible Army Co-operation type *(line 22)*. This interesting aeroplane, marked P3, had been designed as a shipborne torpedo dropper but the

Westland PV.3 P3 in December 1931 for assessment as an Army Co-operation type, although designed for torpedo dropping. (British Crown Copyright/ MOD)

requirement had been cancelled. It had a steel-framed forward fuselage and wing structure of duralumin, with Frise ailerons and Dunlop wheels fitted with Bendix brakes. Generally good handling was spoilt by large trim changes with power and loss of response from the elevator on landing; the armament was poorly arranged. Also, the highly supercharged Jupiter XFA would have been unsuitable for the co-operation role. The PV.3 was not adopted but, extensively modified, flew over Everest in April 1933.

Hawker Hector

Specification 4/35 for an interim replacement of the Audax resulted in a further development of the Hart, namely the Hector with the high revving Napier Dagger III engine (rated at 3,500rpm and containing no fewer than 48 sparking plugs). The prototype, K3719, spent eight months at AAEE and was the subject only of a report on its dual control conversion. K8090 the first production Hector (built by Westland) arrived in March 1937 and handled well *(line 23)*. The power of the Dagger (over 50 percent greater than the Kestrel of the original Hart) made take off tricky due to the swing to the right; although the swing could be contained by rudder, the sideways slip which developed caused three tyre failures during trials. The cockpit was noisy and draughty, the cooling was sufficient for the temperate summer conditions, and the engine contained seven troublesome

Hawker Hector K3719 in April 1936, here shown in standard Army Co-operation configuration but later tested with dual controls. The flared bullet channel near the nose of the cowling is unusual - and due to the Napier Dagger engine's H layout. (British Crown Copyright/ MOD)

components, some of which failed several times in the eight months of testing. Engine replacement time by two men was reduced to 25hr 10min, a time considered excessive on other aeroplanes.

Specification A.39/34

Monoplanes were specified for Army Co-operation (Specification A.39/34) and two types reached Martlesham – the low-wing Bristol 148 and the high-wing Westland Lysander. The Type 148, K6551 made three short visits, starting in March 1938; no type report was written, possibly on account of the prior selection of the Lysander for production, and the collapse of an undercarriage leg on landing; brief comparative trials were made and the power operated gun mounting assessed.

The Lysander K6127 *(line 24)* arrived in November 1936 and was well liked with the automatic flaps and slots working well, although nose-down trim and full forward stick was needed for control on overshooting with full power. Such was the speed range that the pressure error was plus

Bristol 148 K6551 in 1938. No record of any AAEE report has been found for this type. (British Crown Copyright/ MOD)

Westland Lysander K6128 in November 1938, with stub wings for bomb carriage. (British Crown Copyright/MOD)

20mph at the lowest indicated speed of 50mph; diving at 250mph resulted in a panel blowing off. Westland's own rear gun mounting was soon replaced by the more satisfactory Fairey mounting; the two fixed Browning guns in the spats could only be harmonized by jacking the aircraft. Bombs up to 500lb were dropped, and night landings were easy by the light of the lamp in the port spat. Range of the HF radio was satisfactory but readability of aircraft transmissions was poor because the pilot's microphone picked up excessive engine noise.

Although identical to K6127, the second prototype, K6128, *(line 25)* was 12mph slower and failed by 34mph to meet the specified speed of 245mph; the landing run was excessive but otherwise the type met the requirements. It was very noisy, and impossible to spin; stub wings were fitted for bombing trials. On 20 May, 1937, K6128 was nearly lost when half the fabric tore away from one wing during diving tests; the pilot eventually managed to trim out of the steep spiral dive and land. After modifica-

Lysander L4673 in May 1938, with Bristol Mercury engine and bead gun sight on the cowling. (British Crown Copyright/MOD)

tions to the wing, trials continued from August until December; the Fairey free gun mounting was satisfactory and heating acceptable. In March 1938, K6128 with a Mercury XII engine, had improved entry arrangements and more fresh air inlets. Greater engine cooling was required, and the Vokes air filter reduced top speed by a further 7mph.

Lysander K6127 in July 1938, with Bristol Perseus engine and very long message hook hinged aft of the engine cowling. (British Crown Copyright/MOD)

L4673 *(line 26)*, the first production aircraft, incorporated several modifications; most were satisfactory including a friction damper in the elevator but the damper in the slot mechanism resulted in the slots failing to extend before landing. Engine cooling was improved and radio and electrical systems acceptable. Operational trials between December 1938 and March 1939 were used to compile a summary of the various handling and other peculiarities of the Lysander in a form suitable for what later became known as Pilot's Notes.

The Bristol Perseus powered the second version of the Lysander, tested first on K6127 from July 1938 *(line 27)*. It was dived to 320mph (indicated) during which a panel blew out and back pressure on the stick was needed to prevent an even steeper dive at that speed. Several long flights to establish accurate fuel consumption were made; noise was less objectionable than on the Mercury type. In May 1939, L4739 similarly powered but equipped with a Vickers gas-operated rear gun in place of the Lewis was generally satisfactory once modifications were incorporated. A Service aircraft, L4682, spent a month performing from 9 June; the results are unknown.

Army co-operation

Line	Type	Identity	Engine No.	Type	Power (bhp/rpm)	Seats	Wing area (sq ft)	Max speed (mph/ft)	Take-off run (yd)	Landing speed (mph)
1	Weasel	J6577	1	Jupiter	375/1,575	2	344	130/10,000		
2	Bristol Fighter	J6586	1	Falcon III	271/2,000	2	410	110/5,000		
3	Bristol Fighter	J6800	1	Falcon III	264/2,000	2	406	107/10,000		
4	Springbok	J6974	1	Jupiter	403/1,580	2	460	118/6,500		
5	Springbok	J6975	1	Jupiter	391/1,575	2	460	117/6,500		
6	Duiker	J6918	1	Jupiter IV	388/1,575	2	390	119/6,500		
7	Wolf	J6921	1	Jaguar II	333/1,500	2	480	112/6,500		
8	Vixen I	G-EBEC	1	Lion	499/2,100	2	522	137/10,000		
9	Vixen III	G-EBIP	1	Lion II	496/2,100	2	525	129/6,500		
10	Venture	J7277	1	Lion	489/2,100	2	525	137/6,500		
11	Hyena	J7780	1	Jaguar IV	394/1,700	2	443	125/6,500		
12	Boarhound	G-EBLG	1	Jupiter IV	397/1,575	2	463	131/6,500		
13	Boarhound	G-EBLG	1	Jupiter VI	453/1,575	2	463	128/6,500		
14	Vespa	G-EBLD	1	Jupiter IV	400/1,575	2	577	126/6,500		
15	Atlas	G-EBLK	1	Jaguar IV	404/1,700	2	377	141/6,500		
16	Chamois	J7295	1	Jupiter VI	389/1,575	2	440	116/6,500		55
17	Atlas	—	1	Jaguar IV	404/1,700	2	382	135/6,500		
18	Atlas	J8799	1	Jaguar IV	398/1,700	2	391	131/6,500		62
19	Atlas	J9516	1	Jaguar VIC	460/2,000	2	391	130/6,500		54
20	Atlas	G-EBYF	1	Panther III	500/2,000	2	402	148/6,500		

Line	Climb to 10,000ft Time (min-sec)	Rate (ft/min)	Service ceiling (ft)	Fuel capacity (Imp gal)	Weights Empty (lb)	Gross (lb)	Report No	Date	Remarks
1	7-06	1,070	24,350	68	2,080	2,958	299A	6/22	3½hr endurance
2	17-30	370	16,000	45	2,094	3,215	280	2/21	
3	17-30	350	14,800	85		3,215	293A	2/22	6hr endurance
4	14-50	460	17,000	104	2,420	4,080	357	11/23	4hr endurance
5	15-49	405	15,750	104	2,530	4,080	359	12/23	
6	20-25	290	14,550	96	3,098	4,700	364	2/24	3¼hr endurance
7	19-00	333	15,150	66	2,616	4,122	363	1/24	3¼hr endurance
8	10-24	680	19,400	83	3,159	4,717	329	4/23	5hr endurance
9	16-25	410	16,650	126	3,319	5,550	383	6/24	
10	11-59	590	18,800	81	3,217	4,873	385	6/24	
11	13-24	527	19,230	100	2,399	3,875	453	7/26	
12	10-38	748	23,600	102	2,565	4,026	447	4/26	
13	11-42	640	21,000	104	2,508	3,981	447A	6/26	
14	11-48	642	20,300	100	2,631	4,101	454	7/26	
15	9-30	770	20,800	73	2,176	3,637	437	12/25	
16	17-06	350	14,600	98	2,720	4,210	489	11/27	
17	10-59	640	20,025	76	2,242	3,715	437A	7/26	Later J8675
18	13-44	490	17,300		2,243	3,902	437C	4/28	
19	13-58	420	15,900	76	2,914	4,247	437K	4/30	18,200ft – new intake
20	8-43	1,185	23,600	68	3,200	4,599	437D	1/31	

Line	Type	Identity	Engine No.	Type	Power (bhp/rpm)	Seats	Wing area (sq ft)	Max speed (mph/ft)	Take-off run (yd)	Landing speed (mph)
21	Audax	K1438	1	Kestrel IB	480/2,250	2	347	169/5,000	176	
22	Westland PV.3	P3	1	Jupiter XFA	483/2,000	2	500	155/13,000		
23	Hector	K8090	1	Dagger III	709/3,500	2		191/5,300	170	55
24	Lysander	K6127	1	Mercury ME3M(a)		2		236/9,500	135	50
25	Lysander	K6128	1	Mercury XII	786/2,400	2	260	224/9,000	165	50
26	Lysander	L4673	1	Mercury XII	799/2,400	2	248	218/6,000	170	50
27	Lysander	K6127	1	Perseus XII	728/2,400	2		228/7,500	190	50

Line	Climb to 10,000ft Time (min-sec)	Rate (ft/min)	Service ceiling (ft)	Fuel capacity (Imp gal)	Weights Empty (lb)	Gross (lb)	Report No	Date	Remarks
21	8-40	905	21,500	83	2,938	4,386	599	8/32	6.8ampg
22	9-29	1,095	23,300	134	3,963	5,614	602	4/32	
23	6-00	1,290	23,400	90	3,431	4,879	690A	10/37	6.8ampg
24						5,731	694	8/36	
25	6-12	1,335	25,750	95	4,300	5,857	694A	2/38	4³/4hr endurance
26	7-00	1,105	23,850	95	4,474	5,989	694C	1/39	
27	8-18	1,100	22,900			6,006	694B	12/38	3¹/2hr endurance

General Purpose Types

General Purpose (GP) as a class of RAF aeroplanes was in service long before the term was coined in about 1926, when the Air Ministry was drawing up desiderata for replacements of the ubiquitous D.H.9A. For the AAEE there were two main phases of activity for GP machines – the competitions in 1927 and in 1935; the latter phase was concerned with finding a replacement for the 1927 types. Between the two competitions two private venture types appeared; 1935 also saw the testing of two General Purpose developments of existing types.

1927 Competition

The official requirement for a replacement for the D.H.9A was Specification 12/26 sent to the industry in May 1926. Even before manufacturers had submitted their suggested designs, the Air Ministry appears to have reconsidered the requirements, and by the end of 1926 no fewer than eight firms had proposed eleven types for the new general purpose role. There was no formal specification, and all designs were modifications of existing types, or types being built, for other purposes; time, it seems, was of the essence.

de Havilland D.H.9AJ Stag J7028 in April 1927, used many components from the D.H.9A. The fabric between the fuselage and the first rib of the lower wing is absent. The oil cooler under the engine is blanked-off. (British Crown Copyright/MOD)

Fairey IIIF (later N225) in April 1927, with metal frame and three seats otherwise configured as IIIF S1147. (British Crown Copyright/MOD)

The Armstrong Whitworth Atlas was considered too small and too late and the Hawker Horsley too big; the remaining nine types were tested at Martlesham Heath between March and May 1927, *ie* a year before the aeroplanes designed for Specification 12/26. The ten machines (of nine types) in contention included four with inline engines – the private de Havilland D.H.65 Hound, the Fairey IIIF two-seater and three-seater (both owned by the Air Ministry) and the private Vickers Vixen VI. The remainder had Jupiter radials initially, the Bristol Beaver and Vickers Valiant (private ventures) and, owned by the Air Ministry, the de Havilland D.H.9AJ Stag, the Fairey Ferret, the Gloster Goral and the Westland Wapiti. In mid-May 1927, six were eliminated on the basis of AAEE's findings. They were the Vixen VI G-EBEC *(line 1)* with a Condor engine which was considered unsuitable, and the Stag J7028 with a poor performance *(line 2)* and poor equipment stowage. The metal structured three- seat Fairey IIIF N225 was slower than the wooden two-seater, but handled well. A bungee on the rudder pedals was fitted to relieve left foot loads in the climb and standard ailerons replaced the differential type which tended to flutter. A total of 32hr 45min was flown at Martlesham on N225. The Goral J8673 had a worse performance *(line 3)* than the Beaver, was not pleasant to fly and also had poor equipment stowage; the Goral had, however, the merit of using D.H.9A spares of which many existed. The Beaver, *(lines 4 and 5)* (un-numbered) was unstable, had poor handling but good stowage, while the unmarked Hound, had a narrow fuselage which helped bestow the best performance *(lines 6 and 7)* of the contenders but which handicapped equipment stowage. The Hound also floated on landing and was thus considered difficult to get into small fields.

The remaining four were the Fairey IIIF two-seater S1147 *(lines 8 and 9)*, the Wapiti J8495 *(lines 10 and 11)*, the unmarked Valiant, *(lines 12*

Gloster Goral J8673 in April 1927, has, like the Stag, many D.H.9A components and a cut-away panel on the starboard lower wing. (British Crown Copyright/MOD)

and 13) and the Ferret N192 *(lines 14 and 15)*. All had adequate provision for the extensive desert equipment specified – weighing a total of 328lb including 68lb of water, 50lb bedding and equipment, 40lb of fitter's tools and 35lb for spare wheel. The IIIF had heavy controls, was stable but yawed left at high speed, some radiator joints leaked and the wings blocked parts of the pilot's view. The Wapiti, fitted with a larger rudder during AAEE trials handled well in spins and aerobatics as well as in normal manoeuvres but 'bucketted' on the ground, had a poor armament layout and no elevator control on landing; its endurance was 5.37hr at 5,000ft. Pilots also liked the easy handling of the Valiant, but the Establishment criticised the armament layout and the three failures of the spinner. Maintainability and tailplane trim were praised on the

Ferret which had heavy controls. The Air Ministry short listed the IIIF (two-seater), Valiant, Wapiti and Ferret for Service trials (the Ferret was delayed at Martlesham by engine and propeller trouble) as a result of which the Chief of the Air Staff selected in July 1927 the Wapiti for use in Iraq and the IIIF for Egypt and Aden. Production orders for the GP Wapiti (to Specification 26/26) and the General Purpose IIIF (to Specification 27/26) were placed; early three-seat IIIFs already being built

for Naval use were diverted to RAF squadrons.

Westland Wapiti

Development of the two types selected for Service began with incorporation of the recently fashionable leading edge slots. For the Wapiti, a D.H.9A (E9895) was used for tests and the wings then removed on to J8495 which also received the uprated Jupiter VIII. Martlesham pilots flew these innovations in early 1928 at

The Bristol Type 93A Beaver in April 1927. The Vickers gun housing is the bulged metal panel on the left of the pilot's cockpit. (British Crown Copyright/MOD)

A de Havilland D.H.65 Hound in April 1927. Lack of stowage in the narrow fuselage was the major criticism of this fast type. (British Crown Copyright/MOD)

Fairey IIIF S1147 in April 1927. This is the two-seat, wooden-framed version. It has the inboard trailing edges of both lower wings cut away. (British Crown Copyright/MOD)

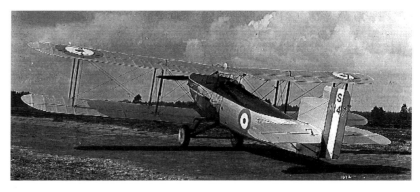

Westland Wapiti J8495 in April 1927. The oil cooler is on the upper right nose and the cut away panel on the starboard lower wing. (British Crown Copyright/MOD)

Westland's airfield in Yeovil, commenting enthusiastically that 'the aircraft is rendered practically foolproof' – an uncharacteristic hostage to fortune in a Martlesham report. J8495 *(line 16)* soon arrived at AAEE with refined Type B slots and other minor improvements for the production machines. Vibration was a recurring problem, which coupled with the harsh undercarriage led to numerous minor breakages. Changes to the pitch and diameter of the wooden propeller were partial palliatives; the metal Fairey Reed propeller gave better results on the initial production version of the Wapiti with Jupiter VI, of which two were tested. J9102 proved satisfactory in July 1930 when spun with ballast in the rear fuselage, and, two years later, J9084 *(line 17)* flew with four types of two-blade wooden propellers without conclusive result.

The major production version of the Wapiti (known as the IIA in service) was represented by J9382 *(line 18)*; it was the subject of no fewer than sixteen AAEE reports between March 1929 and May 1930. A geared Jupiter VIII, a metal fuselage frame and split undercarriage did not change the han-

dling and the controls remained heavy; both cockpits were draughty. A metal propeller reduced vibrations (except in spins) and performance, and the replacement tailskid overcame earlier criticism; seven minor breakages were reported.

Contemporary with J9382 was the private venture Wapiti *(line 19)* at first unmarked. A geared Jaguar produced greatly reduced vibrations, and then as G-AAWA with a Panther engine *(line 20)*, it flew in September 1930. The Panther had both an exhaust ring and, later, a Townend ring; the latter resulted in the engine overheating and a reduction in performance – contrary to expectations. The lengthened fuselage of G-AAWA was liked, and no problems reported in the terminal velocity dive to

The Vickers Valiant in April 1927. Pleasant handling was offset by poor armament layout. (British Crown Copyright/MOD)

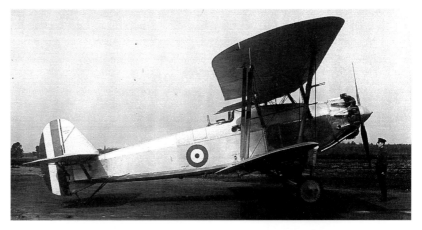

Fairey Ferret N192 in May 1927. The engine and propeller gave trouble early in the trials at AAEE. (British Crown Copyright/MOD)

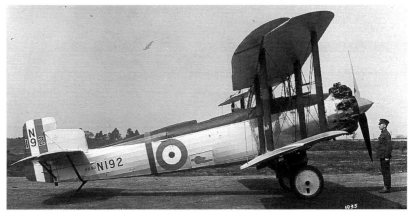

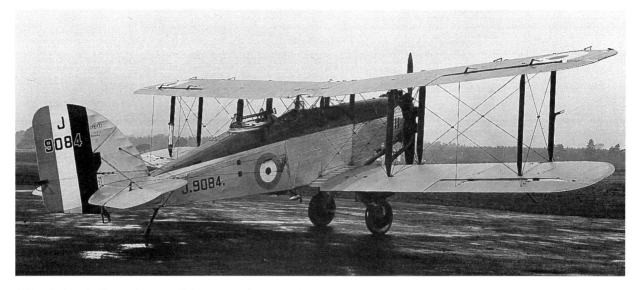

229mph (true). Extensive gun firing and bombing trials were successfully made on this civil registered machine.

For Indian use, the Wapiti was adapted to meet Specification 12/30, and J9728 *(line 21)* was duly put

Wapiti J9382 early in 1929, with geared Jupiter engine, slots and provision for four 112lb bombs. (British Crown Copyright/MOD)

sure gauge. Following complaints in service of lack of elevator control on landing, K1380 had an elevator with 3in extra chord and greater aft stick movement; these changes cured in 1931 a problem first reported by AAEE in 1927.

The last Wapiti to be reported upon was K2262 late in 1932 which was successfully spun at a load representative of the Army Co-operation role.

Westland Wapiti J9084 early in 1932, with one of the four types of propeller tested. The Lewis gun is real, but lacks an ammunition drum. (R C Sturtivant)

Fairey IIIF and Gordon

The other successful contender in 1927 was the IIIF. Before trials of the production version of the GP IIIF, an unmarked but metal-framed IIIF with Lion XA was flown with encouraging performance *(line 22)*. Two types of automatic slot were investigated in 1928. First was S1208 when lateral control was maintained down to the stall, and then, in November 1928, on J9164 when modified slots remained open at too high an airspeed and never fully closed. Heel operated brakes on S1208 were ineffective.

With Frise ailerons, slots and an increase in weight, J9164 *(line 23)*,

Wapiti K1129 in October 1930 with two long-range fuel tanks, each with its own windmill driven pump. (Philip Jarrett)

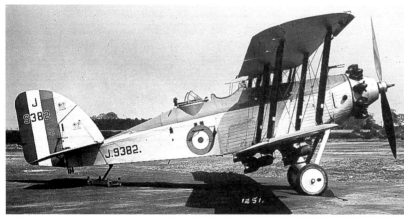

through its paces with the lengthened fuselage, and exhaust ring. The rudder bias was inadequate and although vibration was improved, the cockpit remained draughty. Ground handling was later improved by fitting wheel brakes and a tailwheel.

Between late 1930 and mid-1933, K1129 was tested first with two 60gal long-range tanks, then two 71gal tanks, then with a skid of Virginia type (no good), then with a modification to the windscreen and finally with Dunlop pneumatic brakes with the familiar (in later years) triple pres-

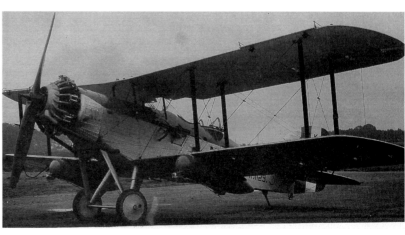

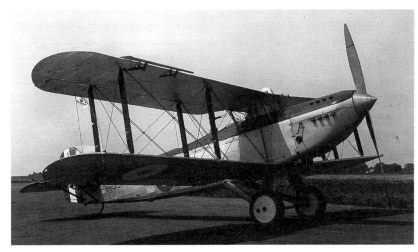

Fairey IIIF J9164, probably in the summer of 1929 during type trials with stub exhausts and starting handle. (British Crown Copyright/MOD)

and mid-1935. The comprehensive range of tests included performance, handling with standard and modified control surfaces (the latter making K1731 a Mk II), Lockheed brakes and long-range tanks; the last led to investigation of the adequacy of the oil supply. Other Gordons included K1697 in 1933, flown at loads typical of both the Gordon and the Seal; its Frise ailerons improved the handling, spins were normal, and dives to 225mph (true) uneventful. K1739 flew at AAEE in late 1933.

represented the standard Service IIIF GP in 1929; performance was disappointing, but lateral control was much better. Attempts in 1930 to improve speed, ceiling and cockpit comfort were scarcely successful. Two extra 75gal tanks *(line 24)* further degraded performance at 7,072lb all up weight, and the modification was not pursued in this Lion-powered version, possibly because better results were expected from the radial engines then in prospect. Such hopes were not realised with J9154 (geared radial Jaguar VIC) *(line 25)* flown from June 1929, and a few months later J9154 was tested with an early Panther. When S1325 was fitted later with a

Panther, performance *(line 26)* was improved, and re-engining of the IIIF for General Purposes and the Fleet began. The former was named Gordon. Type trials took place on Gordon K1731 between early 1931

Fairey IIIF J9164 late in 1930 with two 75gal fuel tanks and long exhausts. (British Crown Copyright/MOD)

Fairey Gordon K1731 in mid-1931 in its original form; the rear gun is stowed well out of sight. (Philip Jarrett)

Fairey Gordon K1731 in April 1935 with modified control surfaces, wheel-brakes, and fittings for Holt flares. (British Crown Copyright/MOD)

Bristol 118 R-3 in November 1931. Although designed as a General Purpose type, the 118 was subjected only to the limited civil C of A trials at Martlesham. (British Crown Copyright/ MOD)

Private Venture Types 1931-1932

Bristol's private venture general purpose Type 118 was tested in November 1931 for a civil C of A as R-3. Its Jupiter XFA engine powered the Type 118 to over 3,000ft in 3min from the start of the take-off run; handling, take off and landing were good. A development, the Bristol Type 120 R-6, had a cupola to overcome the disabling effect of the slipstream on the capabilities of the gunner at the increasing speeds being realised. Trials in July 1932 were temporarily halted when a fin fitting failed at 200mph; three months later strengthened fittings permitted dives to 230mph (indicated), and handling was assessed as generally good, although the response to the elevators was poor at low speeds. Gunnery trials continued after its purchase by the Air Ministry as K3587, and were followed by comparative trials with and without the turret; performance was only slightly degraded by the turret *(line 27)*.

In 1931 Westland built the private venture PV.6 based on the Wapiti but fitted with the new Pegasus IM2 *(line 28)*. Tested (at Westland's risk) at Martlesham in early 1932 it was found to be better than the Wapiti but still heavy on controls and very stable; the new Dunlop brakes were good. The PV.6 returned in June 1932 with the Pegasus IM3 engine (greater supercharging), but achieving a service ceiling of only 24,200ft *(line 29)* – well below the 30,000ft achieved in this aeroplane in 1933 over Everest. Other tests included a new Watts wooden propeller and maintenance trials in preparation for the Service use of the

production type named Wallace; it took two men 7hr 57min to make a complete engine change. Specification 19/32 covered conversions from the Wapiti to Wallace, and the first, K3562 *(line 30)*, was tested in late

The private venture Bristol 120 in August 1932. This was the first example of a turret to protect the gunner, and permit him full use of his gun at maximum speed. (British Crown Copyright/MOD)

1933 with its motor driven generator and slots; it remained easy to fly. Early the following year, K4010 was assessed with dual controls including dual Bendix brakes, and blind flying hood; the latter caused pronounced vibrations above 185mph. By 1934 the dual requirement had been cancelled. Meanwhile, the PV.6 purchased by the Air Ministry as K3488, was fitted with an enclosed and heated cockpit and tested from March 1934; *(line 31)* dives to 215mph (indicated) were

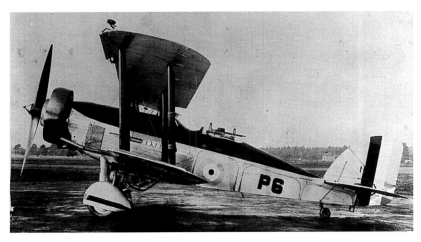

Westland PV.6 P6 in March 1932, for evaluation as a Wapiti replacement. (British Crown Copyright/MOD)

made. Remaining at AAEE, K3488 crashed on Friday 13 December, 1935, when water in the carburettor caused the engine to cut. In its four-year life, it achieved 260 flying hours. To compare performance with K3488, a standard machine, K3673, produced nearly identical figures *(line 32)*.

Vickers Vincent

To investigate the suitability of the Vildebeest as a General Purpose type, the eighth development machine, S1714, was modified with an auxiliary fuel tank holding 129gal (having a special air driven pump), and a message hook.

At Martlesham in early 1931, the extra cocks and levers were found confusing, and the cockpit was cold and draughty. The latter criticism was

Wallace K3488 in March 1934. This was P6 (later G-ACBR of Everest fame) purchased by the Air Ministry and fitted with an enclosed cockpit.

not rectified in view of the intention to operate the production version in hot climates. Handling of S1714 was indistinguishable from S1707 (see Coastal Types), and the performance similar *(line 33)*; fuel and oil systems were satisfactory and gave an estimated range of 1,117 miles at 4.32 air miles per gallon in the cruise. The successful trials on S1714 led to a production contract for the type, known

Westland Wallace K3562 in April 1933, was the first to be converted from a Wapiti. (Imperial War Museum)

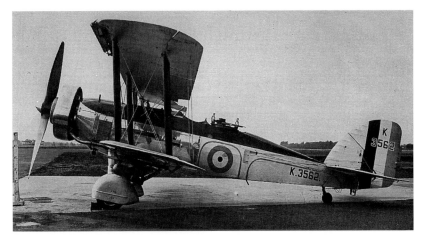

as the Vincent to Specification 16/34. The first production Vincent, K4105, tested early 1935 was disappointing *(line 34)* – there was backlash in both the elevator and the aileron controls, and dives to 210mph were unsatisfactory. Mass-balances were tried in the elevators without significant improvements. Differences from the earlier type included a new type of engine (Pegasus IIM3 instead of Pegasus IM3), strengthened centre section, and a third seat with a new gun mounting (Fairey instead of Scarff). These differences would not account for the criticisms quoted above; it is probable that in the four years since the earlier tests, standards at Martlesham had risen. It may be significant that the Vincent was tested at the same time as the more modern types submitted for the G.4/31 competition, and suffered from the comparison. No handling improvements were recorded when K4105 returned to AAEE later in 1935 with the more powerful Pegasus IIIM3 and a Townend ring *(line 35)*; cooling was, however, satisfactory with the later engine. In 1936 and 1937, 100hr were flown on Vincent K2945 (con-

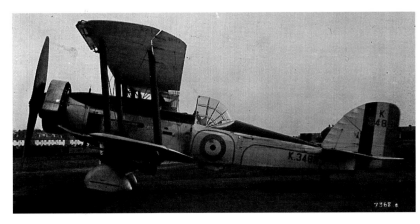

verted from a Vildebeest) fitted with the new Miocarta propeller; no deterioration was noted, although the Coffman cartridge starter failed after seventy engine starts.

Hawker Hardy

Also first tested in 1935 was the Hardy prototype, K3013 *(line 36)* a Hart development with desert equipment. Handling was pleasant, and the low-pressure tyres and brakes were well liked. In 1937 the production

Vickers Vildebeest S1714 in January 1933, modified for the General Purpose role. (Philip Jarrett)

Hardy, K5919, to Specification 23/33 retained very good handling, especially control harmonization, up to the maximum speed tested of 245mph. The tropical radiator and thirteen-element Potts oil cooler kept the water and oil temperatures suitably low for tropical conditions, but additional crankcase cooling was required. The modification to overcome this deficiency was satisifactorily tested in September 1937, the same month as tests of a new propeller optimized for take off which was reduced to 190yd into a 5mph wind.

Specification G.4/31

After years of deliberation and, no doubt, spurred by the economic condition of the country, the Air Ministry drew up G.4/31 for a general purpose aeroplane; the specification was later amended to include the requirement for carrying and dropping a torpedo. By early 1932, Handley Page, Vickers and Parnall were selected on the basis of their tenders for official purchase of one each of their designs. Such was the size of production orders expected that seven other designs were proposed as private ventures; these were by Armstrong Whitworth, Bristol, Blackburn, Hawker, Westland and two by Fairey. The Bristol Type 120

Hawker Hardy K5919 in March 1937, fully equipped for service in tropical climates where wireless was not required. (British Crown Copyright/MOD)

was soon withdrawn after separate tests at Martlesham, and one of the Fairey types, the monoplane, was withdrawn at the end of 1934 by which time flying for the G.4/31 competition had begun. Among the early arrivals, in late 1934, was the Fairey biplane, F-1, but it was plagued by oil cooling trouble and, it appears, performance was not measured nor was a report issued. The Fairey was not considered further, nor was the Parnall, K2772, which arrived very late, in early 1936 – long after the end of the competition. After a period of miscellaneous armament work, K2772 crashed on 9 March, 1937, and was written off.

Vickers Vincent K4105 in May 1935, with Townend ring. (British Crown Copyright/MOD)

The remaining six G.4/31 types all received serious consideration by the Air Ministry in the summer of 1935; Martlesham reports, as usual, formed the factual basis of discussion. By 1935 the torpedo requirement had been withdrawn (although AAEE put torpedoes on the types built to take them), and dive bombing was substituted for which only one type, the Hawker PV.4 was designed. Urgent trials (it arrived only five days before the selection meeting at the Air Ministry) proved the PV.4 to have

Parnall G.4/31 K2772 in March 1936. It arrived too late for the competition for a new General Purpose aeroplane – but posed beautifully for its official photographs. (British Crown Copyright/ MOD)

pleasant handling and good stability in the dive making it a suitable bombing platform. It was however, too slow as a bomber (although the fastest of the G.4/31 contenders at 6,600ft *(line 37)*, and had inadequate armament. It remained at Martlesham until October 1935. For the General Purpose role, both the Handley Page H.P.47, K2773 *(line 38)* and Blackburn B-7 were rejected; both were subject to a rapid assessment following arrival in April 1935. The former type was very

Hawker G.4/31 IPV4 in May 1935, was well liked, but too slow as a bomber according to the Air Ministry who changed the rules for the G.4/31 competition. (British Crown Copyright/ MOD)

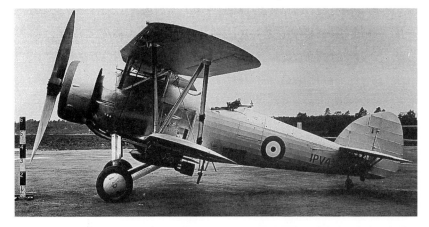

flimsy, and excessive yaw at high speed limited the dive to only 180mph on safety grounds as it was felt that undue fuselage flexing occurred. There were excessive vibrations and the ailerons were too heavy at high speed; trimming was bad and needed essential modification action. Handling and stability of the Blackburn were good, and the brakes particularly well liked; however, the type had the lowest performance of the contenders *(line 39)*. Placed third in AAEE's order of preference was the Arm-

strong Whitworth A.W.19 A3, which had been the first to arrive in June 1934 allowing full trials to be completed *(line 40)*, including full loads of bombs and the alternative load of a Type K torpedo weighing some 1,870lb. The guns were fired – revealing the need for some alterations, maintainability was good and two men could change an engine in 6hr 17min. It was dived to only 200mph (indicated), but handling remained pleasant. A3 could not be spun; with full aft stick the nose merely yawed in the direction of the rudder displacement. Tests with a torpedo loaded were made in mid-1935 with the Tiger VI *(line 41)*, in place of the earlier Tiger IV. Second in Martlesham's opinion was the Vickers K2771 *(line 42)*, flown briefly in April and May 1935, at the bomber loading. Apart from a

Handley Page G.4/31 K2773 in May 1935. The slim rear fuselage flexed excessively with disturbing yaw at high speed. The undercarriage gave no cause for comment as to its adequate rigidity. (British Crown Copyright/MOD)

Blackburn G.4/31 B-7 in May 1935. This had the lowest performance of the contenders for the G.4/31 Specification. (British Crown Copyright/MOD)

cold and draughty cockpit, and engine vibration pulling out of the dive there were no criticisms of the type. The Westland, PV.7, a high-wing monoplane, was flown for some 23hr in the summer of 1934 by two AAEE pilots before structural failure and crash on 21 August. Performance was the best of the general purpose group *(lines 43 and 44)* and the armament arrangements, especially the gunner's field of view, were outstanding. The handling assessment was not complete and yet the Establishment, following an extensive inquiry into the reasons for the structural failure, recommended the Westland for Service use. This recommendation was overruled by the Air Ministry on the grounds that the

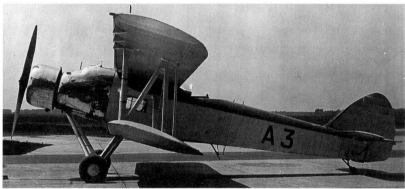

Armstrong Whitworth A.W.19 G.4/31 A3 in June 1934. This clean looking, conventional design was placed third in order of preference by AAEE. (British Crown Copyright/MOD)

cause of the structural failure had not in fact been fully established.

The inquiry established the sequence of the disintegration and concluded that a contributory cause was

the inadequacy of the airspeed indicator. This instrument had a scale up to 180mph, and dives were made to considerably greater speeds when the pilot had to guess how fast he was going as the needle made a second revolution of the dial. It was later estimated that 291mph (indicated) had been achieved at the time of failure.

The Vickers G.4/31 was selected as the winner in June 1935, by which time Vickers had almost completed a new monoplane design and, convinced that the new type was vastly superior, persuaded the authorities to order it instead of their biplane winner. Thus, on 31 July, 1935, the G.4/31 was officially changed to a Medium Bomber requirement, and the appellation General Purpose was dead.

Vickers G.4/31 K2771 in May 1935. This was the ultimate winner of the competition but, by the time a decision on selection was made, the General Purpose type had been removed from official requirements. (British Crown Copyright/MOD)

General Purpose Types

Line	Type	Identity	Engine No.	Type	Power (bhp/rpm)	Crew	Wing area (sq ft)	Max speed (mph/ft)	Take-off run (yd)	Landing speed (mph)
1	Vixen VI	G-EBEC	1	Condor III	723/1,900	2	592	160/6,500		
2	Stag	J7028	1	Jupiter VI	/1,700	2	491	130/5,000	134	
3	Goral	J8673	1	Jupiter VI	492/1,700	2		129/5,000		
4	Beaver	–	1	Jupiter VI	453/1,700	2	464	129/6,500	175	59
5	Beaver	–	1	Jupiter VI	453/1,700	2	464	127/5,000	200	56
6	Hound	–	1	Lion XA	542/2,350	2	462	163/MSL		
7	Hound	J9127	1	Lion XA	542/2,350	2	461	153/6,500	126	59
8	Fairey IIIF	S1147	1	Lion XA	551/2,350	2	443	148/6,500	140	60
9	Fairey IIIF	S1147	1	Lion XA	551/2,350	2	443	144/6,500		63
10	Wapiti	J8495	1	Jupiter VI	482/1,700	2	488	132/6,500	95	54
11	Wapiti	J8495	1	Jupiter VI	482/1,700	2	488	129/6,500		58
12	Valiant	–	1	Jupiter VI	492/1,700	2	597	129/6,500	135	54
13	Valiant	–	1	Jupiter VI	492/1,700	2	597	128/6,500	159	56
14	Ferret	N192	1	Jupiter VI	482/1,700	2	380	133/6,000		57
15	Ferret	N192	1	Jupiter VI	482/1,700	2	380	128/6,500		60
16	Wapiti II	J8495	1	JupiterVIII	542/1,535	2		139/6,500		
17	Wapiti	J9084	1	Jupiter VI	515/1,700	2		119/6,500		
18	Wapiti	J9382	1	JupiterVIII	440/2,000	2	489	128/6,500		
19	Wapiti	–	1	Jaguar VIC	460/2,000	2	488	127/6,500		
20	Wapiti	G-AAWA	1	Panther	516/2,000	2	489	128/5,000	151	56
21	Wapiti	J9728	1	JupiterVIIIF	460/2,000	2	489	126/10,000	150	60
22	Fairey IIIF	–	1	Lion XA	553/2,350	3	443	148/6,500	123	63

Line	Climb to 10,000ft Time (min-sec)	Rate (ft/min)	Service ceiling (ft)	Fuel capacity (Imp gal)	Weights Empty (lb)	Gross (lb)	Report No	Date	Remarks
1	12 – 36	770	25,250	83	4,051	5,550	441A	1/28	
2	24 – 36 to 15,000 ft		19,900				484	7/27	
3	17 – 05	460	20,000		2,943	5,006	486	7/27	Desert Equipment
4	13 – 13	625	19,900	104	2,642	4,262	481	10/27	
5	17 – 24	440	17,400		2,830	4,857	481A	1/28	5.2hr endurance
6	6 – 28	1,185	25,600		3,126	4,640	485	4/27	
7	8 – 48	845	21,500		3,285	4,934	485B	10/28	
8	8 – 30	835	20,500	137	3,452	5,120	482	7/27	Take-off – 9deg flap
9	10 – 44	635	18,500	150	3,452	5,742	482A	7/27	Land 7deg flap
10	10 – 36	750	22,700	108	2,644	4,240	480	2/27	
11	15 – 00	510	18,800	134	2,644	4,838	480A	7/27	Desert Equipment
12	13 – 42	550	19,650	132	2,896	4,519	487	7/27	
13	17 – 12	405	16,400	170	2,896	5,105	487A	7/27	Desert Equipment
14	13 – 25	590	17,750	106	2,583	4,179	488	7/27	
15	17 – 01	410	15,500	115	2,583	4,765	488A	7/27	Desert Equipment
16	10 – 58	1,090	24,200			4,600	480C	3/28	4mph faster – no slots
17	19 – 43	525	15,500			5,070	480M		All 4 propellers similar
18	14 – 06	600	17,500	107	3,322	5,210	480E	3/30	
19	15 – 18	430	16,800	137	3,186	5,185	480F	11/29	30gal aux tank
20	11 – 10	610	18,000	80	3,474	5,323	480I	9/30	
21	11 – 09	715	20,400	107	3,437	5,292	480H	9/30	
22	8 – 54	810	20,150	135	3,524	5,195	483	4/28	All-metal frame

Line	Type	Identity	Engine No. Type		Power (bhp/rpm)	Crew	Wing area (sq ft)	Max speed (mph/ft)	Take-off run (yd)	Landing speed (mph)
23	Fairey IIIF	J9164	1	Lion XIA	530/2,350	2	444	132/10,000		
24	Fairey IIIF	J9164	1	Lion XIA	539/2,350	2	444	133/6,500		67
25	Fairey IIIF	J9154	1	Jaguar VIC	460/2,000		443	126/6,500		70
26	Gordon	S1325	1	Panther II	525/2,000		443	140/6,500		
27	Bristol 120	K3587	1	Pegasus IM3	581/2,000	2	414	164/7,000		
28	Wallace	PV.6	1	Pagasus IM2	565/2,000	2	489	153/6,500		
29	Wallace	PV.6	1	Pegasus IM3		2	489	152/6,500		
30	Wallace	K3562	1	Pegasus IM3	587/2,000	2		155/6,500	138	61
31	Wallace	K3488	1	Pegasus IM3	578/2,000	2	489	150/6,500		
32	Wallace	K3673	1	Pegasus IM3	571/2,000	2		152/6,500		
33	Vildebeest	S1714	1	Pegasus IM3	580/2,000	2	713			
34	Vincent	K4105	1	Pegasus IIM3	576/2,000	3		142/6,500	210	49
35	Vincent	K4105	1	Pegasus IIIM3	672/2,200	3		146/5,000	190	
36	Hardy	K3013	1	Kestrel X	581/2,500	2		161/MSL	210	48
37	Hawker G.4/31	IPV4	1	Pegasus X	820/2,250	2		183/6,600		
38	H.P. G.4/31	K2773	1	Pegasus III M3	659/2,200	2		161/6,000		
39	Blackburn G.4/31	B-7	1	Tiger IV	682/2,150	2		147/7,000		
40	A.W. G.4/31	A-3	1	Tiger IV	706/2,150	2		150/6,500		66
41	A.W. G.4/31	A-3	1	Tiger VI	765/2,150	2		153/12,000		
42	Vickers G.4/31	K2771	1	Pegasus IIIM3	680/2,200	2		159/5,500		
43	Westland G.4/31	PV.7	1	Pegasus IIIM3	686/2,200	2		168/5,000	138	65
44	Westland G.4/31	PV.7	1	Pegasus IIIM3	686/2,200	2		151/5,000		

Line	Climb to 10,000ft Time (min-sec)	Rate (ft/min)	Service ceiling (ft)	Fuel capacity (Imp gal)	Weights Empty (lb)	Gross (lb)	Report No	Date	Remarks
23	11 – 48	550	16,950		3,932	5,896	483C	2/30	
24	12 – 42	500	16,150	141	3,963	5,927	483C	3/30	287gal = 6,904lb.
25	18 – 48	295	13,550		3,576	5,524	483B	7/29	
26	12 – 55	495	17,100		3,891	5,809	483F	11/30	Modified IIIF
27	7 – 58	955	22,000				608	2/34	With Turret
28	8 – 10	990	22,950	107	3,670	5,500	593	3/32	480lb bombs
29	7 – 15	1,140	24,200		3,692	5,522	593A	6/32	Engine gear change
30	8 – 49	895	22,800	105	3,792	5,635	593B	10/32	4.2hr endurance
31	8 – 45	900	22,200	105	3,867	5,792	593D	9/34	Enclosed cockpit
32	8 – 40	920	22,800		3,762	5,664	593E	10/34	
33				150	4,411	7,213	510D	3/33	500lb bomb
34	11 – 40	625	19,500	150	4,613	7,910	665	5/35	4.8 ampg
35	11 – 54	595	18,800	150	4,660	7,978	665A	7/35	Townend ring
36	10 – 12	665	17,800	84	3,194	5,006	669A	3/37	
37	6 – 45	1,150		140	3,748	6,144	675	7/35	
38	9 – 53	750	19,900	138	5,362	7,708	674	7/35	Bomber load
39	9 – 48	735	19,800	170	4,327	6,805	673	7/35	Bomber load
40	9 – 56	765	15,400	147	4,749	7,242	646	6/35	Bomber load
41	13 – 30	500	12,000			8,871	646A	6/35	Torpedo load
42	8 – 30	880	21,700	145	4,365	6,757	672	6/35	Bomber load
43	8 – 24	940	22,000*	141	4,820	7,050	661	6/35	580lb bombs
44	13 – 18	500	18,800*	124	4,820	8,660	661	6/35	1,908lb torpedo

* Absolute ceiling.

Trainers

Avro 504

The Avro 504 was the standard Service training type in the 1920s; it was extensively flown at Martlesham for tests of new equipment and new engines and as the standard training aeroplane on the station. In use from 1919 was H2431 (110hp Le Rhône engine) for consumption, metal and wooden propellers and later, until August 1923, parachute tests. H2007 (B.R.1 engine) flew little between mid-1922 and mid-1923, fitted with metal and wood propellers. Six Monsoupape-engined 504Ks were used, three of them for propeller evaluation - H2041 briefly in 1920, D6308 *(line 1)* throughout 1920 and 1921 (also with metal framed wings) and H2401 for fifteen months from November 1921. H2202 had a modified carburettor in mid-1922, E3269 had a slotted wing in 1925 and finally, in 1926, H9815 had a new undercar-

riage, described by one pilot as 'leaden', and the lowest recorded ceiling of any of the type (3,500ft) *(line 2)*.

On 12 February, 1922, the first Avro 504 with a postwar engine arrived - E9261 *(line 3)* with only the second Armstrong Siddeley Lynx made, on which 100hr flying time was amassed in the following eighteen months. E9261 was an excellent trainer with very pleasant controls; directional instability appears to have been cured by moving the undercarriage forward 2in while at Martlesham - a puzzling remedy. The only criticism was the lack of a fireproof bulkhead - this at a period of general concern over aircraft fire safety. Later attempts at measuring lateral stability were inconclusive and led to consideration of the methods to be used for such tests. E9261 remained in general use until 1925 fitted at various times with a new statoscope and a turn indicator. A second Lynx Avro, E9266, had completed 45hr when it was destroyed in the

Avro 504K E9261 in April 1922, with Armstrong Siddeley Lynx engine. (British Crown Copyright/MOD)

ARS hangar fire in October 1922. J750 with further airframe modifications was briefly assesed in mid-1923, followed a year later by J7301 *(line 4)*, with all the changes planned for the production Lynx Avro - the 504N. J7301 appears to have been used for another two years.

An alternative engine to the Lynx was the less powerful Bristol Lucifer, first at AAEE in G-EADA, between March and June 1923 and the following year in J733 *(line 5)* which was otherwise similar to the 504N. J733 also stayed on after its initial assessment until well into 1926.

In 1928, the Air Ministry purchased a civil development of the 504, the 504R Gosport, J9175 *(line 6)* with a Mongoose engine, but tests at Martlesham revealed no reason to change from the standard Lynx version.

Between 1927 and 1929 the two Squadrons used 504Ns F2575 (previously a prototype and fitted with slots), H1982 (which ended its days on a hangar roof in May 1928) and H9568 for training and communication until destroyed in mid-1929 to test a new fire extinguisher.

de Havilland D.H.53 Humming Bird and D.H.60 Moths

Following an Air Ministry order for the D.H.53 after the Light Aeroplane Competition, two, J7325 and J7326,

Avro 504N J7301 in mid-1924, with Lynx engine, underwing fuel tanks and revised undercarriage. (British Crown Copyright/MOD)

Avro 504K J733 late in 1926 with Lucifer engine and modified fuel and undercarriage arrangements. (British Crown Copyright/MOD)

for special experiments with airships, were flown at Martlesham in late 1924. They appear to have been evaluated as single-seat trainers *(line 7)*.

The de Havilland Moth was represented at Martlesham by more than a dozen of the type between 1925 and 1934; this large number and the lack of available reports make identification of individual aircraft and their associated trials difficult. In November 1925 many pilots flew and enthused over an unknown example for which no report was written. The first military Moth at AAEE, J8030, arrived on 28 April, 1926, and completed full trials *(line 8)*, demonstrating a top speed of over 83mph at 3,000ft carrying two pilots on the power of its 61hp Cirrus engine; this performance confirmed the type as a light trainer suitable for the RAF. Slots were fitted later in 1926 but did not improve handling; J8030 remained in use for many months following completion of its trials. J9109, another Cirrus Moth, was briefly tested in the winter of 1928-9, followed by J9922, the first RAF Gipsy Moth, for six months from May 1929. The latter completed extensive handling and spinning, but not performance. The full performance of Gipsy Moth E-2 *(line 9)* was measured early in 1930, and similar comprehensive trials were undertaken the following year on E-3 *(line 10)* (a version with the Gipsy II engine). Although E-2 and E-3 were subsequently given civil registrations, it appears probable that both were assessed for RAF use. Handling and spins were the subject of trials on

Avro Gosport 504R J9175 in mid-1928, with Armstrong Siddeley Mongoose engine. (British Crown Copyright/ MOD)

K1227 (Gipsy) in mid-1930, followed by its use on communications and armament work until 1937. Minor modifications to the Gipsy Moth led to handling tests on K1839 in 1932; changes to the ailerons of K1864 were

assessed in the winter 1933-4, and K1111 was looped and spun by the pilot sitting under the newly installed blind flying hood in 1934. Finally, in 1936, *K1859* visited the Establishment for an unknown purpose.

de Havilland 53 Humming Bird J7325 in December 1924. Martlesham Heath was a challenge for the small wheels. (British Crown Copyright/MOD)

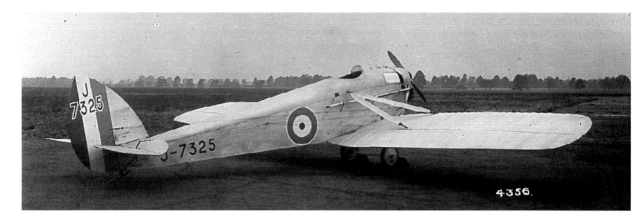

Early in 1931, de Havilland Puss
Moth K1824 *(line 11)* was assessed
for light communications duties; the
cabin was warm and comfortable but
the condensation froze on the win-

*de Havilland D.H.80A Puss Moth
K1824 early in 1931. The rotating strut
is shown in the normal flying position.*
(British Crown Copyright/MOD)

Hawker Tomtit and Avro Avian

Following two years after the first of
the numerous wooden Moths was the
metal-framed Tomtit: the first, later
numbered J9772, arrived at Martlesham on 14 November, 1928, only a
few days after the type's maiden
flight. It was found to be roomy,

*de Havilland D.H.60M Gipsy Moth
K1859 in March 1936, with slots, mass-
balanced ailerons and in pristine condition after five years Service use.* (British
Crown Copyright/MOD)

robust, docile and viceless; construction was far superior to that usually
associated with light aeroplanes. It is
surprising in view of the very
favourable report that only a handful
were ordered for the Royal Air Force.
Performance *(line 12)*, measured
early in 1930, was also superior to
other contemporary training types,
which included the Avian J9182, tested first in mid-1929 with a Genet
engine *(line 13)* and, in early 1930
with a Hermes *(line 14)*. Although
pleasant to fly, the Avian was
draughty, underpowered with the

dows in the winter conditions prevail-
ing. The view from the offset rear seat
was only fair; the rotating strut, acting
as an airbrake increased gliding angle
from 1:10 to 1:9, but the main criticisms were the long take-off and landing runs. Air operated wheel brakes
were tested in May 1931 and reduced
the landing runs from 227yd to
149yd.

*Hawker Tomtit J9772 late in 1929, on
its second visit to AAEE.* (British
Crown Copyright/MOD)

Avro Avian J9182 in mid-1929 with Genet engine. The chocks, placed behind the wheels, belong to 'A' flight of No.22 Squadron. (British Crown Copyright/ MOD)

Genet and, apparently, insufficiently robust for aerobatics.

Avro Tutor

More successful in comparison with the Tomtit was the Tutor, first assessed in Service use *(line 15)* in late 1929 using the civil prototype G-AATK retained after its C of A trials. Maintainability was good although the Establishment was concerned at the lack of trained welders in the Service to minister to the needs of the type's metal airframe. The extreme docility of the handling was the Tutor's outstanding characteristic, although the ailerons were heavy at high speed - a shortcoming rectified on the first Service machine, K1230, tested from April 1930. With the slots locked standard eight-turn spins to left and right were normal; less satisfactory was the rudder hinge bracket on K1237 which bent during a terminal velocity dive in November 1930. With the more powerful Lynx IXC in place of the Mongoose IIIA in earlier Tutors, the second civil prototype, G-AARZ *(line 16)* demonstrated even better handling characteristics, aided by the fitting of ailerons to all four wings. The horn-balance on the elevators felt slightly overbalanced, but all controls were acceptable up to the maximum diving speed of

Tutor K3248 in July 1934, with tailwheel and standard single-bay wings. (British Crown Copyright/MOD)

245mph (indicated). An exhaust ring, fitted after initial trials, reduced significantly the engine noise.

Full type trials of the Lynx-engined Tutor were made in mid-1932 on K1797 *(line 17)* which had the undercarriage moved forward nearly five inches and brakes operable from both cockpits. Other improvements eased maintenance - including

Avro Tutor K1797 in early 1932 with the Lynx engine. (Philip Jarrett)

the time taken to change an engine which was reduced from 6.7 to 4.3 man hours. The type was considered to be a very suitable trainer, and after selection in mid-1932 nearly four hundred were produced for the RAF. K1797 returned to AAEE towards the end of 1932, probably fitted with a Townend ring, followed in early 1933 by K3191 with a Lynx IV Star engine for propeller trials. K3189 was flown late in 1933 with a Townend ring and mass-balanced rudder among other changes; the ring improved top speed by 3mph *(line 18)* without altering the handling. Satisfactory results on K3248 in 1934 led to the tailwheel becoming a standard feature, but two-bay wings to increase torsional stiffness on K3308 two years later were not adopted. K6116 with major strengthening of the wings spun normally with slots closed but could not be coaxed into a spin with slots open; these trials, late in 1937, were probably required by the weight of the extra equipment fitted since the original spinning.

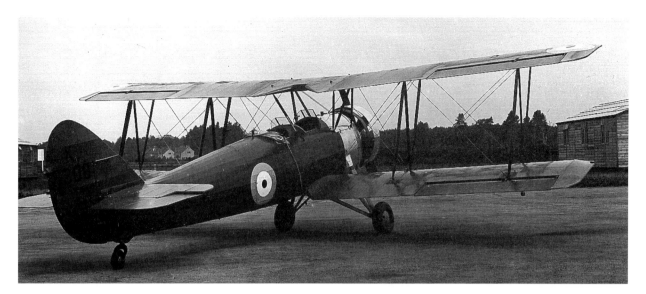

A development of the Tutor, the Avro Type 626 Advanced Trainer G-ABJG, was submitted by the maker for type tests in June 1931. Destined for use overseas, the Establishment assessed it as a trainer, and also for its offensive and defensive gunnery potential. The navigational trainer version for the RAF, the

Prefect K5063, reached Martlesham in mid-1935 but no report has been found.

de Havilland D.H.82 Tiger Moth

Following tests for C of A of the Tiger Moth, a second aircraft, E-5

Tutor K3308 in July 1936 with two-bay wings, blind-flying hood stowed behind the rear cockpit, and inter-aileron strut. (British Crown Copyright/ MOD)

successfully completed full type trials in September 1931 as a military trainer powered by a Gipsy III. Only eight months later, the thirteenth production aircraft, K2579 completed its trials *(line 19)*; the simple construction and easy maintenance were liked but the draught in the rear seat and lack of adjustable seats were criticised. K2579 was dived to 225mph indicated. Between January and December 1933, mass-balances were added in two of the three flying controls - K2578 (ailerons) dived to 215 indicated, K2570 (ailerons) flown inverted from 120mph down to the stall at 60mph and K2583 (rudder) in which there were no detectable differences in handling. Known as the Tiger Moth II in the Service, the first,

Avro Prefect K5063 in July 1935. In addition to a blind-flying hood, the rear cockpit has a mounting (probably for a drift sight) and an enlarged windscreen. The Prefect was a version of the Type 626. (British Crown Copyright/ MOD)

de Havilland Tiger Moth K2579 in May 1932. The indicated diving speed achieved at Martlesham was 225mph; the wing sweep angle remained unaltered. (Imperial War Museum)

British Aircraft Eagle G-ADJO in January 1936. The retractable under-carriage worked well. Visible here are the rudder mass-balance and the venturi tube for the gyroscopic instruments. (British Crown Copyright/MOD)

K4242 (Gipsy Major), arrived in mid-1934 *(line 20)*; moving the accumulator and thus CG forward reduced instability and made dive recoveries safer.

British Aircraft Eagle and Miles Mentor

In the search for a Service instrument and night flying trainer, the Eagle G-ADJO *(line 21)* was assessed in early 1936. Handling, including dives to 185mph (indicated), was good, but at aft CG the aircraft was unstable and speed increased rapidly on releasing the stick. A unique criticism was the bowing of the plywood ailerons and rudder at altitude because they were not vented. The Eagle was not considered suitable.

To meet the requirement for specialised trainers for blind and night flying the Miles Nighthawk, U5 *(line 22)* was assessed in mid-1936 during

its C of A trials. The plywood construction was not considered robust enough, there was only one stick and the view was poor; as a trainer it was rejected but was suitable for communications duties. As a result forty-five Miles Mentors were ordered, notwithstanding its name, for the latter

Miles M.16 Mentor L4392 in March 1938. Around the rear fuselage is a metal band of the type used to secure an anti-spin parachute. It was probably fitted by the maker to meet a contractual requirement for tests of a trainer – the type's original role; there is no record of spinning trials at AAEE. (British Crown Copyright/MOD)

role. Even for this undemanding duty, the Mentor in its initial form, L4392 proved unsuitable - its take-off run was excessive *(line 23)*, the climb poor (impossible with flaps down), and the cabin very uncomfortable on account of engine noise and numerous leaks which let in rain. Fitting a larger fin and rudder resulted in very large changes of directional trim with engine power to such an extent that on the approach there was an excessive tendency to yaw and roll left. In mid-1939, a year after the first trials on L4392, L4393 appeared with a two-pitch propeller; handling and take off were marginally improved but there was still no rudder bias as recommended from earlier tests.

Miles Hawk and Magister

Miles had greater success with its Hawk trainer in spite of the first air-

Miles M.14 Magister L5912 in June 1937. This aircraft was lost on spinning trials shortly after the photograph was taken; no anti-spin parachute was fitted. (British Crown Copyright/MOD)

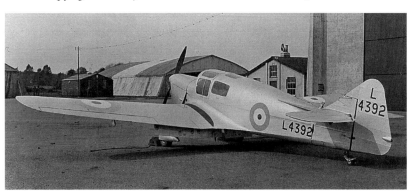

Miles M.9 Kestrel U5 in April 1938. A single Browning gun is visible above the starboard wheel; the latter rotated through 90deg as it retracted rearwards. (British Crown Copyright/MOD)

craft, G-AENT, crashing very early in its spinning programme It failed to recover from what had been intended to be a spin of only three turns; the pilot baled out. Six months later Hawk Trainer G-ADWT, with increased wing span and area, successfully completed its programme of twenty-eight spins paving the way for the similar Magister to enter service. However, on 22 July, 1937, tragedy struck when the pilot baled out during spinning of the first production aircraft, L5912 (line 24), and was drowned. Five days later a company pilot in G-AEZS loaded to represent

The Miles Kestrel as N3300 in February 1939 with lengthened fuselage, lowered tailplane, redesigned rudder and cockpit cover, and an anti-spin parachute fitting. (British Crown Copyright/MOD)

L5912 but including a tail parachute also failed to recover after over thirty turns. Subsequent modifications included raising the tailplane 6in, flattening the top of the rear fuselage and fitting fillets; these were tested on L5933 in October 1937. Forty-six sets of spins were made successfully during the course of which a new stan-

dard recovery technique using full rudder to oppose the direction of the spin (previously centring the rudder was used) followed by centring the stick. Minor criticisms were made of the small windscreen and harsh throttle friction but otherwise this Magister was satisfactory. Maintenance was remarkable for the time taken to change the elevator (10.1 man/hours), longer by over 80 man/minutes than changing an engine - usually the longest item. L5933 tested three types of propeller and more spinning in 1938 with changes to weight and CG

de Havilland D.H.93 Don L2388 in February 1938, has a fairing in place of the gunner's turret. The auxiliary fins under the tailplane are visible on the original photograph. (British Crown Copyright/MOD)

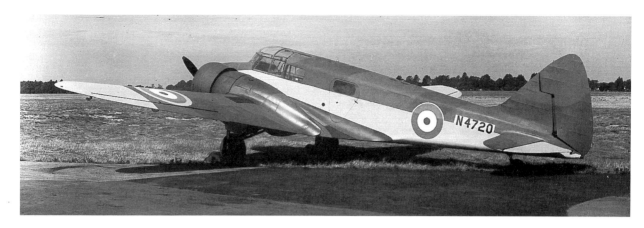

Airspeed Oxford N4720 in July 1939 in the pilot training configuration without turret. The combination of camouflage and training yellow is interesting. (British Crown Copyright/MOD)

at the same time as a standard fully modified aircraft, L6905, was flown; results were satisfactory. In mid-1938 a rudder with a higher aspect ratio gave a general improvement in handling on L8168; this aircraft was with the D Flight until the outbreak of war.

Miles Master

The enthusiastic Miles, perceiving the need for training pilots for the new low-wing monoplane fighters, produced privately the Kestrel and sent it to AAEE in November 1937. Tested as U5, the Kestrel was found to have many serious shortcomings; the view was bad, the stall was without natural warning, the rudder with dashpot damping made taxying difficult, and uncontrollable directional

Miles T.1/37 P6326 in July 1939, with band for anti-spin parachute. Protective tubing on the fin of L7714 was designed to prevent the tail parachute from fouling the rudder. (British Crown Copyright/MOD)

Heston T.1/37 L7706 in November 1938. It possessed unacceptable handling and performance for a primary trainer. (British Crown Copyright/MOD)

oscillations occurred at speeds above 250mph. An aileron mass-balance broke off and wedged the control surface, and the rear cockpit cover failed. Two months of modification by the makers improved the view, taxying and directional behaviour. Take-off distance to a height of 50ft was 540yd, some 40yd longer than usually specified and the landing distance was 110yd longer. In spite of these criticisms, the Kestrel was ordered into production as the Master, and the prototype (by then owned by the Air Ministry as N3300) was further modified including a six-inch fuselage extension, tailplane lowered and a production type rudder. Adverse comments in August 1939 were limit-

ed to the heavy rudder, the lack of stall warning and the ease of pulling into a stall on spin recovery. There was no AAEE comment on the desirability of the last two characteristics in an advanced trainer.

de Havilland Don

The official requirement (Specification T.6/36) for a trainer to prepare pilots for monoplanes also included gunnery and bombing. The resulting aeroplane, the D.H.93 Don, soon exhibited serious shortcomings at Martlesham from September 1937. L2387, the first, had a large wing drop at the stall accompanied by snatching of the ailerons; fitting strips four feet long on the leading edge improved matters. Fitting auxiliary fins and larger elevator tabs on L2388 further improved handling but there remained the problems of poor view, difficulty in entering, excessive take-off distance and very heavy elevator. With a three-bladed propeller take off was acceptable by April 1938, but increasing engine boost and revolutions were required to achieve acceptable initial rate of climb. The single fixed Browning II gun proved erratic in spite of several modifications during the trials in which 3,396 rounds were fired. The type was rejected for training in favour of the Miles

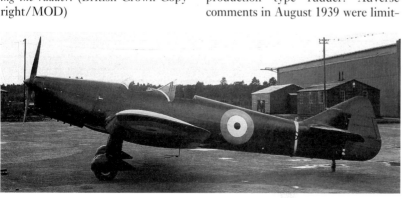

Master. Don L2391, without a turret, was briefly tested for the communications role. Take off was too long, view bad, rudder bias useless and the cockpit layout poor. On a fuel consumption test on 22 September, 1938, the throttle linkage to the engine broke, the engine failed and L2391 crashed. The Don was a disappointment; one feature, however, was liked - the new Breeze electrical system, which reduced the risk of fire.

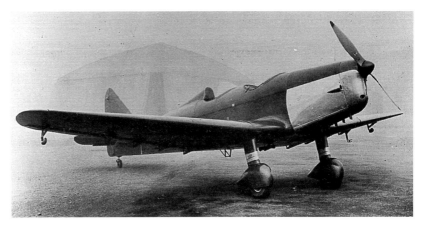

Airspeed Oxford

For conversion of pilots to twins, Airspeed received orders for a modified Envoy, named Oxford. The first, L4534 *(line 25)*, reached Martlesham on 9 November, 1937, and was immediately assessed for single-engine performance; height could not be maintained on the port engine alone but could on the starboard. In December the first two of several undercarriage failures occurred - the first when one leg collapsed while taxying, and the second when the other leg failed to lock down before landing. L4540 continued the testing, and suffered a collapse of the tailwheel caused by an excessive swing on landing - behaviour frequently experienced on the type. Rotating the turret caused loss of effectiveness of the elevator and vibration on dives up to 260mph indicated. Although the cockpit was generally well laid out, the undercarriage lever was selected on the ground in mistake for the flap lever alongside before take off with embarrassing results. Gunnery, bombing and radio were satisfactory. N4560, the first Oxford built by de Havilland and tested early in 1939 handled similarly to the Airspeed aircraft. N4720 with no provision for gunnery training arrived in July 1939.

Specification T.1/37

Two constructors not already fully engaged on work for the RAF Expansion were selected to build a robust primary training type to Specification T.1/37. Both the Heston, L7706, and Miles, L7714, had the Gipsy Queen I engine specified, but otherwise seem to have been well below requirements. Both arrived early in 1939, both well overweight with resulting lengthy take-off distance and poor climb. Aerobatics were unpleasant in the Heston and impossible in the Miles - the latter due to the engine overspeeding. Minor improvements were incorporated in the second Miles T.1/37, *P6326*, in 1939, but both types were rejected. The private venture to T.1/37 by Parnall, J I, was however pleasant to fly, stall, spin, and aerobat; it was suitable with three major changes and eight engineering modifications.

Yet another trainer was submitted privately by Miles in early 1939 - the

Miles M.18 U2 in March 1939. It was insufficiently robust for use as a primary trainer. (British Crown Copyright/ MOD)

Parnall T.1/37 J1 in February 1939. It was pleasant to fly but failed to secure an order. (British Crown Copyright/ MOD)

M.18, U2. Although easy and pleasant to fly it was considered to be insufficiently robust, and needed thirteen modifications to be satisfactory as a primary trainer.

North American Harvard

Following the placing of large orders in the USA for the Harvard, the first, N7000, arrived at Martlesham on 2 December, 1938, and was subjected to handling and diving. In its initial form with fixed slats, the aircraft was pleasant to fly, with the notable exception of the vicious dropping of the starboard wing at the stall which occurred without warning and with the stick only a third of the way back from neutral. With the leading-edge beading removed, the stall was much less violent, even with flaps and undercarriage down. On 16 February, 1939, N7000 crashed, and the visiting RAE pilot was killed. The replacement Harvard, N7013, continued full type tests *(line 26)* until after the start of the war. In the meantime N7001 was assessed as a bombing and gunnery trainer; apart from some difficulty of seeing the target through the windscreen the type was suitable in this role. At night the noise of the near supersonic propeller tips was particularly noticeable, but otherwise the five night flying pilots found the Harvard acceptable with use of the type's landing lamp; switch layout was particularly liked. With slats removed and wingtips faired, N7001 was assessed as a very satisfactory spinning trainer.

Trainers

Line	Type	Identity	Engine No. Type		Power (bhp/rpm)	Seats	Wing area (sq ft)	Max speed (mph/ft)	Take-off run (yd)	Landing speed (mph)
1	Avro 504K	D6308	1	Gnome/Mono	113/1,250	2	329	75/6,500		
2	Avro 504K	H9815	1	Gnome/Mono	109/1,244	2		74/1,000		
3	Avro 504K	E9261	1	Lynx	145/1,700	2	329	86/6,500		
4	Avro 504N	J7301	1	Lynx III				93/6,500		
5	Avro 504K	J733	1	Lucifer	127/1,700	2		81/4,000		
6	Gosport	J9175	1	Mongoose	135/1,620	2	313	93/6,500		
7	D.H.53	J7326	1	Tomtit	22/	1	121	70/		
8	Moth	J8030	1	Cirrus	61/1,800	2	227	83/3,000		
9	Moth	E-2	1	Gipsy	85/1,900	2	244	96/6,500		48
10	Moth	E-3	1	Gipsy II	105/2,000	2	244	97/6,500		46
11	Puss Moth	K1824	1	Gipsy III	108/2,000	3	209	126/1,000	226	54
12	Tomtit	J9772	1	Mongoose II	130/1,620	2	238	115/6,500		50
13	Avian	J9182	1	Genet II	70/1,850	2	244	87/1,000	166	46
14	Avian	J9182	1	Hermes	104/1,900	2		99/6,500	85	
15	Tutor	G-AAKT	1	Mongoose IIIA	150/1,850	2	302	104/6,500		
16	Tutor	G-AARZ	1	Lynx IVC	229/1,900	2	301	120/5,000	102	47
17	Tutor	K1797	1	Lynx IV	180/1,620	2	299	108/5,000	142	41
18	Tutor	K3189	1	Lynx IV★	212/1,900	2	299	120/2,000	130	40
19	Tiger Moth	K2579	1	Gipsy III	105/2,000	2	239	105/MSL		
20	Tiger Moth	K4242	1	Gipsy Major	123/2,100	2		104/MSL		
21	Eagle	G-ADJO	1	Gipsy Major				136/MSL	300	
22	Nighthawk	U5	1	Gipsy VI	185/2,100	2		159/5,000	282	42
23	Mentor	L4392	1	Gipsy Queen I	190/2,100	3	158	151/MSL	450	51
24	Magister	L5912	1	Gipsy Major I	124/2,100	2	162	133/MSL	210	42
25	Oxford	L4534	2	Cheetah X	609/2,100	3	348	184/8,400	360	55
26	Harvard	N7013	1	Wasp S3H1	550/2,200	2		207/5,000	235	67

Line	Climb to 10,000ft Time (min-sec)	Rate (ft/min)	Service ceiling (ft)	Fuel capacity (Imp gal)	Weights Empty (lb)	Gross (lb)	Report No	Date	Remarks
1	30 – 00 to 6,500ft		7,900			1,820	286	9/21	
2	14 – 50 to 3,000ft		3,500	30		2,000	391A	4/26	New undercarriage
3	27 – 00	222	13,700	20	1,401	1,850	315	11/22	
4	20 – 20	300	14,200	30	2,066		391	8/24	
5	41 – 30 to 8,500ft		8,100	20	2,018		391B	7/26	
6	12 – 09 to 6,500ft		14,000	31	1,268	1,975	463A	11/28	
7	46 – 12 to 6,500ft		5,700	2	349	551	401	1/25	
8	31 – 30 to 6,500ft		7,550	15	827	1,340	465	10/26	Slots added 33lb
9	24 – 45	224	13,100	17	964	1,548	465D	5/30	
10	26 – 54	210	13,400	19	1,070	1,636	465H	6/31	
11	24 – 40	260	15,000	35	1,207	2,050	564A	2/31	
12	17 – 29	352	14,900	22	1,235	1,851	516	4/30	
13	35 – 18	100	6,500		887	1,460	519	8/29	
14	26 – 15	207	12,600	17	1,022	1,574	519/2	5/30	
15	26 – 40	190	11,900	30	1,571	2,230	548	12/29	
16	13 – 06	517	17,450	30	1,720	2,375	548C	10/30	
17	20 – 40	260	12,900	31	1,816	2,464	574A	6/32	
18	18 – 50	325	15,300	30	1,844	2,493	574D	1/34	
19	22 – 05	280	14,500		1,073	1,624	586B	5/32	
20	29 – 54	225	14,000		1,116	1,725	586F	2/35	
21	20 – 36		15,000	39	1,594	2,400	686	2/36	
22	16 – 06	425	17,600	33	1,680	2,650	691	6/36	
23	20 – 06	300	14,300	35	1,686	2,884	725	9/38	
24	18 – 48	360	16,500	21	1,220	1,804	708B	9/37	
25	11 – 40	750	19,750	156	5,215	7,347	718	12/38	6.9 hr endurance
26	8 – 18	1,010	21,000	84	4,003	5,200	732	12/39	

MSL = Mean Sea Level

Coastal Types

Blackburn Cubaroo and Avro Ava

Coastal defence by aeroplanes in 1920 was considered feasible only if they had the capability of carrying the 21in torpedo weighing some 2,967lb (3,195lb including release gear). The first relevant Air Ministry requirement (Specification 8/21) resulted in the Cubaroo, of heroic proportions powered by the immense Napier Cub engine of a nominal 1,000hp. With a span of 91ft 8in and a loaded weight of 20,600lb, the Cubaroo underwent many design changes before its first flight; N166, the first of two, reached Martlesham in October 1924 where it completed manufacturer's trials before undergoing official evaluation *(line 1)*. The latter was delayed by several engine failures (none catas-

trophic), but eventually type tests were completed in December. The Cubaroo had balanced controls, was manoeuvrable yet extremely stable and had a good view. However, the water boiled before reaching the service ceiling of 4,975ft (9,000ft was specified). The poor performance led in mid-1925 to the Air Ministry abandoning the type which, in any case, had been superseded by the Ava to Specification 16/22 for a four-seat twin-engined Coastal Defence Torpedo Carrier. The Ava N171 was half a ton heavier and spanned 10in less than the Cubaroo. By the time the Ava was tested in 1926-7 a lighter torpedo was available, and the type was abandoned. The size of both Cubaroo and Ava was remarkable; the former was the heaviest single-engined aeroplane weighed at Martlesham between 1920 and 1939, and the Ava the heaviest of any aeroplane in the 1920s; only the Armstrong Whitworth Awana and Beardmore Inflexible exceeded their wing spans. A second Ava, N172 with

square wingtips, appeared at AAEE in 1927 – for performance tests *(line 2)*, (achieving a ceiling of 9,750ft).

Hawker Horsley

In 1926, Hawker modified a bomber Horsley, J8006, to take the lighter torpedo of 2,069lb. After showing the combination to the Air Ministry in January 1927, Hawker sent J8006 to Martlesham the following March. Performance *(line 3)* was sufficiently encouraging for a Specification (17/27) to be written for a production Horsley Torpedo Bomber. With production modifications incorporated J8006 was again tested early in 1928 *(line 4)*, followed by the first production aircraft, S1236 *(line 5)*, in the summer of 1928. Handling was similar to the bomber version, and performance acceptable – although the ceiling was 1,750ft lower in the production version. At the end of 1930, Horsley J8620, a wooden frame machine fitted with the first Leopard III engine, was tested with bombs and then with a dummy torpedo *(line 6)*. Without bombs or torpedo it was found impossible to spin with slots free and CG fully aft. The rudder was heavy and (some three and a half years after J8006 had first been tested), the view for torpedo dropping was criticised; the elevator and rudder out of trim forces in a dive were unacceptably large. The engine gave out much oil, smoke and noise from its fourteen cylinders; the report concluded that the engine needed replacing. At Martlesham at the same time as the Leopard III Horsley was the Rolls-

Blackburn Cubaroo N166 in October 1924, complete with 3,000lb torpedo, and plenty of drag. The Cubaroo was, at 20,600lb, the heaviest single-engined aeroplane at Martlesham Heath during 1920-1939. (British Crown Copyright/MOD)

Avro Ava N171 in late 1926. Features include the two-piece propellers, the radiators mounted in the top wing and the hinged door under the roundel. The wheels under the tail belong to the ground handling trolley which supported the skid. (British Crown Copyright/ MOD)

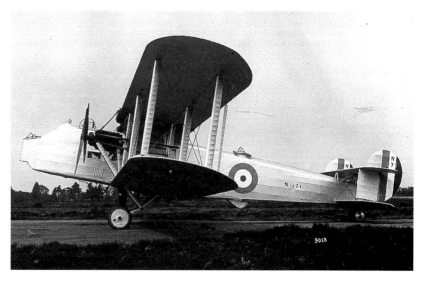

Royce H-engined version; the latter was fitted in J8932 *(line 7)* with all metal airframe. The H engine was No.1 – the first of its kind; the carburettor regularly froze at height, and much cooling water was thrown out; the rudder was, typically for the type, unpleasantly heavy. Both J8620 and J8932 were considered for torpedo carrying replacements of the Condor-engined version then in service. In mid-1931 Horsley S1436, the first of the production version with all metal airframe, was tested with a Condor IIIB engine and slightly reduced span; it had increased fuel capacity but reduced performance *(line 8)*. Target towing equipment on the torpedo Horsley (probably S1452) was assessed in late 1930.

Specification 24/25

In January 1926 the Air Ministry invited tenders for a new coastal defence type to Specification 24/25; two designs were initially proposed – the Blackburn Beagle and Vickers Vildebeest (the official spelling without the final 'e' is used here). Contemporaneously, the Horsley bomber replacement was specified in 23/25, and four designs were built – the Gloster Goring, Handley Page Hare, Hawker Harrier, and Westland Witch. These last four were initially assessed at Martlesham Heath as bombers in late 1928 by which time the similarity of the two Specifications was recognised, and all six types competed for the production

Hawker Horsley S1236 in July 1928, with standard Condor engine. It was the first production Torpedo Bomber of the type. (British Crown Copyright/ MOD)

contract which eventually focussed on the more demanding torpedo carrying requirement. During the course of the competition, the Air Ministry decided to include the two Horsley developments mentioned; both were late and were not seriously considered.

Of the six contenders, Goring J8674 spent an unhappy eight months at AAEE from January 1929. Shortly after arrival, a mainwheel sheared twenty-two of its forty rivets, followed a week or so later by the tailskid collapsing on the hard frosty ground. Then, in the dry summer, a further failure of the tailskid coupled with the type's inability to carry a torpedo (a single axle was fitted) led to the

Goring's elimination. Initial trials of the remaining five were completed by October 1929; all five had Jupiter VIII engines. The Harrier, J8325, *(lines 9 and 10)* suffered, like so many aircraft, from Martlesham's notoriously uneven surface and burst a tyre when loaded to maximum weight with the Type VIII torpedo of 2,800lb. Two oil system breakages did not prevent some trials from being completed. However, the take off was excessively long even when pilots opened the throttle through the gate to get maximum (unauthorized) power and the upper wing seriously obscured the view of the target when diving; the

Horsley J8932 in November 1930, with Rolls-Royce H engine. Outwardly similar to S1236 and J8932 it has an oil cooler visible on the rear of the cowling and a modifed exhaust arrangement. (British Crown Copyright/MOD)

Gloster Goring J8674 in December 1928. It was of conventional appearance, but with weak wheels. (Royal Air Force Museum)

structure was also criticised. The Harrier was eliminated. Despite good controls, the Witch, J8596 *(line 11)* with its distinctive parasol monoplane wing, was also eliminated as unsuitable due to the excessive number of breakages (three tailskids, main undercarriage struts, bowed structure and three fittings). The report praised the Witch as a good bombing platform, but found it unsuitable for Service use.

The Beagle, N236, tested at bomber and torpedo loads *(lines 12 and 13)* had differential, shrouded Frise ailerons and automatic slots; it was easy to fly. In 1929 it had suffered the usual series of tailskid and undercarriage failures and was criticised accordingly. The maintenance report of March 1929 concluded that the type was spoilt by details which could have been seen by the makers had they made suitable tests. The Hare had many vicissitudes during maker's trials in 1928-9, and had been delayed by the requirement to accommodate a torpedo and thus the need for a split undercarriage. It arrived in June 1929 and was the last of the six contenders. Initial vibration with the four-bladed propeller was improved by replacing the engine. The elevators were slightly

too heavy and ineffective on take off resulting in a long run as the tail could not be raised sufficiently early; the Palmer pneumatic brakes were praised. Handling with a single 500lb bomb asymmetrically loaded under the left wing was satisfactory, and vibration and performance *(line 14)* improved with a two-bladed propeller.

First flown at Weybridge by an Establishment pilot in September 1928 the Vildebeest N230 handled well, but vibration from the geared Jupiter VIII caused continuous movement on the rudder pedals. At Mart-

Hawker Harrier J8325 early in 1929, armed with four bombs but clearly showing the split undercarriage necessary for loading a torpedo. (British Crown Copyright/MOD)

lesham two months later, the initial impression of easy handling was confirmed; in addition, at both bomber *(line 15)* and torpedo *(line 16)* loadings performance was superior to the Beagle. The Vildebeest had a well laid out cockpit, and the report concluded, 'The aircraft has very good general qualities from the Service standpoint and is recommended for Service trials'.

In October 1929 it was decided to re-engine the three remaining contenders, the Beagle, Hare and Vildebeest, with the new Jupiter XF. So powered, all three arrived at AAEE, but tests on the Vildebeest, the first to arrive, demonstrated that the new engine was prone to overheating (both with and without the Townend ring) with consequential

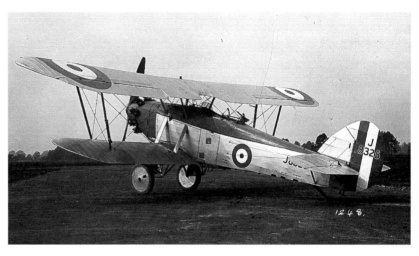

engine failure and forced landing. The Jupiter XF was rejected for torpedo aircraft, and no reports appear to have been written on the Beagle and Hare, although there was some flying of both types with the engine, including at least one engine failure on the latter. The Beagle was abandoned at this stage, and a further engine change, to the Panther II (a development of the Jaguar), made on the remaining two types.

Returning to AAEE in 1931 for a third time, the Hare suffered a recurrence of earlier wheel failures, preventing full assessment with the Panther until 1932 *(line 17)*, when the take off was still considered too long, the elevators insufficiently powerful and the view poor. Full- and partial-span slots were tried, the latter 'chattering' at cruising speeds. By this time the Vildebeest had already been selected as the Horsley replacement.

Vickers Vildebeest

The Panther IIA was also initially disappointing when fitted to the private venture Vildebeest O1 starting at Martlesham in mid-1930. In Sept-

Vickers Vildebeest N230 late in 1928. The skid looks particularly well braced — by this date Vickers had had plenty of experience of Martlesham's way with this vulnerable excrescence. (British Crown Copyright/MOD)

ember an induction pipe split, followed in November by a complete engine failure at 20,000ft resulting in a long glide back to the aerodrome; in January 1931 a piston broke. A fourth failure two months later in the same engine (No.AS7514) occurred in Vildebeest N230. From the Establishment's report numbering system it

Blackburn Beagle N236 early in 1929, with split undercarriage, shown armed with four bombs. The pilot has a Vickers gun and there are four ailerons. (British Crown Copyright/MOD)

would seem that N230 and O1 were the same machine; indeed, the performance report *(line 18)* dated before the fourth failure is written on N230 yet the attached photograph shows O1. With the Panther N230 retained its pleasant handling, but some details were criticised including the poor operation of the brakes and the position of the brake lever; new intakes improved performance but fitting the Townend ring reduced top speed.

A private Vildebeest, G-ABGE *(line 19)* with a Jupiter XFBM engine was at Martlesham at the same

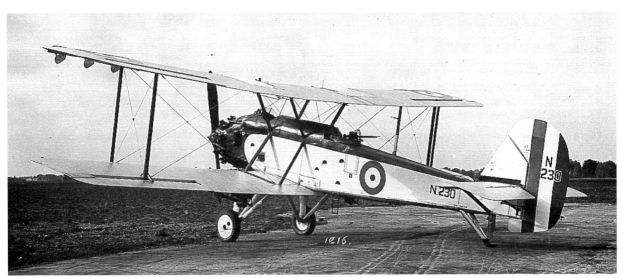

time as N230 in early 1931 and the only criticisms of G–ABGE were rudder over-balance and the need for a collector exhaust ring for night flying. A similar (or the same) engine fitted to N230 *(line 20)* indicated the need for a reduction in horn-balance which subsequently cured the rudder over-balance. The search for a successful engine for the winner of the 24/25 competition ended with the Pegasus IM tested in the long suffering N230 in mid- to late-1932. Oil cooling was the only problem (solved by fitting a larger sump and a new oil cooler); performance *(line 20)* was increased by fitting wheel fairings and a re-designed Townend ring.

Full type trials from late 1932 on the first production Vildebeest, S1707 *(line 21)*, revealed no surprises. The offset fin (1½deg to starboard) was adequate in the cruise, but significant left rudder was necessary for the climb; the controls were not considered well harmonized. Modifications to the windscreen did not cure earlier criticisms of the wet and draughty cockpit for the pilot; the rear position was too narrow for the fully rigged gunner. With new electro-mechanical bomb release gear, S1707 underwent possibly the earliest electro-magnetic compatibility trials; the HF radios

Vickers Vildebeest O1 in March 1931, complete with 'tinfish'. The darker panel just forward of the registration is marked 'CW crate'; however, there are no aerials and the radio seems, therefore, not to be fitted. (Royal Air Force Museum)

produced no adverse effects. In 1933 and 1934, this machine was flown at Martlesham with over a dozen different propellers including several with two blades, both wooden and Fairey Reed metal, Miocarta three-bladed types and three versions made of magnesium; performance was scarcely affected but one sort of Fairey Reed caused serious vibrations. A Curtiss variable-pitch propeller completed 111 flying hours on K2819 between February 1936 and January 1937, the only problem was occasional overspeeding.

Although no fewer than forty-five modifications were made to the Vildebeest Mk II, it was considered unnecessary to test the performance of the first, K2916, during its brief visit towards the end of 1933. The final version, fitted with the sleeve valve Perseus engine, was first tested in 1936 in K4164 when the best

Handley Page Hare J8622, probably in 1931, powered by an Armstrong Siddeley Panther engine. (British Crown Copyright/MOD)

results with least vibrations were obtained with a metal propeller. The production version, represented in late 1937 by Mk IVs *K6408 (line 22)* with a Schwarz three-bladed propeller and K8087, retained the pleasant handling of earlier versions, but the original difficulties with oil cooling and high cylinder-head temperatures were again manifest on the new engine. As a result, the Mk IV was not considered suitable for service overseas.

de Havilland D.H.89 and Avro Anson

The first RAF Expansion scheme included a new class of aeroplane –

coastal reconnaissance. Single examples of the Avro 652 and D.H.89 airliners with minimum alterations were ordered for comparison at Martlesham; both arrived in early 1935. The D.H.89A K4772, handled pleasantly up to 193mph (true) in a dive, but stiffness in the aileron control runs made lateral stability difficult to measure. As a military aircraft, it was assessed as generally too fragile.

Vildebeest K6408 in March 1937, with torpedo and four smoke bombs under the starboard wing. The Bristol Perseus engine has a full cowling, and drives a fixed-pitch three-bladed propeller. The raised ailerons on the port wings are of the Frise type, while the venturi is uniquely placed on the port forward strut. (British Crown Copyright/ MOD)

There was no intercomm and the bomb aimer's position was cold and draughty; four light bombs were dropped. The D.H.89A had a performance *(line 23)* inferior to the Anson (as the Avro 652 was later named) K4771 *(line 24)*. The latter type was chosen for production. Trials of K4771 revealed many points for improvement including a heavy rudder, a flat glide, cockpit layout and longitudinal instability making prolonged flights tiring; the undercarriage took 2min and 140 turns of the handle to wind up and down. Rapid work by Avro cured the instability with a larger tailplane, replacing the Cheetah VI engines with Cheetah IXs and moving them forward 4in; the rudder, modified without a horn-balance, was also better and the type thus acceptable for Service use.

K6167, the first with detachable trailing-edges to the wings, was the next Anson at Martlesham in May 1936; there was no detectable difference in air handling, and the modification was a decided improvement for ground handling. The following month K4771 returned with flaps, reduced span ailerons and a horn to warn pilots of an unsafe undercarriage; all features were satisfactory. Late in 1936, the first production Anson, K6152, started type trials including tests on various further improvements including sealing of the turret, a metal rudder and five-element oil coolers which reduced the warming up period. K6152 later had a cable braced tailplane and was successfully dived to 237mph (oscillations had previously been felt at 211mph); in late 1938 some 500 rounds were fired from the Browning Mk II fitted on the left side of the nose. The final prewar improvement to be tested was the fitting of variable-pitch propellers in K4771 *(lines 25 and 26)* starting early in 1938; performance was greatly improved, especially single-engined ceiling which was increased from 1,000ft to 6,800ft, and take-off distance which was halved. L7928, without the benefit of variable-pitch propellers, was used to extend the approval of the Anson to

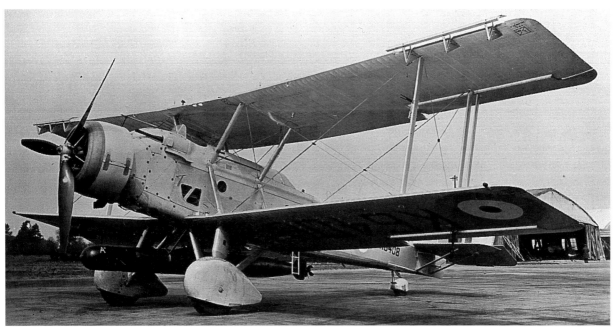

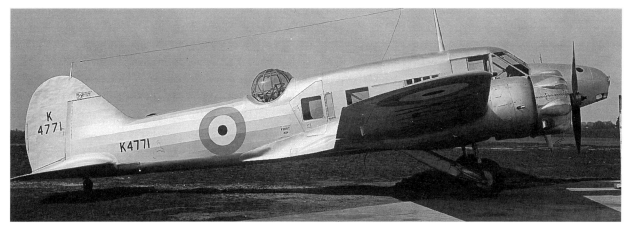

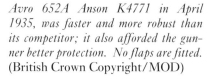

Avro 652A Anson K4771 in April 1935, was faster and more robust than its competitor; it also afforded the gunner better protection. No flaps are fitted. (British Crown Copyright/MOD)

8,000lb. The Establishment's recommendation was that at the new weight, the CG must be well forward of the aft limit with flaps down as full forward control column would not prevent the aircraft from pitching up and stalling when full power was applied at the aft limit.

Bristol Beaufort and Blackburn Botha

The Air Ministry Specification (10/36) for the replacement of the Vildebeest was a combination of earlier separate reconnaissance and torpe-

Blackburn Botha L6104 in May 1939. The Establishment had little good to say about this type. (British Crown Copyright/MOD)

Bristol Beaufort L4441 in May 1939, with ample flap. One of the earliest ground locks for the undercarriage is visible inboard of the port wheel. (British Crown Copyright/MOD)

do bomber requirements – M.15/35 and G.24/25 respectively. Some delay ensued to the chosen contenders by Bristol and Blackburn, and so a Specification 11/36 for an interim type was introduced. The Bristol Bolingbroke resulted from 11/36, but the requirement was cancelled before the type reached Martlesham, although some features were tested on a Blenheim. The Beaufort L4441 *(line 27)* arrived on 17 April, 1939, for a three-week stay for limited trials. Oil cooling and cylinder temperatures

were considered of higher priority than diving, endurance and military qualities. It was assessed as promising, but it was cold, very noisy and the throttle friction was not progressive. The auto lock to prevent movement of the undercarriage lever on the ground was liked. The stall was conventional but at the high speed of 70mph with undercarriage and flaps down and 80mph with them retracted.

The Botha L6104 *(line 28)* had even higher stalling speeds (82mph and 93mph) when tested in April and May 1939. Initial impressions were almost entirely unfavourable – the propeller controls were useless, fumes entered the cockpit, the heavy elevator combined with longitudinal instability made handling unpleasant and tiring, and rotating the turret caused rudder buffet. Long before Martlesham's assessment 242 Bothas had been ordered. L6105 arrived just in time to fly to Boscombe Down on the outbreak of war.

Lockheed Hudson

Ordered in the United States in June 1938, four Hudsons (N7205, N7206, N7207 and N7208) reached AAEE in June 1939. The only prewar report on the type records results of their formation flight of 5hr 15min at 10,300ft. Only N7207 had a turret (a mock-up), and it was concluded that the range from the 536gal that each carried was some 1,750 air miles, double that of the Anson.

Coastal Types

Line	Type	Identity	Engine/s No. Type		Total power (bhp/rpm)	Crew	Wing area (sq ft)	Max speed (mph/ft)	Take-off run (yd)	Landing speed (mph)
1	Cubaroo	N166	1	Cub	986/1,796	3	2,154	93/3,000		
2	Ava	N172	2	Condor III	1,369/1,900	4	2,163	100/6,500		64
3	Horsley	J8006	1	Condor III	687/1,900	2	696	129/MSL		
4	Horsley	J8006	1	Condor III	687/1,900	2	696	124/6,500		65
5	Horsley	S1236	1	Condor IIIA	665/1,900	2	696	125/6,500	252	56
6	Horsley	J8620	1	Leopard III	813/1,700	2		128/3,000	153	58
7	Horsley	J8932	1	Rolls-Royce H	810/2,000	2		127/1,000	241	57
8	Horsley	S1436	1	Condor IIIB	665/1,900	2	687	118/6,500		56
9	Harrier	J8325	1	Jupiter VIII	546/2,000	2	497	135/6,500		59
10	Harrier	J8325	1	Jupiter VIII	545/2,000	2	497	126/6,500		
11	Witch	J8596	1	Jupiter VIII	555/2,000	2	533	138/6,500	199	62
12	Beagle	N236	1	Jupiter VIII	526/2,000	2		130/5,000	152	60
13	Beagle	N236	1	Jupiter VIII	526/2,000	2	569	124/5,000		67
14	Hare	J8622	1	Jupiter VIII	545/2,000	2	453	136/6,500		67
15	Vildebeest	N230	1	Jupiter VIII	536/2,000	2	711	128/5,000	228	59
16	Vildebeest	N230	1	Jupiter VIII	536/2,000	2		128/5,000		53
17	Hare	J8622	1	Panther II	525/2,000	2	453	139/6,500		
18	Vildebeest	O-1	1	Panther IIA	525/2,000	2	711	120/5,000	231	61
19	Vildebeest	G-ABGE	1	Jupiter XFBM	540/2,000	2	711	137/5,000	194	58
20	Vildebeest	N230	1	Jupiter XFBM		2		134/5,000		

Line	Climb to 6,500ft Time (min-sec)	Rate (ft/min)	Service ceiling (ft)	Fuel capacity (Imp gal)	Weights Empty (lb)	Gross (lb)	Report No	Date	Remarks
1	52 - 00	55	4,975	700	12,389	20,600	399	1/25	Torpedo 2,967lb
2	16 - 54	245	9,750	700	13,100	21,770	456	4/27	Torpedo 2,967lb
3	8 - 12 to 6,000ft				5,086	9,342	418	6/27	120gal on trials
4	9 - 12	510	14,000	230	5,064	8,342	418D	3/28	
5	10 - 30	485	13,250	230	5,170	9,486	418E	8/28	Torpedo 2,069lb
6	6 - 48	735	17,750	230	5,358	8,230	418F	1/31	Bomber load
7	7 - 45	650	16,300		5,510	9,569	418I	12/30	
8	11 - 42	400	11,950	250	5,680	9,334	418J	10/31	
9	14 - 36	670	20,000		3,278	5,656	522	3/29	Bomber load
10	29 - 15	254	13,050	191	3,293	7,179	522/2	7/29	Torpedo load
11	14 - 12	600	20,000		3,703	6,156	518	5/29	Bomber load
12	16 - 45	430	15,800		3,739	6,047	501	12/28	Bomber load
13	25 - 30	300	11,200	124	3,770	7,445	501	2/29	Torpedo load
14	17 - 50	420	15,650	188	3,270	5,742	534	7/29	Bomber load
15	21 - 30	415	14,200	124	3,897	7,528	510	12/28	Torpedo load
16	16 - 21	540	18,500		3,822	6,130	510	12/28	Bomber load
17	8 - 30	615	15,200			6,056	534	5/32	Slotted wing
18	13 - 53	345	12,300	176	4,226	7,778	510A	2/31	
19	8 - 37	705	17,400	161	4,254	6,641	510B	2/31	Bomber load
20	6 - 45 to 5,000ft				4,306	7,649	510A	5/31	Oil cooling trials

Line	Type	Identity	Engine/s No.	Type	Total power (bhp/rpm)	Crew	Wing area (sq ft)	Max speed (mph/ft)	Take-off run (yd)	Landing speed (mph)
21	Vildebeest	S1707	1	Pegasus IM3	587/2,000	2	713	139/5,000	306	
22	Vildebeest	K6408	1	Perseus VIII	678/2,200	2		156/5,200	225	64
23	D.H.89A	K4772	2	Gipsy Six	372/2,100	3		148/5,000		
24	Anson	K4771	2	Cheetah VI	585/2,100	3		188/7,000		
25	Anson	K4771	2	Cheetah IX	620/2,100			182/6,600	245	
26	Anson	K4771	2	Cheetah IX	620/2,100			185/6,800	235	
27	Beaufort	L4441	2	Taurus TEIs		3		303/15,000	330	
28	Botha	L6104	2	Perseus X		3		253/15,600	350	

Line	Climb to 6,500ft Time (min-sec)	Rate (ft/min)	Service ceiling (ft)	Fuel capacity (Imp gal)	Weights Empty (lb)	Gross (lb)	Report No	Date	Remarks
21	9 - 57	625	16,250	153	4,437	8,103	510C	9/33	4.2hr endurance
22	7 - 30	800	17,550	72	4,755	8,500	510M	3/38	
23	9 - 00	565	17,700	90	3,368	5,372	643A	6/35	
24	7 - 00	880	19,500	120	5,104	7,342	680	5/35	
25		960	20,700				680A	3/38	Fixed-pitch props
26		1,115	22,700				680A	3/28	Variable-pitch props
27	6 - 45	1,070	26,000			17,000	740	6/39	
28	7 - 36	915	23,600			14,955	742	6/39	

MSL = Mean Sea Level

Special Purpose Types

Aeroplanes sent to Martlesham for testing but with no thought of obtaining a C of A nor of entering normal service with the Royal Air Force are the subject of this short section.

Several captured German machines found their way to Martlesham after the War, and in 1920 three of particular interest were overhauled with the intention of their flying. Fokker D VIII (110hp Oberursel) was flown between December 1921 and March 1922, while Roland D VIB was extensively overhauled in the summer of 1921, its constructional details noted, and then scrapped. A Junkers-J 10 of all-metal construction, was nearly ready for flight in September 1922, but was destroyed in the hangar fire.

Gloster Mars G-EAXZ; in December 1921 it raised the British speed record to 196mph. It is here shown with two Lamblin radiators. (British Crown Copyright/MOD)

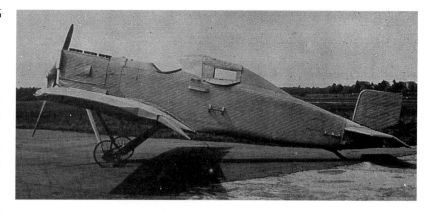

Junkers-J 10 (a CL I with cockpit cover) in August 1921. All surfaces were covered with corrugated metal sheet. (British Crown Copyright/MOD)

The Gloster Mars racer G-EAXZ raised the British speed record to 196mph in December 1921 in the hands of a Gloster pilot. A year later official trials were witnessed by the Royal Aero Club and several rate of climb records established. The outstanding speed and climb of this aeroplane *(line 1)* were combined with stability and well harmonized controls, but at the expense of a cramped yet very draughty cockpit and too high a landing speed compounded by a poor view. By the end of 1923 the

aircraft, as J7234, was stored at Martlesham; in May 1924 it returned to Glosters for modification.

The Gloster Grouse G-EAYN and its B.R.2 rotary motor was a development of the Nighthawk but with experimental wing sections; it arrived at AAEE on 11 May, 1923, and was extensively flown over the following few months. Results were sufficiently impressive for a version, named the Grebe, to be ordered for Service use.

Powered by an early Jaguar III radial engine, the Martinsyde F.4 G-EBKL was another racer, tested in the winter 1924-5. Performance *(line 2)* was inferior to the earlier Mars. Two experimental cantilever wing fighters were hastily constructed by

Handley Page as the H.P.21 and the second machine (unmarked but known as S2) started tests by the makers at Martlesham. Despite several improvised aerodynamic modifications handling was unsatisfactory and flying ceased after the company's pilot made an emergency landing in March 1924 when the elevator controls became disconnected.

Originally conceived as three-seater medium-range postal aeroplanes (Specification 11/20), the Parnall Possum and Boulton Paul Bodmin appear to have had only curiosity value by the time they reached Martlesham. The triplane Possum J6862 arrived in April 1924 and promptly broke its undercarriage; its fuselage-mounted Lion drove two wing-mounted propellers via chains. After repair, investigation of the novel power transmission was delayed by engine failure and finally terminated by serious damage while taxying in January 1925. Possum J6863 was tested from August 1925; its handling was described as 'nice' by one pilot, but it was damaged beyond repair in March 1926. Bodmin J6911 with two Lion engines was briefly flown in August 1925; pilots said it was 'a curious craft' and had 'a heavy rudder'.

Three of the foreign aircraft purchased by the Air Ministry in the mid-1920s found their way to Martlesham. Dornier Komet I J7276 arrived in spring 1924, and was briefly

assessed before its metal monoplane characteristics were fully investigated at the RAE. From France came the Breguet XIX J7507, flown between November 1924 and August 1925. It was written off when an airman, running the engines, ran into a hangar; he forgot that the throttle worked in the

Gloster Grouse G-EAYN in the summer of 1923. (Philip Jarrett)

Martinsyde F.4 G-EBKL early in 1925. (British Crown Copyright/ MOD)

Handley Page H.P.21 – flown at Martlesham only by the company's pilot early 1924. (Royal Air Force Museum)

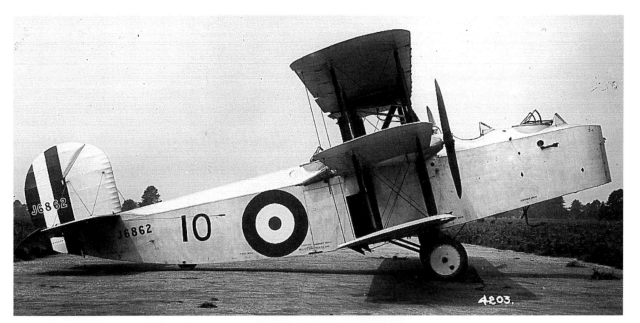

Parnall Possum J6862 in May 1924, with fuselage-mounted Lion and chain-driven propellers. The dark area ahead of the roundel is a radiator. The Scarff rings for the two gunners seem inappropriate for a postal aeroplane. (British Crown Copyright/MOD)

Dornier Komet I J7276 in the spring of 1924. (British Crown Copyright/ MOD)

reverse sense to the British practice. One pilot commented, 'Lord help the Frenchmen – laterally solid and long-ways ANEC-ish', (*ie* very twitchy) 'view bad at eye level – buckets on land and T-off', and another 'terrible thing – all out of proportion.' By contrast the third type, the Dutch Fokker F.VIIb.3M, J7986, was well liked; it had caused astonishment on arrival by looping in the hands of the Fokker pilot. One Martlesham pilot said, 'very nice, 3 engine job, practically non-stallable', another, 'wizard' and a third, 'very good on all controls'. In the Establishment's report, the Fokker F.VII's large load carrying capacity was attributed to the high-lift wing section used; the ability to fly easily with one wing engine inoperative was also praised but in stalled flight the ailerons were ineffective. The enclosed cabin caused no comment.

To Air Ministry order, Beardmore built a large cantilever monoplane on the lines favoured by the German Dr Adolph Rohrbach. Named Inflexible,

the sole machine of its type, J7557, had a wing span of 156ft 7in and made its journey by road to Martlesham in the spring of 1928. Once assembled it dominated the other types there, and ground trials revealed excessive back-lash in the controls of the three Condor III engines. Unusual precautions were taken before its first flight,

Breguet XIX J7507 in early 1925, with radiator extended. (British Crown Copyright/MOD)

but the take off took only a fraction of the run allowed for; later it was measured at 338yd into a 2mph wind at maximum weight. Performance was stately *(line 3)* and handling satisfactory in rough air. The Establishment report states: 'easy to taxy into the shed'; as there are no accident reports, it may be assumed that entry into the hangar was intentional although difficult to believe in view of the 100ft width of the open doors. The statement should, it seems, have read '...in

Fokker F.VIIb-3m J7986 in early 1926. Among advanced features were the high-lift cantilever monoplane wing and gyro instruments (the venturi is mounted on the fuselage above the undercarriage struts). (British Crown Copyright/MOD)

towards the shed'. Some 48hr were flown by AAEE by the end of 1929.

A French-built Wibault Type 12.C2 was purchased through Vickers, numbered J9029 and flown at Martlesham between August 1928 and early 1931. A series of short reports was written as breakages occurred on this all-metal parasol design during endurance tests. Most reports concerned fuel and radiator leaks from the Lion engine; the most serious structural weakness was discovered in the tail spar – only discovered after the machine was blown over taxying at the end of 1928.

Three special British designs were briefly tested between 1929 and 1935; the Handley Page H.P.39 (Gugnunc), the Fairey Long-range Monoplane and the de Havilland D.H.88 Comet. The Gugnunc G-AACN, designed for the American Guggenheim safety competition, was the subject of pressure error checks on 14 and 15 August 1929. Frederick Handley Page did not trust the correction of plus 9.2mph at an indicated 40mph, and a more accu-

rate check in September using an air log revealed a maximum correction of plus 7mph at an indicated 50mph. At 29mph (indicated) asymmetric slot closing caused a wing to drop suddenly; thus controlled flight at 35mph (true), a major requirement of the competition, was barely achievable *(line 4)*.

Beardmore Inflexible J7557 in mid-1929. The six-foot scale serves its purpose by the nose. All flying control surfaces have ample aerodynamic balancing – particularly the rudder. The wing dihedral is clearly shown in the shadow. (British Crown Copyright/MOD)

On 3 February, 1932, one flight was made by two pilots of No.22 squadron at Fairey's works on their second Long-range Monoplane, K1991. Vibration was bad, but control and stability were satisfactory, although the slight overbalance of the elevator and pronounced adverse aileron yaw made flying tiring in bad weather. A week later, K1991 broke the world's distance record with a nonstop flight of 5,397miles.

The Comet E-1 was assessed at Hatfield in October 1934, only a few weeks before the race to Australia for

Vickers-Wibault Type 122 (Type 12.C2) J9029, probably in late 1928. (Philip Jarrett)

de Havilland D.H.88 Comet K5084 after its landing accident on 2 September, 1936.

Cierva C.30A Rota K4230 in March 1935. The freely-rotating blades were found to lack rigidity. (Royal Air Force Museum)

Vought V-66E Corsair K3561 in December 1934. (British Crown Copyright/MOD)

which it was designed. Features commented upon included light and effective controls, lateral instability, a flat glide even with flaps down and the excessively long time to complete undercarriage retraction. The two propellers coarsened automatically after take off, not always simultaneously, but could only be reset to fine pitch on the ground; taxying was just possible in coarse pitch. At light load, 5,000ft could be maintained on the power of one engine. The third Comet was bought by the Air Ministry as K5084 and sent to Martlesham for comprehensive testing shortly before seizure of a pulley on 30 August, 1935, led to a wheels-up landing. After repair and some flying, a further failure in the under-

carriage locking system resulted in extensive damage during heavyweight landing.

Following tests with the Avro-built Cierva Autogiro in 1932, a batch for Service evaluation was ordered as the Rota. In January 1935, K4230 arrived for investigation into behaviour while diving; a limit on maximum speed was imposed as it was found that blade twisting occurred under extreme air loads causing nose-heaviness. K4239 paid a brief visit to Martlesham in May 1935, K4775 at the end of 1935, followed by K4236 which crashed on 18 June, 1936, just

Dewoitine 510 L4670 in October 1936, with cannon port in the spinner. (British Crown Copyright/MOD)

four weeks after arrival; K4232 was in general use between September 1936 and October 1937, by which time doubts existed about the strength of the rotor blades.

In the five years before the start of the war in 1939, six special foreign types flew at Martlesham. In mid-1934 the German Heinkel He 64 G-ACBS/K3596 (Gipsy III engine), was handled to assess the effects of slots and flaps on flight path angle at slow speed *(line 5),* The slots opened below 50mph, and at slower speeds it was found that very small changes in airspeed gave large changes in the flight path on the approach. It was also found that landing speeds were below the free air stalling speed and the extent of ground effect on this low-wing monoplane was measured. Among constructional criticisms was the lack of inspection panels in the wooden fuselage. The Vought Corsair V.66E from the United States was numbered K3561, and used in mid-1935 to measure performance *(line 6)* with the supercharger of its Wasp engine changing gear at 7,500ft. The cockpit was free from draughts up to 235mph, the controls light and effective and spins easy to enter and recover from. Performance was not outstanding. The two-seat American Northrop A-17 dive-bomber K5053 remained in general use for some months after its initial assessment in the summer of 1935.

Arriving at Martlesham on 21 August, 1936, the French Dewoitine 510, later L4670, possessed an outstanding climb but modest top speed *(line 7)*. The ailerons were heavy, due to a friction device in the control runs, but aerobatics were easy and the stall, at 68-70mph (indicated) was gentle. Features particularly liked were the automatic supply of oxygen above

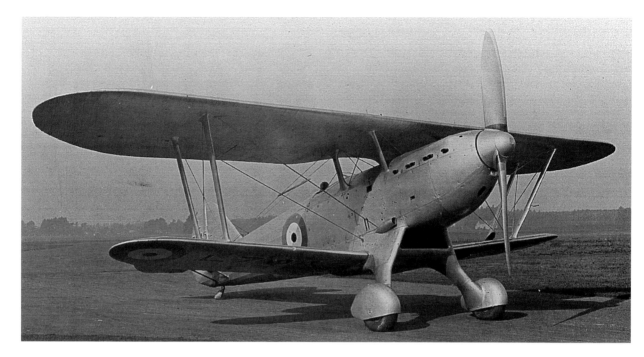

Fairey Fantome L7045 in February 1938. It has the same type of Hispano Suiza 12Ycrs engine as the Dewoitine 510, but without the cannon. (British Crown Copyright/MOD)

7,000ft, the electric heater in the oxygen mask, and the superior restraint of the five-point harness. Trials of the Dewoitine continued at RAE from January 1938.

The elegant Belgian-built Fairey Fantome L7045 was something of an anachronism as a biplane fighter on arrival in January 1938. Tests were limited to handling at 4,674lb, and cooling of its Hispano-Siuza 77.13 Ycrs engine. Handling was easy, but the aerodynamic controls were unusually heavy, while engine temperatures were adequately controlled by a single lever for both radiator and oil cooler. The type remained in use well into 1939.

Major Seversky brought his Type 2PA Model 202 NX2586, to AAEE,

in April 1939 and piloted the machine while Establishment pilots flew as observers. It had an exceptional rate of roll, a remarkable range, claimed to be 2,650 miles at economical speed,

Seversky 2PA/200 NX2586 in March 1939. The directional loop aerial is visible, as are the fairings for the rearward retracting main undercarriage. (British Crown Copyright/MOD)

Cunliffe-Owen O.A.1 G-AFMB in July 1939. This view hides the almost square planform of the fuselage. (British Crown Copyright/MOD)

was only slightly slower *(line 8)* than the current Hurricane and the workmanship was to a very high standard. The exceptionally comprehensive radio equipment was largely unuseable in the United Kingdom, and the gunner could not traverse his gun at high speed. Perhaps the most advanced feature was the constant-speed propeller.

Later in 1939, the unusual Cunliffe-Owen O.A.1 flying wing G-AFMB with two Perseus XIVC arrived for C of A trials. It failed to meet the take-off criteria, but achieved 218mph (true) at 6,700ft, and the design gave a large square floor area in the main cabin. It remained at Martlesham on the outbreak of war.

Special purpose types

Line	Type	Identity	Engine/s No.	Type	Power (bhp/rpm)	Crew	Wing area (sq ft)	Max speed (mph/ft)	Take-off run (yd)	Landing speed (mph)
1	Mars I	G-EAXZ	1	Lion	526/2,100	1	200	180/6,500		
2	Martinsyde F.4	G-EBKL	1	Jaguar III	363/1,620	1	324	149/6,500		
3	Inflexible	J7557	3	Condor III	2,065/1,900	3	1,892	101/6,500		65
4	H.P.39	G-AACN	1	Mongoose III		2			66ft after 474yd	
5	Heinkel He 64	K3596	1	Gipsy III	109/2,000		149	126/MSL	155	42
6	Corsair V-66E	K3561	1	Wasp D1	500/	2	322	151/7,500	174	58
7	Dewoitine 510	L4670	1	Hispano-Suiza 12	860/2,400	1		230/13,000	225	66
8	Seversky 2PA	NX2586	1	Pratt & Whitney R-1830	1,100/2,700	2	223	316/15,500		

Line	Climb to 6,500ft Time (min-sec)	Rate (ft/min)	Service ceiling (ft)	Fuel capacity (Imp gal)	Weights Empty (lb)	Gross (lb)	Report No	Date	Remarks
1	2 – 30	2,220	26,600	50	2,133	2,770	317	11/22	Racer
2	4 – 12	1,315	22,000	55	1,981	2,800	402	2/25	Racer
3	18 – 06	232	9,350	546	24,923	31,400	495	3/30	
4	3 – 00 to 1,980ft			36		2,140	541	8/29	
5	12 – 04	420	14,500	28	1,115	1,780	621	4/34	
6	6 – 10	835	21,400	78	2,841	4,040	645	6/35	8.3ampg cruise
7	5 – 18 to 15,000ft		32,000	315		4,400	705	1/37	
8	3 – 40 to 10,000ft		33,100		4,581	7,658	736	5/39	11hr endurance

MSL = Mean Sea Level
ampg = Air Miles Per Gallon

Deck Landing Torpedo and Bomb Droppers

Blackburn Swift N139 in December 1920. The split undercarriage is shown with the torpedo crutching arrangements under the fuselage. (British Crown Copyright/MOD)

Three roles were formulated in 1919 for the Royal Air Force operating afloat – reconnaissance, defence and offence. The last named was limited initially to carrying and dropping a torpedo – either a Mk VIII★ of 1,500lb or a Mk IX of 1,100lb. A dummy example of each was received at Martlesham in 1920 for carriage on the aircraft designed to meet the recent Air Ministry requirement (Director of Research Type VIII). Before arrival of the new designs, a wartime torpedo carrier, the Sopwith Cuckoo, N8005, spent several months in 1920 on parachute testing.

Blackburn Swift and Dart, Handley Page Hanley and Hendon

First of the Type VIII aircraft was the Swift *(line 1)* a private venture recently purchased by the Air Ministry and numbered N139 for Martlesham trials, starting in December 1920. After decreasing the fin area and altering the rudder shape, directional and elevator control at low speed were improved, and handling was assessed as easy for the large aeroplane. Meanwhile, orders had been placed for three developments of the Swift, known as the Dart, and for three Handley Page

Hanleys; in 1921 the Specifications for the two types were numbered 9/20 and 3/20 respectively.

The first Dart, N140, spent only four weeks from October 1921 at Martlesham on handling assessment before carrier trials on HMS *Argus*. Shortly afterwards N141 completed the full performance trials twice *(lines 2 and 3)*, once with each of the two torpedoes. N142 soon followed with divided control column, a tail incidence gear giving greater movement, and deck landing claws. The wheel control of N141 was preferred. Trials of the fuel jettison system (so that the empty tanks could provide buoyancy after a ditching) revealed that some petrol was blown into the bottom of the fuselage. In May 1922 N142 was fitted with a new propeller which increased performance slightly *(line 4)*, and was adopted for the produc-

tion versions; N9542 was the representative for rapid trials lasting twelve days in November 1922 and taking 3hr 45min of flying. An oleo undercarriage, tested on N9545 was also adopted as standard. Three other Darts featured at AAEE: N9557 in early 1925, probably including bombing trials, N9822 in 1927 for an unknown purpose and N9806 *(line 5)* with automatic slots in 1928.

The Hanley N143 arrived in March 1922 and was an immediate failure; the ailerons gave a slow response and the rudder was ineffective and considered dangerous when a torpedo was fitted. The cockpit was small and uncomfortable, the CG, at 35 percent of mean chord resulted in tail heaviness. A larger fin and rudder

Handley Page Hanley N143 after the collapse of its undercarriage in April 1922. Interesting features visible are the full-span slots, the small control wheel and the tube running along the fuselage and terminating at the fins. The last item is probably the fuel jetison pipe. (British Crown Copyright/MOD)

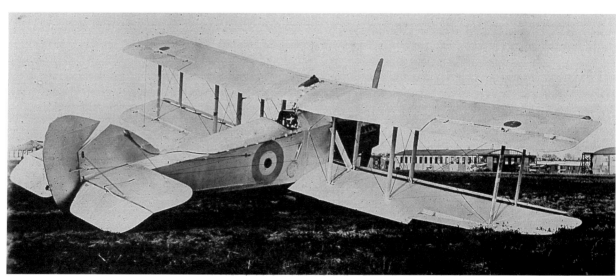

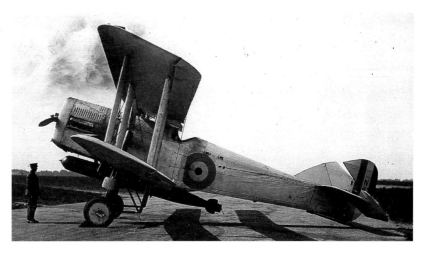

Handley Page Hanley N143 in June 1923, with improved slots, a balanced elevator and revised control cable arrangements alongside the cockpit. (British Crown Copyright/MOD)

were made and fitted by AAEE, but encouraging results were terminated when the weak undercarriage failed. Meanwhile, the company had crashed N144; N145 *(line 6)* arrived in May 1922 and broke an engine mounting. Engine change on the Hanley took two men 12hr, twice as long as on the Dart. Although N145 had full-span slots on both wings, any benefit was lost due to ineffective elevator and aileron control at low speed. The Establishment summarised the Hanley as inferior. On return in April 1923, N143 had many improvements incorporated, included better slots, differential ailerons and a larger rudder; handling and performance *(line 7)* improved. This aircraft continued on various tests including new air intakes until at least March 1924. N145 also returned, but was struck off charge after the stern post broke.

A two-seat development of the Hanley was the Hendon. N9724 was tested by Handley Page at Martlesham in August 1924 – but was tail heavy; sweeping back the wings moved the centre of pressure rearwards and restored balance. N9727 completed trials in October 1924, but performance *(line 8)* was inferior to the modified Hanley.

Specification 21/23

Specification 21/23, dated June 1924, for a two-seater Ship Plane capable of carrying the 1,500lb Mk VIII torpedo

Handley Page Hendon N9724 in late 1924, with swept wings and fully-equipped including a little ballast under the wings. (British Crown Copyright/MOD)

produced three types for testing at AAEE in 1926 and 1927. The types were the Avro Buffalo (a private venture), Blackburn Ripon and Handley Page Harrow. All three arrived by

October 1926 powered by the Lion VA for the first phase of trials lasting until early 1927. The Buffalo G-EBNW possessed very poor handling qualities, the ailerons being particularly bad and performance appears not to have been measured. The Ripon N203 *(line 9)*, had an over-balanced rudder and poor ailerons; violent yawing was cured by fitting 15lb of ballast in the rudder horn-balance. The first Harrow, N205, possessed good and positive handling but a weak undercarriage which collapsed before trials had been fully completed. Replaced by the similar second prototype, N206, performance *(line 10)* tests were completed. All three types were returned to their makers for aerodynamic improvements and the fitting of the more powerful Lion XA (probably the Lion XIA in the private venture Buffalo). The trio

Blackburn Ripon N203 in late 1926, in original form with Napier Lion V engine. (British Crown Copyright/MOD)

Handley Page Harrow N206 in late 1926, with its Lion V enclosed in a cowling different from that of the Ripon. (British Crown Copyright/MOD)

Avro Buffalo G-EBNW in July 1927, in its interim form with Lion X in streamlined cowling, but lacking the Frise ailerons and slots fitted and tested later in 1927. (British Crown Copyright/MOD)

completed the second phase of the competition at Martlesham between May and November 1927. The Buffalo G-EBNW with the new engine and metal-framed wings was delayed by undercarriage failure in May; handling was improved but there is no evidence of performance measurements. Later in 1927, G-EBNW paid a third visit with slots and four Frise ailerons. The Harrow was again represented by N205 and N206; the latter suffered initially from inadequate cooling of the engine in its streamlined cowling. With a larger radiator N205 completed trials but suffered no fewer than thirteen reportable failures, and was further modified with equal dihedral on both wings and finally, in early 1928, a metal propeller. The Ripon, initially N203 and,

Handley Page Harrow N205 in August 1927 with revised and acceptable cooling, and a new cowling. (British Crown Copyright/MOD)

then, from late 1927, a new prototype N231 *(line 11)*; both had increased sweepback and, in N231, a streamlined cowling with retractable side radiators. The Ripon possessed satisfactory handling with light and effective controls in all three axes; it had the best performance. It was selected in late 1927 for Service use and S1268 duly arrived in April 1929 for production checks, including dives

to 195mph (indicated). A year later S1266 and S1267 were also dived in an attempt to reproduce tail flutter as reported on these aircraft in Fleet Air Arm use. At the same time S1270 was handled and spun with a cropped rudder and improved tail actuating gear, but without a torpedo; with a 'tinfish' its performance *(line 12)* was mediocre. S1424 and S1468 with slight structural and aero-

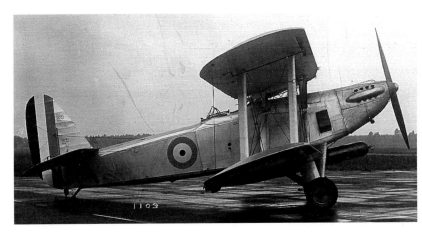

Blackburn Ripon N231 in September 1927, with a Lion X and a new, taller fin and rudder. (British Crown Copyright/MOD)

with a Pegasus IM3. Both were subject to performance, handling and armament trials, and, in addition, B-5 underwent oil cooling tests. Another trial, propeller suitability later in 1933 was made on a Pegasus-engined machine – K3589; the AAEE report numbering system indicates that K3589 was the same machine as B-5. As a result of trials on B-5, the pro-

dynamic changes followed in 1930 and 1931 respectively for handling and performance measurement. In September 1931 S1571 completed fuel jettison trials, and the following year S1670 was successfully spun without a torpedo, after repairs to the air intakes.

First of several developments of the Ripon was S1272 *(line 13)*, with redesigned fuselage and fin and with metal frame. Criticisms in March 1930 included the lack of hand holds for mechanics when hand-cranking the engine and the poor view on take off and when diving, the latter due to the wing position. Two months later

Ripon S1272 in March 1930, with Lion XI, side radiators, enlarged observer's cockpit and revised fin and rudder. Like N231 it has interconnected ailerons and slats. (British Crown Copyright/MOD)

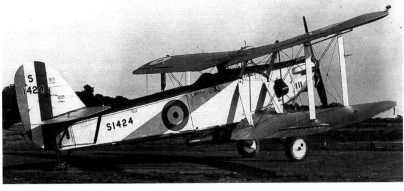

S1272 *(line 14)* returned with the top wing raised which improved the view, but slightly degraded the performance. Various breakages occurred in succeeding months during trials of the ammunition box and link chute for the fixed gun.

Two radial-engined Ripons arrived almost simultaneously in January 1933 – B-4 with a Tiger I and B-5

Ripon S1424 in mid-1930; it had minor structural modifications and was the first of the version known as Mk IIA in service. The torpedo appears without its fins. (Royal Air Force Museum)

duction type K3546, known as the Baffin, had a hook, generator windmill, revised instrument layout and several armament and other minor

modifications incorporated. The controls were good up to the maximum diving speed of 185mph indicated; however, the cockpit was narrow and uncomfortable and several instruments were obscured by the control wheel. The last fault was cured by fitting an articulated control column, tested in S1142 by eight pilots nearly two years later in November 1935. Meanwhile, late in 1934, S1665 the first Ripon to be converted to Baffin configuration completed performance measurements.

Specification M.1/30

The Ripon replacement Specification, M.1/30, called inter alia, for extremely low structural weight on the three officially sponsored contenders. The Handley Page H.P.46 was virtually unflyable and the Vickers 207 broke up in a dive; neither type reached Martlesham. The Blackburn M.1/30, S1640, reached AAEE in January 1933 after lengthy trials at Brough, but during performance tests, it

crashed and was destroyed on 30 June, 1933, when its Buzzard engine cut out on take off; no reason was adduced. In 1932, Blackburn privately built a second M.1/30 but with a metal monocoque fuselage containing a watertight compartment. As B-3 (later K3591) *(line 15)*, it was found in 1933 to have heavy and sluggish controls, unreliable brakes and excessive trim change with application of power; the cockpit was narrow and cold. Martlesham commented that

Blackburn Baffin S1665 in July 1934 was the first conversion from a Ripon by fitting a Pegasus engine and other changes - including wireless. (Royal Air Force Museum)

K3591 was 1,000lb overweight, 9kt slow and 4,000ft low on ceiling compared to the requirements of its modified Specification, M.1/30A. As a private venture, Vickers submitted a modified Vildebeest, O-7, with a span just 12in less than the maximum

Blackburn M.1/30 K3591 in May 1933. Features include the neat stowage of the Lewis gun at the rear of the aft cockpit and the large-span ailerons on all wings which could also act as flaps. (British Crown Copyright/MOD)

Vickers Vildebeest O-7 in November 1933. The slats are of unusually short span; visible in front of the tailwheel is the arrester hook. (British Crown Copyright/MOD)

Blackburn Shark K4880 in March 1936, with redesigned oil cooler, and exhaust muffs for cockpit heating. (British Crown Copyright/MOD)

allowed of 50ft. At Martlesham from September 1933, O-7 *(line 16)* was dived to 210mph (indicated), and handled well; its new Fairey mounting for the Lewis gun was liked but other aspects of the armament were criticised. The Pegasus engine did not comply with the requirement for a Buzzard or Leopard; however, the Vildebeest met the stringent load and endurance requirements.

Specification S.15/33

While the M.1/30 designs were experiencing their vicissitudes, the Specification was rewritten as S.15/33. With the lessons of the M.1/30 in mind, Blackburn built a private venture torpedo shipplane which arrived at AAEE in November 1933 at about the time that S.15/33 was issued. This aeroplane, later to become the

Shark, was initially B-6 and was tested against the requirements of the new Specification. Spending most of the year until November 1934 undergoing full tests B-6 (bought by the Air Ministry as K4295 in May 1934) with a Tiger IV engine was ordered for Service use. The first production Shark K4349 *(line 17)* spent two periods of five months each at Martlesham the first from 31 December, 1934, and the second period from

Shark K4882 in March 1936, with Pegasus engine and heater muffs on the exhaust pipes. (British Crown Copyright/MOD)

September 1935 when it had its Tiger IV replaced by a Tiger VI; the cockpit remained too cold in spite of improved draught proofing. Similarly powered, K4880 *(line 18)* had increased fuel capacity (not fully filled for trials) and was spun with and without a torpedo. The brakes, flaps and controls (heavy but effective) were satisfactory; dives to 243mph (indicated) no doubt served to highlight the very cold and draughty accommodation. Contemporary with K4880 at Martlesham in the spring and summer 1936 was K4882 *(line*

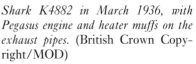

Gloster TSR.38 S1705 in June 1934. The entire leading edge of the upper wing appears to be the condensation pipe for the steam from the engine. (British Crown Copyright/MOD)

19) with the cleaner, simpler but too cool Pegasus III engine. K4882 had jig-made ailerons which overcame earlier inconsistent handling of the Shark and later an enclosed cabin to cure the perennial cold. K8902 had barely begun its trials before it made a forced landing on 20 May, 1937.

Following difficulty with stainless steel, Specification S.9/30 was dropped early in 1933, and the two companies affected, Gloster and Fairey, redesigned their proposed aircraft into the TSR.38 and TSR II respectively, for the S.15/33 requirement, combining gun spotting and reconnaissance with torpedo dropping. Both arrived at Martlesham in the first week of June 1934, the Gloster S1705 with an experimental Goshawk engine and the Fairey, K4190, with the well tried Pegasus. The Gloster had a marked swing to the left on take off and the flying qualities were poor due to lack of control at speeds less than 90mph and heavy controls above 115mph; the undercarriage and brakes were praised. After deck landing trials (for which the lack of low speed control appears to have been acceptable) S1705 *(line 20)* returned to AAEE and stayed until May 1935. The Fairey *(line 21)* was immediately praised for its light, quick and positive controls throughout the speed range, although the ailerons snatched at the stall; flying with three 250lb bombs, all under one wing, presented no problems. No fewer than 2,500 rounds were fired from the fixed Vickers gun and over 1,200 from the rear Lewis gun but the rear gunner's cockpit was draughty and he could not traverse his gun above 100mph. For the spotter loading, the Fairey TSR II carried three crew and, for the torpedo loading a crew of two. The only adverse comment was that the production Swordfish, as the TSR II was named, needed another 20gal of fuel.

The extra capacity was provided in K5660 *(line 22)* (type trials April to October 1936) also fitted with a new three-bladed propeller. Loadings for reconnaissance (162gal), torpedo dropping (137gal) and catapult launching (42gal) confirmed the type's pleasant handling characteristics up to the maximum diving speed of 182mph indicated (K4129 had reached 214mph). With an increase in the range of elevator movement, K5660 reached 210mph in mid-1937, by which time a redesigned oil cooler was assessed as suitable for tropical flying in the Swordfish. At the end of 1938, the growing diversity of armament available, even for Naval aircraft, was tested on L9776 *(line 23)*, in various combinations of Small Bomb Containers; armed with the load giving the greatest drag, a range of 435 miles was calculated.

Fairey Albacore L7075 in May 1939. It was intended as a replacement for the Swordfish. (British Crown Copyright/MOD)

Fairey Albacore

The replacement for the Swordfish, specified in early 1937, was the Albacore the second of which, L7075 appeared briefly at Martlesham between 16 and 25 May, 1939, for assessment before deck landing trials. The rudder was heavy, but otherwise the Albacore handled well and was judged to be easy and pleasant for ship work; the type required a trickle of power to prevent an excessive rate of descent and heavy landing on the spongy undercarriage.

Blackburn Skua

In December 1934 the advanced requirements for a deck landing dive-bomber were formulated in Specification O.27/34 and the Skua monoplane duly arrived at Martlesham; other companies, whose projects failed to materialize were daunted perhaps by the thought of adding folding wings and robust undercarriage to the complexity of a modern monoplane.

K5178 arrived in time to be flown by an Establishment pilot at the RAF Display in June 1937; it then returned

to its makers. Trials proper occupied four weeks from 9 October, 1937, and concentrated on handling and stability. Ballast, to bring the CG 18in forward, produced pleasant and easy handling except near the stall when a small rearward pressure on the stick produced a 10mph loss in speed and a stall. The Establishment criticised the position, on the right side of the cockpit, of the levers for the undercarriage and flaps; the undercarriage oleo legs were also poor. The following March, full armament trials were made; both wing guns had an inadequate 50 watt heater and the rear Lewis gun mounting was unsatisfactory. Slots were fitted to K5179, flown in June 1938; the approach was characterized by longitudinal instability, but pilots soon became familiar with the tendency of the nose to rise, and accepted the need for small compensating stick movements. In November a spring in the elevator improved handling on the

Skua K5179 in June 1938 with turned up wingtips, landing lights and four wing-mounted Browning guns. (British Crown Copyright/MOD)

Blackburn Skua K5178 early in 1938 with straight wing and unarmed. (British Crown Copyright/MOD)

approach, but made pitch control worse with power on; slots were considered to be unnecessary. The prototypes' Mercury was replaced by a Perseus in the production version and L2867 completed radio, oil cooling, diving and night trials from September 1938. Prolonged climbs resulted in the engine running slightly too hot; the aircraft was dived to 300mph indicated. L2868 (armament trials) had a much improved rear gun mounting, and a novel method of ejector arm to carry the 500lb bomb clear of the airframe before release. The ejector was satisfactory for release but unacceptable when the arm was later restowed. The two wing-mounted Browning guns (one made by Vickers and one by BSA) were unheated but nevertheless satisfactory on account of the Skua's low ceiling and the reliability of the guns. L2871 crashed on 6 January, 1939, during performance trials which were completed on L2888 *(line 24)*. The latter had the elevator spring fitted and the aeroplane appeared to be unstable in the climb. The plots of elevator angle and trimmer against angle of attack show longitudinal stability; the plots were made at cruising power. Performance was disappointing, particularly take-off distance and initial rate of climb and the type was relegated to target towing. L2867 returned suitably accoutred for this new secondary role six weeks before the war; trials were completed at Boscombe Down.

Deck landing torpedo and bomb droppers

Line	Type	Identity	Engine No.	Type	Power (bhp/rpm)	Crew	Wing area (sq ft)	Max speed (mph/ft)	Landing speed (mph)
1	Swift	N139	1	Lion IB	462/2,000	1	712	106/3,000	
2	Dart	N141	1	Lion II	470/2,000	1	654	106/3,000	
3	Dart	N141	1	Lion II	470/2,000	1	654	107/3,000	
4	Dart	N142	1	Lion II		1		107/3,000	
5	Dart	N9806	1	Lion II	468/2,000	1		103/5,000	
6	Hanley	N145	1	Lion II	474/2,000	1	593	97/3,000	
7	Hanley	N143	1	Lion	486/2,000	1	596	114/MSL	
8	Hendon	N9727	1	Lion II	471/2,000	2	562	104/MSL	
9	Ripon	N203	1	Lion VA	463/2,000		681	104/6,500	
10	Harrow	N206	1	Lion VA	470/2,000		564	113/3,000	64
11	Ripon	N231	1	Lion XA	566/2,350	2	682	129/6,500	62
12	Ripon	S1270	1	Lion XIA	530/2,350	2	682	106/MSL	61
13	Ripon	S1272	1	Lion XIA	530/2,350	2	711	111/MSL	
14	Ripon	S1272	1	Lion XIA	530/2,350	2	711	110/MSL	53
15	Blackburn M.1/30A	K3591	1	Buzzard IIIMS	825/2,000		651	142/MSL	
16	Vildebeest	O-7	1	Pegasus IIL3	621/2,000	2	713	133/5,000	
17	Shark	K4389	1	Tiger VI	780/2,150	2		147/6,500	
18	Shark	K4880	1	Tiger VI	763/2,150	2		150/6,500	
19	Shark	K4882	1	Pegasus III	670/2,200	2		147/5,000	
20	Gloster TSR.38	S1705	1	Goshawk III	694/2,600	2		151/5,200	
21	Swordfish	K4190	1	Pegasus IIIM3	677/2,200	2	542	143/5,000	
22	Swordfish	K5660	1	Pegasus III	656/2,200	2	547	142/5,000	
23	Swordfish	L9776	1	Pegasus IIIM3	690/2,200			136/4,200	
24	Skua	L2888	1	Perseus XII	730/2,400	2	319	224/6,500	

| Line | Climb to 6,500ft | | Service ceiling (ft) | Fuel capacity (Imp gal) | Weights | | Report | | Remarks |
	Time (min–sec)	Rate (ft/min)			Empty (lb)	Gross (lb)	No	Date	
1	11 – 42 to 5,000 ft		11,550	80	4,425	6,495	281	3/21	Mk VIII torpedo
2	17 – 24	260	10,300	78	3,599	6,373	294	2/22	Mk VIII torpedo
3	15 – 30	304	11,350	78	3,599	5,973	294	2/22	Mk IX torpedo
4	14 – 20	340	12,700		3,989	6,333	303	5/22	Mk VIII torpedo
5	12 – 24	305	9,700		3,640	6,297	294A	8/28	
6		120	10,550	81	3,595	6,349	300B	5/22	2.5hr endurance
7	11 – 15	460	14,700	80	3,659	6,413	336A	6/23	3hr endurance
8	18 – 48	255	9,500	82	3,968	6,970	398	10/24	
9	18 – 15	230	9,500	161	3,802	7,071	468	10/26	
10	18 – 45	210	8,700	156	4,236	7,460	470	6/27	
11	11 – 00	430	12,950		4,117	7,303	468A	1/28	
12	20 – 30	194	8,700		4,569	7,556	468C	6/30	
13	15 – 30	270	10,000	162	4,676	7,663	553	3/30	
14	20 – 00	200	9,150		4,776	7,763	553/2	5/30	Raised wing
15	11 – 25	410	12,000	255	6,138	10,393	621A	4/34	
16	11 – 40	410	12,700	183	4,687	8,738	510G	1/34	4.66ampg
17	7 – 06	730	15,650	171	4,459	8,111	639A	3/36	3.82ampg
18	8 – 30	580	14,600	175	4,596	8,250	639C	9/36	4.25ampg
19	8 – 18	610	14,600	172	4,431	8,086	639B	9/36	4.34ampg
20	7 – 45	660	16,100	156	4,573	8,038	653	6/35	Torpedo load
21	8 – 19	605	16,500	142	4,110	7,580	648	4/35	Torpedo load
22	9 – 48	500	13,100	162	4,689	8,230	648A	11/36	Torpedo load
23	6 – 18 to 5,000 ft		13,550			8,250	648B	2/39	Bomb load
24	7 – 42	900	19,100	163	5,859	8,228	717A	8/39	500lb bomb

MSL = Mean Sea Level
ampg = Air Miles Per Gallon

Deck Landing Fighters

Nieuport Nightjar

Among the standard types of aeroplane chosen by the Air Ministry in 1920 was the Nieuport (later Gloster) Nighthawk for use as a single-seat fighter from land and at sea; the official requirement was Director of Research Type I. Persistent trouble with the original ABC Dragonfly engine led to the fitting of the proven but old Bently B.R.2 rotary engine for the Naval version. Renamed Nightjar, H8535 arrived at Martlesham in May 1922 by which time the rotary engine had been abandoned for operational use, although some twenty-two Nightjars later entered service. Trials of H8535 were brief and the performance *(line 1)* poor. In 1923, the production version J6941 was tested even more briefly in 1hr 22min of flying.

Specification 6/22

The promise of the Jaguar radial engine led to Specification 6/22 for a

Gloster Nightjar H8535 in May 1922, with port Vickers gun visible in front of the cockpit. (British Crown Copyright/MOD)

deck landing fighter; Parnall and Fairey each received contracts for three aeroplanes. The Parnall Plover flew in December 1922, but difficulties with the early Jaguar engine delayed progress. The third Plover, N162 temporarily fitted with a Jupiter engine, arrived at Martlesham in May

1923 for performance trials *(line 2)*. N162 soon had a Jaguar fitted and the performance tests *(line 3)* were repeated in August. N160 followed, with its second or third replacement Jaguar, in November 1923; no report has been found. A small pro-

Nighthawk J6941 in May 1923, in production form but lacking armament. Seen between the undercarriage struts is the fuel pump windmill. (British Crown Copyright/MOD)

duction contract was placed to Specification 27/23; N9609 completed full performance *(line 4)* trials powered by a Jupiter IV, and later, armament tests. Flying took over a year (May 1924 to mid-1925) to complete due partly to bowed spars and rigging trouble. N9702 *(line 5)*, performed with a supercharged Jupiter IV in the summer of 1924, followed in September by N9708 with a strengthened centre section. It seems that the final decision in favour of the rival Fairey Flycatcher was made as a result of Service experience with both types; only a few Plovers were used in the Service Flights.

With its Jaguar II engine running satisfactorily, the first Flycatcher, N163, completed initial trials *(line 6)* in February 1923, including evaluation of its unique camber-changing device on the wing trailing-edges. The handling qualities were not praised by test pilots – logbook comments included 'rather heavy - tail gear slips'. N163 soon left for Gosport and deck landing trials with Plover N160, the latter without preceding handling at Martlesham. In mid-1923, Flycatcher N164 had its consumption measured – while handling was reported as 'tail heavy – beastly'. Later, in 1924, N164 was used for gun firing and then performance measure-

ments *(line 7)* with an experimental cowling in place of a spinner. Also in mid-1923 N163 returned for maker's trials with a Jupiter engine; no official trials appear to have followed until the end of 1924 when full performance *(line 8)* was measured with a Jupiter IV, and many other changes incorporated including strengthened wings and special air inlets. N9616, representative of the production version was flown as early as July 1923; per-

Fairey Flycatcher N164 in mid-1923, with Jaguar engine. (British Crown Copyright/MOD)

Plover N9702 in June 1924, with supercharged Jupiter. The panel just behind the cockpit is labelled 'Engine Starting'. (British Crown Copyright/MOD)

formance *(line 9)* was unchanged from the Jaguar prototype. Supercharging in the Jaguar IV engine of N9619 increased top speed and rate of climb both with *(line 10)* and without *(line 11)* a spinner in the summer of 1924. Other Flycatchers at Martlesham were N9882 (December 1925 to May 1927 propeller tests) for which a pilot's logbook records the opinion 'v. sluggish', N9952 (June 1926 to April

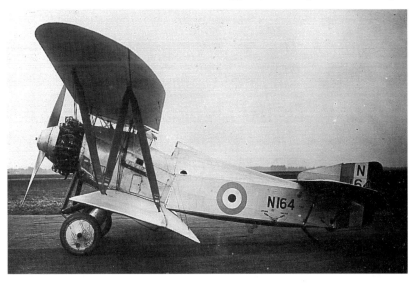

Flycatcher N9662, probably late 1927, showing all the ailerons lowered to increase camber. (British Crown Copyright/MOD)

1929) for tests including brakes and N9662. No reports appear to survive indicating any improvement in handling – yet in service, the Flycatcher was renowned for its delightful handling.

Specification 17/25

A metal-skinned airframe and relatively low power were features of Specification 17/25; two types were built – the Avro Avocet and the Vickers Vireo. Both were officially sponsored, both were usually unserviceable at Martlesham and both were rejected. Their Lynx IV engines failed to provide the expected output

during trials in the summer of 1928; the Vireo arrived on 1 April. The report on the Avocet, N210, is missing but that of the Vireo, N211, *(line 12)* praised its excellent view but criticised the rapid loss of speed on roundout because of the difficulty this characteristic would pose on deck landing. During the Vireo's second visit in mid-1929 to mid-1930, firing the guns almost stopped the engine. Any remedies tried are not known.

Specification 21/26 (later N.21/26)

No fewer than eleven types of aeroplane were seriously proposed by manufacturers to replace the Flycatcher and meet the requirements of Specification 21/26. Ten of them reached AAEE for handling, performance and armament assessment; trials on floats, catapult launching and deck handling were held elsewhere. Due to delays with the engine specified, the Mercury II, and a revised require-

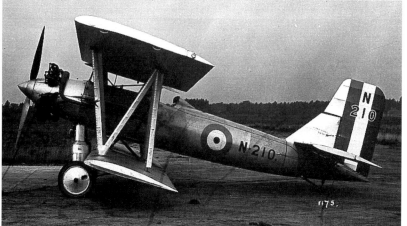

Avro Avocet N210 in February 1928, with metal propeller and ample rudder. (British Crown Copyright/MOD)

Vickers Vireo N211 in May 1928. The corrugations of the metal wing are visible. The pitot tube is parellel to the ground and thus at an angle of at least 10deg to the mean chord. (British Crown Copyright/MOD)

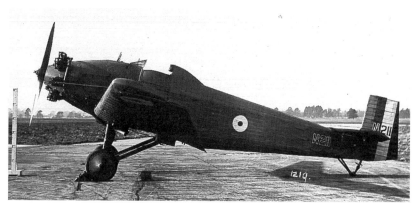

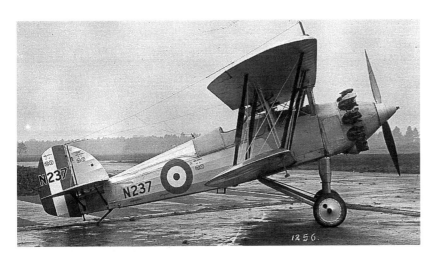

Hawker Hoopoe N237 in April 1929, for the first phase of the N.21/26 competition. Copious radio aerials are visible in the original photograph, plus liberal stencilling to indicate electrical bonding. (British Crown Copyright/MOD)

rapid throttle opening (the same fault occurred on the Flycatcher II); it was draughty and possessed poor ground control qualities in spite of its wheel brakes. Subsequently, deck handling was deemed unsatisfactory. Vickers' private Type 141 (Rolls-Royce FXI) had a narrow cockpit, slightly over-balanced controls but was neverthe-less easy to land slowly; the wheel brakes could be applied by moving the stick fully aft. The fifth type was the Hawker Hoopoe N237 (Mercury) which was comfortable, handled well at mid-speeds, but needed lots of left rudder at high speed, and lots of ele-vator at slow speed; the brakes were harsh. In spite of the tricky landing, the Hoopoe was sent for the more demanding deck landing trials. The Flycatcher II, Gnatsnapper and Vickers 141 also were considered sat-isfactory for sea trials; but the Flycatcher II crashed at Gosport on 8 May, 1929, before embarking.

The second, and ultimately con-clusive, phase of the N.21/26 competi-tion began in the spring of 1930. Six types appeared (a seventh, a private venture by Gloster failed to material-ize), and while all had metal air-frames, no fewer than four types of engine were used. The Hoopoe and Gnatsnapper, modified after the 1929 trials, were officially funded and pow-

ment for an all-metal structure, AAEE trials for the 21/26 competi-tion were in two phases – the first in spring 1929 and the second in the spring of 1930. Even before the first phase, one contender, the Parnall Pipit, selected by the Air Ministry for prototype construction, had been eliminated. The first of the type, N232, had a weak rudder, heavy ele-vator and a strange tendency to drop the starboard wing at high speed. It crashed on 20 September 1928, seri-ously injuring the pilot, when at-tempting to land at Martlesham with the starboard tailplane crumpled dur-ing high-speed flying. The second, N233, with a much modified fin and rudder originally built for N232, Frise ailerons, a braced tailplane, Palmer brakes and other changes, had better

Gloster Gnatsnapper N227 in May 1930, with the fashionable Townend ring cowling around its Jaguar engine. (British Crown Copyright/MOD)

handling, but the elevator remained heavy and the rudder became unmov-able above 100mph. N233 crashed after the rudder post broke during tri-als from the maker's aerodrome at Yate near Bristol; the pilot baled out successfully.

In addition to the Pipit, five other types underwent brief handling trials during the first phase in April and May 1929 to assess suitability for car-rier flying; no performance figures were obtained. The Fairey Flycatcher II N216 (Mercury) had heavy rudder and elevator and was very tricky on overshooting; it was difficult to manoeuvre on the ground and had no brakes. The same company's private Firefly III (F1137) (Rolls-Royce FXI) was cramped, and had poor low-speed handling; the consequent high approach speed rendered it unsuitable for deck landing. Good air handling qualities characterized the Gloster Gnatsnapper N227, but the Mercury II engine was prone to cut out on

Armstrong Whitworth Starling A-1 in April 1930; an unusual feature is a lamp on the top centre section. (British Crown Copyright/MOD)

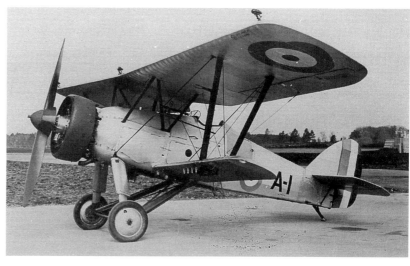

ered by Jaguar VIII engines; the remaining types were privately entered by their makers. The first to arrive was the Vickers 177 *(line 13)* (Jupiter XF) in February 1930. Its pleasant handling and easy take off were liked, but its poor view and awkward armament were considered bad; it was also a large aircraft for its role. A larger rudder (modified in a single day) improved spin recovery marginally; a horn-balance made spin

Hawker Nimrod S1577 in November 1935. The prominent oil cooler and radiator are well shown. (British Crown Copyright/MOD)

recovery acceptable by June 1930 and increased terminal velocity to 360mph (true) The brakes reduced landing roll by 12 percent. The Gnatsnapper N227 *(line 14)* with its new supercharged Jaguar VIII was particularly robust, but had sluggish controls and was found to be unsuitable for both deck landing and air fighting. In June 1930 the Gnatsnapper crashed on landing, due, it was thought, to the pilot using full aft stick at touch down thus applying full wheelbrake pressure. It was returned to its makers. The Hoopoe N237 complete with a Townend ring, which spoilt the view around its Jaguar VIII engine, was

Hoopoe N237 in May 1931 with double Townend ring around its Panther engine. It has an extended tailskid – but lacks the wheel spats fitted later. (British Crown Copyright/MOD)

pleasant to fly and well constructed. Its stable mate, the unmarked Hawker N.21/26 (later Nimrod) with its sleek Rolls-Royce FXIS engine, was highly praised for handling, spinning, armament and maintainabilty. The report says 'it is considered a splendid aircraft to handle and should be very easy to land on deck'. Its wide speed range was from an indicated 50mph to 385mph true in a terminal velocity dive, and its performance was the best

(line 15) in the group. The Nimrod won the Fleet Fighter Competition of 1930, but not before it and the Firefly completed deck landing and catapult trials elsewhere. The main report of the 1930 trials of the Firefly III *(line 16)*, which suffered four failures including ripped access panels, damage to the Townend ring and a bent axle, indicates that very good handling was gained at the expense of an unacceptable armament installation; the view was good but the cockpit cramped. The Starling, inspite of its number A-1 *(line 17)*, was inferior in many respects with heavy and unresponsive controls at high speed making gun aiming poor at operational speeds. On return to AAEE two months later in June 1930 *(line 18)*, the aileron gap had been reduced, but roll response was still poor; maximum speed was 305 mph true.

After the competition, five types returned for further trials including the Nimrod in its various production forms. Nimrod S1577 *(line 19)* completed extensive trials from late 1931

to early 1933; handling remained impeccable, metal (Fairey Reed) and wooden propellers were equally suitable and maintenance normal – an engine change took two men 230 minutes. The only criticism of the production aircraft arose from the aftwards shift of the CG caused by the weight of the tail hook and other nautical impedimenta. The remedy, sweeping back of the wings (tested on K2823 in October 1933), produced a poor spin to the left. A month later K2823 returned with a larger tailplane; results were acceptable to No.22 Squadron pilots. Complaints by a Nimrod Squadron led to a trial in April 1934 involving flying ground attack manoeuvres in K2823 (swept wings) and K2824 (old standard wings) for comparison; the CO of No.800 Squadron was satisfied with both configurations. In 1935 K2823 was fitted with an uprated Kestrel – the Mk V Full Power; performance improved *(line 20)*.

The Firefly (now numbered S1592) returned early in 1931 for consumption measurements (14.7gal/hr at 10,000ft at 118mph (true) or 8.03 miles per gallon) before joining the High Speed Flight at Calshot as a floatplane. Between May 1931 and May 1932 the Hoopoe N237 *(line 21)* re-engined with a Panther completed minor trials, including satisfactory spinning with full Service equipment and armament fitted. A second Gnatsnapper, N245, visited Martlesham in October 1930 but trials were terminated when the wind-driven generator disintegrated and damaged the centre section; a further lengthy visit in 1932 was spent on armament trials. Reports covering the 1932 handling, armament and wireless trials of an eleventh type designed to meet Specification N.21/26, the Armstrong Whitworth A.W.XVI S1591

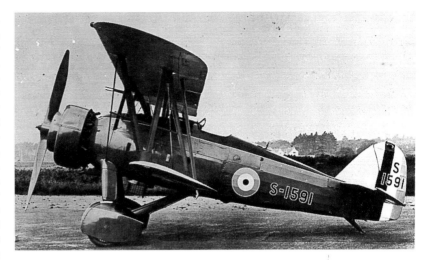

Armstrong Whitworth A.W.XVI S1591 in June 1931 for armament and handling trials with double Townend ring. (British Crown Copyright/ MOD)

are missing, as are those covering 1933 trials of the type with the Panther IIIA.

Gloster Sea Gladiator

It is an interesting commentary on the low priority given to the Fleet aircraft that the latest Specification that produced a prewar single-seat fighter in service was issued in 1926. The only other aircraft of this class to be assessed at Martlesham was the Gladiator, a type long since in RAF service. No performance measurements appear to have been made (or photographs taken), presumably

Blackburn Roc L3057 in May 1939, complete with hook, radio, flush navigation lights and turret, but no guns. Below the rudder is a ring attached to a cable running to the pilot's cockpit cover; the purpose is apparently to release the cover. (British Crown Copyright/ MOD)

because of its similarity to the RAF version. Two machines were used: K8039 in 1938-9 for comparative test of propellers which showed that the old two-blade Watts type gave a 30 percent shorter take off than the three-blade Fairey Reed type, and K6129 in late 1938-9 for trials of modified ammunition stowage and cartridge ejection. These were, in fact, not true Sea Gladiators but modified RAF aircraft.

Blackburn Roc

The last in this class of aeroplanes, the Blackburn Roc is included as it was tested purely as a Naval fighter; the type is notable in this class as the first monoplane, the first with a gun turret and for being ordered into production without a prototype because of its similarity to the Skua. L3057, the first Roc, arrived at AAEE on 24 February, 1939, but problems arose with trim, control and stability, and acceptance was delayed; meanwhile L3058 joined in March for armament trials which were concentrated on assessment of the Mk II turret. L3058 was dived up to 260mph without problems on turret operation, but five armament modifications were recommended to be made before Service use. L3057 resumed tests with L3059; controls were heavy at high speed and sloppy at low speed but handling overall was acceptable, and assessed as superior to the Skua. Performance, however, was poor *(line 22)*, and inferior in many respects to the biplane Nimrod of eight years earlier. L3061 with armament and other modifications was tested briefly in July and August 1939.

Deck landing fighters

Line	Type	Identity	Engine No.	Type	Power (bhp/rpm)	Seats	Wing area (sq ft)	Max speed (mph/ft)	Take-off run (yd)	Landing speed (mph)
1	Nightjar	H8535	1	B.R.2	251/1,300	1	270	108/6,500		
2	Plover	N162	1	Jupiter	399/1,623	1	305	139/6,500		
3	Plover	N162	1	Jaguar	354/1,500	1	305	134/6,500		
4	Plover	N9609	1	Jupiter IV	410/1,575	1		132/6,500		
5	Plover	N9702	1	Jupiter IVS	390/1,575	1		133/6,500		
6	Flycatcher	N163	1	Jaguar II	345/1,500	1	284	132/6,500		
7	Flycatcher	N164	1	Jaguar				129/6,500		
8	Flycatcher	N163	1	Jupiter IV				124/10,000		
9	Flycatcher	N9616	1	Jaguar	341/1,500	1	284	135/6,500		
10	Flycatcher	N9619	1	Jaguar IV	391/1,700	1		134/6,500		
11	Flycatcher	N9619	1	Jaguar IV	391/1,700	1		132/6,500		
12	Vireo	N211	1	Lynx IV	220/	1	208	115/5,000		57
13	Vickers 177	—	1	Jupiter XF	525/2,000	1	337	186/13,000		
14	Gnatsnapper	N227	1	Jaguar VIII	440/2,000	1	318	180/10,000		
15	Nimrod	—	1	FXI	480/2,250	1	301	200/13,000		
16	Firefly	—	1	FXI	480/2,250	1	271	188/10,000		
17	Starling	A-1	1	Panther IIMS	525/2,000	1	289	168/6,500		
18	Starling	A-1	1	Panther IIMS	525/2,000	1	289	166/6,500		55
19	Nimrod	S1577	1	Kestrel IIS	477/2,250	1	301	195/13,000		
20	Nimrod	K2823	1	Kestrel VFP	608/2,500	1		192/13,000		
21	Hoopoe	N237	1	Panther III	500/2,000	1	301	188/13,000		
22	Roc	L3057	1	Perseus XII	748/2,400	2		223/10,000	260	

Line	Climb to 15,000ft Time (min-sec)	Rate (ft/min)	Service ceiling (ft)	Fuel capacity (Imp gal)	Weights Empty (lb)	Gross (lb)	Report No	Date	Remarks
1	41 – 22	100	15,000	40	1,489	2,087	304	6/22	2hr endurance
2	12 – 57	695	23,000	50	1,912	2,851	341	7/23	2.2hr endurance
3	17 – 52	390	18,800	50		2,793	350	10/23	
4	16 – 30	475	20,500	52	2,070	3,019	382	5/24	
5	15 – 26	506	21,200	52		3,033	389	7/24	
6	18 – 50	380	19,000	47	1,980	2,894	321	2/23	2hr endurance
7	19 – 19	380	19,150			2,937	379	5/24	With cowling
8	17 – 15	400	18,760		2,128	3,107	400	12/24	
9	18 – 15	383	18,850	52	1,980	2,937	345	8/23	
10	16 – 23	490	20,600		2,141	3,029	394	9/24	
11	16 – 23	490				3,029	394A	9/24	Without spinner
12	46 – 42	90	14,750	52	1,951	2,700	499	9/28	180yd land run
13	9 – 57	1,390	26,000	81	2,944	3,962	558	4/30	
14	12 – 50	1,030	24,500	75	2,786	3,804	529/2	4/30	
15	7 – 39	1,650	27,500	62	2,640	3,559	61	4/30	
16	12 – 58	910	27,000	66	2,702	3,616	562	5/30	
17	11 – 39	755	22,600	60	2,686	3,722	496B	4/30	
18	12 – 34	690	23,300	60	2,698	3,734	496B	6/30	
19	9 – 14	1,360	26,900	61	2,901	3,867	594	9/32	
20	8 – 06	1,415	28,800	61	3,115	4,058	594A	11/35	
21	9 – 02	1,370	30,600	73	2,522	3,539	526/3	10/31	
22	25 – 06	290	18,200	116	6,124	7,815	741	8/39	

Deck Landing Reconnaissance Types

Type VII Aeroplanes

Among the roles for the permanent Royal Air Force was that of gunnery spotting for the Fleet; the requirement was detailed as the Director of Research's Type VII. The Type VII designs at Martlesham were numerous, often ugly, and usually ungainly. The first was a D.H.9A much modified by Westland with a Lion engine, three seats and known as the Walrus; the poor wireless operator was probably happy to stay inside the aft cockpit during firing over his head by the gunner standing in front of him. The first Walrus, N9500, arrived on 27 May, 1921, and performed creditably *(line 1)* considering the increased weight and drag of the flotation gear, extendable radiator and robust undercarriage. The low-speed handling was poor, because the elevator lost effectiveness at about 70mph – too high a speed for deck landings.

In August 1921, N9515 *(line 2)* with 64 Section (high-lift) wings was flown under control down to 50mph; below this speed there was a sudden loss of control; the rudder heaviness was absent although the ailerons were overbalanced. N9515 also had the earlier hydrovanes and flotation bags

Westland Walrus N9515 in August 1921, introduced high-lift wings to the type. This development of the de Havilland D.H.9A gives early indication of the low priority afforded to aerodynamics by the inter-war naval authorities for whom the aeroplanes in this section were designed. (British Crown Copyright/ MOD)

removed, but the undercarriage was too harsh for deck landings.

The bouncy undercarriage was replaced by an oleo type in N9523; tests involved forty landings, many heavy, in early 1923 with excellent results. The Establishment commented that the rubber in the oleo strut was unsuitable for use in Eastern climates.

Two new Type VII designs were the Blackburn Blackburn and Avro Bison; three of each were ordered and all six reached Martlesham. Blackburn N150 and Bison N153 arrived and left together in August 1922 for deck trials on HMS *Argus* after brief handling

assessments. Blackburn N151 *(line 3)* followed in September; the view was exceptional, the offset fin effective but the response to ailerons and rudder was slow. The wallowing aircraft could be flown under control at 42½ kt (50mph) with four crew on board. Three modifications were considered necessary for service, most notably in the fuel system to cure fuel surging and consequent cutting of the engine when the tanks were less than full. Fuel surging was responsible for the forced landing of N152 on its delivery flight to Martlesham; this aircraft was destroyed in October 1922 in the ARS hangar fire. Further criticism of the type concerned the undemanded pitching oscillations associated with

Blackburn Blackburn N150 in August 1922, in almost pristine condition – only a little oil on the lower fuselage spoils the effect. Two claws are fitted just inboard of the wheels. (British Crown Copyright/MOD)

Avro Bison N153 in August 1922, in the original configuration of the type before deck landing trials for which three claws are fitted in the centre of the undercarriage axle. (British Crown Copyright/MOD)

Bison N154 in mid-1923 with raised wing, fins over the tailplane, bracing struts to the inboard lower wings and increased lower fin area. (British Crown Copyright/MOD)

periodic airframe vibrations; control was adversely affected by the observer standing in the slipstream.

Meanwhile Bison N154 made slow progress due to poor performance and an undercarriage collapsing in January 1923; very little flying was done – until the arrival of N155 *(line 4)* in the same month. The latter completed type trials with a modified fin and tailplane, but performance *(line 5)* remained poor, even when fitted with a two-bladed Blackburn propeller. N154 *(line 6)* then returned, in mid-1923 with many aerodynamic changes including a raised wing; a further undercarriage breakage delayed flying which revealed marginally acceptable handling and performance.

Last of the types built to meet the D of R VII requirements was the amphibian Supermarine Seagull, the first of which, N158 *(line 7)*, spent the first three months of 1923 undergoing trials at Martlesham. The Seagull had a very long take-off run and poor control response.

Preceding the Seagull by four months was another amphibian, the Vickers Viking N156 *(line 8)*, ac-

quired by the Air Ministry for tests of this form of aeroplane in hot climates. Designed for four people, only two could be carried with full military load. Although N156 was the first aircraft to be tested with a retractable undercarriage, the wheels remained down throughout its brief trials at Martlesham. Take off was short (157yd into a 10mph wind) and the controls good, but very large trim changes were produced by altering the power of the engine, and, at constant power, there was a continuous half minute phugoid over 7 deg of pitch.

The Fairey IIID N9451 *(line 9)* arrived on 24 July, 1922; normally a floatplane, N9451 had a wheel under-

carriage for the AAEE trials. Of primary interest was the variable-camber control of both wings; the range was 0 deg to 21 deg and early trials were made to establish optimum setting for the take off (20 deg reduced the run by 30 percent compared with 2 deg) and climb (12 deg best). The ailerons were heavy but responsive, and the elevators poor near the stall; stalling speed was reduced by 6mph to 44mph with use of 12 deg camber. The oleo undercarriage was exceptionally good but entry to the cockpit and the view

Supermarine Seagull N158 in early 1923, built to meet the same requirement as the Bison and Blackburn. (British Crown Copyright/MOD)

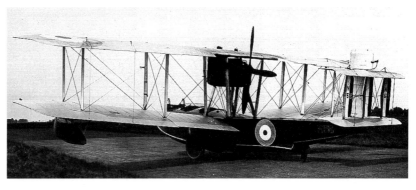

,Vickers Viking N156 in August 1922 with pusher propeller, was tested before hot weather trials in Iraq. (British Crown Copyright/MOD)

were poor. The Establishment was very interested in the IIID's variable-camber, and recommended that a range of wing sections and slots should be tried; the recommendation was accepted, but the various wings were flown later on different aeroplanes. Fairey IIID S1023 with a Lion V in place of the earlier Lion II spent the last months of 1927 at Martlesham.

Early in 1923, the Establishment compared in a report, the five Fleet Spotters, *ie* the three to D of R VII specification plus the Viking and IIID. The IIID had the best performance, but did not meet the Admiralty's requirement for a crew of four; the Viking was better all round than the Seagull but failed to satisfy the Admiralty; the Blackburn had an excellent performance while the Bison was acceptable at this stage (April 1923) only with the redesigned tail and strengthened undercarriage tested on N155. Nevertheless, both Bison and Blackburn were ordered for service, and a few Seagulls purchased – probably to keep Supermarine in business.

The production Blackburn N9581 completed standard trials successfully in June 1923, followed two years later by the prototype N150 modified with a raised top wing, internal fuel tanks and other refinements which marginally improved top speed but reduced rate of climb *(line 10)*. In June 1925, a dual control Blackburn, N9589 *(line 11)*, with enhanced built-in drag, performed marginally and, in the words of one pilot was 'very heavy and unanswerable', although a stalled glide could be maintained for one minute at 45mph indicated. Finally, in April 1929 N9982 with raised wing completed dummy deck landings on Martlesham's rough but stationary airfield.

The second Bison, N154 *(line 12)*, with further changes including internal fuel tanks was tested in mid-1925

together with the production Bison N9844 *(line 13)* with a Lion V in place of the Lion II of the prototypes. A pilot's cryptic comment remained, 'a poor kite'.

Specification 37/22

Long before the Blackburn and Bison entered service, their replacement was detailed early in 1923; three types were tested against Specification 37/22 – the Hawker Hedgehog, Blackburn Airedale, and Fairey Ferret. The Hedgehog was apparently privately produced as it was unmarked for its initial trials in September 1924 a year ahead of its rivals. However, it was purchased by the Air Ministry while at Martlesham and numbered N187; two Airedales and three Ferrets were ordered at the same time. The 1924 tests on the Hedgehog were favourably reported – 'a nice kite', but performance was not much better than the Blackburn *(line 14)*. In 1925, N187 returned to Martlesham with drooping ailerons among other changes, and although no report was written on these later trials one pilot commented 'damn bad'. The first Airedale, N188, crashed on leaving Brough for Martlesham in mid-1925, and the second, N189 with unique

Fairey IIID N9451 in August 1922; its Lion engine displaying copious pipery (including a large horn exhaust to the right of the propeller hub) and large radiator on the fuselage beside the pilot. (British Crown Copyright/MOD)

Blackburn (Dual Control) N9589 in April 1925, shows clearly the overwing tanks, raised top wing and the wide upper fuselage accommodating side-by-side seating. A ladder for the left-hand pilot is also visible. (British Crown Copyright/MOD)

Avro Bison N154 in April 1925 showing port wings folded and large dorsal fin, and stub exhausts. (British Crown Copyright/MOD)

wing folding arrangements, did not arrive until February 1926. Very little flying was done on this Jaguar-engined monoplane and no report

written, probably because the requirement had by then been cancelled. The Ferret N190 *(line 15)* with the original Jaguar engine was assessed in mid-1925 and returned a year later re-engined with a Jupiter with a markedly beneficial effect on performance *(line 16)*. Handling was also improved by lightening the controls with horn-

balances. One pilot commented, 'Not bad – poor landing view'. Ferret N191 also spent some months in 1926 at AAEE during which the undercarriage failed. The third Ferret was modified for general purposes.

Fairey IIIF

Cancellation of the 37/22 requirement was due in part to the poor performance of the three contenders, and, in greater part, to the markedly superior qualities of the Fairey IIIF, originally required as a seaplane for spotter-reconnaissance duties, but tested as a three-seat landplane in prototype form, N198 *(line 17)* from September 1926. Handling was very good, although excessive left rudder was initially required in the climb (cured by fitting a bungee). The outstanding advantage of the IIIF was its

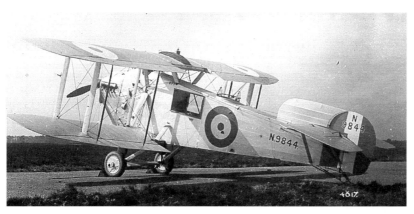

Bison N9844 in late 1924, in production form and lacking the portholes of the prototypes. Other changes include elevators of increased area and cut-away rear centre section. (British Crown Copyright/MOD)

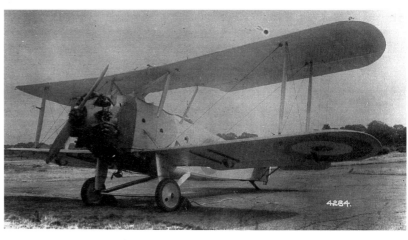

Hawker Hedgehog (later N187) in September 1924. Although of clean aerodynamic design with single-bay wings, the Hedgehog performed poorly. (British Crown Copyright/MOD)

Blackburn Airedale, N189 early in 1926, with Jaguar engine and metal propeller. (British Crown Copyright/MOD)

Airedale N189 early in 1926, with wings folded. The deck handling problems in this configuration may have been considered but were never tested. (British Crown Copyright/MOD)

exceptional take-off and landing distances using 9 deg of flap (cambered trailing edge); take-off in still air took only 140yd. Night flying was not undertaken because there was no exhaust manifold.

Tests on IIIFs for general purposes were made at Martlesham in 1927 to 1929 (and at the RAE Farnborough, and MAEE on floatplanes); deck landing IIIFs with wheel undercarriage were not tested at AAEE in production form until mid-1930. At that time the metal-framed S1316 *(line 18)* completed full trials at reconnaissance load giving a take-off weight approaching 6,000lb, some 700lb heavier than the prototype. Tests included measurement of consumption at 5.000ft; the figure of 4.9 air miles per gallon at 98mph (true) was good; handling was acceptable, although the ailerons were heavy and the aeroplane unstable longitudinally. S1474 with minor modifications for catapulting was also handled late in 1930. Flotation gear was initially assessed on S1226 at the end of 1930. The two bags stowed under the wings took 50 seconds to inflate and were found to be too weak; the installation

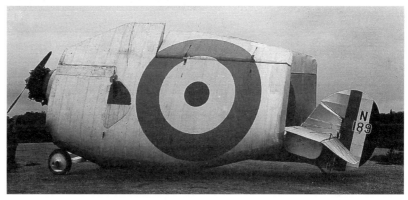

was rejected. A new stowage on the fuselage on S1504 was an improvement, but during the ditching trial, the cock to release compressed air and inflate the bags required one and half turns to operate during the last seconds before impact; after settling in the water the pilot was unable to get to the dinghy. S1504 was salvaged, modified and ditched again on 7 May, 1931, with satisfactory results. The long standing problem with vibration on the IIIF was finally cured on the three-seater S1532 at the end of 1932 using a slightly finer wooden Watts propeller after unsuccessful tests over six months with various Fairey Reed

metal designs. S1847, one of a small batch of IIIF trainers, was handled, spun and dived to 206mph (indicated) with the robust flying hood raised and stowed; there were no adverse comments.

Specification 22/26

Reconnaissance combined with fighting was a new role for a ship-plane in

Fairey Ferret N190 in July 1925, showing the operating mechanisms for the variable-camber trailing-edge, double arrester claws and bomb carriers. (British Crown Copyright/MOD)

Fairey IIIF N198 in October 1926, with wooden propeller, arrester claws, interplane strut close to the fuselage, and fixed radiator. The exhausts for the top row of four cylinders are on the starboard side only. (British Crown Copyright/MOD)

1926 when the Admiralty and Air Ministry agreed Specification 22/26 (later O.22/26). During the tendering period the speed required at 15,000ft was increased from 120kt (138mph) to 130kt (150mph), but the choice of water- or air-cooled engine remained the maker's. Five aircraft of four types were tested; the Hawker Osprey*, the Fairey Fleetwing, the Blackburn Nautilus and two Short Gurnards. All five arrived within a few days in May/June 1929 for brief handling tests before deck trials on HMS *Furious* in the latter month. All completed ship landings safely, but the Gurnard N228 *(line 19)* (the only contender with a radial, a Jupiter X with 0.5 reduction ratio) had heavy controls, needed rudder in straight and level flight and swung left on landing. In addition the heel-operated brakes were useless; deck landings were probably interesting, particularly as the landing view was poor. In September 1929 an aileron jammed at 240mph in a dive from 16,000ft; vigorous operation of the controls freed the ailerons for landing where failure of some weak ribs was revealed. Gurnard N229 *(line 20)* (powered like the three other types with an FXII engine) was assessed in May 1929 as unsuitable for deck trials as the report states, 'the turning tendency is so great as to make it impractical for ordinary work – even apart from deck landing'. Full right rudder was required on take off and for normal flying. Speedy modification action improved handling to a standard just acceptable for deck landing – but, even with further aerodynamic im-

provements after sea trials, the controls were heavy and a constantly leaking radiator led eventually to complete loss of cooling water. Martlesham's opinion was summarised as, 'the Gurnard needs a complete redesign.'

The Fleetwing N235 *(line 21)* was sturdy with very good ailerons, but the elevator was heavy and lost effectiveness near the stall resulting in the need for a high landing speed. After deck trials, N235 had a metal-framed wing and slots fitted. Spinning characteristics were particularly suscepti-

Fairey IIIF S1504 with the successful flotation gear stowed (upper) and inflated (lower). (British Crown Copyright/MOD)

---

* Known until the end of 1929 as the Hart O.22/26

Short Gurnard N228 in mid-1929. This was the only contender for the 22/26 competition with a radial engine. (British Crown Copyright/MOD)

ble to CG position; spins in both directions were possible only at mid-position and impossible to the left at both aft and forward position. To the right, at aft CG, a fast spin developed, so straining the aircraft that wires buckled, one of which broke. As with most Fairey aeroplanes of the period, the Fleetwing had a low fuel consumption, and achieved 5.8mpg at 1,000ft and 108mph (true) during a later visit in 1931.

The Nautilus N234 *(line 22)* had a good view, landed slowly and had good controls making it ideal for deck landing. Spinning was restricted because the engine tended to stop, but dives to 297mph (true) were very steady. The Nautilus's Bendix brakes were poor due to backlash, even after modification, and lacked strength in the wheels, one of which broke up. In November 1929 the Nautilus was judged to be better than the Fleetwing and the Gurnard, but larger than the Osprey. Such was the importance of overall dimensions for shipborne operations that the Osprey, which also had excellent handling characteristics was selected for Service use.

The Osprey J9052 *(line 23)* converted from the Hart prototype with swept and larger, folding wings, pedal-operated brakes and a supercharged Kestrel, retained the latter's excellent handling and was entirely suitable for deck operations. Absence of a Sutton harness precluded aerobatics at first. With the harness fitted, the one serious shortcoming of the type was revealed – it was very reluctant to come out of a spin, full power

being needed to effect recovery. The culprit was thought to be the swept and larger wings which had two effects – moving the CG aft and reducing the tail volume*. By October 1929 the fin had been increased by 15 percent and the rudder by 9 percent; there was a slight improvement, but recovery from a spin followed only

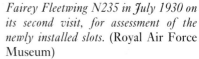

Blackburn Nautilus N234 in mid-1929. The duralumin-covered forward fuselage is well shown. (Royal Air Force Museum)

Fairey Fleetwing N235 in July 1930 on its second visit, for assessment of the newly installed slots. (Royal Air Force Museum)

after full and violent forward movement of the stick. Two months later with a further 60 percent increase in fin area and 9 percent in the rudder area, together with a reduction in lower wing area, spinning characteristics were satisfactory, without any adverse effects on the excellent controls. With the reduced wing area, the take-off run was 128yd and landing run 179yd.

In Fleet Air Arm service the fighter role predominated over the reconnaissance; at Martlesham the latter function was of primary importance in the prototype Osprey. Production aircraft were not tested at AAEE until

---

* Tail Volume. A non-dimensional number used to indicate the effectiveness of the tail organs – usually the fin and the rudder.

mid-1934 when Osprey III (metal propeller and more forward CG) K3615 *(line 24)* confirmed the type's pleasant handling, although the brakes were assessed as poor. In common with many open cockpit aircraft of the period, the effectiveness of the gunner at speeds over 150mph was criticised. K3615 was successfully dived to 275mph (indicated). S1700 in a dive as part of brief handling of the experimental stainless steel type of airframe, suffered near catastrophic failure on 1 April, 1935. Air pressure at 240mph was sufficient to operate the hydrostatic valve to inflate the rubber dinghy which burst out of its housing and wrapped itself temporarily round the tailplane; a safe landing was made. To improve performance, the Kestrel V (unsupercharged) was tested in

Fairey Seal K4779 in mid-1937 with extended tailwheel strut. (British Crown Copyright/MOD)

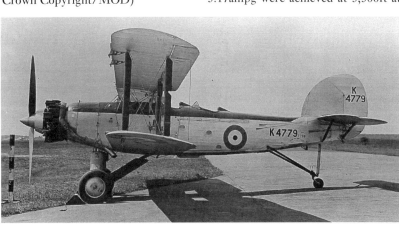

mid-1935 in K3954 with very satisfactory results *(line 25)*. In early 1936, the last Osprey at Martlesham, the Mk IV K5742 with an alloy propeller, recorded 7.12ampg at 10,000ft at 112mph (true) – a consumption figure indicating the advance in aerodynamic and engine efficiency since 4.9 of the IIIF.

Fairey Seal

Appearing before the production Ospreys was the radial-engined Fairey IIIF renamed the Seal. The first, K3477 *(line 26)*, arrived towards the end of 1933 and demonstrated the docile handling of its predecessor, with a very light elevator, although atmospheric bumps caused marked wallowing which needed aileron control to correct. The W/T and Fairey rocking mounting for the free Lewis gun were satisfactory; in the cruise 5.17ampg were achieved at 5,500ft at

Hawker Osprey S1700 in September 1935, with stainless steel frame, after repair. The Lewis gun is a dummy, and the gyroscope venturi is placed behind the extendable radiator. (British Crown Copyright/MOD)

110mph (true). Developments on K3477 were tested satisfactorily in 1934 and included mass-balancing of the ailerons and rudder, and later, reduced chord slats and a self-centring tailwheel. Three experimental Seals were tested. In 1934 the unarmed and dual control K3485 *(line 27)* had normal handling, but the view from the back seat was poor for landing. In mid-1937, six Martlesham pilots flew K4779 with a novel undercarriage comprising the normal mainwheels (moved forward one bay) and the tailwheel mounted on a long strut; taxying and take off presented no difficulty, but landings were tricky requiring a fast approach and flat touchdown to avoid hitting tail first with ensuing porpoising. No definite conclusions were reached as to the suitability of the configuration for deck landing for which it was designed; the trial ended when the aircraft was damaged. A similar undercarriage but with a self-centring tailwheel was flown in January 1938 on K4203. Taxying required much use of brake and engine, but the landing was found to be easy and suitable for deck operations.

Deck landing reconnaissance types

Line	Type	Identity	Engine No.	Type	Power (bhp/rpm)	Seats	Wing area (sq ft)	Max speed (mph/ft)	Landing speed (mph)
1	Walrus	N9500	1	Lion	472/2,000	3	482	116/5,000	
2	Walrus	N9515	1	Lion	474/2,000	3	543	114/5,000	
3	Blackburn	N150/1	1	Lion	475/2,000	4	650	122/6,500	
4	Bison	N155	1	Lion	480/2,100	4	622	92/6,500	
5	Bison	N155	1	Lion	480/2,100	4	622	96/6,500	
6	Bison	N154	1	Lion	470/2,100	4	622	104/6,500	
7	Seagull	N158	1	Lion	492/2,100	3	593	98/3,000	
8	Viking	N156	1	Lion II	489/2,100	2	637	117/3,000	
9	Fairey IIID	N9451	1	Lion	458/2,000	3	468	119/10,000	
10	Blackburn	N150	1	Lion II	491/2,200	4		106/6,500	
11	Blackburn DC	N9589	1	Lion II	474/2,000	2	642	96/3,000	
12	Bison	N154	1	Lion	483/2,000	4	614	104/6,500	
13	Bison	N9844	1	Lion V	469/2,000	4	620	105/6,500	
14	Hedgehog	N187	1	Jupiter IV	398/1,575	3	481	116/6,500	
15	Ferret	N190	1	Jaguar IV	402/1,700	3	387	119/6,500	
16	Ferret	N191	1	Jupiter VI VT	407/1,700	3	379	129/5,000	
17	Fairey III F	N198	1	Lion V	481/2,000	3	443	137/6,500	
18	Fairey III F	S1316	1	Lion XIA	530/2,350	3	444	117/3,000	
19	Gurnard	N228	1	Jupiter X	525/2,000	2	429	162/11,000	52
20	Gurnard	N229	1	FXIIMS	513/2,250	2	429	125/6,500	

Line	Climb to 6,500ft Time (min-sec)	Rate (ft/min)	Service ceiling (ft)	Fuel capacity (Imp gal)	Weights Empty (lb)	Gross (lb)	Report No	Date	Remarks
1	6 – 15 to 5,000ft		17,000	118	3,392	4,800	283	7/21	Easy to overload
2	5 – 39 to 5,000ft		15,800	118		4,800	285	8/21	64-Section wings
3	12 – 00	390	13,000	90	3,929	5,962	312A	10/22	3.2hr endurance
4	15 – 30	310	11,000	93	3,780	5,813	328	3/23	4hr endurance
5	13 – 18	355	11,900	93	3,780	5,813	328B	7/23	4hr endurance
6	11 – 00	440	12,850	93	3,680	5,713	356	11/23	4.5hr endurance
7	20 – 30	210	9,150	100	3,820	5,691	327	3/23	
8	10 – 48	460	14,250	112	4,129	5,650	314	10/22	
9	6 – 48	750	17,400	101		5,050	311	8/22	
10	14 – 30	325	11,750			5,962	409	4/25	
11	15 – 30	302	11,350	100	4,184	5,962	422	7/25	
12	11 – 15	440	13,800	95	4,152	5,713	416	7/25	
13	10 – 36	495	14,900	93	4,275	5,713	417	7/25	
14	12 – 30	385	13,500	134	2,882	4,791	395	9/24	
15	9 – 42	537	15,070	110	2,620	4,425	424	7/25	
16	7 – 42	711	17,200	110	2,619	4,585	464	9/26	
17	6 – 18	850	19,400	125	3,272	5,300	466	9/26	
18	8 – 10	629	16,100	124	3,976	5,874	483D	9/30	
19	5 – 54	1,100	28,500		3,243	4,785	530	9/29	
20	6 – 25	960	17,850	100	3,498	4,854	530A	3/30	

Line	Type	Identity	Engine No.	Engine Type	Power (bhp/rpm)	Seats	Wing area (sq ft)	Max speed (mph/ft)	Landing speed (mph)
21	Fleetwing	N235	1	FXIIS	525/2,250	2	362	176/4,000	
22	Nautilus	N234	1	FXIIS	525/2,250	2	435	147/4,000	74
23	Hart O.22/26	J9052	1	FXIIS	525/2,250	2	363	174/4,000	
24	Osprey III	K3615	1	Kestrel IIMS5	575/2,350	2	339	167/MSL	
25	Osprey IV	K3954	1	Kestrel V	607/2,500	2		175/13,000	
26	Seal	K3477	1	Panther IIA	523/2,000	2	443	120/MSL	
27	Seal (T)	K3485	1	Panther IIA	529/2,000	2	443	140/3,000	

Line	Climb to 6,500ft Time (min-sec)	Climb to 6,500ft Rate (ft/min)	Service ceiling (ft)	Fuel capacity (Imp gal)	Weights Empty (lb)	Weights Gross (lb)	Report No	Report Date	Remarks
21	5 – 18	1,170	18,950		3,390	4,730	532	11/29	
22	5 – 18	1,060	18,700		3,400	4,748	533	11/29	
23	4 – 30	1,430	22,850		2,886	4,242	512A	9/29	
24	5 – 06	1,030	18,500	93	3,521	4,976	644	3/35	
25	4 – 00	1,245	25,400	93	3,518	4,979	644A	11/35	
26	7 – 36	690	16,500	121	4,061	6,000	617	2/34	
27	6 – 45	800	18,500	126	4,171	5,637	617A	5/34	

MSL = Mean Sea Level

Deck Landing Trainers

Specification 5/24

Three aeroplanes were officially sponsored in this small group – the Blackburn Sprat N207, Parnall Perch N217 and Vickers Vendace N208; all were built to meet Specification 5/24. No record has been found of the Perch being tested at Martlesham; the Sprat and the Vendace arrived in April 1926, and probably made sec-

Blackburn Sprat N207 in June 1927, probably on its second visit. (British Crown Copyright/MOD)

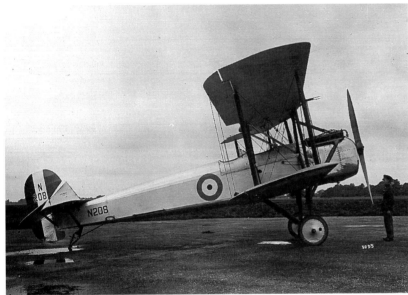

ond visits in 1927. Apart from the photographs and the performance figures *(lines 1 and 2)* the only comment found is in the log-book of a pilot who said of the Sprat 'No speed, lands like a brick, no control'. The requirement was cancelled, and none of the three went into production.

Vickers Vendace N208 in mid-1926 provides a good example of the quality of print produced by the Establishment photographers. (British Crown Copyright/MOD)

Deck landing trainers

Line	Type	Identity	Engine No.	Type	Power (bhp/rpm)	Seats	Wing area (sq ft)	Max speed (mph/ft)
1	Vendace	N208	1	Falcon III	282/2,000	2	524	101/MSL
2	Sprat	N207	1	Falcon III	290/2,000	2	373	109/MSL

Line	Climb to 6,500ft Time (min-sec)	Rate (ft/min)	Service ceiling (ft)	Fuel capacity (Imp gal)	Weights Empty (lb)	Gross (lb)	Report No	Date
1	10 – 24	485	13.700	61	2,791	3,728	469	4/27
2	12 – 30	385	12.570	59	2,489	3,447	473	2/28

Armament Trials

Introduction

From 1924 to 1939, the testing of air armament and associated equipment developed for use by the British Services was the preserve of AAEE; aerial torpedoes were notable exceptions. The armament squadron was supported at first by specialist officers of Flight Lieutenant rank; by 1937 the specialists were headed by a Wing Commander, and the work of the flying section was his responsibility. It has earlier been explained how the work of No.15 Squadron, later the Armament Testing Section, included armament, wireless and general equipment tests on new aeroplanes, proof testing from batches of bombs and gun ammunition and assessment of all new aeronautical offensive and defensive weapons and ancilliary mechanisms. The results from trials on new aeroplanes are included in earlier sections of this book; proof testing, although requiring a considerable number of flying hours, was not reported (after 1925) in any documents which have survived, and is not described here. This section summarises the results of 15 years of tests on new and modified armament as described in existing reports – the M/Arm series.

Some one thousand reports in this series were written before the Second World War, the great majority of which survive. Just under a half concern bombing, one-third gunnery, one-sixth flares and the remainder are about other topics.

The material on which the reports were written originated from several sources; bombs and ammunition usually came from the Royal Arsenal at Woolwich, sights and some fuses from the RAE, while guns, turrets and other equipment came from Industry. All were submitted under instructions from the Air Ministry – the Directorate of Technical Development initially, later the Directorate of Armament Development. Some work for Industry was on a repayment basis, as in the case in 1934 of the 100kg anti-submarine bombs submitted by Vickers-Armstrongs, and intended for overseas. Facilities at Martlesham included bomb stores (moved in 1927 away from the new married quarters), cold chamber, workshops and the gunfiring butts. Part of the airfield was used in the 1920s for dropping some small bombs, but predominantly the range at Orfordness was used for bombs, flares and air firing. By May 1939 the Armament Section had in addition to seven new types under test, no fewer than 22* aeroplanes on permanent allotment for the various dropping, firing, target and communications duties. Between 1924 and 1939 the methods of testing changed considerably; suffice it here to say that the Establishment's expertise in test techniques at least matched the advances of the equipment under evaluation. By 1939, the AAEE handbook on armament testing was probably unique in the world; it was certainly used later by the USA.

Bombing

Martlesham's pre-flight work on offensive weapons included loading with particular emphasis on safety of live munitions, sighting, carriers, and release characteristics; and finally in-flight dropping tests determined ballistics (after 1931), behaviour of the various elements of bombs (fusing, pistols and detonators) parachutes and, after 1937, the effect of impact.

The first ground equipment examined was a jack for loading bombs (550lb capacity was sufficient in 1926) followed by various trolleys, including in 1931, one for a torpedo, and, from 1934, a number of hoists for lifting bombs up to their carriers. A hoist designed by Handley Page for their Heyford was particularly liked. Bombsights for many years were variations on the standard type, but some so-called emergency sights were attached to the outside of the fuselage. Of the latter, that fitted to the Bristol Fighter for use by the pilot was not a success in 1925; the following year another for use by the observer was more practical. The standard aiming positions in other machines were either in the nose or under the pilot's seat with the observer acting as bomb aimer. The former involved opening a window and admitting a cold blast of air. The Establishment's comments on the debilitating effect of this arrangement became increasingly critical as speeds increased. In the 1920s, the standard sight was the Course Setting Bomb Sight (CSBS), used in two versions, the Mk I and Mk IIA, developed during the war and capable of accommodating airspeeds between 70mph and 150mph. In 1926 the Establishment approved a version modified for use up to 190mph to cope with the speed of the Fairey Fox. Later in the same year, the CSBS Mk IVA was flown in an Avro Aldershot to assess the sight's ability to bomb moving ship targets – the so-called fourth vector. The Establishment's comments were limited to practicability and did not address accuracy. The Mk IIC (for the Fleet Air Arm) and Mk VI (increased altitude and speed)

The first armament trial in April 1924 involved this Blackburn Dart, N9693, carrying the 700lb SN bomb shown. (British Crown Copyright/MOD)

---

* Battle (3), Blenheim (3), Demon (1), Fantome (1), Fury (1), Gladiator (1), Hardy (1), Harrow (1), Hart (1), Hind (1), Henley (1), Hurricane (2), Moth (1), Monospar (1), Tutor (1), Valentia (1), and Virginia (1).

Somewhat crudely roped to a convenient piece of timber, the new '230lb skeleton Bomb Carrier' of 1925 demonstrates its ability to carry four types of bomb. Top to bottom: 230lb, 250lb, 100lb and 112lb. (British Crown Copyright/ MOD)

were flown in 1927. The popularity for dive bombing in mid-1935 included a trial using a Whitley, Blenheim and Battle; the pilot dived at about 20 deg, sighted with the aid of convenient cockpit structure and released the bomb. Results were encouraging – unlike the experimental Dive Bombsight Type A in a Hart which gave poor accuracy. Similarly, inaccurate bombing resulted in 1938 from the trial of a Scatter sight for formation attacks. More promising in 1939 was the Auto bombsight Mk II tried in a Blenheim; two comments were that the hitherto accepted flat (*ie* yawed) turns were no longer possible and that gyroscopic stabilization was necessary. In the Hampden a Vector sight Type C was found satisfactory.

Bomb Carriers

Bombs designed and largely manufactured before 1920 remained standard for many years. There were over twenty types* of bombs and flares, each with its own requirement for attachment, crutching to hold it steady, and fuse wire to arm it on release. A single carrier with great adaptability was required. Martlesham, which had by 1926 unrivalled experience of all types added many improvements to what later became known as the 'Universal Carrier'. The first was tested in 1926 on the Ava with promising results, but weight was excessive and operation of the slip was unsatisfactory for accurate results. Over the following few years manufacturers (not only the established armament firms of Vickers and Armstrong but also smaller companies like Hawker and Handley Page) sub-

---

* 112lb Mk V, Mk VI, Mk VIII; 230lb RFC Mk II, Mk III; 230lb RL Mk I, Mk II, 520lb RAF Mk I, RL Mk I; 550lb RAF Mk I, RL Mk I, 500lb HE Mk I, 500lb SAP; HE 50lb, 120lb, 250lb; 250lb Mk I; 250lb and 500lb lightcase; 439lb AP; 5½-in and 8-in flares with parachutes.

A 1938 bomb trolley capable of carrying four 1,000lb bombs (top), with its own loading arm; another hoist was necessary to load the bombs on to the aircraft. (British Crown Copyright/ MOD)

mitted lighter weight designs, usually with restricted choice of bomb. To improve release, friction was reduced in the cable between the operating lever and the slip (one cable for each bomb). Then, in 1928, a pneumatic system invented by Boulton Paul was tried, followed in 1929 by electrical signalling to fire a cartridge and open the slip. The first test of the cartridge system was inauspicious; as the Virginia laden with two 500 pounders was completing the usual long distance taxying before the first test flight, one bomb fell off. On another occasion a 250-pounder hung up (failed to release in the air) but promptly dropped onto the ground on landing. Concrete filling was invariably used for early tests of new carriers. In 1930 designs by Vickers and Fairey were tested, but the first acceptable design, by Vickers, appeared in 1933, and the electro-magnetic system was introduced into the

Service in 1934, initially restricted to light bombs. Later the Vickers was approved for weights up to 550lb and for catapult launching from ships; in 1936 the EMRU was further improved in its Mk III version and the following year the carrier itself was approved for all of the current bombs (very similar to the 1926 list). By late 1938, a successful electrical selector (known as the 16-way distributor) had been developed and tested.

Bombs

Development of bombs was slow in the 1920s with the notable exception of an experimental series of 1,000lb models in 1926. Results were inconclusive and incomplete, and the next test of missiles of over 550lb was in 1939 – and then only on the ballistics of half-scale 1,000lb general-purpose type. For over ten years, AAEE was involved in sporadic minor trials of

modifications to existing bombs such as new types of explosive filling, attachments and casing construction. Later the effects of increased altitude were studied, and the ballistics were rechecked once the special hut was opened in 1934, and subsequently the release of the various sizes of bomb was tested in dives. Among new weapons was a 30lb light case container for the Establishment at Porton; subsequently, it was found that the liquid gas froze at altitude and that bomb bay heating was therefore required. Practice bombs received a great deal of attention throughout the period 1924-1939, and improvements were assessed in safety, ballistics, visibility of explosion by day and night, and methods of carrying. A great number of trials was reported on bomb accessories – fuses, pistols, detonators and parachutes (for flares). Fusing in the early 1920s involved the pilot or observer pulling a lever before release to remove the safety pin in the bomb. Later developments, starting in 1925, were fusing by fan (after release), then in 1929, fusing for all types of bomb on the Universal Carrier, tail fusing, and improved fuse wire. Pistols and detonators initiating the explosion were tested for operation on various surfaces including water, and under water, at various angles of striking the surface and after release at low, medium and high level. Parachutes met with little success at first, but gradually improvements were made, and the standard 3½in, 5½in and 8in flares were finally assessed as acceptable for their various functions suspended from a properly developed canopy. In addition to reconnaissance (including photography), navigation and wind finding, flares were also important for night landings and two developments were hailed with acclaim – the first in 1934 was the Flare, Landing, Mk III which burnt for as long as four minutes to allow leisurely landing of the Vickers B.19/27. The other was an effective shield under the wing on fighter types which allowed pilots to land at night looking out of the cockpit on the same side as the incandescent flare. As late as 1938, specifications for some new types of aeroplane still included a fitting for a landing flare, even though a landing lamp was also required.

Miscellaneous trials were made on containers for small bombs (or bomblets), an RAE height computer, an ingenious but totally impractical camera to replace actual bombing, sea markers of aluminium, signal rockets; from 1935 a new series of incendiaries ranging from 5oz to 25lb in weight received attention.

Gunnery

From 1920 until about 1937 the standard gun armament for British aeroplanes remained virtually unchanged – single-seat fighters had two fixed Vickers 0.303in, two-seaters (apart from trainers) had one fixed Vickers

Although the shields were placed in front of the pilot on Hawker Horsley J8611, the rear gunner was intended to be the beneficiary of this first attempt, in 1929, at protecting him from the effects of slipstream. (British Crown Copyright/ MOD)

gun plus one free Lewis 0.303in gun in the rear, and multi-engine bombers had an appropriate number of free Lewis guns. As gunnery developments were fewer in number than bombing, Martlesham's work reflected the ratio (3:2) in its test reports. In addition, any new ideas on guns and gun accessories were often incorporat-

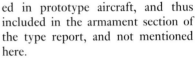

In 1935, this Armstrong Whitworth Atlas (G-ABKE) had an unpowered cupola for the gunner; airflow forced the turret to turn when aiming to the side. (British Crown Copyright/MOD)

ed in prototype aircraft, and thus included in the armament section of the type report, and not mentioned here.

Guns

Apart from a few tests on 0.5in calibre Vickers and BSA designs in 1924, trials on guns were for many years limited to improvements to the standard Vickers and Lewis. On the former, glare on firing was reduced, an improved cocking handle approved, and a modified muzzle lock introduced; in 1933, a Mk V version produced very good results in the Audax and, in 1935, also in the Demon. Meanwhile, the age old bugbear of frequent stoppages in the earlier Mk III version was comprehensively examined in 1934; results were inconclusive but seem to indicate that no real improvement was possible with this make of weapon. On the Lewis, tests were made on an improved extractor, new mounting brackets on the Mk III model in 1930 and on the hand grip; various improvements of the collector bag used for spent cartridges were tried. Both types of gun were cold-soaked in the refrigerating chamber in 1931, and the need for better lubrication and/or heating established for installation in high-flying aeroplanes. The following year, both guns were extensively fired at high altitude in several single- and two-seat types with various improvements made including heating of the guns in the Hart; an insignificant improvement in reliability was reported. To replace the Lewis, on which accuracy trials had recently proved disappointing, a Vickers Berthier gas-operated

gun was tested successfully and introduced with several modifications into the Service in the late 1930s. Other makes were also assessed, the Darne and Hotchkiss in 1932, and found to be inferior to the Vickers gas-operated design; the Browning in 1934 was mechanically unacceptable, liable to fouling and causing damage by blast. By the end of 1935, however, a very successful trial (involving the firing of 7,500 rounds) had been completed on a pair of improved Brownings in place of the Vickers in a Gauntlet. The Browning became the standard 0.303in calibre fixed gun, and was later sufficiently reliable to be placed out of reach of the pilot, thus making the eight-gun fighter a practical proposition. The first 20mm calibre cannon to be tested at Martlesham was fitted in the Dewoitine 510, and some 352 rounds were fired (mostly in the air) in 1937.

Interrupter Gear

To permit guns to fire through the propeller arc without hitting the blades, the Constantinesco interrupter gear was adopted during the First World War, and remained standard equipment on British fighters until just before the Second. Martlesham's routine included tests on every type of aeroplane so equipped, and used a circular wooden disc fixed to the rear of the propeller. The Vickers guns were then fired and the exact position of the path of the bullets noted in relation to the blades as they rotated at various speeds. The interrupter gear involved the use of varying lengths of pipe containing oil under pressure; early trials at AAEE were concerned with improving joints and minimiz-ing leaks generally. An improved version, the Type E was tested in 1928 and after incorporation of modifications made by Martlesham, was adopted. Later changes included a new reservoir, revised gearing and strengthened cam. A Bristol type of gear was not adopted after tests in 1937, but an electrically controlled interrupter

Handley Page Heyford K3489 has an experimental Stieger mounting for a remote Lewis gun; among poor features was the need for frequent and lengthy magazine changing in a trial in 1936. (British Crown Copyright/MOD)

Gun Firing

The various methods of reducing the time between squeezing the trigger and the firing of the guns has earlier been described. Among the first experiments using hydraulic pressure to transmit the firing signal was on a Demon with a Browning mounted under the wing.

Sights

A few trials at Martlesham were made on sights which attempted to improve on the standard Aldis model for aiming fixed guns. The first, in 1925, was insufficiently advanced to warrant a change in Service equipment; over the following five years ideas, usually involving a reflector device, were not adopted. In 1936, an AAEE suggestion of using a fixed bead with a rela-tive speed ring was simple and gave good results – but by then the RAE had more advanced concepts under development. A reflector sight, the GM1 (later GM2) was soon under test at Martlesham, and other types were fitted in new fighters.

No Allowance Sighting

A special form of sighting was employed on fighters designed to fly under their target and fire upwards, making no allowance for the effect of gravity, range or relative movement, and thus concentrate firepower. The special aeroplanes have already been described. Work on the large COW gun in the Westbury continued after type trials were complete. In 1929 new ammunition and propellant suc-

Good results were obtained using the 'no allowance' method of firing this Vickers IIIN gun from Bristol Bulldog J9567 in 1934; the idea was not pursued. (British Crown Copyright/MOD)

7374

cessfully overcame earlier problems with flash on firing. An Oerlikon gun fitted in the Westbury and firing at an elevation of 40 deg to 60 deg was abandoned on account of unserviceability. In 1932, special tracer ammunition was found to be unreliable above 15,000ft in the Westland F.29/27, and in the same aeroplane in 1934 a developed, Mk III version of the COW gun was tested.

Two related trials were flown in Bulldogs (1934) and a Wallace. A pair of Vickers was mounted in one Bulldog and a pair of Lewis in another, both pairs elevated at an angle of 60 deg; flying 1,000ft under their target, over 90 percent of rounds fired hit their target – a very creditable result. In the Wallace three Lewis were fixed with a depression of 50 deg; the result was inaccurate firing – a dive attack with the guns firing ahead gave better results for ground attack.

Mountings

The observers' free Lewis gun had as a standard mounting the Scarff ring from 1920. Early trials with two guns were not successful and a back rest improved comfort but prevented firing. Various new models were tried, the first, known as a No.15 Ring Mounting, had several drawbacks in 1928, reduced to only a few in 1929; the No.17 (1932) and the No.19 (1935) mountings were unacceptable. Westland produced a new mounting on the Wizard, and Fairey on their Fox. The Fairey was developed successfully for high-speed, and performed well on, inter alia, the Hart. Other companies, notably Vickers (used on the Wallace and Gordon), Bristol and Blackburn submitted their designs with varying degrees of acceptability. A more ingenious model was made by Steiger, first tested in 1934. Full trials followed on a Heyford in 1936; its main drawback was its inability to mount more than one gun.

Turrets

The need to protect the observer/gunner from the increasingly debilitating effect of the slipstream led to the turret; most protective devices were on aeroplanes already described. The first trial at Martlesham involved fitting spoilers on the wing of a

Horsley in 1929 together with screens on the fuselage; the aerodynamic effects so reduced control and top speed that the gunner needed no protection. The cupola on the Bristol 120 gave good results, and was preferred in 1933 to the clamshell on the Demon. Late in 1933, the first powered-turret in the nose of the Overstrand was cramped, offered no stowage and suffered a sticking valve; nevertheless, good shooting could at times be obtained and the conclusion was favourable for further development. Pending improvement, unpowered cupolas by Armstrong Whitworth were tested on the Atlas (well liked) and the company's Bomber Transport (C.26/31). A Demon had the General Aircraft Company's so-called balanced cupola; it offered no advantages, and the standard Frazer-Nash was preferred.

A great improvement in smoothness of operation was eventually achieved during lengthy trials in 1937 of the Boulton Paul Turret Mk IA in an Overstrand; the four Brownings also represented a significant increase in firepower. Less success attended the Trojan turret in a Heyford, also tested in 1937; it was slower, less smooth and less serviceable than the Boulton Paul type. In 1939, the Air Ministry reviewed turrets by Frazer-Nash, Boulton Paul, Vickers and Bristols largely on the basis of AAEE reports; the conclusion, that Frazer-Nash designs were the best, resulted in part from the significant improvements suggested by the Establishment.

Ammunition, Boxes and Stowage

Of the small number of trials on these items, wooden bullets were, not surprisingly, found to be useless, the blinding effect of firing at night in a Siskin (1929) was reduced by flashless ammunition; later various designs of flash eliminator on Brownings in a Fury (1934) and on the Spitfire and Hurricane (1938-9) were eventually successful. Tracer and 20mm ammunition were also briefly tested, as were two designs of machine for filling magazines for Lewis guns; stowage pegs for the magazines were tested in the 1920s. The far greater ammount of ammunition carried for the fixed

The pilot of this experimentally-armed Westland Wallace was unable to see the target when he needed to fire the three Lewis guns. (British Crown Copyright/MOD)

guns, especially in fighters, demanded considerable ingenuity in stowing and feeding the rounds to the guns. Stowage for safe inverted flight was investigated in the Siskin in 1929, and several manufacturers submitted their ideas, incorporated into various prototypes, such as the Supermarine F.7/30, the Fairey 12/26 and Blackburn M.1/30. All had ingenious features, but were found to have shortcomings. The wing-mounted guns in later fighters eased the stowage problems, and the well designed arrangements for reloading and maintaining the armament in the Martin-Baker M.B.2 of 1939 were redeeming features in an otherwise unacceptable design.

Minor Trials

Items not falling into the categories already described included a rear view mirror, several tests of signal guns and ammunition, tools for cleaning and clearing stoppages in guns, lubricants for low temperatures, and an assessment of the damage by the wads used in filling gun ammunition. With the advent of enclosed cabins and turrets, the effects of firing from them, and of their being fired at, were investigated for the various materials used, such as Triplex and Rhodoid and others; Triplex was adjudged the best.

Conclusion

This section summarises a selection of the very wide range of armaments and associated equipment subjected to the probing and criticism of Martlesham between 1924 and 1939. Even more than the testing of the aeroplanes by No.22 Squadron/Performance Testing Section, armament trials were conducted in conditions of great secrecy, and rarely seen by the public. Nevertheless, the work of No.15 Squadron/Armament Testing Section was a complementary and increasingly important part of the AAEE.

Miscellaneous Trials

This short section is based on the 500 or so reports (80 percent extant) in the E, F, M/I, M/Q and M/Tech series. The E (Engine) was discontinued in March 1924, and the F series in March 1927. Topics covered in the F series were continued in failure (F suffix) parts of the main, M, reports, and in the M/I (instruments), M/Q (general equipment) and M/Tech (technical) classifications. Many reports are contained on a single side of foolscap (some a mere paragraph); others, particularly the M/Tech, are lengthy.

Engines

Before the transfer of engine development work to the RAE, presumably to

The aircraft seat by Boulton and Paul; it was comfortable but appears somewhat lacking in restraint when tested in 1921. (British Crown Copyright/MOD)

make way for the imminent transfer to Martlesham of armament testing, the latter had responsibility for endurance flying of new engines. The ABC Dragonfly could rarely be persuaded to endure for the standard 50 hr test; two Armstrong Siddeley Jaguars, later joined by a third did better, although engine No.6 in a Nighthawk seized after 50½hr of running. The Bristol Jupiter was briefly tested in 1923 in a Nighthawk, and the Armstrong Siddeley Lynx was in good condition after 50hr in an Avro 504. However, the Remy ignition system of the Jaguar and Lynx was unreliable and a magneto system was recommended. Little, if any, flying was done on the Handley Page V/1500 after arrival in May 1920 as each of the four Rolls-Royce Eagle engines used between 37 and 56 pints of cooling water on the 30-minute delivery flight. A semi-automatic altitude control in a D.H.9A gave good results, but pilots preferred manual control. Other tests included extra tanks on a D.H.9A (for a total capacity of 175gal), cooling trials on a Martinsyde F.4 and an assessment of the oil system and accessibility of the engine of the Aldershot. Some propeller tests were included in the E reports.

The F Reports

An appraisal of the corrugated aluminium alloy of the Junkers monoplane and its engine and petrol system were exceptions in this series concerned with equipment both inside and outside of aeroplanes. Instrument reports comprise the bulk of the subjects, including altimeters, revolution indicators (one of an advanced electrical type) and various recording devices for test purposes (air speed and altimeter). In 1929 an accurate assessment was made of the effect of temperature on the uncompensated instruments then in use; the errors found exceeded expectations on altimeters but not rpm gauges. A stroboscopic device for accurate determination of propeller speed was found entirely satisfactory and subsequently developed for Establishment and other use. A series of trials involving much flying in a Bristol Fighter in 1925-6 proved the Reid to be superior to turn indicators by Sperry, RAE, Vickers and the Electric Company; the lamps on the Reid were particularly liked as an aid to recovery from spins. Less favoured were cockpit mounted oil pressure gauges in the Westbury on account of the time (up

to 6 minutes) taken after starting to obtain a reading; nacelle mounted instruments on this twin-engined machine were preferred. Harnesses for pilots were tried with modifications – a quick release fastening and a locking device among them; a strengthened wicker seat in the Boulton Paul Bourges was found to be too weak.

On the ground, Odier and Crossley starters were reported upon, and a Kegress tractor excelled in pulling a fully laden Virginia. Damage to a Baghdad hangar was attributed to the failure of the supporting structure to withstand very high winds. From 1926, the bulk of the reports concern various failures in aeroplanes under test, such as the cowling on Horsleys, the ailerons of the Westbury and radiator on the Harrow.

Equipment and Instruments

Various aids to the ground handling of aircraft dominated the equipment section – jacks, scaffolding, shear legs, trollies, folding chocks, trestles and power cutters are among items tested. The many scrap aeroplanes that were the invariable occupants of the Establishment's dump frequently ended their days in tests of new fire fighting equipment – Avro 504 H9568 was put to good use in 1929 in proving the efficiency of a Froth extinguisher, and Grebe J7587 in 1931 to prove an Essex model. Protective hoods and asbestos aprons proved useful while Ferret N190 perished in the flames. Another gale in November 1928 wrecked a second Baghdad hangar, destroying Blackburn N150 and an Avro 504K in the process. Various petrol filters, nozzles and pumps appeared at Martelsham, and, in 1930 a portable tank for hot oil to assist

starting recalcitrant engines. Liquid oxygen equipment (a Vapouriser Vessel Mk VIIIB and an Evaporator), reported in December 1927 after a year's use, was a great improvement on earlier models in ensuring a steady supply to the pilot – unfortunately problems, including freezing, in the mask persisted. Further difficulties with storage, maintenance and transport of liquid oxygen led to its abandonment in the RAF in 1928. High-pressure gaseous oxygen was tested in a Siskin in 1928 up to 33,000ft (-53 deg C); together with a modified regulator (a Mk VIIA) the new system was found to be acceptable. Later RAE and other oxygen equipment was not reliable. Early flame damping exhausts on the Blackburn involving lengthened exhaust pipes blocked at the end and drilled on the side effectively eliminated flames from ground observers; the effect on performance was not measured. Later, extensive exhaust trials were made on Merlin-engine types and have already been detailed. Exactor-type hydraulic throttle linkage on Valentia K3603 was found to be better when serviceable than the original rod and lever system. Four electrically heated suits by the RAE with their own special windmill generator were still functioning after three months trial in the winter of 1928 – an achievement made in spite of practical drawbacks. Four years later, the crew of three on a ceiling climb in the Heyford prototype escaped serious injury when their electrical clothing overheated and burned; a faulty voltage regulator was to blame. Cabins on aircraft were not a universal boon – one problem was constant misting. Some types of specially treated sponges were useful in reducing the effects. In 1939 wipers were tested on the outside of the windscreens on Wellington L4221; a better squeezee blade was required.

In 1929, the Establishment produced a compendium of good design features including accessibility for maintenance, drawing on its unrivalled experience of British and some foreign aircraft; several suggestions for improvements were made in the report subsequently widely distributed in the industry. Another report, dated 1930, compared the three earlier systems of brake operation – pneumatic (Palmer), cables (Bendix) and hydraulic (Lockheed). The hydraulic was found to be the best – but considerable work remained to be done on the method of operation. Revisions to the methods of measuring air speed position error, in defining the stalling speed and in allowing for compressibility were subjects of investigation in the 1930s. The lateral trim of monoplanes could not be successfully adjusted by the old method of affixing an appropriate length of cord to the trailing edge of the aileron. Various improvements were tried, including an unsatisfactory method of adjustable wingtip (Wellesley); the conclusion was that a tab operable by the pilot was the best method. Among special instruments for test purposes in 1930 was a photographic device by RAE for periodically recording six parameters, a recording rate of descent instrument, a maximum recording accelerometer in 1931 (tested at over 5g in the Wizard monoplane) and, in 1938 an indicator, devised by AAEE for control column position. The search for an acceptable fuel flowmeter continued throughout the period, the best being the JFH type in 1938, its drawback was lack of a safety bypass.

The selection of items for inclusion in this section is far from complete – but nevertheless illustrates the wide range of the more mundane tasks undertaken.

Appendices

Appendix A: Senior RAF Staff

Commanding Officers

February 1920	-	Sqn Ldr A Sheckleton DSO
January 1921	-	Sqn Ldr A C Maund CBE DSO
March 1922	-	Wg Cdr N J Gill CBE MC
September 1924	-	Wg Cdr H Blackburn MC AFC
November 1928	-	Wg Cdr V O Rees OBE (Grp Capt January 1930)
September 1931	-	Wg Cdr R M Field (temporary)
January 1932	-	Grp Capt H L O'Reilly DSO
September 1933	-	Grp Capt A C Maund CBE DSO
January 1937	-	Grp Capt H G Smart OBE DFC AFC
December 1938	-	Grp Capt B McEntegart

Armament Technical Officers

January 1935	-	Sqn Ldr E D Davies
October 1936	-	Sqn Ldr W Wynter Morgan
September 1937	-	Wg Cdr R St H Clarke AFC
March 1939	-	Wg Cdr C N H Bilney

Squadron Leader Administrative

December 1933	-	Sqn Ldr (Rtd) A Rowan
September 1935	-	Sqn Ldr W E Swann
June 1937	-	Sqn Ldr J E W Bowles
March 1938	-	Sqn Ldr A H Owen MC

Appendix B: Squadron Commanding Officers

Performance

January 1920	-	Sqn Ldr M Henderson DSO
July 1921	-	Sqn Ldr C H Nicholas DFC AFC
March 1925	-	Sqn Ldr T H England
May 1927	-	Sqn Ldr E R L Corballis OBE DSO
July 1927	-	Sqn Ldr J Noakes AFC MM
January 1929	-	Sqn Ldr E S Goodwin AFC
March 1933	-	Sqn Ldr C E Maitland DFC AFC
October 1934	-	Sqn Ldr E G Hilton DFC AFC
July 1937	-	Sqn Ldr C E Horrex AFC
March 1939	-	Sqn Ldr J F X McKenna AFC

Also Officer Commander Flying No.22 Squadron 24 July, 1923, Performance Testing Squadron 1 May, 1934, Performance Testing Section 30 June, 1934.

Armament

March 1924	-	Sqn Ldr P C Sherren MC
November 1927	-	Sqn Ldr C E H James MC
September 1929	-	Sqn Ldr J K Wells AFC
March 1930	-	Sqn Ldr G H Martingell AFC
March 1933	-	Sqn Ldr E S Goodwin AFC
May 1933	-	Sqn Ldr R M Foster DFC AFC
June 1935	-	Sqn Ldr R St H Clarke AFC
June 1937	-	Sqn Ldr E D M Hopkins
September 1937	-	Sqn Ldr W Wynter Morgan MC
April 1939	-	Sqn Ldr D W F Bonham Carter

No.15 Squadron 20 March, 1924, Armament Testing Squadron 1 June, 1934, Armament Testing Section 30 June, 1934.

Appendix C: Senior Civilian Staff, Martlesham Heath 1920-1939

Chief Technical Officer (Appointment)

1920 - 1923	T M Barlow
1923 - 1927	P T Capon #
1927 - 1931	H L Stevens#
1932	F W Meredith#
1932 - 1935	E J H Lynam*
1935 - 1937	N E Rowe*
1938 - 1939	E T Jones#

Grade - # Principal Scientific Officer
        * Principal Technical Officer

Engineer Officer

1920 – 1936	H W McKenna (RAF until 1928)
1936 – 1939	F Rowarth

Scientific Officer

1926 – 1927	W G Jennings
1927	L P Coombes
1928 – 1931	A E W Nutt
1931 – 1933	J L Hutchinson
1934 – 1935	H C Pritchard
1936	A R Low
1937	G J Richards
1938 – 1939	A Daniels
1937 – 1939	A S Hartshorn

Technical Officer

1926 – 1929	N E Rowe
1926 – 1932	D Rollinson
1929 – 1933	S Scott-Hall
1932 – 1939	A L Lingard
1933 – 1936	W Dancy
1937 – 1939	S Scott-Hall (Senior Technical Officer from 1938)
1937 – 1938	G O Smith

Appendix D:
The Competitions

Martlesham Heath involvement in the process of selecting types to meet Air Ministry requirements (Specifications), in chronological order of trials:

Text (page)	Specification	Manufacturers' Proposals (Number)	Types Reaching Martlesham	Date of Trials	Winning Design	Remarks
78	5/20	2	2	1923	Victoria	
216	6/22	2	2	1923	Flycatcher	Plover built in small numbers
223	3/21	5	5	1921–4	Bison Blackburn	Three types to other requirements
225	37/22	3	3	1924–5	None	Requirement cancelled; see O.22/26
64	26/23	4	4	1925	Horsley	
159	30/24	5	5	1926	Atlas	
207	21/23	3	3	1926–7	Ripon	
233	5/24	3	2	1927–8	None	Requirement cancelled
167	None	11	9	1927	IIIF Wapiti	IIIF – water-cooled Wapiti – air-cooled
67	12/26	5	3	1928	Hart	Fairey types too late
90	9/26	7	7	1928	Bulldog	
218	17/25	2	2	1928	None	Requirement cancelled
227	O.22/26	4	4	1929	Osprey	
93	F.20/27	12	10	1929–30	Fury	Firefly close second
191	24/25	6	6	1928–30	Vildebeest	Four types originally to 23/25
218	N.21/26	6?	6	1929–30	Nimrod	Two phases
48	B.22/27	2	2	1931	None	Requirement cancelled
48	B.19/27	6	4	1931–2	Heyford	Hendon later ordered
114	F.29/27	2	2	1931–2	None	Requirement cancelled

99	F.9/26(mod)	4	3	1933	Gauntlet	Originally private venture competition
80	C.16/28	3	2	1933	None	Requirement cancelled
210	M.1/30	3	1	1933	None	Requirement cancelled (see S.15/33)
174	G.4/31	10	8	1935	Vickers G.4/31	Biplane winner cancelled in favour of Wellesley
100	F.7/30	7	3	1935	Gladiator	
194	None	2	2	1935	Anson	Minimum alterations to existing civil design
211	S.15/33	4	3	1934-35	Swordfish	Shark ordered as interim type
80	C.26/31	3	2	1936	Bombay	
163	A.39/34	2	2	1936-38	Lysander	Not treated as competition
187	T.1/37	3	3	1939	None	Requirement cancelled

Appendix E: Report Numbering

Aircraft The principle series of reports, prefix M for Martlesham, was devoted to results of aircraft tests and ran from M271 (1920) to M745 (1939). Before 1927 it was customary for individual aircraft to be given a separate M number; thus it is not possible to derive the number of different types tested by reference to this system, *eg* the early Vickers Virginias were allocated six M numbers. From 1927 each new aircraft type was allocated a number in this series, and tests on subsequent versions were denoted by a suffix letter to the report, *eg* the Armstrong Whitworth *Atlas* reached M437T. From 1938, reports were issued in Parts as tests on individual systems were completed.

Armament M/Arm/1 (1924) to M/Arm/552 (1939) covered bombing, bombsights, guns, flares and turrets. Reports on modifications were given a letter suffix.

Research S1 (1923) to S14 (1927) and M/Res/15 (1927) to M/Res/127 (1939) were devoted, typically, to performance reduction methods, spinning and acceleration in turns.

Engines E167 (1920) to E225 (1924) covered engine subjects before the removal of engine testing to the RAE in 1924.

Equipment F261 (1920) to about F401 (1927) were allocated to such items as tests on parachutes and instruments.

Appendix F: Standard Report Layout – 1927

Air Ministry Form 897

Page

1	Summary
2	Dimensions, areas
3 } 3a }	Armament
3b	Electrical system and miscellaneous
3c	Wireless
4	Weight and Centre of Gravity
5	Actual weight and CG on trials
6	Aerodynamic areas, tail volumes
7	Propeller and engine
8	Petrol and oil system
9	Climb performance and ceilings
10	Speed performance and landing speed
11	Assessment of power unit
12 } 12a } 12b }	Equipment and maintainability
13	Flying qualities
14	Fuel consumption
15	Radiator suitability
16	Propeller suitability
17	Loading details for three CG
18	Gliding and slow speed
19	Control and maneouvrability
20	Stability
21	Armament – position and handiness
22	Fixed gun
23	Free gun
24	Pyrotechnics
25	Bomb gear
26	Bomb sighting
27	Instruments and communications

These 32 pages were later increased as more guns, wireless, and equipment were fitted.

Appendix G: Comparison of Flying Hours 1927–1937

	1927	*1928*	*1929*	*1930*	*1931*	*1932*	*1933*	*1934*	*1935*	*1936*	*1937*
Martlesham Heath											
No.15 Sqn/ArmT	763*	782	570	906	1,055	1,158	1,289	1,453	1,601	1,196	1,356
No.22 Sqn/PerT	1,670	1,967	1,799	1,578	1,393	1,558	1,707	1,885	1,728	1,660	1,742
Two standard squadrons											
No.12 Sqn Bomber	2,879	2,579	1,814	4,163	3,457	3,012	3,222	3,418	4,753	3,197	3,938
No.41 Sqn Fighter	2,051	2,309	2,267	2,759	3,172	3,706	3,212	3,523	3,482	2,703	2,782

* Includes 282hr of Training Flight.

Appendix H: Names on Menu Card at 1923 Dinner

Left		
Fred Green	–	Designer Sir W G Armstrong Whitworth Aircraft
Rex Pierson	–	Designer Vickers (Aviation)
J H B Carson	–	RAF accounts
A H Orlebar	–	RAF pilot
F T Courtney	–	Freelance test pilot
F A Bumpus	–	Designer Blackburn Aeroplane & Motor Co
J D Breakey	–	RAF pilot
H F V Battle	–	RAF pilot
V Nicol	–	Designer Fairey Aviation
J Potter	–	RAF pilot
B G Drake	–	RAF accounts
Oswald Short	–	Designer Short Brothers
C C Walker	–	Designer de Havilland Aircraft Co
C E Horrex	–	RAF pilot
H W McKenna	–	RAF technical officer
G de Havilland	–	Designer de Havilland Aircraft Co
C H Nicholas	–	RAF pilot – OC Flying
F Handley Page	–	Designer Handley Page
F Sigrist	–	Designer Hawker Aircraft

Right		
H S Broad	–	Test pilot de Havilland Aircraft Co
J A Gray	–	RAF pilot
J L Parker	–	Test pilot Short Brothers
R Ivelaw Chapman	–	RAF pilot
H J Payn	–	Test pilot Vickers (Aviation)
D Townsend	–	RAF technical
P G H Winter	–	Representative D Napier & Son
T J West	–	RAF
E Bird	–	RAF
A M Saywood	–	RAF stores
M C Head	–	RAF technical
S Marker	–	Representative ?
W F Dry Unidentified	–	RAF technical
N J Gill	–	RAF Commanding Officer
H B Greene	–	RAF medical
H Bolas	–	Designer George Parnall & Co
Tom Sopwith	–	Designer Hawker Aircraft
L V Sippe	–	Designer Hawker Aircraft
H Wells	–	RAF armament
T M Barlow	–	AAEE Chief Technical Officer
R J Parrott	–	Designer A V Roe

Abbreviations

AAEE	Aeroplane and Armament Experimental Establishment
ABC	All British Engine Co Ltd
AEE	Aeroplane Experimental Establishment
AFC	Air Force Cross
AMOA	Air Ministry Order – permanent
AMWO	Air Ministry Weekly Order
AP	Armour Piercing
ARS	Aeroplane Repair Section
ATS & Arm T	Armament Testing Section
°C	Degrees Celsius
C of A	Certificate of Airworthiness
CAC	The Civilian Aircraft Company
CFS	Central Flying School
CG	Centre of Gravity
CTO	Chief Technical Officer
d	Pence (2.4 old pence = 1p)
Dept	Department
D.H.	de Havilland
DTD	Director of Technical Development
ETPS	Empire Test Pilots School
ft	Feet or foot (1ft = 0.305 metres)
HE	High Explosive
HF	High frequency
HMS	His Majesty's Ship
lb	Pound (1lb = 0.454kg)
MAEE	Marine Aircraft Experimental Establishment
mph	Miles per hour (1mph = 0.447m/sec)
NAAFI	Navy, Army and Air Force Institute
NCO	Non-commissioned officer
psi	Pounds per square inch (1 psi = 0.07 bar)
PTS & PerT	Performance Testing Section
RAE	Royal Aircraft Establishment
RAF	Royal Air Force (or Royal Aircraft Factory – bomb design)
RDF	Radio Direction Finding (Radar)
RFC	Royal Flying Corps
RL	Royal Laboratory (Woolwich)
s	Shilling (1 Shilling = 5p)
SAP	Semi-armour piercing
SN	Corruption of Essen
TV	Terminal Velocity
W/T	Wireless telegraphy

Bibliography

The following books contain references to the subject of this work:

BALFOUR, H H, *An Airman Marches*, Hutchinson & Co, 1933

BATTLE, H F V, OBE DFC, *Line – The Reminiscences of a Royal Air Force Pilot*, Privately published, 1984

BOWEN, E G, *Radar Days*, Adam Hilger, 1987

CLARK, R W, *Tizard*, Methuen, 1965

CLOUSON, A E, *Dangerous Skies*, Cassell and Co, 1954

KINSEY, G, *Martlesham Heath*, Terence Dalton Ltd, 1975

PEGG, A J, *Sent Flying*, MacDonald, 1959

PENROSE, H, *No Echo in the Sky*, Cassell and Co, 1958

—, *British Aviation: The Adventuring Years*, Putnam, 1973

—, *British Aviation: Widening Horizons 1930-1934*, HMSO, 1979

—, *British Aviation: Ominous Skies 1935-1937*, HMSO, 1980

POWELL, H P (Sandy), *Men With Wings*, Allan Wingate Publishers Ltd, 1956

—, *Test Flight*, Allan Wingate Publishers Ltd, 1956

ROBERSON, N J, *The History No 15/XV Squadron*, Privately published, 1975

TAYLOR, J W R, *C F S Birthplace of Air Power*, Putnam, 1958

SCOTT HALL, S and ENGLAND, J H, *Aircraft Performance Testing*, Pitmans & Son, 1933

Index

Page numbers in italics represent illustrations, and those in bold performance summaries. Illustrated pages also contain relevant text.